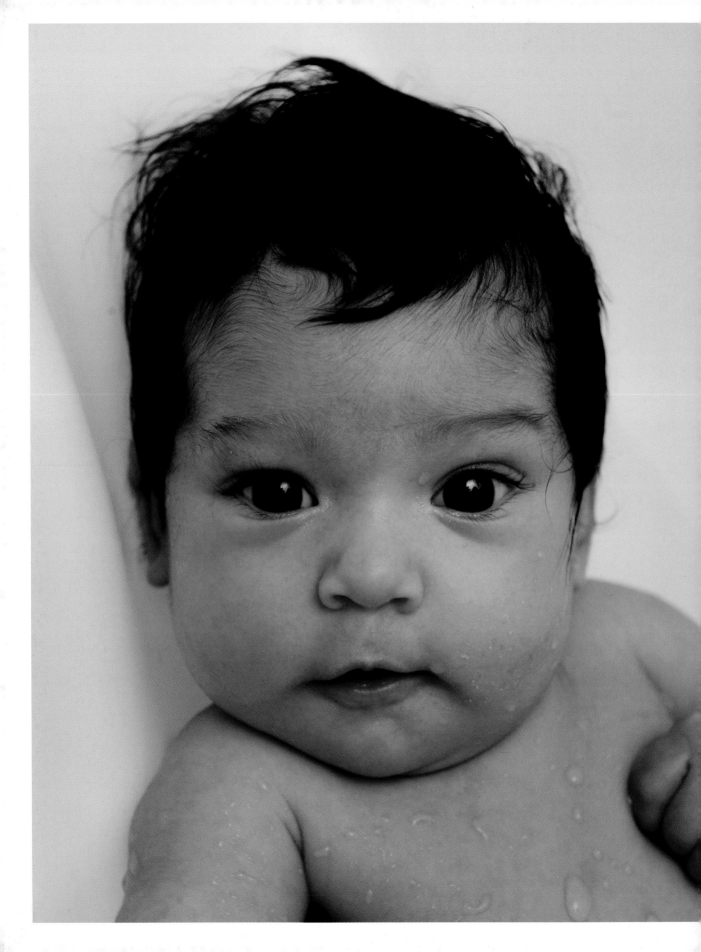

EXPECTING *a Baby?*

A complete guide to pregnancy, birth and your baby's first six weeks

DR PENELOPE LAW BA (HONS), MRCOG

with Debbie Beckerman

Quadrille
PUBLISHING

Contents

INTRODUCTION

I wanted to write this book for many reasons. Firstly, there seemed to be a gap between the information that was available to doctors and what was 'out there' for pregnant women and their partners. Doctors have a multitude of sources that they can use and, although much of this is also available to the general public, many people don't know this, so I wanted to ensure that readers were aware of what information they could access themselves and from where.

I also wanted this book to provide answers to many of the questions I am frequently asked by the women I care for. For example, they often want to know why a certain treatment or intervention is offered, so I have tried to include, wherever possible, the evidence that obstetricians make use of themselves when weighing up a situation. I have also tried to explain why a mother's choice may sometimes need to be tempered by concern for her well-being and that of her baby. My role is to ensure that women fully understand the risks and benefits of each choice they make and its implication for their immediate and long-term health, as well as that of their baby.

Finally, I remember all too well what it was like to be pregnant and give birth. I was a third-year medical student when my daughter was born and, looking back, I realise my knowledge was patchy, at best! The two midwives who helped me through my delivery shed a few tears when my daughter arrived, even though they had delivered over twenty babies that week alone. We never forget our labours, and midwives and obstetricians can help make the experience as positive as possible for women and their partners. Being an obstetrician is a huge privilege, and few people get to experience so frequently the amazing event that is birth. I hope that, through the pages of this book, I am able to pass on to you some of the best things I have learned from all the women I have looked after, from my own experience of pregnancy and birth, and from the midwives and fellow doctors I have been lucky enough to work with. Whether you are embarking on this exciting adventure for the first, second or seventh time, I hope all this experience will be helpful to you.

DR PENELOPE LAW

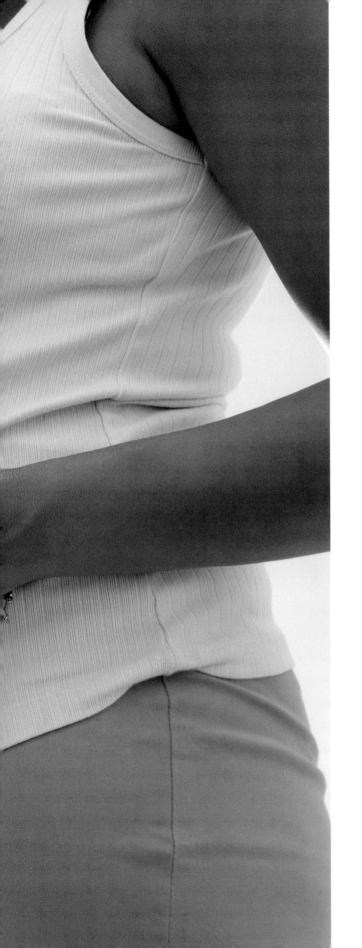

You are pregnant

Your pregnancy is confirmed! Now what happens? The moment when you discover you are pregnant is unforgettable and you may now be keen to know what has been happening to your body and to your developing baby since the moment of conception. This is also the time to start thinking about your antenatal care and where you would like to have your baby.

Like most women, you may be a bit hazy about what actually happens during your menstrual cycle and what physiological processes are required for conception to take place. In fact, without your knowledge, the body undergoes immense changes in the few weeks from the start of your period to the moment you discover, a few weeks later, that you are pregnant.

The length and type of menstrual cycle varies from woman to woman, but on average a period occurs every 28 days, although if the cycle is regular (i.e. it happens every month) and is between 23 and 35 days long, it is also considered perfectly normal.

Day 1 of a woman's cycle – the first day of her period – is the start of the 'follicular' phase. The hypothalamus, deep inside the brain, releases gonadotrophin-releasing hormone (GnRH), which in turn instructs the pituitary gland just beneath it to begin secreting follicle-stimulating hormone (FSH). As a result, about twenty eggs, each in their own fluid-filled follicle, start to ripen. We still do not understand why certain egg follicles mature and others do not, nor why it is that, by the time ovulation takes place, only one (or occasionally more than one) gets to ripen fully, while the other follicles and the eggs inside them simply shrivel away. Furthermore, the ovaries do not take it in turns to produce this 'dominant' egg, and it is still unclear why one ovary does so rather than the other in any given cycle.

The egg itself is surrounded by granulosa cells, whose job it is to produce the oestrogen hormone and also the nutrients that feed the egg. Oestrogen stimulates the growth of the endometrium (the lining of the uterus), thins cervical secretions and gradually reduces the secretion of FSH. The oestrogen level continues to rise and eventually it causes the hypothalamus to 'tell' the pituitary gland to release a burst, or pulse, of luteinising hormone (LH). About 36 hours later, the follicle ruptures and the egg is released into the Fallopian tube. This is called ovulation and, in a normal 28-day cycle, it occurs on or around Day 14.

The second part of the menstrual cycle, the luteal phase, now begins. The ruptured, empty egg follicle is now a small cyst-like swelling called the corpus luteum, which starts to produce the hormone progesterone. This stimulates growth of the endometrium and produces nutrients that help to support a pregnancy in the early stages. Progesterone causes the body temperature to rise by about 0.2°C until the start of the next period. It also thickens cervical secretions and, along with oestrogen, causes the breast tenderness felt by many women in the later stages of their cycle.

The newly released egg contains one of the two sets of chromosomes that carry the genetic information needed to make a human being (*see* Box opposite), and it has now reached exactly the right stage of maturity to enable it to be fertilised by sperm. It measures 0.1 mm in diameter and is the biggest single cell in the human body. The egg is wafted into the Fallopian tube by fimbriae, the wand-like projections at the entrance to each tube. From there, muscular contractions of the Fallopian tube, together with the microscopic, hair-like cilia that line it, start to move the egg down the tube towards the uterus. The egg needs to be fertilised within 24 hours of ovulation. If it is not, production of LH gradually stops, the corpus luteum collapses and oestrogen and progesterone reduce to a level at which the blood-filled, thickened endometrium can no longer be maintained. It begins to be shed and this is the start of a woman's period.

Fertilisation

The process of fertilisation (conception) – the fusion of egg and sperm to create a life – usually takes place in the Fallopian tube (*see* Ectopic pregnancy in Complications, p. 285). While the egg is making its way down the tube, sperm (which are twenty times smaller than the egg) have arrived in the vagina and now have to undertake an arduous journey to reach the egg. Of the 100–300 million present in the seminal fluid at ejaculation, only about one per cent make it as far as the cervix. By the time the sperm reach the Fallopian tubes, which can be up to 72 hours after ejaculation, there are only around 200 left. These are now swimming up towards the descending egg – swimming against the tide, as it were – so only the strongest manage to reach the egg and bind to its thick, outer layer. Just one sperm successfully manages to break through to the oocyte, the innermost part of the egg. Once it has done so, its tail breaks off and disintegrates, while the head, which contains the other set of genetic information, remains.

The just-fertilised egg, now called a zygote, quickly creates a thick outer layer that prevents any further sperm from entering. The initial single-cell zygote will start to

BOY OR GIRL?

The human genome is made up of around 40,000 genes, which determine our sex, our physical and mental characteristics and our predisposition to certain illnesses. These genes are arranged in pairs along the two strands of chromosomes that are contained in the nucleus of every cell. The man's sperm and the woman's egg each contain 23 single chromosomes, so that, at fertilisation, the resulting single-cell embryo has a total of 46 chromosomes, or 23 pairs. When this single cell multiplies, the same genetic pattern is repeated. The 23rd pair of chromosomes is called the sex chromosome and it determines what sex a baby will be. A woman's egg always contains the female chromosome, known as X. A man's sperm contains either an X (female) or Y (male) chromosome. An embryo that has two X chromosomes will be female, whereas one with an XY combination will be male. It is therefore the man's sperm that determines whether a baby is male or female.

divide within 24 hours and multiply into further cells, called blastomeres. The cells get smaller and smaller with each division, until they are eventually as small as other cells in the human body. By Day 3, there are about twelve blastomeres and this cluster of cells, known as a morula, makes its way slowly down to the uterus. When the rapidly dividing cells reach the 32nd cell division, they become differentiated into two different types: the outer, trophoblast, layer of cells, which goes on to form the placenta, and the inner cell mass, which will develop into the fetus. By the time the mass reaches the uterus, about 60 hours after Day 3 (i.e. sometime on Day 5), it consists of about 60 cells and is known as a blastocyst.

Following ovulation, progesterone and oestrogen have thickened the endometrium in preparation for a possible pregnancy and, two to three days after entering the uterus – about a week after fertilisation – the blastocyst, now numbering about 100 cells, embeds in the lining. The blastocyst starts to produce a hormone called beta human chorionic gonadotrophin (BhCG), which tells the corpus luteum to keep producing progesterone, thus maintaining the uterine lining and preventing menstruation from starting. Both progesterone and BhCG are essential for maintaining the pregnancy in its first stages. Your body temperature,

If you have become pregnant following assisted conception, you should feel reassured that your pregnancy is likely to be normal, although it may have certain physical and psychological characteristics that make it different from a spontaneous pregnancy (see below). In addition, your antenatal care may be handled differently; for example, even if yours is an uncomplicated pregnancy and you are cared for primarily by midwives, you will probably be seen by an obstetrician at least once during your antenatal visits.

There are regular scare stories in the media regarding the possibility of higher rates of pregnancy complications, fetal abnormality or future illness following conception using in vitro fertilisation (IVF) or intra-cytoplasmic sperm injection (ICSI). The latest research indicates that for mothers:

▸ there is a slightly increased chance of pre-eclampsia, high blood pressure, gestational diabetes, placenta praevia and first trimester bleeding
▸ miscarriage rates are similar to those for spontaneous conception
▸ there is an increased chance of having a Caesarean section and of obstetric haemorrhage.

For the baby, the results showed that:

▸ the risk of low birthweight risk is increased by 40 per cent
▸ there is an increased risk of stillbirth
▸ three per cent of all babies (conceived spontaneously or not) are diagnosed with some form of congenital abnormality soon after birth; the rate for IVF/ICSI babies is 30 per cent higher (i.e. four per cent of IVF/ICSI babies), which means that the overall risk of congenital abnormality is still very low
▸ there is no evidence of a higher rate of cancer in IVF/ICSI-conceived babies
▸ babies born as a result of frozen eggs or embryos have similar risks to those born following 'conventional' IVF/ICSI.

Undergoing fertility treatment can be very stressful and you may subsequently be quite anxious through some or all of your pregnancy, because babies conceived in this way are often much waited-for. It is not uncommon to need additional psychological support during this time, so do not hesitate to speak to your GP or midwife if you think you might need some professional help.

which rose by 0.2°C just after ovulation because of the rise in progesterone, will now remain raised, whereas if you were not pregnant, it would fall back down to normal shortly before your next period was due.

As the trophoblast cells embed further into the lining of the uterus, the inner mass of cells continue to multiply to form what is now referred to as the embryo. Two weeks after fertilisation – at around the time when a woman's period would normally be due – this tiny mass of cells is still barely the size of a pin head. However, it has now developed three distinctive cell layers, called germ layers, each of which are destined to become different parts of the body. See Chapter 4, p. 84 for further information.

Although a few women say that they 'know' they are pregnant at this stage even before their period is due, most women do not yet know, as there are usually no obvious symptoms, and only a blood or urine test would be able to confirm a pregnancy. Yet, unbeknown to them, their bodies are already changing, the embryo is fast developing and its human form is already planned. See Chapter 9, p. 264 for information about your response to the pregnancy.

DID YOU KNOW…?
Hospitals now use exactly the same type of pregnancy test as the ones you can buy over the counter in shops, so the test you may do at home to confirm your pregnancy is as accurate as any carried out by your GP or hospital.

YOUR ANTENATAL CARE

As soon as your pregnancy is confirmed, you will be looked after by a team of healthcare professionals. Antenatal care has greatly improved pregnancy outcomes: it offers healthcare advice and monitors the progress of the pregnancy, so that any problems can be identified and, if possible, treated. It is also an opportunity for you to receive information that can help you make choices about your welfare and that of your baby.

The main thing to bear in mind when thinking about your options is that your needs and those of your baby are paramount, and you should not feel obliged to conform to anyone else's expectations when it comes to your care and what you decide to do for the actual birth. You will discover that pregnancy and birth are highly emotive subjects on which some people have very strong views – and they won't hesitate to share them with you. Differing opinions are often polarised and it is easy to become confused and anxious when faced with conflicting and overwhelming information. However, if you remain focused on what feels right for you and your baby, it should help you to feel confident in the decisions you make regarding your antenatal care and birth.

The first GP visit

Although you don't actually have to see your general practitioner (GP) as soon as you know you are pregnant, I would nonetheless advise you to do so. Try not to be disappointed if they don't leap off their chair in excitement when hearing your news, because although they will be very pleased for you, in reality, they will have a professional rather than a personal interest in your pregnancy. Your GP will be able to give you information about the type of antenatal care on offer in your area (*see* below), as well as answers to questions that you may already have about the months ahead. An early visit to the GP also allows them to ensure that you are starting your pregnancy in the best possible conditions, and you may be given advice about nutrition and your lifestyle (*see* Chapter 2, p. 20). Most women are between six and eight weeks pregnant at this point; this means that there is time

to arrange appointments with the midwife and hospital, so that you can take advantage of the screening programme for abnormalities offered to all women between twelve and thirteen weeks (*see* Chapter 3, p. 72).

Before your GP appointment, note down the date of the first day of your last period, so that your estimated delivery date (EDD) can be calculated. If your period is regular, your EDD is calculated as being 40 weeks from the first day of your last period. This means that by the time you miss your first period, you are already four weeks pregnant (if you have a 28-day cycle). If you have irregular cycles or cannot remember the date, a hospital ultrasound scan will enable your healthcare professionals to calculate the exact gestation of your pregnancy (*see* Chapter 3, p. 66).

During the visit, your GP will probably ask you whether you are considering giving birth at home or in a hospital (*see* pp. 16 –19. If they don't discuss the possibility of a home birth with you and this is something you might be interested in pursuing, do make sure you bring this up. You don't have to make any decision just yet; you can simply have an initial talk now and think things through in your own time. You will also have the opportunity to discuss this more fully with your midwife at your booking appointment (*see* Chapter 3, p. 60). Remember that you are within your rights to change your mind at any stage during your pregnancy – nothing is cast in stone. This is your pregnancy and it is always your choice.

Antenatal care options

There are a number of ways in which your antenatal care can be provided, depending on how services are structured in your area and whether you opt for a home or hospital birth. Some options may not available where you live, as they require careful planning, as well as a midwife-to-births ratio that many local authorities cannot provide.

Team midwifery

Some hospitals and GP surgeries have teams of community midwives who care for women throughout their pregnancy. As its name implies, a team of midwives is allocated to a group of women. You will have a named midwife, but will also meet the others in the team who may also provide care both throughout pregnancy and during labour. The aim is to provide continuity of care, although this is sometimes difficult to achieve, as midwives work shifts and can be away on your clinic days or when you go into labour.

The two principle figures in your antenatal care are the midwife and the obstetrician. For information on the different systems by which care can be delivered, see main text.

Midwife

Midwives are experts in normal births and are trained to look after women during pregnancy, labour and after delivery. Midwives are not nurses – it is a completely separate profession – although many are also trained nurses, and they often work alongside obstetricians (*see* below) in hospitals, referring to them when there is a medical need in your care. If yours is an uncomplicated pregnancy, you are likely to have most of your antenatal appointments, as well as your labour, with a midwife. She will also provide counselling before and after your routine screening tests (*see* Chapter 3, p. 72), should you choose to have them.

A community midwife provides care outside the hospital, although she is usually attached to either a hospital, Children's Centre or GP surgery. She attends you if you are having a home birth and will also assist you in a hospital birth, if you are under a system of antenatal care such as team midwifery. You will also have a community midwife if you have chosen to give birth in a midwifery unit (also called a 'Birth Centre' – *see* p. 18).

A hospital midwife runs antenatal appointments, helps women through labour (working, where relevant, with an obstetrician) and cares for them in the immediate postnatal period before they return home. You might have all your antenatal appointments at hospital with a midwife, either because of a pre-existing medical condition or because your GP surgery or local Children's Centre does not provide shared care. Alternatively, you might go to the hospital only for specific antenatal appointments (e.g. if you are due to have one of your routine antenatal scans).

Obstetrician

An obstetrician is a doctor specialising in women who are pregnant. Obstetricians and midwives in hospitals work closely together to make sure you have the best care. You are unlikely to see an obstetrician unless you are over 40, have a BMI of more than 30 (*see* Chapter 2, p. 29), have a pre-existing medical condition, have had a previous abdominal operation or became pregnant as a result of assisted conception. They may, however, be called upon to perform an assisted or Caesarean delivery.

Shared care

The most common form of antenatal care if you are giving birth in a hospital is known as 'shared care': your appointments are shared between your GP and the hospital itself. Your GP – or the one at your practice who specialises in antenatal care – will check your weight, blood pressure and urine, as well as your baby's heartbeat and growth, at each of your antenatal appointments. Unless any problems occur, you will only need to go to the hospital for routine ultrasound scans and blood tests. When you give birth, you will be attended by a hospital midwife and, once back home, you will be visited by a community midwife (*see* Box) or health visitor until you and your baby can be discharged into the care of your GP and local health clinic or Children's Centre.

Independent midwife

Whether you choose to give birth in hospital or at home, you may prefer to pay for an independent midwife to provide your care throughout pregnancy and birth. You can still, of course, access NHS care when you need it. An independent midwife will carry out the same antenatal checks as a hospital or community midwife, but the visits take place in your home. If you are having a home birth, she will attend to you there during labour. If you deliver in hospital (either because you have been transferred from home or because you have booked a hospital birth), your independent midwife can stay with you. She cannot assist you during labour, although a few independent midwives do have honorary contracts with their local hospital and can provide midwifery care. However, most independent midwives feel that they are better able to be your advocate by staying with you as your birth supporter (*see* Chapter 5, p. 137) and the hospital midwife will therefore provide your clinical care. If a Caesarean section is needed, most hospitals will allow your independent midwife into theatre with you and your partner. See Useful Resources for information on how to hire an independent midwife.

BIRTH OPTIONS

Early in your pregnancy, usually at your booking appointment, you will be asked where you would like to give birth: at home or in a hospital. Within the hospital setting, there may be several types of unit offering different styles of care, depending on where you live.

It is useful to be aware of the facts about the different birth settings and of the reasons why one option might be preferable to the other – you may find the information below helpful. When making your decision, bear in mind that nothing is ever guaranteed in a pregnancy. For example, you might have had a straightforward pregnancy and birth on a previous occasion, but this does not mean that it will happen again. It is therefore advisable to keep an open mind about all the options and to be flexible, because sometimes a medical complication can arise during your pregnancy or labour, which means that a home birth or one in a midwifery unit is no longer advisable or possible.

Home birth

Many women are drawn to the idea of giving birth in the comfort and familiarity of their own home. Home births can offer a very positive experience of childbirth, allowing your partner and, if you wish, other family members, friends and your other children to be fully involved. In addition, you are more likely to be attended to by the midwives who cared for you during your pregnancy, you don't have to travel to hospital while you are in labour, and you won't be separated from your partner for any reason after the birth. You can also guarantee access to a birthing pool or other specialist equipment, if you would like to use them, by hiring your own. The home setting may be especially important to you if hospitals make you feel anxious.

Home births are particularly suited to women having their second or subsequent baby in an uncomplicated pregnancy, having had a previous vaginal delivery. However, if this is your first baby, there are several factors that may make a home birth a low-risk option for you:

▸ you are under 40
▸ your BMI is under 30
▸ you have no medical complications
▸ your pregnancy is progressing without any problem

▸ you live close to a hospital, in the event of requiring a transfer to deliver your baby – your hospital can advise you on what their time limit would be (some hospitals provide specific information).

Most women are offered a home birth when they initially see their GP or midwife, unless it is clearly contraindicated for them from the outset. If, for any reason, your GP does not support your plan for a home birth (and yours is a low-risk pregnancy), you should be able to find another doctor, either in your practice or in the area, to whom you could transfer for the duration of your pregnancy.

If you choose a home birth, you will be under the care of a team of community midwives, as it is rare that you will see the same midwife all the way through your pregnancy. The midwives will carry out all your antenatal care, either at a clinic or in your home, and you will only attend the hospital for specific ultrasound scans or if you need to see an obstetrician. One of the team will assist you during labour and after your baby is born. In order to help you to decide whether this is what you would like, you could ask your midwife the following questions:

▸ How many babies are delivered at home from that GP practice or maternity unit per year?
▸ How many were born to first-time mothers?
▸ How many women needed to be transferred to hospital after the start of labour, and for what reasons?
▸ How many deliveries has the midwife planning to deliver you performed at home that year?

Alternatively, you can book and pay for an independent midwife; the pattern of care will be broadly the same, except that all midwife visits will take place in your own home. Although it is likely that the person you hire will be the one who delivers you, your midwife may introduce you to a colleague, who may be called upon if, for some reason, she herself is unavailable (e.g. she is ill, she is delivering another woman).

Despite an increase in recent years, the percentage of women who give birth at home remains very low and the majority who do so are not first-time mothers. If you have had a previous straightforward delivery and yours is a low-risk pregnancy, studies show that home births pose no more risks than hospital ones. (That said, you should be aware that, for unforeseen medical reasons, you may need to be transferred to a hospital at some stage during or after labour.) If this is your first birth, the risks of a home birth are three times higher, although it should be stressed that the actual number of negative outcomes is still very low (*see* Box opposite). In addition, if you live a long way from a hospital that has full

emergency and maternity services, this could affect the advice given to you by your healthcare professionals.

Remember that, although the choice of a home birth is ultimately yours, it is worth seeking advice from your midwife or obstetrician: your welfare and that of your baby is their prime concern and should be central to any decision you make. As with all matters in pregnancy, you are entitled to change your mind at any point, and may indeed be advised to do so, if the circumstances of your pregnancy or your home life change.

Is my home suitable for giving birth?

As long as you feel comfortable there, most homes are perfectly adequate for giving birth. When your due date approaches, the midwife will discuss with you what preparations need to be made, if any, to ensure your home is suitably set up. She will also let you know what equipment she will be bringing. Many women are concerned that giving birth at home might be very messy, but a few plastic decorating sheets can protect furniture and surfaces and the midwife will bring large, disposable pads on which you can deliver. After the birth, she will also clear up and take away the placenta and cord if you wish. See Chapter 5, p. 140 for more information on preparing your home for a home birth.

HOME BIRTHS – THE LATEST FINDINGS

Women are often concerned as to whether giving birth at home is safe and want to know the facts before making their choice. The most recent large-scale study, looking at 65,000 births across a variety of birth settings (both obstetric and non-obstetric), provides the following statistics on low-risk, planned home births:

▸ slightly more than ten per cent of women who had previously given birth needed to be transferred to a obstetric or midwifery unit before or after delivery
▸ around 40 per cent of women who had never given birth before had to transfer to a obstetric or midwifery unit
▸ first-time mothers giving birth at home were three times more likely to suffer complications during or after labour than those who had previously had straightforward births, although the absolute risks remained relatively low at approximately one per cent.

Hospital birth

Within the hospital setting, there are three different types of maternity unit:

▶ **obstetric unit (OU):** part of a hospital, where obstetricians, anaesthetists and other specialists work alongside midwives; all obstetric facilities (e.g. operating theatres) and full pain relief options and some or all levels of neonatal care are available

▶ **alongside midwifery unit (AMU):** either next to or part of an obstetric unit; staffed by midwives, with limited pharmacological pain relief and with easy access to specialist doctors and obstetric and neonatal facilities if a transfer is needed

▶ **freestanding midwifery unit (FMU):** geographically separate from an obstetric unit; staffed by midwives, with limited pharmacological pain relief and will require a transfer by ambulance if specialist doctors or obstetric or neonatal facilities are needed.

The majority of births take place in an OU, as they cater for all types of birth, irrespective of risk; they can guarantee prompt medical attention if it is needed. The latter two settings, which are sometimes called Birth Centres, are staffed by midwives and care only for low-risk births requiring minimal pain relief (e.g. epidurals are not available). All three settings can offer equipment such as birthing pools, beanbags and balls, and will allow you to create the atmosphere you want using, perhaps, mood lighting, music and so on. Which of the three units you opt for will depend on what is available in your area, as well as on your own personal circumstances. It is a good idea to check which of the systems of antenatal care explained on pp. 14–15 is offered by the unit, as this may also affect your decision.

There are a number of reasons why you might choose a hospital birth:

▶ this is your first baby (first labours tend to need more medical intervention than subsequent ones)
▶ you have a pre-existing medical condition, such as diabetes, that needs careful monitoring during labour
▶ antenatal tests have shown that your baby is likely to require medical assistance after delivery
▶ you have had complications with previous births
▶ you have already had a Caesarean section
▶ you are over 40 (the risk of complications increases with age)
▶ you have a BMI over 30 (increases the risk of complications)
▶ your home is too far from a hospital to risk having your baby at home, in case you need an emergency transfer to hospital

▶ you are unsure of your pain threshold and what might happen during labour and want the option of pharmacological pain relief should you need it (*see* Chapter 6, pp. 180–6)
▶ you feel comforted by the idea of having immediate access to medical support for you and your baby
▶ you feel that your home environment is not suitable for a home birth – it lacks privacy or you have other children who might be alarmed about what is happening
▶ you want to be 'looked after', if only for a short time: your meals and drinks will be brought to you and your bedding changed, if required. (Sometimes, women who have a baby at home find themselves up and about very soon after delivering.)

Before deciding, it is worth researching each option fully and visiting the different birth settings. You should do this even if you have given birth there before, as facilities can often change in the space of a few years. Many women also find it helpful to speak to other mothers who have recently had a baby. However, while anecdotal evidence can be useful, each woman will have a unique experience of labour, so what might have been satisfactory for someone you know may not turn out to be so for you. And remember that, should you be opt for a midwifery unit, you may begin your labour there but may at some stage need to be transferred to an obstetric unit – you should therefore know what this has to offer when making your choice.

Most hospitals organise regular tours of their unit(s) so that you can get a chance to see the facilities for yourself and ask the questions that are important to you. I have outlined some common questions (*see* Box opposite), although not all will be relevant to your particular situation. When you have made your choice, you will need to book your hospital birth with your GP, midwife or the hospital itself. Again, you are entitled to change your mind later on about which hospital you have opted for, or even that you would now prefer to have a home birth.

Antenatal care

▸ What type of antenatal care does the unit offer: shared care or team midwifery?

▸ How many antenatal appointments will you have? (Ten is the normal amount for a first-time birth, seven for subsequent births.)

▸ How many ultrasound scans will you have? (You should be offered as standard a dating scan at eight to fourteen weeks of pregnancy, and a fetal anomaly scan at eighteen to twenty weeks – see Chapter 3, p. 66–71.)

▸ Which screening test(s) for Down's syndrome does the unit offer? (This partly depends on when you have your booking appointment – see Chapter 3, p. 72.)

▸ All units now offer either access or referral to nuchal fold screening, part of the screening test for Down's syndrome – ask which of these is offered by the unit.

▸ Does the unit organise antenatal classes and how early do you have to book them?

▸ Which of the three levels of care provided by neonatal units (NNU) are provided here (see Chapter 7, Prematurity, p. 225)? Where do babies get transferred to if they need a different level of care?

▸ What is the earliest gestational age of a premature baby that the NNU will accept into each level of care? (This differs from one unit to another, with some very premature babies requiring transfer elsewhere.)

General facilities

▸ How many delivery beds are there per 1,000 births? (This information may be available on the internet.)

▸ Do any delivery rooms have en suite bathrooms (more likely in a midwifery unit)?

▸ Can partners stay the whole time? (More and more units – not just midwifery units – are encouraging this because it is beneficial for both parents and babies.)

▸ Can I see the bathrooms and toilets in both the labour and postnatal wards (to check for cleanliness)?

Labour and pain relief

▸ Who will review the birth plan, if you decide to make one?

▸ What is the hospital's Caesarean section rate? (Bear in mind that, if this is a teaching hospital or a large district hospital, the rate might be higher than the current average for England and Wales of 25 per cent, because these types of hospitals

look after women with medical complications.)

▸ Is 24-hour anaesthesia available?

▸ Does it have epidurals and, importantly, mobile epidurals?

▸ How long are the shifts for midwives? (If the shifts last twelve hours, you are more likely to have the same midwife to assist you, at least for the main part of your labour, than if the shift lasts eight hours.)

▸ What is the policy on water births?

▸ Does the unit have birthing pools and if so, how many? (If there are only a few birthing pools, you might not be able to count on one being available.)

▸ What is the policy on non-pharmacological pain relief, including TENS, acupuncture, reflexology; by extension, are practitioners of certain alternative methods of pain relief allowed to assist you during labour?

▸ How many people are allowed with you in the delivery room?

▸ Are you encouraged to give birth in any position that feels comfortable, for example, squatting on the floor?

▸ What is the policy on induction (e.g. if your baby is overdue) and routine electronic monitoring during labour?

▸ What is the policy on episiotomies versus vaginal tears (some women indicate a preference in their birth plan for one rather than the other)? Who will do the suturing, a midwife or a doctor?

Post-birth

▸ What is the average length of stay after the birth? Is there a difference between first and subsequent births?

▸ How many beds are there in the postnatal ward and how many midwives are present at any one time?

▸ Are there any amenity rooms (single rooms) and do they have en suite bathrooms? How much do they cost? On what basis are they allocated: for example, are they only for women who have had a difficult birth?

▸ Can partners stay overnight? (Even if you don't have your own room, some hospitals do nonetheless allow husbands to stay.)

▸ What are the visiting hours? How many visitors are allowed, who can visit, and what is the policy on children visiting?

▸ Is there a breastfeeding counsellor available and what are their hours?

▸ What items will you need to bring into hospital (e.g. pillows, towels, nappies)?

▸ Are special diets catered for (especially important if you have a food allergy)?

2

Looking after yourself

Many women want to reassure themselves that they are doing everything they can to maximise their chances of having a healthy pregnancy and a healthy baby. This can include eating a nutritious diet, exercising, taking sensible precautions to avoid harmful substances and attending antenatal classes to help you prepare for the birth and your new life as a parent.

A varied, balanced and nutritious diet will not only support your well-being during pregnancy but also can help to establish a healthy approach to food for your whole family – one that will hopefully last a lifetime.

If you feel good and eat well, you will be better prepared for pregnancy, birth and life with a newborn baby. However, it is a sad fact that many women already feel guilty about much of what they eat even when they are not pregnant. Once you are, you can feel overwhelmed by the amount of supposedly scientifically proven dos and don'ts regarding your food choices. Furthermore, common side effects of pregnancy, such as morning sickness, indigestion and heartbearn (*see* Chapter 4, pp.123–4), can wreak havoc on your appetite and ability to tolerate or digest certain foods.

Let me tell you that much of the alarmist diet and lifestyle information that is published in the media is scientifically questionable, so try not to worry too much about what you might be doing right or wrong. And remember: if your digestion prevents you from eating much at certain points in your pregnancy, this is unlikely to harm your baby, which will draw all it needs to thrive from your nutritional reserves. So, as long as you eat reasonably healthily most of the time and include a wide range of foods in your diet, you are eating well enough for your pregnancy.

The basis of a healthy diet

A healthy diet in pregnancy is the same as a healthy diet when not pregnant: it contains proteins, fats, carbohydrates, fibre and vitamins and minerals from as wide a variety of sources as possible. However, rather than getting too hung up about the precise ratios and quantities of different foods that you should be consuming, just focus on eating something every day from each of the four main food groups listed below.

Bread, cereal, rice, potatoes, pasta

Starchy staples, which are rich in carbohydrates, are an excellent source of energy and should form the main part of your meal. Wholegrain versions of these foods, for example, brown rice and wholemeal pasta and flour, have a fuller vitamin, mineral and fibre content and so are more nutritious than the refined (white) varieties.

Fruit and vegetables

Fruit and vegetables – fresh, frozen or dried – contain essential vitamins, minerals and fibre and it is good to eat plenty of these every day. However, fruit is high in sugar, so while the fruit itself is good for providing, among other things, the fibre needed to prevent constipation (which is common in pregnancy – *see* Chapter 4, p.124), you should consume fruit juice in moderation (the amount of sugar contained per 100 ml should be listed in the carbohydrate column on the label), as repeated intake of sugary foods raises the likelihood of

IRON: THE ESSENTIAL MINERAL

Iron is the mineral used to transport oxygen around the body and, in pregnancy, it helps to build and maintain muscles in both the mother and the fetus. Your iron requirements are two to three times higher than normal when you are pregnant. Consequently, iron deficiency (leading to anaemia – *see* Chapter 4, p.127) is very common in pregnant women, especially after the twentieth week. You should be actively aiming to increase your intake of foods that are high in iron, the main ones being red meat, poultry, eggs and fish. Meat is particularly good, as it contains compounds that facilitate the absorption of iron, whereas vegetable sources, such as lentils, oatmeal, almonds, green leafy vegetables, dried apricots and prunes, are less easily absorbed. However, vitamin C (ascorbic acid) in the form of orange juice, for example, does increase the absorption of iron. Conversely, tea and coffee, which contain tannin, inhibit absorption if taken during a meal or shortly afterwards.

You will be tested for anaemia at least twice during your pregnancy, by ten weeks and again at 28 weeks (*see* Chapter 3, p.62). If you are found to be deficient in iron, you will probably be prescribed an iron supplement, because diet alone cannot make up for the shortfall of this nutrient in your blood. This is likely to be 100–200 mg daily in pill form, on an empty stomach, taken with some orange juice to maximise its effectiveness. It is important that you do not self-diagnose anaemia and take over-the-counter supplements, as overconsumption of iron can damage organs such as the heart and liver. Conversely, obtaining iron from your diet is safe, because it is unlikely you will ingest excessive amounts and any surplus will be easier to eliminate naturally.

developing gestational diabetes (*see* Chapter 3, p. 64) – it is better to drink water to quench your thirst.

Meat, fish, eggs, beans, nuts, pulses

Eating widely from this food group will provide you with protein, and many of these foods also contain iron (*see* Box opposite). Note, however, that certain fish should be limited or avoided altogether (*see* p. 25). Half of your daily main meal should consist of protein. They are an especially important part of your diet during pregnancy, as they play a key role in enabling the healthy growth of your baby's muscles, bones and internal organs, as well as your own cell growth and repair. Protein molecules are made up of twenty amino acids. Of these, our bodies produce twelve naturally and these are called 'non-essential' amino acids. However, the other eight can only be obtained from food sources and are called 'essential' amino acids. Animal sources of protein (lean meat, fish, well-cooked eggs and dairy products) contain all the essential amino acids, as do soya products. Vegetable sources, however, do not, which is why if you follow a vegetarian – and particularly a vegan – diet, you will need to eat a variety of vegetable sources of protein (*see* p. 24) to make sure that your nutritional needs are met.

Milk and dairy products

Dairy foods are an excellent source of the calcium, which is essential for building healthy bones and muscles, as well as of vitamins A, B and D. The lower the fat content, the more digestible they are and the greater the proportion of nutrients they contain (as these are not present in the fat). Your baby derives calcium from your existing reserves, so it is important to keep up your intake during your pregnancy, as depletion could result in loss of bone density, which can lead to osteopaenia (a precursor to osteoporosis) in later life.

Vegetarians and vegans in pregnancy

Vegetarians, and vegans in particular, are at risk of becoming anaemic during pregnancy (see Box on iron on p. 22). If you eat fish and dairy products, and eat as varied a diet as possible, you should be able to maintain your levels of iron, as well as calcium and vitamins D and B12 (which is only found in animal products), and obtain all the essential nutrients you need for your pregnancy. Dried apricots and prunes are a good source of iron, but they also provide fibre (which helps prevent constipation), so are particularly good during pregnancy.

If you are a vegan, you should increase your intake of nuts, pulses, tofu, leafy green vegetables and wholegrains to ensure you do not become deficient in essential proteins, vitamins and minerals, particularly those mentioned above.

If you have any concerns about your diet, do not hesitate to speak to your GP or midwife, as it may be necessary for them to prescribe a special multivitamin supplement for you to take during pregnancy.

Vitamin and mineral supplements

There are two specific supplements that you must definitely take while pregnant, as the amounts needed are difficult to obtain from diet alone: folic acid and vitamin D.

Folic acid

A 400 mcg daily dose of folic acid is known to help prevent neural tube defects, such as spina bifida, and it may also protect against other birth defects. Ideally, you should have started taking it for three months before you conceived, but as long as you begin as soon as you are pregnant and continue throughout the first trimester, it will still be beneficial.

Vitamin D

About 25 per cent of the population are deficient in vitamin D, and this is even more prevalent among vegetarians and vegans (see above). Although vitamin D can be obtained from certain foods (e.g. eggs, oily fish, butter, cheese), the best source is from exposure to natural light (not necessarily sunlight). We need about 40 minutes of natural light per day to produce the level of vitamin D that is required for good calcium absorption. If you are vitamin D deficient, your baby's development is unlikely to be affected, but it can mean that you yourself may later suffer from calcium deficiency. Women are now advised to take a 10 mg daily supplement of vitamin D during pregnancy and until they are no longer breastfeeding. These are available to buy over the counter in a chemist's or supermarket, either as a single vitamin or as part of a combination with folic acid.

Kitchen hygiene and food safety

Pregnant women are more susceptible to gastroenteritis caused by bacteria and viruses, as well as being more likely to suffer from the complications that can arise from these types of infection. Although the risks of bacteria in food are low, it is better to err on the side of caution while pregnant and, if you take the following basic steps of kitchen hygiene, you will further protect yourself:

- Wash and rinse your hands thoroughly with soap and water before and after handling food.
- Change tea towels and dishcloths regularly.
- Wash all kitchen knives and utensils in hot, soapy water and rinse well.
- Don't use the same knives and utensils (including chopping boards) to prepare different types of ingredients (e.g. vegetables and raw meat).
- Wash all fruit and vegetables well.
- Defrost food thoroughly.
- When heating/reheating food, make sure it is piping hot all they way through, especially if using a microwave.
- Do not reheat a dish more than once.
- If in doubt whether food you have kept in the fridge is still safe to eat, throw it away.

In addition, there are certain foods that should be avoided altogether during pregnancy because they could potentially harm you or your baby. If you need further clarification, or if you begin to have any of the symptoms described below, consult your GP or midwife.

Liver and liver products (e.g. sausage, pâté)

Liver contains high doses of vitamin A in a form called retinol and excessive levels of this may cause fetal abnormalities. Vegetable products (especially orange-coloured fruit and vegetables such as carrots, mangos and apricots) contain good levels of vitamin A in a form called betacarotene that is safe to eat.

Raw or undercooked eggs and chicken

Eggs and chicken can contain the salmonella bacterium, which crosses the placenta and can, in some cases, lead to miscarriage, premature labour, intrauterine death and other neonatal problems. (Free-range hens can carry it, but it is usually found in battery hens.) Salmonella is killed by heat, so it is important to cook or reheat these foods fully (for eggs, that means hard-boiled). Mayonnaise and mousses can contain raw eggs, although the more mass-produced they are, the less likely they are to contain *fresh* raw eggs – pasteurised egg or egg powder are more common and are safe to eat, and some varieties contain no egg at all. Symptoms of salmonella poisoning appear within 12–48 hours of eating the affected food and include vomiting, diarrhoea and fever.

Raw or undercooked meat, unwashed fruit and vegetables

Toxoplasmosis is a fairly common infection to which most people are immune (*see* also p. 43). It is caused by a parasite that is present in raw meat and is also found in animal (especially cat) faeces. Make sure you wash all shop-bought fruit and vegetables thoroughly (and wash your hands if you pick any yourself or do some gardening) and that meat is thoroughly cooked. Toxoplasmosis infection can be very harmful to the fetus in the first trimester, so if you think you may have been infected, ask your GP for a blood test (symptoms are similar to a mild dose of flu, and so it is difficult to diagnose yourself).

Unpasteurised or blue cheeses

Very rarely, soft, unpasteurised or blue cheeses can contain listeria. This bacterium causes mild flu-like symptoms with nausea and diarrhoea, but it can be potentially fatal for the fetus. Semi-soft cheeses (e.g. mozzarella), pasteurised processed cheeses, hard cheeses and cream or cottage cheese are the safer options.

Pâtés and cooked meats

If they are kept at the wrong temperature, pâtés and cooked meats can contain listeria (*see* above) as well as e-coli (although this is extremely rare). Cooked meats are fine to eat if they have been kept in hygienic conditions, but don't store them for longer than a few days. E-coli symptoms begin about a week after eating contaminated food and include severe cramps and diarrhoea (containing blood). It can lead to kidney failure and ultimately can be fatal for mother and baby.

Fish and seafood

Fish is a good source of the fatty acids that are needed in pregnancy, but certain types should be eaten in limited quantities and others avoided altogether. Those containing high levels of mercury – shark, swordfish and marlin – should not be eaten while pregnant, as this can affect the developing baby. Only eat oily fish, such as fresh tuna, salmon and mackerel, up to twice a week, although tinned tuna is fine. There is a higher risk of food poisoning and parasitic infections from raw seafood and shellfish, but thoroughly cooked versions are safe to eat, as is the raw fish used in sushi if the fish has been frozen first (because this kills any parasites).

Bagged salads

Bagged salads and other prepared chilled foods can contain salmonella or listeria bacteria, although this is rare. Nevertheless it is wise to avoid them – better to buy a whole lettuce and wash it thoroughly yourself.

Easy ways to begin eating healthily

Many of us start off with the best of intentions when embarking on a healthy eating programme, only to be undone by setting the bar too high for ourselves and by the environment we live and work in. Before we know it, we have given in to temptation when we open a kitchen cupboard at home, when colleagues bring in cakes or when our partner decides to get a take-away on the way back from work.

If you suddenly adopt a totally different diet from your normal one, or try to stick to it too rigidly, you could end up failing after a few days, leading you to binge on all the high-fat, high-sugar processed foods that you tried so hard to cut out. Accept that you are not going to break poor habits overnight: healthy eating should be a lifelong goal and so it needs to be appealing in the long term. Make changes gradually and it will be easier to maintain them, and remember that you are allowed to eat treat foods that might not be 'ideal', as long as you do so occasionally and in moderation.

> **Believe it or not, I actually went off chocolate in both my pregnancies, which is very strange, as I'm a chocoholic normally!** KATE

To begin with, probably the single best thing you can do is to reduce your intake of refined sugar. For example, if you have sugar in tea or coffee, cut this out and, after a week, I guarantee you that you will have forgotten what it tasted like. Try switching your breakfast cereal to one that contains less added sugar (*see* below) and add a banana or some strawberries to sweeten instead.

You can have a couple of snacks per day, but instead of a few biscuits or a packet of crisps, make it a dozen shelled almonds or half a dozen dried apricots – these will stop you feeling hungry and will also boost your iron and energy levels. Steer clear of 'empty' foods, ones that increase your calorie count but have little or no nutritional content (*see* Box). In addition, the following ploys may help you to avoid some of the pitfalls of snacking and unhealthy eating:

- ▸ At home, wrap treats such as plain biscuits individually (in foil or cling film) or portion off some nuts/low-fat crisps into separate containers or bags – don't have the larger packet on display.
- ▸ Plan all meals for the whole week and make a shopping list – buy only what is on the list.
- ▸ Never shop on an empty stomach.
- ▸ If you must have a take-away, limit it to once a week and choose healthier options, avoiding deep-fried foods and those with rich sauces.
- ▸ If restaurants and fast-food outlets list the calories contained in their different dishes, choose their healthier options.

If you take your own lunch and snacks to work (or have them delivered – *see* Useful Resources), you are much less likely to be tempted by celebratory cakes or fancy biscuits in meetings, or to eat on a whim the closest thing you can get hold of (usually from a vending machine or a coffee bar/work canteen). The following are easy to prepare and transport:

- ▸ chopped carrot, cucumber, cherry tomatoes and peppers with a hummus dip (small, individual pots can be bought from supermarkets)
- ▸ small packets of oatcakes
- ▸ cold chicken breast (no skin) in a wholemeal roll/bagel
- ▸ wholemeal pasta salad
- ▸ fresh fruit (e.g. clementines, apples, strawberries, blueberries) – there is no place for tinned fruit in the 21st century!
- ▸ yoghurt (natural, unsweetened is best – you can add honey or your own fruit)
- ▸ nuts, seeds, dried fruit.

'EMPTY' FOODS
Foods that add to your calorie count but provide little or no nutritional benefit are considered 'empty'. While they often provide a short-term boost to energy, they can result in a dip later on that will lead you to crave more. These include:

- ▸ white/brown sugar and artificial sweeteners
- ▸ chocolate (minimum 70 per cent cocoa content is better and can boost your iron levels)
- ▸ sweets
- ▸ fizzy drinks
- ▸ artificial cream (mainly sugar and chemicals)
- ▸ cereals with high levels of added sugar (*see* main text)
- ▸ biscuits and cakes made with refined sugar and flour
- ▸ breakfast biscuit or cereal bars (all high in sugar).

Finally, eating healthily works best when it applies to all the family. Many of the large supermarket chains now publish menus to help busy mothers cook budget-conscious, nutritious family meals. For example, easy ways to increase fibre, protein and slow-release carbohydrates are to use oats as a crumble topping, and add beans to stews and casseroles, peas to fish pies or risottos, lentils to soups and grains and seeds to salads. If your children are finding it difficult to kick-start a good eating pattern, simply take the junk food out of the house. They don't need any of it, and you should be in control of the dietary habits of the household, not them.

Breakfast cereals: the healthy option?

Most of us have grown up assuming that breakfast cereals are healthy. However, a recent independent survey, which compared the sugar, salt and fat content of 50 well-known cereals (based on the manufacturers' information) found that most contained significant levels of sugar. Specifically:

- ▸ 32 were high in sugar (defined as more than 12.5 g per 100 g of cereal) – in only two of these cereals was this due to the fruit they contained; for the rest, it was due to *added* sugar
- ▸ most met the target of a maximum of 1.1 g salt per 100 g, although three did not
- ▸ most were low in fat (three per cent or less), although one contained medium levels (fifteen per cent)
- ▸ those that had the lowest sugar content had medium levels of either fat or salt.

You might think that once you are pregnant, you can – and even *should* – 'eat for two'. However, this is a myth and it is only in the third trimester that your calorie requirements increase slightly. In the first two trimesters, your calorie intake should remain that of a normal, healthy woman (i.e. 2,000 calories per day). In the last trimester, you need to increase it a little, but only by 200–300 calories. Before you rejoice and reach for the nearest bar of chocolate (a small bar is equivalent to around 250 calories), it goes without saying that this additional calorie intake should comprise nutritious foods, that is, useful calories for you and the baby! Equally, it is hardly a green light to eat as much as you want, because 200–300 calories represents only the equivalent of a banana and a low-fat yoghurt, or of a piece of buttered toast.

There are, however, increasing numbers of women whose extremes of weight can lead to problems during or after pregnancy. If you are overweight or clinically obese (with a BMI of 26 or above), this can increases the risk of miscarriage and premature birth and of developing complications such as hypertension, gestational diabetes and pre-eclampsia. If you are very slim, with a BMI that is below 19, and if your diet has been poor, you may be depleted in certain essential nutrients, most commonly vitamin D and iron, and find that you become exhausted by meeting the needs of pregnancy. If you are underweight, overweight or obese, you can speak to your GP or midwife about the best way to manage your weight during your pregnancy.

A diet high in sugar and salt increases the likelihood of developing hypertension (high blood pressure – *see* Complications, p. 286) or diabetes and, as with consumption of high levels of fat, raises the risk of becoming overweight or obese (*see* Feature on pp. 30 –1). Women who were diabetic before they became pregnant should consult also the Feature on diabetes in Chapter 3 on p. 64 –5.

It is therefore important to look at the food labels when shopping and choose cereals and other food items that are lower in salt, sugar and saturated fats where possible. Compared to a full cooked breakfast, the average breakfast cereal is still probably a better option and, indeed, most are fortified with vitamins and minerals. However, there are many other healthier breakfast choices, such as scrambled eggs on wholemeal toast accompanied by a glass of orange juice. Adding fresh fruit to a low-sugar cereal can make it more appealing and also increases its nutritional value. For more ideas about better breakfasts, see Useful Resources.

Your weight in pregnancy

If your body mass index (BMI) is within the normal range (*see* Box on right), you should put on around 13 kg in weight while you are pregnant. Very little of this – only up to 1 kg – is gained during the first trimester. However, your weight increases significantly over the next two trimesters, when you will gain about 500–700 g a week, up until the final two weeks when weight gain usually tails off. Just over one-third of this additional weight is the baby, the placenta and the amniotic fluid, with the rest accounted for by the elements needed to support your pregnancy, such as your enlarged breasts and uterus, as well as your increased blood volume and body fat (*see* Box above).

Obesity

Obesity can have serious consequences in particular for pregnant women and for their babies. Your healthcare professionals should help you address any underlying health and lifestyles issues, so that you are better able to manage your weight while you are pregnant.

You are clinically obese if your body mass index (BMI) is more than 30 (see Box on p. 29 for how to calculate your BMI). Your health and that of your baby may require more frequent monitoring during pregnancy and after the birth. This is because a high BMI, with or without pre-existing type 2 diabetes (see Feature in Chapter 2, pp. 64–5), increases the risk of virtually all pregnancy complications (the higher the BMI, the greater the risk) and of an adverse outcome for you and your baby. Specifically, obese women are much more likely than women with a healthy BMI to suffer from pregnancy-induced hypertension, gestational diabetes and pre-eclampsia. The Caesarean section rate (especially the emergency rate) is significantly higher among obese women, as are induction and instrumental deliveries, and postpartum haemorrhage (PPH) is four times higher. Stillbirths are twice as likely, the risk of death of a baby during childbirth is up to three times higher and newborn babies are more likely to need admission to a neonatal intensive care unit.

How your antenatal care is affected

If your BMI is more than 30, you should be prescribed a daily 5 mg folic acid supplement for the first three months of pregnancy, rather than the usual 400 mcg, as well as a 10 mcg vitamin D supplement (which you should continue to take until you have finished breastfeeding). You should be helped and supported during pregnancy to minimise the amount of weight you gain, so please don't feel affronted or upset if your GP or midwife weighs you regularly throughout your pregnancy or if they refer you to an obstetrician or to a specialist clinic. They are simply trying to establish your risk of complications and to keep you and your baby as safe as possible during your pregnancy.

It is harder for the sonographer to monitor and visualise your baby effectively using ultrasound scanning if you are significantly overweight, and this makes screening for fetal abnormalities and surveillance of fetal growth, position and well-being more difficult. If the sonographer cannot see all the elements that need checking (e.g. the palate), you will be asked to move around the clinic or hospital for 30–40 minutes to see if the fetus changes position or, alternatively, you will be given another appointment at a later date. If it is still difficult, a second sonographer or obstetrician may be asked to review the scan or observe the procedure, but in some cases it is still not possible to see every organ and you will be told that, as far as can be seen, the fetus appears to have no abnormalities, but that certain features have not been visualised.

Similarly, fetal monitoring during labour is more challenging and it may be harder to site and administer an epidural in obese women. Indeed, you may need to see an anaesthetist antenatally in order to avoid discovering this in an emergency. Caesarean sections can be more complicated if you are obese and are more likely to lead to problems with recovery, such as PPH, venous thromboembolism and wound infection. As a result, women with a BMI of more than 35 are advised to give birth in an obstetric unit with appropriate neonatal facilities, and those with a BMI of 30–35 should be individually assessed and be made aware of the increased risks to them and their babies during and after birth.

Managing your weight in pregnancy

While you are pregnant, you should be considering weight maintenance (i.e. not putting on weight during pregnancy) rather than weight loss. This does not mean that you should go on a diet (they don't work during pregnancy), but rather eat healthily (see below) – your baby will still get all the nutrition they need, but you will not actually put on any weight (or very little). There is evidence that if you are supported in your efforts to maintain a healthy weight during pregnancy, you are less likely to put on more weight than is recommended than if you are left to manage the situation by yourself. If you are keen to minimise the risk of complications to your baby, but feel your healthcare professionals are not as supportive of your efforts to maintain your weight as you would like them to be, you should ask to be referred to a consultant obstetrician with a special interest in plus-size pregnancies. Postnatal nutritional and exercise advice should also be made available to you, so do let your GP or midwife know beforehand if you feel this would suit you.

If you are struggling to maintain a healthy weight and have been piling on more kilos than you would like, consider getting help from weight-loss organisations (see Useful Resources), which will welcome and support you during your pregnancy so that you don't put on any actual weight. Some even have specific programmes for pregnant women, but all are keen to help women find ways of changing their eating habits by providing psychological strategies and habit-busting advice to break the cycle of unhealthy eating and thus help you to keep the weight off once your baby is born. If you do contact a weight-loss organisation, check that your local group has someone experienced in helping pregnant women, but the chances are that you will find other pregnant women in the group already and that you will derive much-needed encouragement and support from others.

The notion that you must at all costs avoid weight-loss programmes run by experienced organisations during pregnancy should be balanced with the fact that you are at much higher risk of harming your health and that of your unborn child by remaining significantly overweight. Without necessarily losing weight, a sensible weight-management programme, overseen by a professional, can allow you to maintain your current weight despite your growing baby. As long as your baby is growing well, there is no evidence that such programmes harm either you or your baby, yet they enable you to lose some of you own excess body fat during your pregnancy.

How to keep weight gain to a minimum

Reading the information given about diet (*see* pp. 22–9) and exercise (*see* pp. 32–6) can help you find ways to eat healthily and gain physical fitness as a means of managing your weight. It will be helpful if you enlist the help and support of your partner by getting them to do the food shopping and remove the 'rubbish'/junk food from your cupboards to help you avoid temptation. Write down what you eat and plan meals in advance, especially what you eat at work. Take your lunch in with you if you have limited access to healthy eating.

Start by reducing your sugar intake. Sugar is addictive: once it has been absorbed into the bloodstream, you end up craving more. This rise and fall in blood sugar levels can also affect your baby's growth pattern and their ability to process sugar, which the body then 'programmes' for life. In addition, limit your intake of refined carbohydrates, such as white flour and sugar, and increase your consumption of fibre-rich, slow-release carbohydrates and vegetables. Check packaging for the nutritional value of foods, especially sugar (carbohydrate) levels (remember that some so-called 'healthy' or 'low-fat' options are actually very high in sugar). Switch from sweetened fizzy drinks to sparkling water as often as possible and make sure that you eat breakfast every morning, even if it is a yoghurt or a banana, so that you reduce your craving for unhealthy snacks later in the day. When making a meal, bear in mind that half of your plate should consist of lean protein, a third of vegetables (not potatoes) and the rest should be

slow-release carbohydrates (e.g. wholewheat pasta, brown rice, lentils, pulses). It may help you to watch your portion size if you try eating on a smaller plate, in order to give the impression of having a larger portion.

Going to restaurants can be the undoing of many a careful eater, so aim in advance of eating out to have a maximum of two courses. Turn away the free bread, ask for dressing/sauce on the side and for vegetables rather than potatoes or other carbohydrates to accompany the main course. You should be aware that main course salads can actually be higher in fats and calories than other simply cooked main courses, because of the high calorie content of salad dressing.

Try to remain active for as long as possible into your pregnancy. Exercise doesn't always have to mean going to the gym. Cleaning the house vigorously – preferably to music that has a lively, energising rhythm to keep you going! – can be just as good, but remember that walking or swimming should make you feel breathless if it is to count. Physical activity for 20–30 minutes, especially after a meal (even if you are just clearing up after the evening meal), helps to keep blood sugar levels more stable, both immediately after the meal and once the peak levels have passed. Try, above all, to make exercise fun – then you will have an additional incentive to continue.

Making lifestyle changes such as those listed above can be challenging, but you are more likely to be successful in your new regime if you:

▸ try to address the reasons why you find it difficult to maintain a healthy weight, as well as the triggers that lead you to eat unhealthily or to overeat
▸ identify the barriers to change
▸ set yourself goals and track your progress
▸ are consistent in your approach: long-lasting habits take a while to form, so try not to make drastic changes that you cannot stick to
▸ adjust not just your own diet, but that of your partner and children, so that you are all eating the same foods – this is a great opportunity to change the eating habits of your family.

While you are pregnant, your new healthy eating and exercise pattern is not just for you, but for your baby as well. However, after the birth, it is important to continue with the adjustments you have made, otherwise your good intentions will be short-lived and all your hard work easily undone.

EXERCISE

Exercise is good for everyone, partly because it is a mood enhancer and partly because it is essential for long-term cardiovascular health. It is a good idea to stay active and do some form of exercise when you are pregnant, as the fitter you are, the better your body is likely to cope with pregnancy, labour and the weeks that follow.

Research has shown that exercising during pregnancy does not increase the risk of harm to the pregnancy or the fetus. Fears that exercise can trigger a miscarriage are also unfounded. On the contrary, a normal, healthy pregnancy can certainly withstand regular exercise and your baby may indeed cope better with the stresses of labour if you have exercised throughout. In addition, many of the common but unpleasant side effects of pregnancy (*see* Chapter 4, pp. 122 –31), including tiredness, varicose veins and insomnia, are reduced in women who exercise. Aerobic and strength and conditioning exercise are therefore beneficial to both you and the baby, as long as they are not done to excess.

Suitable forms of exercise when pregnant are ones that are low-impact, raise the heart rate within safe levels, don't dehydrate you excessively and improve muscle tone without overstretching ligaments or abdominal muscles. They should not put undue strain on your joints, your back or your growing uterus. In particular, you should avoid:

▸ exercise that involves lying on your back for any length of time, as this can affect blood flow to the placenta
▸ contact sports
▸ sports where you might fall (e.g. skiing, horse riding)
▸ jogging/running or similar activities that involve jumping up and down
▸ scuba diving or, conversely, sports at altitude (more than 2,500 m).

When exercising, you should avoid overheating, drink plenty of water to stay hydrated and keep up your blood sugar levels by eating sufficient amounts before and after exercise. Stop exercising at once and seek medical advice if you become light-headed or overly short of breath, you feel pain of any sort, especially in the abdomen or lower back, or if you develop chest pain, palpitations or a headache. Remember that, even if you are not particularly sporty or keen on the gym, brisk walking, swimming and generally staying active all help you to stay fit. However, make sure you do these activities until you are out of breath and your heartbeat is slightly raised – sauntering along or bobbing around at the shallow end of the pool chatting to your friend do *not* count as exercise!

HELP FOR SWOLLEN FEET AND ANKLES

Ankles and feet can swell in pregnancy (known as oedema – see Chapter 4, p. 131), especially in the third trimester. This is because more water collects in your body and this can particularly affect your lower limbs, especially if you have been standing up for a while. To help prevent the problem, rest whenever you can with your feet raised up (e.g. propped up in front of you on cushions), try to avoid standing for long periods – now is definitely the time to ask for a seat on public transport! – and wear comfortable shoes, preferably ones without straps. Drink plenty of water (this will not increase retention of fluid) and try to keep active in order to maintain good circulation. In addition, practising the following exercises can help to allieviate the discomfort:

▸ Flex your feet towards you and then point the toes away in a gentle up-and-down movement. Do this around 30 times.
▸ Rotate each foot in a circle, eight times one way and then eight times the other.

While a little swelling is a normal side effect of pregnancy, particularly if the weather is hot, any *sudden* swelling of the hands, ankles or feet should be investigated immediately by your GP or midwife, as it is a symptom of the serious condition of pre-eclampsia (*see* Complications, p. 289).

Dealing with back pain

Back pain is not an inevitable part of pregnancy, and I don't believe women have to put up with it, however bad it becomes. Here is some general advice for good posture and alleviating symptoms, plus some exercises that will strengthen your back.

Carrying a heavy bump in front of you puts pressure on your lower back in particular. Protect your spine by:

▶ standing as upright as possible with your shoulders back
▶ avoiding wearing high-heeled shoes
▶ making sure your lower back is properly supported when sitting down or driving (e.g. with cushions behind you)
▶ sleeping on your side using pillows for support
▶ pushing up on your hands and arms to bring you up to sitting when getting up from lying on your side
▶ bending your knees, keeping your back straight and using your legs to push up when lifting any heavy object.

If you are in pain, try applying heat to the area, having a massage or visiting a registered osteopath who has experience of treating pregnant women. Bear in mind that if you need to take a painkiller, use paracetamol only (anti-inflammatories, such as ibuprofen, are contraindicated in pregnancy). If you are in any doubt about the nature of your pain, however, you should always speak to your GP or midwife.

The following exercises are safe in pregnancy. Do them on a regular basis, even if you are not currently suffering from back pain, as they will keep you strong and flexible in advance of labour. In later pregnancy, avoid lying on your back for longer than a few minutes and always listen to your body: if you feel any sharp pain, stop at once.

Spinal stretch
▶ Sit on your heels, with your feet together and knees slightly apart.
▶ Slowly lean forwards, creeping your hands along the floor until your arms are fully stretched out in front of you.
▶ The sides of your bump should be lightly supported by your thighs, but if your head cannot reach the floor you may need to place a cushion or folded-up blanket under your head, so that you can rest in this position.
▶ Hold for as long as you wish and enjoy the stretch in your back.

Cat humps
▶ Position yourself on all fours, hands and knees shoulder-width apart, with your spine flat but relaxed.
▶ Arch your back upwards like a cat, tucking your pelvis in and tightening your buttock and abdominal muscles.
▶ Hold for a few seconds, then slowly roll your spine back down so that it is level once more. Repeat three times.

Spinal twist
▶ Lie on your back, with your knees bent, feet together on the floor and arms out at right angles to your body.
▶ Gently lower your knees to one side, while turning your head the other way. Try to keep both shoulders on the ground.
▶ Slowly raise your knees to the upright position and turn your head back to the centre.
▶ Now make this movement to the other side. Repeat three times, alternating sides each time.

Pelvic tilts
▶ Lie on your back with your knees bent hip-width apart.
▶ Roll your pelvis towards you so that the small of your back presses against the floor. Squeeze your pelvic floor muscles and buttocks as you do this.
▶ Hold for ten seconds and slowly return to the start position. Repeat five to ten times.

Knee hug
▶ Lie on your back, with knees bent up to your chest either side of your bump and your arms lightly clasping them.
▶ Roll gently from left to right as many times as you wish.

Lower back stretch
▶ Lie on your back with your legs stretched out.
▶ Keeping one leg firmly on the floor, slowly bend the other one into your chest and clasp it, without arching your back. Feel the stretch in your lower back and buttock.
▶ Hold for a few seconds and lower slowly back to the floor.
▶ Now do this with the other leg. Repeat this three times.

Knee squeezes
▶ Lie on your back with your knees bent, holding a small object (such as a tennis ball) between the knees. Squeeze your knees together for up to ten seconds, then release for ten seconds. Repeat up to ten times.
▶ Once you have mastered this, move on to a larger object and proceed as above.
▶ This exercise strengthens the inner thigh muscles and is particularly helpful for pubic symphysis dysfunction (see Chapter 4, p. 129).

Exercise in the first trimester

If exercise has been a part of your life before you conceived, the chances are that you will want to continue doing some form of physical activity during your pregnancy. Unless you are suffering from a medical problem and your doctor has advised you to steer clear of exercise, you should be safe to continue doing whatever activity you were doing before you became pregnant, as your body will already be used to the physical exertion. The only word of warning I would give is about lifting weights: bear in mind that the pregnancy hormones now flooding your body are loosening your joints, ligaments and tendons in preparation for the birth (particularly those in the pelvic and lower back areas) and, by lifting heavy weights, you risk overstretching and permanently damaging them. By all means continue to lift weights, but use lighter ones. And if you are in any doubt about the exercise you are doing, speak to your GP or midwife.

If you are not a regular exerciser, now is not the time to take up a new sport, but physical activities such as yoga and Pilates (ideally, classes tailored specifically for pregnant women), cycling, swimming (an excellent aerobic and anaerobic form of exercise) and brisk walking are safe to start now if you have not been doing them before and are fine to continue through all stages of pregnancy.

Tiredness and morning sickness mean that women often cut back on exercise during the first trimester. This is absolutely fine, as it is important to listen to your own body. If you cannot face doing any gym classes for a few weeks, don't force yourself. Try to keep walking, or perhaps go swimming instead. And if any sort of exertion really is too much, then don't feel guilty. In all likelihood, you will feel re-energised once the symptoms disappear at the end of the trimester, and you will want to start exercising again, particularly if it is an established part of your weekly routine.

Exercise in the second trimester

The second trimester is often when you feel your best and so exercise becomes a more appealing prospect. However, you will find that, fairly soon, the size of your bump means that you are no longer able to keep up the sort of physical activity that you may have been doing up until now. Throughout this time you can continue to do aerobic exercise, such as cycling, swimming or brisk walking, as well as resistance training (using light weights only). If you cannot face dragging yourself to a yoga or Pilates class, or cannot find a suitable and convenient one, DVDs and apps are now available so that you don't even have to leave the comfort of your own home (see Useful Resources). You should stop doing abdominal exercises, otherwise these will eventually damage the band of muscles running vertically down your abdomen that need to be able to separate to make way for your growing uterus. As ever, listen to your body and, if you have any pain, stop what you are doing at once.

Exercise in the third trimester

You can continue to exercise right through to the end of your pregnancy if your GP or midwife says it is safe for you to do so. You will know your body well enough to feel which activities are comfortable to continue and which you should stop. Swimming, cycling, yoga and Pilates are all still suitable for this stage of pregnancy and you may also want to consider specific pregnancy exercise classes. Whichever activity you choose, make sure that you focus on posture and aim to do some back-strengthening exercises to help prevent or reduce back pain (see Feature on pp. 34 and Chapter 4, pp. 128–9). Swimming is especially wonderful during the later stages of pregnancy: simply standing in water takes the baby's weight off your back and lower abdomen and may also help reduce swollen ankles and feet.

" I love the gym and keeping fit and active has always been a big part of my life, so when I fell pregnant I knew I didn't want to stop exercising. I was lucky, because my personal trainer specialises in ante- and postnatal exercise, so he was able to guide me and tell me the most appropriate exercises for each trimester. I was even at the gym two days before having my baby! Someone once told me that active mothers produce active babies and, so far, the theory is proving right: my little boy is so active, he never keeps still! " SARAH

Pelvic floor exercises

Even if you do no other exercise for the entire time you are pregnant, you should definitely make pelvic floor exercises a part of your daily routine – indeed, these should be continued for life.

Pelvic floor muscles surround the urethra, vagina and rectum and support, like a hammock, the bladder, uterus and bowel (*see* diagrams). They can be damaged by the weight of the uterus during pregnancy and by the passage of the baby during a vaginal birth. Stretched or damaged pelvic floor muscles lead to stress incontinence during and after pregnancy – this is when urine is leaked when you cough, laugh, sneeze, jump or run (*see* Chapter 4, p. 128). More severe urinary and faecal incontinence can also occur after labour (*see* Complications, pp. 288). Although Caesarean deliveries can limit the damage, the weight of the uterus during pregnancy still stretches and puts a strain on the muscles.

Postnatal problems are less prevalent among women who do regular pelvic floor exercises. Because of the drop in oestrogen levels (which exacerbates weakened pelvic floor muscles), one-third of post-menopausal women suffer from incontinence. The reality is that the stronger your pelvic floor muscles are, not only during pregnancy but thereafter, the less likely you will be affected by these problems. And strong pelvic floor muscles are good for your long-term sex life, too.

Pelvic floor exercises are quick and easy to do, regardless of where you happen to be. There are two types of exercise and you should aim to do both sets three or four times per day:

▸ Slowly squeeze the muscles around the anus, vagina and urethra – as if stopping the passage of wind or urine. Hold for as long as you can (up to a maximum count of ten), making sure you are breathing normally throughout, then let go. Repeat ten times.
▸ Quickly squeeze and release the pelvic floor muscles ten times, but do not hold this time.

The contraction is internal – you should not see any movement in your leg, bottom or stomach muscles – but you should feel a 'lift' inside your lower body when you squeeze. It doesn't matter if you can only hold for three seconds to start with; just try to increase the length of time you hold for as you continue to practise. However, it is important to exercise your muscles until they are tired and not to where they are comfortable. So, when you can hold a slow contraction for ten seconds, increase the length of the hold to thirteen or fifteen seconds and when you find ten fast contractions easy, increase to fifteen.

The best way of remembering to do pelvic floor exercises is to do them at a particular time, such as when you brush your teeth, so that the other activity becomes associated with them. In addition to these daily exercises, you can squeeze your pelvic floor muscles in the same way when you cough, sneeze, laugh or carry out an activity that is strenuous in order to help prevent leakage of urine. If you are not sure how to do the above exercises correctly, speak to your GP or midwife.

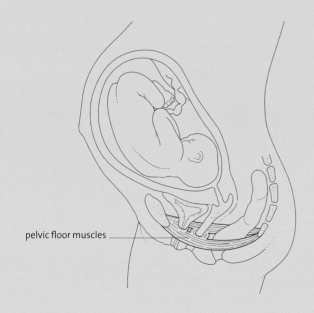

pelvic floor muscles

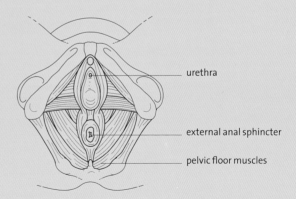

urethra

external anal sphincter

pelvic floor muscles

Pelvic floor muscles The perineum is made up of a hammock-like arrangement of muscles surrounding the urethra, vagina and rectum, which supports the uterus, bladder and bowels.

There are certain precautions that you may need to take to safeguard your general health during pregnancy. Some common infectious diseases can be harmful to the developing fetus, as can some medication that you may be taking for a pre-existing medical condition.

Pre-existing medical conditions

If you suffer from a medical condition, during your pregnancy you will doubtless be under the care not only of the relevant maternal medicine team but also of the specialist consultant who normally looks after you. They will have detailed knowledge of how to achieve the best possible outcome for you and your baby. If you take medication to treat or control your condition, you should speak to your GP and/or specialist as soon as you discover you are pregnant so that you can receive the correct advice about treatment. On no account should you stop medication, as this could leave you and your baby in greater danger than if you were to continue. Information on the drugs commonly used for some medical conditions is outlined below.

Steroids

Steroids in the form of an inhaler are commonly prescribed for asthma and are completely safe to use, as are topical creams for the treatment of eczema. If you are taking steroids in tablet form, however, consult your specialist in case the dosage needs to be amended.

Drugs for hypertension

Ideally, you will have spoken to the doctor responsible for managing your hypertension (high blood pressure) in advance of getting pregnant so that, if necessary, alternative medication can be prescribed for you. The following drugs are contraindicated, as they may cause problems with fetal development:

▸ angiotensin-converting enzyme (ACE) inhibitors,
▸ angiotensin 11 receptor blockers (ARBs)
▸ Thiazide diuretics.

If you are taking one of these when you discover you are pregnant, see your doctor, preferably within two days, to seek alternative medication. See Complications, p. 286 for more on hypertension in pregnancy.

Statins

There is no evidence that use of statins (given to lower cholesterol), particularly during the first trimester, has any harmful side effects for mother or fetus.

Diazepam

Used to relieve the symptoms of anxiety, the drug diazepam increases the risk of the fetus developing a cleft palate (*see* Chapter 3, p. 70).

Anti-epilepsy drugs

Some of the drugs used to treat epilepsy have an increased chance of teratogenicity (harmful effect) on the developing fetus, the most common of which is a cleft palate. Ideally, you would have seen a specialist in advance of getting pregnant to discuss the most appropriate medication to take during conception and the first trimester. However, if yours is a surprise pregnancy (*see* Box opposite), you should be reassured that the risk of malformation is ten per cent or less, and you will be offered an ultrasound to look for specific abnormalities (*see* Chapter 3, p. 70). Thereafter, you should be seen by a specialist obstetrician familiar with epilepsy, as well as a neurologist, to ensure that any adjustment in your drug regime does not increase the chances of an epileptic fit.

Anti-acne drugs (Roaccutane)

This particular drug is not safe to take while pregnant. Consult your doctor at once if you are taking it and discover that you are pregnant.

General medical treatments in pregnancy

Neither prescription drugs nor over-the-counter medication can be tested on pregnant women, so although it is highly likely that a drug is safe in pregnancy, no trials have ever been conducted to confirm this. Consequently, you should err on the side of caution and avoid taking any medication unless it is absolutely necessary. That said, if you have already taken something before you realised you were pregnant, please don't worry, as in all likelihood it will have had no harmful effect on either you or your baby. Listed below are some of the more common medicines and information on their safety for use throughout pregnancy.

If you find you are unexpectedly pregnant, there will, without doubt, be considerable psychological adjustment as you come to terms with the news (see also Chapter 9, p. 264 for more about your response to the pregnancy). However, don't start worrying about what you might or might not have done in the weeks before realising you were pregnant, or trying to remember whether any of it might have been harmful to your baby. Look forwards instead to what you can do from today onwards: start taking folic acid and vitamin D supplements (see p. 24) and aim to eat a well-balanced diet, to stop smoking and to limit your alcohol intake (see p. 44). It may help you to know that about 30 per cent of pregnancies that go on to deliver are not fully planned, yet in the overwhelming majority of cases, the resulting babies turn out to be healthy.

Although general medication is unlikely to have caused any harm to the fetus, you should consult your specialist if you are already being prescribed something for an on-going medical condition. If your pregnancy is due to a failure of your contraception method, it depends on what type you were using as to whether you need to see a healthcare professional (see below).

Barrier methods: spermicidal gels, condoms and caps
All types of barrier methods of contraception are perfectly safe for the fetus, so need no further medical advice.

Contraceptive pills (including the mini-pill)
The combined pill contains oestrogen to inhibit ovulation and progesterone, which thickens cervical mucus to prevent sperm getting through and makes the endometrium less receptive to implantation. The mini-pill and injection-only contraceptives contain only progesterone. None of these hormonal methods of contraception has ever been found to be harmful to the fetus. The same is also true of the 'morning-after' pill (an emergency contraceptive). However, you should stop taking your oral contraceptive at once to avoid exposing your baby to additional oestrogen.

Intrauterine devices (IUDs) and intrauterine systems (IUSs)
Depending on whether the string or device is visible on vaginal examination, your doctor will decide whether the risk of infection posed by leaving your IUD or IUS in place outweighs the possibility of a miscarriage caused by the removal of it.

Painkillers
While paracetemol is safe to take, avoid taking aspirin (except if you are deemed to be at risk of hypertension), ibuprofen and codeine for pain relief.

Diuretics
If you think you are suffering from fluid retention (oedema), a common side effect of pregnancy (see Chapter 4, p. 131), it is important that you do not self-medicate with diuretics or even with herbal remedies, as this could mask an underlying problem such as pre-eclampsia (see Complications, p. 289). If your fingers, feet or legs suddenly swell up markedly, see your GP or midwife as soon as possible.

Antihistamines
In almost all cases, there is no evidence of any harmful effect by antihistamines on the fetus, although versions containing sedatives taken in the third trimester may cause some irritability in the newborn baby. If in doubt about which specific brand to buy or whether your existing medication is safe, consult your GP or pharmacist.

Cold and flu remedies
Over-the-counter medication to relieve the symptoms of colds and flu often contain caffeine and antihistamines, so should be avoided during pregnancy. Take paracetamol and a hot drink instead, and see your GP if your symptoms don't improve within a few days.

Antibiotics
It is common for antibiotics to be prescribed during pregnancy. If you require them, your GP will prescribe the safest one at the lowest dose in order for it to be effective – but be sure to finish the course so that the infection is properly eliminated. If you took antibiotics before knowing you were pregnant, don't worry, as many of the commonest forms are considered safe. These include:

▸ amoxicillin
▸ ampicillin
▸ clindamycin
▸ erythromycin
▸ penicillin.

Certain other antibiotics, however, should be avoided. These include tetracyclines (a family of antibiotics), which can discolour the baby's future adult teeth and affect your liver.

Immunisations

Your immune system changes during pregnancy and your response to a vaccine can be different from what it would be if you were not pregnant. However, if you do need to travel to a part of the world they are required, the tetanus, polio and cholera vaccines are known to be safe for pregnant women. For information on the safety of other vaccines in pregnancy, consult the Department of Health's website for health advice for travellers or the National Travel Health Network and Centre (see Useful Resources).

If you are eligible for an annual flu vaccine, which now includes the vaccine for the H1N1 virus ('swine flu'), you should aim to have it, as there is no evidence that it is harmful to the fetus, whereas if you were to catch flu itself, the high fever could cause you to miscarry. The vaccine also protects your baby during the first months of life.

Due to the sharp rise in the number of cases in the UK, all women are offered the whooping cough (pertussis) vaccination between 28 and 38 weeks of pregnancy to help protect newborn babies from this serious illness. Since babies are not vaccinated against whooping cough until they are two months old, the immunity they need to cover this period is gained through receiving your antibodies via the placenta. Even if you were vaccinated as a child, your immunity is likely to have waned and will therefore provide little protection for your baby, so it is worth having this booster. You can have the whooping cough vaccination at the same time as your flu jab, although you should not delay the latter just so that you can have both at the same time.

Anti-malaria drugs

Some anti-malarials are contraindicated for pregnancy, but there are others that are safe to use. If you are travelling to a part of the world where malaria is a problem, I should stress that *not* taking anti-malaria medication is far more dangerous than taking drugs that are known to be safe, because if you do contract malaria, you are at definite risk of miscarrying as a result of the high fever that develops.

Anaesthetic drugs

Some women undergo surgical procedures during pregnancy, sometimes before they realise they are pregnant. While anaesthesia would only be given if absolutely necessary when it is known that you are pregnant, if the pregnancy does continue following surgery, there is no evidence that the fetus is harmed by anaesthetic drugs. If your pregnancy is advanced, surgery may be performed under regional anaesthesia (see Chapter 6, p. 182) or local anaesthesia if appropriate, which means you will be conscious during the operation and the fetus will be monitored throughout.

Herbal and homeopathic remedies

Women often ask if it is safe to take herbal or homeopathic remedies for certain ongoing conditions, to relieve some of the side effects of pregnancy or to help them during labour and birth (see Chapter 6, p. 189). As a doctor, my principal reaction is that you should consider only treatments that have been rigorously tested in properly conducted scientific trials, on the basis that those that have not are either ineffective or potentially dangerous.

When it comes to homeopathy, I believe that it falls into the 'placebo' category of complementary therapies, so it is safe to use if you want to: it cannot harm you and some women find it helpful. But the reality is that there is no solid *scientific* evidence for its benefit.

Herbal remedies, on the other hand, are not always safe. They can be potent, with some containing natural plant steroids. Others, such as St John's Wort, can be harmful and can interact badly with other medication, so must not be taken during pregnancy. Remember that just because something is 'natural' does not mean it is safe – quite the reverse: arsenic, after all, is natural. That said, herbal teas, such as peppermint, ginger or chamomile (which many women find very helpful when suffering from morning sickness), are completely safe to drink. If you do decide to use herbal remedies during your pregnancy or through labour, please talk to your GP, midwife or obstetrician before you do so and only ever take them after consultation with a qualified practitioner.

Other complementary therapies

Many complementary therapies, including acupuncture, reflexology, massage and osteopathy, are safe for pregnancy and labour, and women make increasing use of them alongside modern medicine in order to treat ailments, such as backache, morning sickness and indigestion and labour pains. It is hard to say how and why some of these therapies work. However, as with herbal remedies, don't assume that because they don't involve the use of orthodox drugs, they are safe. Certain aromatherapy oils, for example, are contraindicated and, ideally, you should avoid all aromatherapy oils during the first trimester (see Chapter 6, p. 188). So if you are thinking of using some complementary therapies, always consult an experienced practitioner and discuss your plans with your GP or midwife.

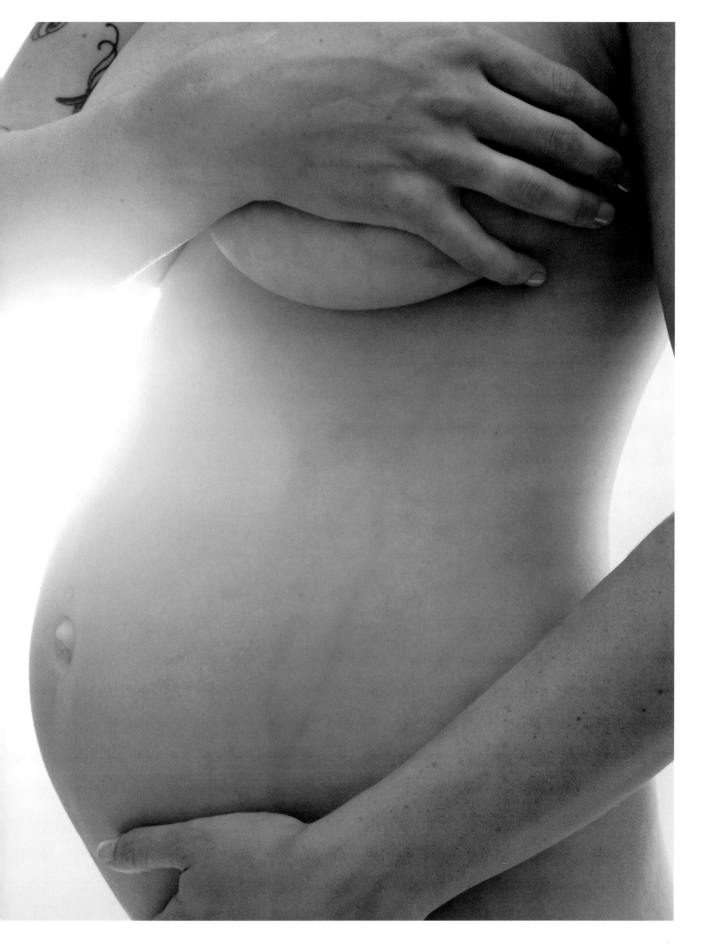

Infectious diseases

Infections caused by viruses or bacteria are sometimes difficult to avoid. Mostly they pose no threat to your developing baby, but you should take steps to protect yourself from certain common infections that could be harmful. If you think you may have been exposed to any of the following in the first trimester, speak to your GP or midwife.

Rubella (German measles)

Most women of reproductive age have had the MMR (measles, mumps and rubella) vaccination, but it doesn't always give total immunity from these illnesses. All pregnant women are tested for rubella and, if you are found not to be immune, you will be advised to have the vaccination *after* you have given birth (it is not possible to have it while you are pregnant, as it is a 'live' vaccine, which could cause infection in the fetus). Rubella infection contracted during the first three months of pregnancy causes, in 50 per cent of cases, miscarriage or major impairments to the fetus, such as blindness, deafness, heart defects and severe learning difficulties (*see* also Chapter 4, p. 88). Because of the lower rate of immunisation among children in the UK in recent years, rubella has now become more prevalent.

Rubella is caught through airborne transmission (coughing or sneezing) and appears two to three weeks after becoming infected. Symptoms are usually mild, though less so in adults, and can include swollen glands in the head or neck, cold-like symptoms and a temperature. A distinctive, slightly itchy rash of red-pink spots appears, which often starts behind the ears before spreading to other areas of the body. Some people do not experience any symptoms or have such mild symptoms that they do not realise they have been infected.

If you are reading this before you have been tested at an antenatal appointment, and especially if you are in contact with young children, you should ask your GP for a blood test if you think you may not be rubella immune (you have neither had rubella nor been vaccinated against it). If you were recently vaccinated and became pregnant within three months, you can reassure yourself that no abnormalities have ever been detected in babies conceived during this time period. Finally, if you know you have had the MMR vaccination or had rubella as a child, it is very unlikely you will be infected again.

Measles

Many people have been vaccinated against measles so, despite a rise in cases in recent years, this highly infectious disease remains rare. Measles can, however, be very serious, and if caught during pregnancy, can result in a miscarriage, stillbirth or premature delivery.

SEPSIS IN PREGNANCY

Women have a lower immunity when pregnant and can be prone to developing bacterial infections, such as genital tract, urinary or streptococcal infections. In addition, factors such as obesity, diabetes or anaemia also increase the risks. If left undiagnosed and untreated, bacterial infections can lead to a severe inflammatory state – known as sepsis – that can have serious consequences if it is not diagnosed sufficiently early. In fact, sepsis is the most common cause of maternal death in the UK.

Typical symptoms of sepsis include fever, shaking, diarrhoea, vomiting, abdominal/pelvic pain, lower back pain and tenderness, offensive vaginal discharge, a thick cough, pain on urination and blood in the urine. As some of the above symptoms are very similar to those of the flu, do see your GP if you develop any flu-like symptoms so that you make sure of the diagnosis. See Complications, p. 291 for more information.

The measles virus is very easily spread through the air by droplets from coughs and sneezes. Most people develop symptoms about ten days after exposure, but this incubation period can vary from between six and 21 days. Early symptoms include a cold with a fever, cough, red eyes and tiny spots in the mouth. A red-brown spotty rash appears three or four days later and lasts for up to seven days.

If you are planning on getting pregnant and you don't know if you have had either measles itself or the measles vaccination, your GP may suggest you have the MMR jab to make sure you are immune. If you know you are not immune and think you have come into contact with someone with measles when pregnant, you should see your GP immediately. You cannot have the jab, because the vaccination contains a live virus. (For the same reason, you should not become pregnant for at least a month after having the MMR jab.) However, your GP may treat you with human normal immunoglobulin (HNIG). This may reduce the severity of your measles, but there is no evidence that it prevents miscarriage, stillbirth or premature delivery.

Mumps

Many adults, but not all children, have been vaccinated against mumps as part of the MMR jab. It is transmitted through airborne droplets from the coughing and sneezing of infected people and symptoms appear two to three weeks after infection. These include fever, headache, swelling of glands and the swelling of cheeks or jaw. Mumps does not cause any problems for the fetus, but because it causes a fever, it can slightly raise the risk of suffering a miscarriage, especially in the first trimester.

Chickenpox

Most pregnant women are already immune to the very common and highly infectious chickenpox virus, because they developed the illness as a child. However, about three in 1,000 are not immune and this can cause problems for their pregnancy. If chickenpox is caught in the first trimester, the risk of miscarriage does not appear to increase. If you are between eight and twenty weeks pregnant, the risks to the fetus are very small, although they can potentially lead to abnormalities. If chickenpox is caught just before delivery and the baby develops it soon after birth, this can cause severe complications for the newborn. If you are unsure whether or not you have already had chickenpox, you can ask for your immunity to be checked for at your booking appointment.

Chickenpox is infectious 48 hours before the rash appears and continues to be so until all the spots have crusted over; the incubation period is between one and three weeks. If you think you may have been exposed to it (usually from a child who had or went on to develop the illness), you should see your GP as soon as possible, who will assess the significance of the contact and establish your immunity, either by ordering an immediate blood test or by asking the laboratory to check the blood sample that was taken at your booking appointment. If it is confirmed that you are not immune and that your exposure has been significant, you should be offered an injection of the human immunoglobin VZIG, which supplies immediate but temporary immunity if given within ten days of contact with the virus. You should assume you are potentially infectious from 8–28 days after the injection and manage your hygiene accordingly.

If you are unaware of your exposure and start to develop chickenpox, you may be prescribed an antiviral drug (depending on your gestation) and this will greatly reduce the severity of the symptoms. A vaccine is also available for those who are not pregnant and not immune and are at risk of more serious complications or who are in regular contact with people in the at-risk category.

Shingles

You can only get shingles if you have already had chickenpox, because they are caused by the same virus. If you develop shingles during pregnancy, there is a low risk to you and the fetus and symptoms are usually mild, but do see your GP in case you require antiviral medication (*see* above). You should also let your GP or midwife know, in case you have been in contact with other pregnant women who may not already have had chickenpox.

Toxoplasmosis

Toxoplasmosis is a parasitic infection found in cat faeces (and therefore cat litter), raw/undercooked/cured meat and contaminated soil on fruit and vegetables. It is virtually symptomless, but can cause mild, flu-like symptoms or more long-term ones similar to glandular fever. If caught, the risk to the fetus is low, but it can sometimes cause miscarriage or stillbirth, as well as birth defects. Fortunately, most people are immune because they have already been infected in the past. To reduce the risk of infection, wear gardening gloves when gardening and rubber gloves when cleaning out cat litter. See also p. 25 for information about food safety. If infection is suspected and subsequently confirmed via a blood test, antibiotics can reduce the chances of transmission to the fetus. About 2,000 pregnant women per year are infected for the first time by toxoplasmosis. About 800 pass the infection on to their babies and about 80 babies a year are born with serious abnormalities.

Appendicitis

Although rare, appendicitis does sometimes occur during pregnancy. Symptoms usually begin as a pain in the centre of the abdomen, which may come and go. Within hours, the pain has moved to the lower right-hand side of the abdomen and gradually increases. Pressing on the area, walking and coughing make it worse. In addition, you may feel sick, or lose your appetite.

Appendicitis in pregnancy can be quite difficult to diagnose, because the expanding uterus displaces the appendix, but failure to identify the condition can lead to peritonitis or a ruptured appendix, which are very serious. It is therefore important that you are seen by a doctor – either a GP at your surgery or one at your nearest hospital – as soon as you develop any symptoms.

SUBSTANCES TO AVOID

There are some substances that you should avoid while pregnant, particularly between the sixth and tenth week when organ development is taking place, as they could potentially cause harm to the developing fetus. These substances (called teratogens) could increase the risk of either miscarriage or some form of fetal abnormality.

However, you may read scare stories in the media about a something being harmful in pregnancy. Although there may be little scientific evidence of its potential for damage, it is often very difficult to know where the truth lies. Below is a list of some of the more common areas of concern, with information on whether or not they are potentially harmful.

Cigarettes

There is no doubt that women who smoke are at greater risk of miscarriage, placental abruption (*see* Complications, p. 288), having a premature and/or low-birthweight baby and other pregnancy complications. This is because smoking reduces the supply of oxygen and nutrients being delivered to the fetus via the placenta. If you need advice on giving up, see your GP or midwife and there are also many organisations and books that offer specific support (*see* Useful Resources). Nicotine patches can also be effective and most maternity units have a 'stop smoking' specialist midwife who can offer help and advice, and who understands how difficult it is!

If your partner smokes, they too should stop. Not only will this help you give up, but it has been shown that passive smoking still exposes the fetus to the effects of tobacco and increases the risk of stillbirth and fetal malformation. There is also clear-cut evidence that when one or both parents smoke, even when not in the baby's presence, this is harmful to a baby's health and can increase the risk of Sudden Infant Death Syndrome, or 'cot death' (*see* Chapter 8, p. 255).

Alcohol

There is a mass of conflicting information regarding alcohol and how much you should drink when you are pregnant. You will not be surprised to read that regular, excessive alcohol intake is not good for you, even when you are not pregnant. If you drink more than the recommended maximum allowance for non-pregnant women (fourteen units per week), it is well-established that this increases your chances of developing certain severe pregnancy complications. It can also have a harmful effect on the fetus during the first ten weeks of gestation (when organ formation is taking place) and will be toxic for the fetus in the remainder of the pregnancy. That said, having a couple of glasses of wine, spread over a week, has no significant effect, and research now indicates that one unit of alcohol per day does not increase the likelihood of having a premature birth or a baby that is small for gestational age (*see* Complications, p. 290). However, you should avoid consuming the weekly allowance all in one go because of the increased work this gives your liver.

Many women go off alcohol entirely during the first trimester due to morning sickness, and voluntarily cut down or stop drinking during the rest of their pregnancy. If you had a heavy night out and subsequently discovered you were pregnant at the time, please don't worry. It is unlikely that one drunken evening will have proved dangerous for the fetus – just avoid repeating the experience until after the birth! However, if you are a regular heavy drinker and are finding it difficult to reduce your intake, make an appointment with your GP, who can refer you for appropriate help.

Caffeine

Caffeine is present in coffee, tea, certain fizzy drinks and colas and even chocolate (albeit in much smaller quantities), and is now regarded by some as something to be avoided in pregnancy because of certain studies linking it to a higher rate of miscarriage. However, these studies are inconclusive at best and, in any event, focused on the effects of consuming very large quantities of strong, caffeinated drinks. Nevertheless, caffeine is a diuretic and drains your body of fluid at a time when you should be staying well hydrated. It also interferes with the absorption of vitamin C, calcium and iron and, because these are important during pregnancy, it is therefore sensible to limit how much caffeine is in your diet. Due to changes in their digestion and tastes, many women find they go off all such drinks – and coffee in particular – during the first trimester and are then happy to cut down or cut them out altogether for the rest of their pregnancy. Be aware that some coffee chains serve varieties that are higher in caffeine than others or use double shots to prepare lattes and cappuccinos, so do enquire if you are concerned about your caffeine intake.

Recreational drugs

All recreational drugs are potentially damaging to you and especially to the fetus. Cannabis, cocaine, heroin, amphetamines and the like cross the placenta and enter the fetal bloodstream. They may all be associated with premature labour and low-birthweight babies, as well as, in the case of ecstasy and cocaine, serious placental bleeding. In addition, a baby born to a regular drug user will have withdrawal symptoms at birth and is likely to need to stay in hospital until the drugs have cleared from the system and sufficient weight has been gained. These babies may need extra help in the neonatal unit. Every pregnant woman will be asked about drug use at the booking appointment (*see* Chapter 3, p. 60), but you can be sure that doctor-patient confidentiality means that you are safe to tell a GP/midwife the truth about your situation, as they will never contact the police regarding your drug use. On the contrary, they will be very supportive and will do all they can to help you not to take any drugs during your pregnancy. If you cannot stop using, you will be cared for by a consultant obstetrician. You *must* attend all your antenatal appointments to ensure the fetus is growing well and so that your own health can be monitored.

Environmental factors: safe or not?

The following are a few of the many environmental factors that women are often concerned about, particularly during the crucial first weeks of pregnancy. The information below is scientifically correct and is based on firm evidence.

Hair dyes

Small studies have, in the past, suggested that some chemicals penetrate the scalp, and hair colourists exposed to dye on a daily basis have been shown to have a slightly higher rate of miscarriage. However, there is no hard evidence that hair dyes harm the fetus and many of these studies were based on extremely high levels of chemicals. Normal use of hair dye is therefore perfectly safe and you don't have to go nine months without attention to your roots!

Household and industrial chemicals

There is no evidence to suggest that exposure to the chemicals found in everyday household products is in any way dangerous for the developing fetus. You could, however, take a few sensible precautions:

▸ Avoid inhaling fumes from paint, petrol, glue, cleaning fluids and oven cleaners. Ventilate the room if you are using them.
▸ Delegate paint-stripping (if you are redecorating) to someone else in case the old paint contains lead.

If you work in a dry-cleaner's, laboratory, garage, artist's studio or certain type of factory, minimise your exposure to the fumes caused by paints, solvents, cleaning agents and lacquers by ensuring that you work in a well-ventilated room and wear suitable protective clothing, as well as a mask, if necessary.

X-rays

The dose of ionising radiation given in one x-ray by today's machines is minimal, so unless you have been given a large number of pelvic or abdominal x-rays before the eighth week of pregnancy, there will be absolutely no risk to the fetus. Even if you had many, the chances are still extremely small that they will have caused any damage. Once you know you are pregnant, doctors will avoid giving you an x-ray; however, if one is necessary, it will not cause any harm at all.

Computers, printers, photocopiers and other office equipment

Large, scientifically sound studies have consistently shown that normal office equipment is completely safe to use and does not increase the rate of miscarriage or birth defects. Tiny amounts of low-frequency electromagnetic radiation are emitted from the backs of computers, and none from the front, and the levels are too minuscule (particularly now that LCD screens are used) to have any effect on a developing fetus. What is a greater risk is developing carpal tunnel syndrome (*see* Chapter 4, p. 131). This is a very painful wrist complaint, which can flare up during pregnancy as a result of prolonged use of a keyboard, combined with bad posture and the fact that ligaments are more lax.

Microwaves

Despite some media scare stories, microwaves are completely safe to use, whether you are pregnant or not.

Ultrasound scanners

Again, there are occasional media-led scare stories suggesting that repeated ultrasound scans can endanger the pregnancy or harm the fetus. Transvaginal ultrasound scans (an internal scan with a vaginal probe, which is done in early pregnancy – *see* Chapter 3, p. 66) do not endanger the pregnancy or cause miscarriage, even when a woman is at risk of losing her baby. A few studies over the years have suggested that abdominal ultrasound scans might cause changes in the development of the cells, affecting later embryonic and fetal growth and even, perhaps, increasing the risk of childhood leukaemia. However, several large studies have disproved these claims completely, even when women have had repeated ultrasound scans.

TRAVEL

Many women decide to take a break when pregnant as a 'final holiday before the birth', especially during the second trimester when airlines still allow pregnant women to fly and it is unlikely that anything will happen during their time away.

Unless you have developed a pregnancy complication or have a history of later pregnancy problems, it is true that this is an ideal time to go away. However, if you are in any doubt about the safety of this, speak to your GP or midwife. In addition:

▸ take your hand-held notes with you, so that all the information about your pregnancy is there if needed
▸ find out where the nearest hospital is to where you will be staying, in case you need to seek medical attention
▸ if you are travelling to an EU country, make sure you have an EHIC card, which entitles you to emergency medical care
▸ if you are going to a part of the world which requires immunisations, seek advice from a medical expert in foreign travel, as information on which vaccines are safe and necessary is complex (see also p. 40)
▸ ensure that you have travel insurance and inform the insurance company that you are pregnant.

Whether you are travelling by plane, train or coach, sit in an aisle seat: it will be easier for you to to move around and to make frequent trips to the toilet! In addition, take plenty of water and snacks to avoid having to queue for them.

Air travel
Women are sometimes worried that reduced cabin pressure and decreased humidity, particularly on long-haul flights, could damage their baby, cause their waters to break or make them go into labour prematurely. There is no scientific evidence that this is the case: the fetus receives all the oxygen and nutrients it needs from you, irrespective of whether the oxygen supply to you is a little less than normal, and occasional flights do not present a risk of increased exposure to radiation to you or your baby.

If you have had a previous first trimester miscarriage, however, you may think about postponing any foreign trips until you have reached the second trimester, simply to avoid the upset of a possible miscarriage either during the flight or while you are abroad. Should you wish to fly after 28 weeks, although there is not any specific risk to pregnancy, many airlines require a letter from your GP confirming your due date and that yours is a low-risk pregnancy. Every airline also has a cut-off date after which it will not allow you to fly (based on your return date, not your outgoing one), so check with your particular carrier before booking, as each will differ. If you have had a previous premature delivery, think about flying earlier than the airline's final date. This is to avoid the possibility that you might go into premature labour on your journey, *not* because the flight might actually cause you to go into labour.

Long periods spent sitting down increase the risk of blood clots, which can lead to venous thromboembolism (see Chapter 3, p. 60), including deep vein thrombosis (DVT). If you are flying medium- or long-haul (longer than four hours):

▸ get up and move around the aircraft at least hourly
▸ rotate, extend and flex your feet ten times every hour
▸ avoid alcohol and caffeine (stay hydrated by drinking water at regular intervals throughout the flight)
▸ wear 'flight socks' (special compression stockings).

You may want to discuss things with your GP before flying. If you are at particular risk of VTE or DVT (e.g. because you are overweight), you may also be advised to take a dose of aspirin. If you are at risk of giving birth prematurely, consider having a pre-flight cervical length scan (see Chapter 7, p. 223).

Travelling by car, train and coach
Other methods of transport, such as train, car and coach are safe during pregnancy, although you must always wear a seatbelt (under and above your bump), however large your abdomen becomes. As your pregnancy advances, you will need to make increasingly frequent stops to stretch your legs and use the toilet, so factor this in when travelling by car, and if you are taking the train or coach, find a seat close to the toilet.

Pregnancy complications and premature birth abroad
If you are thinking of going abroad before your pregnancy has reached 34 weeks, check that the country you are visiting has adequate medical facilities, in case you develop any complications – this should include provision for premature babies. Make sure that you know where your nearest hospital will be and that you are not far from a neonatal unit. You should also ensure that your travel insurance covers medical costs in pregnancy and a premature delivery abroad, particularly if you are travelling to the USA, otherwise your trip could turn out to be an expensive one!

TELLING OTHER PEOPLE

Only you can decide when you tell anyone other than your partner that you are pregnant. Many women prefer to wait until they are beyond the first trimester, however much they are bursting to let everyone know the good news, on the basis that it is unlikely anything will go wrong after this date.

Although telling others about your pregnancy is, on the whole, a joyful experience, you should be prepared for the fact that people often change the way they perceive you from that moment on. You suddenly become a pregnant woman, rather than simply a woman, and can be subjected to an endless stream of well-meaning advice, as well as horror stories of pregnancy and childbirth. You will need to stay clear and firm about how much of this information you want to receive, and from whom, in the months to come.

In addition, people might casually comment on your appearance in a way that they would never dream of doing if you were not pregnant: "Goodness, you're big – you're obviously eating for two!" or, equally hurtfully, "Goodness, you're far too small – are you eating enough?" If you find yourself unable to brush these comments off, you will have to find a way of tactfully telling the person in question that you are not particularly receptive to their remarks. Similarly, some people want to touch your bump in a way that makes you uncomfortable – you are allowed to say that you would prefer they didn't. For the most part, people simply do not realise (or have forgotten) how vulnerable women can feel emotionally and physically during this time in their lives, and if they are gently reminded of this, they will not usually take offence.

Telling parents and in-laws
Invariably, soon-to-be-grandparents are delighted by the news. What can sometimes happen, though, is that their opinions on pregnancy, working and parenting begin to emerge. You may find that theirs coincide with yours or that, even if this is not the case, it does not cause you any problems. However, you may feel a bit of tension creeping in between you and the older generation. "When are you planning to give up work?" may be said innocuously enough (or maybe not!), but you end up taking it as a loaded question. You may also find yourself having to fend off unwanted advice and offers of future help

(including the assumption that you will want your parents or in-laws to come and stay the minute you have given birth). Before you know it, what was once a good, relaxed relationship has become rather fraught.

Given that every family functions in its own particular way, I can only advise you to try to discuss any issues you might have as calmly as possible with your partner. Now that the two of you are going to be parents, it is vital that you act as a team to resolve any problems between yourselves and your families. That said, once you see the love and attention that grandparents can offer your child, you may find it easier to put these differences aside. Indeed, many women find that they become closer to their parents and in-laws once they have had their own baby and that the experience offered by the previous generation becomes invaluable.

Telling friends and wider family
While the vast majority of friends and family will be delighted when they hear about your pregnancy, you should bear in mind that, for some, the news may be tinged with sadness, perhaps because they are having trouble conceiving or have had past miscarriages or pregnancy complications. Although you should proceed with tact, they will nevertheless find out at some stage, and it is better that you inform them yourself rather than let them discover it very late or via some other source. However painful it is for them to hear, most women are impressively generous when it comes to accepting other people's good news.

Telling girlfriends
However excited they appear to be about your pregnancy, you may find your girlfriends are, in reality, a bit less interested in it

than you. Don't be shocked, but try to see it from their perspective: there is now a whole new side to you that they will have to take on board. Friendships that you thought were rock solid can come under considerable strain if the basis on which they were built suddenly shifts. In addition, those who do not have children may be slightly appalled if you seem unable to discuss anything other than stretch marks and constipation. Conversely, some friends may think that all you now want to talk about is your pregnancy – perhaps because they are very excited about it themselves – but you should feel able to steer the conversation back to the latest film releases or the world economy if that is what you would prefer to discuss. You may be pregnant, but you are still able to focus on things other than childbearing.

It is important to reassure girlfriends that you fully intend to go out with them after the birth. Some women do drop off the radar once their baby is born and are not seen out again – at least in the evening – for years. Make a decision to organise babysitting or to leave your partner at home with the baby so that you can stay in touch with your girlfriends. In this way, although you will be a mother, you will also keep your identity as a woman. For more information on rediscovering yourself after pregnancy, see Chapter 9, p. 280.

Telling children

There is no doubt that the arrival of a new baby will change the lives of other children within the unit. You may be desperate to share your good news with them but, unless you are experiencing problems in the first trimester that mean you have to spend time in hospital or in bed, I would advise you to wait until the second trimester before telling them a brother or sister is on its way. They will need to adjust to the situation when you do inform them, so it is better to wait until the pregnancy is a bit more advanced and will almost certainly have a successful outcome. Otherwise, should anything go wrong, you will have to handle their disappointment, which may be an added burden for you at a difficult time.

Exactly how and when you decide to tell any existing child(ren) or step-child(ren) that you are pregnant depends on your own circumstances and on the ages of those concerned. Bear in mind that, whatever their age, a child's initial excitement may mutate into a period of uncharacteristic behaviour, where they display signs of naughtiness, attention-seeking or of regressing to more babyish or childish ways. This may be their method of showing that they have mixed feelings about the arrival of someone whom they may subconsciously view as a rival for your love.

> **" We told people very quickly because we were so excited to be pregnant, as it had taken us over eighteen months to conceive and we had both started to believe it was never going to happen. "** DAWN

However, reassuring your other child – both verbally and through actions – that you will still love them just as much is essential not only through your pregnancy but after your baby is born. Children of all ages want to feel that they are the centre of their parents' world, so finding opportunities to chat (car journeys can be good) about what they were like when they were babies can be very precious and beneficial. As the children themselves cannot remember that time, telling them funny or touching stories about their first few months and years can make them feel very special and wanted, and will show them that those times were wonderful and unique for the two of you. Similarly, going through photo albums and any mementos of their baby years is a good way of bringing home this message and, hopefully, of limiting feelings of jealousy towards the new arrival.

Older children

Older children should be told about your pregnancy before they realise that your growing bump means they will be acquiring another sibling or before they hear it accidentally from someone else. After they have absorbed the news, they may begin to see this baby as getting in the way of the special relationship they currently have with you, particularly if they have been the only child up until now, or if they are a step-child and this is the first baby you and your partner are having together. (If they are teenagers, the worst aspect of hearing you are having a baby is the confirmation that you and your partner are actually having sex!) It is almost impossible for a child to imagine that a parent has boundless love, irrespective of how many children there are in the family. You will need to explain this and to show it by making a fuss of them, and ensuring that other friends and family talk about them and not just about the arrival of the new baby. Promise them that, even once the baby is born, you will have time with them on your own – then make sure you stick to this vow.

You can also try to keep them involved in the preparations for the baby's arrival, but only if they appear interested – and don't expect much if they are a teenager, particularly a boy. If they want to help pick out some baby clothes, or even advise

you on names, then fine. But don't drag them to the shops or sit them down with a name book if, as is likely, they would rather spend time with their friends instead.

Younger children

Telling a child under the age of two presents different issues. As young children have no concept of time, I would advise you to wait until you are well into your second trimester before telling them about the pregnancy. They are unlikely to notice your growing bump and, even if they do, will definitely not have made the link between that and a new baby. Because they will find the concept of mummy expecting another baby quite confusing, you may have to tell them in a casual way, for example, when other babies are around. Point out other families that have a baby and a toddler, so that they understand and get used to the notion. You could also find a story suitable for their age that involves a young child with a new baby, as this might help to talk about the subject (though make sure the story is positive!) – a good bookshop or parenting websites will be able to recommend the best titles. While they may be worried about their place in the family being usurped, they will not be able to voice that thought, so ensure that, as with older children, you reassure them that you love them and will continue to do so as much as ever once the new baby arrives.

Telling work colleagues

Despite legislation and changing attitudes in the work place, my advice, in essence, would be to wait as long as possible before you tell your employer and colleagues that you are pregnant. Although they are likely to be very pleased for you on a personal level, they may be wondering about how this is going to affect them professionally. Some may doubt your on-going commitment to your job, even though the law forbids them from voicing those doubts, and this may unconsciously alter the view they have of you and of your role within the workplace. The Feature on pp. 50–1 deals with work and maternity rights in more detail, and provides advice on pregnancy issues relating to work.

Maternity leave

The decisions of when to stop work before the birth and of choosing whether or when to return afterwards will be based on a range of factors, including your financial and professional situation, your partner, your childcare options and any other children you might already have. Some of the practical considerations that are involved are outlined here.

Maternity legislation and pay

Legislation concerning maternity leave, rights and pay is regularly amended, but there are various organisations that can provide you with the latest, accurate information, notably the Department for Work and Pensions (DWP), Maternity Action (a national charity providing information and advice on maternity and pregnancy rights) and the Citizens Advice Bureau (*see* Useful Resources). In addition, they will give you further information on any benefits you may be entitled to during your pregnancy.

Currently, you are entitled to 52 weeks' maternity leave. Proposals are in place to allow your partner to take the remainder of your maternity leave, should you return to work within the year. See also Chapter 4, p. 112 for information about Paternity Leave. If you qualify for Statutory Maternity Pay (SMP), 39 weeks of your maternity leave will be paid by your employer (but not at full salary, unless you have more a generous package). If you do not qualify for SMP, you may still be entitled to Maternity Allowance (MA) from the DWP. In order to claim either SMP or MA, you need to obtain a MAT B1 certificate from your GP or midwife, which will confirm that you are pregnant and your expected week of childbirth (EWC). The earliest you can obtain this is twenty weeks before your EWC (i.e. in the 21st week of your pregnancy).

The latest that you can tell your employer you are pregnant is in the fifteenth week before your baby is due. The majority of women will have told their employers before that date, partly because they have the right to take reasonable (paid) time off for antenatal appointments and classes, and also because they may benefit from certain health and safety rights. The earliest that SMP or MA can begin is eleven weeks before your EWC.

Key employment rights for pregnant women and women on maternity leave

Pregnant women and those on maternity leave have certain rights enshrined in law:

- ▶ You cannot be dismissed, made redundant or treated unfairly because of pregnancy or childbirth, or because you have taken maternity leave or exercised any of your maternity rights at work.
- ▶ The same rights apply whether you are a part-time or full-time employee, on a fixed-term or temporary contract.
- ▶ You are still entitled to maternity leave if your baby dies after the birth or is stillborn after the end of week 24.
- ▶ During maternity leave, you have the same statutory rights as other employees (e.g. annual paid leave, notice period in your employment contract, redundancy pay after 2 years' service).

Managing your maternity leave as an employee

You will need to think carefully about how soon you tell your employer that you are pregnant and when to start your maternity leave. If you resist informing them of your pregnancy until you are well into your second trimester, you will have had more time to decide what your future intentions will be. In addition, it may help to minimise the effect your maternity leave may have if you make some suggestions for how your job could be done in your absence (if you are aiming to return to work after the birth), and leaving it longer will give you more time to come up with a plan. Your company will still have plenty of time to decide if your suggestion works for them and, if not, to work out the best solution for everyone.

Beware of going for the 'cheap' option of asking a colleague or two to cover for you on an ad hoc basis, as this implies that your current full-time job can be done by others without much trouble. Outside help may be needed, or a colleague may need to switch roles for a while – whatever you suggest, try not to undersell yourself (a common female trait). It might be appropriate to prepare a document in advance in which the details are set out, so that your employer can consider these for a while. They may have an established way of handling such situations, so be prepared to be flexible but firm throughout your discussions.

It is a personal decision as to how long to start your maternity leave before your baby is due and this decision may be influenced by your health, how far you have to travel to work, and so on. When thinking about how long you plan to take off after the birth, there are a few issues to bear in mind, some of which are more applicable if you are an employee rather than self-employed. For example, your employer may have generous maternity leave benefits on paper, but you need to assess whether there will be a negative impact on your career if you take the full amount of time off.

Although you will need to tell your employer how long you intend to be away for, you can adjust the dates at a later stage, including while you are on maternity leave. However, leaving your employer in the dark about your plans or repeatedly changing your mind about the dates is not advisable, as it could cause them to doubt your commitment. If you are unsure about what you want to do, say that you are returning to work. If you change your mind, which you are perfectly entitled to do, you would simply resign from your job.

You have the right to ask to return to work part-time or with flexible hours and your employer has an obligation to consider your request. To help your case (especially if your employer has no particular experience in flexi- or part-time work), draw up a schedule for how this option might work in your particular job. It may be that your employer has not yet had to consider the situation but that, with proper planning, it may nonetheless be possible. Job-sharing may even be an option worth considering. If your request is turned down, which your employer is entitled to do, they should do so in writing, citing valid business reasons.

If you decide not to return to work after you have had the baby, you don't have to refund any SMP, although any amounts that you are paid in excess of the minimum by your employer may have to be reimbursed.

If you are self-employed

Increasing numbers of women are self-employed or run a small business and this poses particular questions when it comes to telling others they are pregnant and deciding how much time to take off. Essentially, the same advice about how early to tell people applies: because you rely on clients to give you work, you do not want to give them too much time to look for other people to take over your hard-won position! So, unless your pregnancy is regularly preventing you from carrying out your work for your clients, there is no particular need for them to know until it becomes absolutely necessary. And the good thing about being self-employed is that it gives you more flexibility than a traditional work environment, so if you are not feeling your best one day, you can probably make adjustments to your schedule and catch up on your work when you do feel better, without having to reveal anything about this to anyone.

Being self-employed is not the same as being an employee, so try to avoid making any drastic decisions about your work-life balance until after the baby is born: you will then have had a chance to settle in to your dual role and work out whether you need to shift the emphasis in one direction or the other. Furthermore, most mothers find that they work even more efficiently than before, and this may enable you to reduce the amount of time you will actually need to be working. It is impossible to cover all situations, but there are some aspects that might be worth considering when deciding what to do in your own particular case:

▸ Work out if it is possible or necessary for someone to take over some or all of your job in your absence.
▸ Once you have decided what the best option is, you can decide when the best time is to tell existing clients and anyone else you work with. However, beware of telling them too early in your pregnancy, as this could give them time to consider using other people.
▸ Explain what your plans are and how these will – or will not – affect them, and clarify how you plan to continue working. Continuity is important, and people want to feel you are still going to be available for them.
▸ Technology should enable you to stay in touch with others as little or as much as you want to once the baby is born, as well as to work whenever suits you best.
▸ Avoid telling clients that you are unavailable because you are at an antenatal check-up or a mother-and-baby yoga class! Simply say you are unavailable at that time. They don't need to know why, and it is better that they think you are in demand.
▸ Try to delegate tasks as much as possible (including to your partner). This may be an uncomfortable thing to do at first, but it will prove important for juggling the demands of motherhood and self-employed work. Delegation may also mean paying for help at home.
▸ If you are going to have childcare based at home and you also work mainly from home, make sure your work environment is kept well separate from the rooms where your baby and their carer will be. It makes a carer's job harder if their boss is forever 'dropping in' to say hello to their baby or to make a cup of coffee, as this is very disruptive and undermines the carer-baby relationship.
▸ Finally, you do not have to be 'superwoman'. Most women who are portrayed as such in the media only survive thanks to copious amounts of back-up and money.

Remember that thanks to modern technology, it has never been easier to stay in touch with the office and with clients, either through Skype, Facetime or other means, so while this can sometimes mean you are never 'off', it can also be used to great advantage during pregnancy and maternity leave.

MATERNITY CLOTHES

As your pregnancy progresses, your normal clothes will start to feel a bit tight, especially around the waist. Aside from a maternity bra, try to resist buying other maternity clothes until you are some way into your second trimester, so that you need only invest in one season's worth of outfits.

Some women expand more quickly than others, especially those who have previously been pregnant (abdominal muscles are never as firm as before). If you find that your clothes are too tight around the waist during the first trimester, try to get by with looser-fitting tops that allow you to undo the top button of your trousers or skirt, or employ the 'elastic waistband' trick (*see* Box). Tops worn over leggings and dresses that are not too fitted can also be a good way round the problem.

Buying a maternity bra

Your breasts start to change from early on in pregnancy: they enlarge and often feel very tender, even painful, to the touch. If you have breast implants, your skin may feel very tight and your breasts particularly uncomfortable because the breast tissue is growing around the implants. The changes to your breasts will take place largely during the first trimester, which is why it is worth investing in a couple of good maternity bras in the eighth or ninth week, so that your breasts are properly supported from the start. Don't wait until the second

trimester, as by then you will probably have been wearing the wrong size bra and your breasts will have been insufficiently supported for several weeks, risking irreversible damage to them that will only become apparent once you are no longer pregnant. The maternity bras you buy should see you through the remainder of your pregnancy, as it is only just before the birth that your breasts will expand again, in advance of your milk coming through. (At that point, you will need to buy bras that allow you to breastfeed, if that is what you choose to do.) On average, your bust increases by one or two cup sizes during pregnancy, although this can vary considerably from one woman to another.

There is no hard medical evidence to indicate that wearing underwired bras during pregnancy is harmful to breasts, but shops and midwives usually advise against them, as there may be a potential risk: the wire may hinder the natural changes in the breasts during pregnancy, including the development of milk ducts. When buying a bra, go to a shop or department store that has a specialist bra measuring and fitting service (this is usually free) rather than try to guess your new size, and buy specific maternity bras, as these have wider side and back sections to ensure maximum support. They are also comfortable enough to wear at night, something which many women find is necessary during the first three months when their breasts are at their most tender.

Buying maternity clothes

Gone are the days when being pregnant meant waving goodbye to looking remotely stylish. There is now an increasingly wide range of fashionable maternity clothes available, both on the internet and on the high street, so it pays to browse around and have catalogues sent to you. However, if you start wearing special maternity clothes in the first trimester, I can guarantee that you will be so bored with them by the time you deliver that you will never want to set eyes on them again (you will still need them for a while after the birth). Plus, by waiting just that bit longer, you can make do with clothes for one season, as you will effectively need them for less than six months. To further limit the expense, take stock of your existing wardrobe and identify tops, jumpers, cardigans, jackets and shirts that you can continue to wear throughout your pregnancy and see if you can borrow larger-size clothes from your partner and friends. Adjust normal trousers and skirts with elastic and a safety pin for as long as possible (*see* Box) and invest in a simple, black bump

---

THE 'ELASTIC WAISTBAND' TRICK

If your ordinary clothes are starting to feel tight around the waist, loop a length of elastic around the button on the waistband and fasten through the button hole with a safety pin. Then wear a tight-fitting, long-length top that covers and smooths out your newly improvised arrangement and helps to keep the trousers in place. By employing this handy trick, you can wear your normal outfits for longer before having to buy (more expensive) maternity clothes (*see* also Useful Resources for a similar kit you can buy).

support band to cover the increasing gap between your top and bottom halves (there are many versions available online – *see* Useful Resources), as both techniques will allow you to postpone buying (more expensive) maternity versions. Lastly, see if you can borrow as many maternity clothes as possible from other people.

When you can last no longer and have worked out where the gaps in your wardrobe are, I suggest the items listed below. Remember that you will be feeling hotter and – particularly in summer – will be sweating more, so you should avoid buying synthetic fabrics.

Skirts and trousers

Specially designed skirts and trousers are essential items in your maternity wardrobe, as they have panels and/or button and elastic systems that can expand with your growing bump. These will keep you feeling comfortable as your pregnancy progresses – there is nothing worse than wearing an item of clothing that is not made for pregnancy and that feels too tight around your abdomen. You will need a couple of skirts or trousers for work and two pairs of casual trousers/jeans for the weekend; leggings or (as I can hardly bear to call them) jeggings also work well.

Tops

Maternity tops (jumpers, shirts, T-shirts) are longer at the front than at the back to allow for your bump. A couple of specific maternity tops are useful for the last four or five months of your pregnancy. Before then, there are any number of on-trend styles of top that you can buy for very little on the high street, simply in a larger size. From drop-waisted and empire line to slouchy or shift-style, longer tops that fit over your bump can be found without having to go anywhere near a maternity clothing range. Paired with trousers or leggings, these can make stylish outfits, particularly in those mid-season weeks when the weather is neither particularly hot nor cold.

DID YOU KNOW…?

Nipple concealers, those sticky plastic gel discs known to all fashion insiders (and available online or in large pharmacies), also help conceal protruding belly buttons.

Dresses
As with tops, there are many styles of dress to choose from on the high street, depending on your tastes, that will work for much of your pregnancy. If you need something smarter to go to a one-off function, hire an outfit from a dress hire company or, once again, borrow if you can. In summer, you may need looser-fitting dresses because you will be feeling a lot hotter than usual.

Jackets
If you normally wear a suit to work, you will probably have to invest in one or two maternity jackets, tailored to allow for your expanding bump. For other occasions, it is fine to wear normal jackets from good-value high street chains that are just one size bigger. In fact, thanks to the structure of the shoulders and the slightly cinched waist, a tailored, non-pregnancy jacket worn over a loose top will give you a great line and, even though you will not be able to do up the buttons, will make you feel less enormous.

Maternity tights and pants
Channel your inner Bridget Jones and invest in some big maternity pants for comfort. There are styles that go both under and over the bump (and some are even quite attractive!). Maternity tights provide more support than their normal counterparts and are a good investment, particularly if you are on your feet a lot during the day.

Shoes
Avoid high heels on a daily basis (*see* Feature on p.34 on back pain) and stick to low heels or flat shoes (but avoid pumps/ ballet flats, as they provide next-to-no support for long-suffering feet). For the odd party or evening out, you can still, Cinderella-like, wear some gorgeous shoes, but bear in mind that in later pregnancy you will not be able to see your feet and your centre of balance will be affected, so be careful as you walk down the red carpet or work that room. You may need to invest in shoes that are one size larger than normal in the third trimester, as your feet tend to swell and, indeed, do not return to their former slim-ankled selves until about a month after delivery (don't panic: they really will return to normal some day). Don't forget: given you can't buy many non-pregnant clothes at the moment, and provided your feet are the same size as usual, you can still indulge in a bit of retail therapy by buying shoes!

Swimming costume
Swimming is a wonderful form of exercise in pregnancy (*see* p.36) and, particularly in the last trimester, a specific maternity costume is much more comfortable than simply wearing a normal one in a bigger size, which does not provide the same sort of support.

ANTENATAL CLASSES

Antenatal classes aim to prepare you for the arrival of your baby, covering what to expect in pregnancy and birth, as well as some basic parenting skills to help you in the first few weeks. It is a good idea to start thinking early in your pregnancy about whether you would like to attend a course, as popular classes can get booked up.

Your local hospital and often your GP surgery will run free antenatal classes (or parentcraft classes, as they are sometimes called), led by specially trained midwives. The hospital ones can be very useful if you are planning a hospital birth, as they give you the opportunity to ask questions to midwives who work there, as well as to other obstetric staff who may help to run the classes. By the time you arrive at the hospital's maternity unit to give birth, you will probably feel much more relaxed about the labour ward and your delivery and may even recognise a few faces.

Private, independent classes, such as active birth classes and National Childbirth Trust (NCT) courses, have different, very specific philosophies. They will not necessarily be run by midwives, but could be led by teachers that are trained in a particular approach to labour and birth and who will have had a child themselves. There is also a wealth of antenatal advice available on the internet and even classes are offered online (*see* Useful Resources).

All classes get booked up a long way ahead, especially private ones where the groups tend to be smaller. Start researching what is available in your area in your first trimester and aim to sign up by the start of your second. You will discover which one will suit you best by finding out for yourself what they offer and also by talking to people who have attended the various classes. Your decision should be based not only on your own personality and budget (independent ones charge a fee), but also on the type of birth you are planning and other practical aspects, such as when and where the classes are held. Whichever option you choose, you should check that the classes cover the following:

▸ specific exercises to do in the lead-up to the birth to help with your flexibility and strength during labour

▸ the physiology of labour (what happens to your body during the birthing process)
▸ the different breathing techniques to help you during the various stages of labour
▸ pain control options
▸ Caesarean sections (more than lip service should be paid to this method of delivery, as it accounts for 25–30 per cent of births)
▸ induction procedures
▸ water births
▸ assisted deliveries
▸ caring for your baby immediately after the birth (including information on how to breastfeed, bath and change your baby).

You should also ask:

▸ Is there is any particular emphasis in the course?
▸ Who are the teachers (midwives or lay people)?
▸ Is there a cost involved?
▸ What are the various start dates and times?
▸ Do partners attend your classes or do they run a specific one-off session for partners (this can be very useful if your partner can't attend the regular classes with you)?

Generally, a course lasts for six to eight weeks, so it is best to start it around the 30th week of pregnancy, which should give you time to complete it before giving birth. Remember that you are legally allowed to have time off from work to attend antenatal classes (although many are run in the evenings). However, it is better to book one that is near to where you live rather than to where you work, so that you can meet women who are local to you and who are due to give birth at around the same time. That way, it will be easier to stay in touch during your maternity leave and, because you have something in common, this network of women will be invaluable for providing support in those (sometimes difficult) weeks and months after the birth and beyond: antenatal classes are well known for being the start of many life-long friendships, not only for mothers-to-be, but for the fathers, too.

Finally, even if this is not your first pregnancy, I still would advise you to sign up for classes. Refresher courses are very helpful for reminding you about the various breathing techniques and what happens during labour. It may also be that the hospital you are giving birth in is not the same as the one where you had your previous children. Even if it is, the facilities and labour ward may have changed since you were last there. Refresher courses are often shorter than those for first-time mothers, but they will give you the confidence to go into labour fully prepared and in a relaxed state of mind.

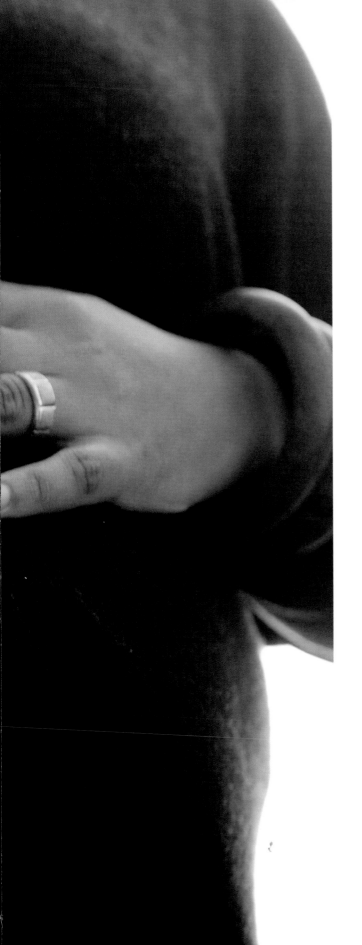

Antenatal tests

Your pregnancy will be monitored regularly to make sure that everything is progressing as it should. You will also be offered a range of antenatal tests, many of which will need to be done in hospital or in a dedicated antenatal centre. While these are not obligatory, they can be helpful in alerting you and your healthcare professionals to any issues regarding your health and that of your developing baby.

Seeing your GP or midwife throughout your pregnancy helps them to check that all is progressing normally for you and your baby. You will also be able to obtain useful information and ask questions about any aspect of your pregnancy and care.

If you are a first-time mother, you should have about ten antenatal appointments. These will be approximately every four weeks, starting with the booking appointment, your first meeting with the midwife (*see* below). From 34 weeks, you should be seen every two weeks, and after 38 weeks, your appointments may be weekly until the birth. If you develop a medical condition or your pregnancy goes beyond 40 weeks, you may have more appointments. If you have had a baby before, you will have seven appointments, but the pattern is generally similar to that of first-time mothers, with the appointments becoming more frequent as your pregnancy nears term. You will be informed of the planned schedule of antenatal care at your booking appointment. These routine appointments can be with your GP, obstetrician or midwife (or a mixture of these), depending on the type of antenatal care you are receiving (*see* Chapter 1, pp. 14 –5). If your pregnancy is high-risk, you may see a specialist doctor for the majority, if not all, of these appointments.

The booking appointment
The first appointment in your scheduled antenatal care is known as the 'booking' appointment. This usually takes place by the time you are ten to twelve weeks pregnant, and is most often conducted by a midwife. It lasts approximately one hour, although you should allow extra time for waiting, especially if you are in a busy hospital. The midwife will take a detailed medical history from you, and will also ask for the date of your last period (note it down in advance), so that your estimated delivery date (EDD) can be calculated. Please bear in mind that this often gets adjusted at the dating scan when more accurate information of gestation is available. This information will be recorded in a special book, your hand-held notes, that will be given to you to keep for the rest of your pregnancy and which you will need to bring to all future antenatal appointments and tests.

Try and be as accurate as possible when answering questions, as this will help the midwife to get a full picture of your general health. If there is any information that you feel particularly sensitive about (e.g. drug use, a previous termination, treatment to your cervix that your partner might not know of), it will still be useful for the midwife to know about it so that she can assess how this might affect your pregnancy. However, you can request for the information not to be written in your hand-held notes.

ASSESSING YOUR RISK OF THROMBOEMBOLISM
Pregnancy can increase the risk of developing a blood clot, known as a venous thromboembolism (VTE). This can take the form of a deep vein thrombosis, which is a clot in the leg (usually the calf) and is often referred to as DVT, or it can be a pulmonary embolism (PE), which is a clot or an air bubble obstructing an artery in the lung – this can be highly dangerous, if not fatal. As a result, all women have a VTE risk assessment at their initial booking appointment. You are considered at risk if you are:

▸ over 35
▸ obese
▸ a smoker
▸ suffering from pre-eclampsia
▸ undertaking long-distance air travel.

If you have no more than one risk factor, you are deemed to be at low risk and no further action is taken. If you have two risk factors, you are considered to be at intermediate risk, so further expert advice will be sought and some preventative treatment (known as thromboprophylaxis) may be considered. This treatment is likely to take the form of a drug called heparin, which prevents blood clots. If you have three or more risk factors, you will be in the high-risk category and will be given thromboprophylactic treatment throughout your pregnancy and beyond and may be offered dietary and lifestyle advice, if appropriate. In addition, all women will be advised in early pregnancy to stay hydrated and to remain as mobile as possible, both during pregnancy and immediately afterwards.

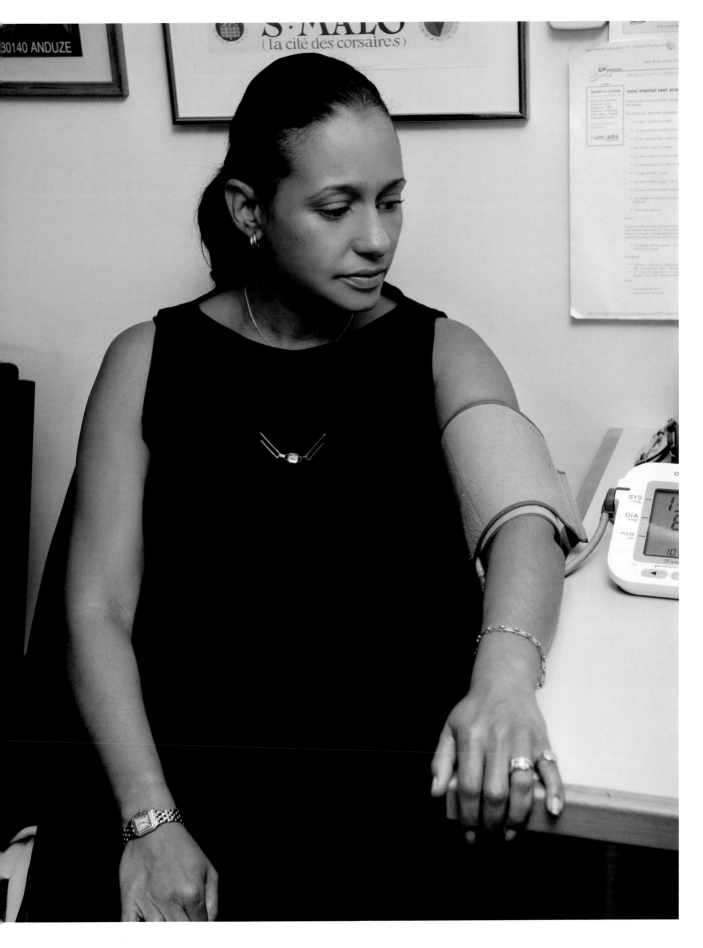

The midwife will also measure your height, weight, blood pressure, and will calculate your body mass index (BMI – *see* Chapter 2, p.29); she may also examine your legs and abdomen. You will be asked to provide a urine sample, which will be tested for the presence of sugar and protein (*see* Box opposite) and for signs of a urine infection, as this is common in pregnancy and doesn't always cause symptoms (*see* Chapter 4, p.128). You may also have a blood test during this initial visit, or be asked to come back shortly to have it. This will confirm your blood group and your Rhesus factor (*see* Box below), will check, among other things, your rubella immunity, and will screen

for anaemia, syphilis, Hepatitis B and HIV. If you are wondering why you are screened for these last two conditions, it is because women may have no idea they have contracted them. Yet if you and your healthcare professionals know at the start of your pregnancy that you have tested positive, there are many things that can be done to significantly reduce the chances of transmission to your baby. However, if you would prefer not to be tested, let your midwife know.

The results of the various tests and measurements done at the booking appointment enable the midwife to assess your need for any special monitoring during your pregnancy. Your booking appointment is also an opportunity to get information about maternity benefits and antenatal classes, and to have further discussion (if you have already seen your GP) on where you would like to give birth (*see* Chapter 1, pp.16–8). Screening tests for abnormalities are offered to all women (*see* pp.67 and 72–3), and your midwife will talk these through with you now to make sure you understand what is involved, so that you can decide whether or not to have them.

Other routine antenatal visits

At each of your subsequent antenatal appointments, your blood pressure and urine will be checked, and your fingers, hands and legs may be examined for any signs of swelling, as this can be an early indicator of pre-eclampsia (*see* Complications, p.289). Your weight may also be re-assessed – this is especially important in the third trimester.

Your GP or midwife may also place a Doppler fetal monitor over your uterus to listen to your baby's heartbeat. During pregnancy, the fetal heart beats at 110–160 beats per minute (i.e. around twice as fast as your own) and the first time you hear it is always very exciting.

By the time you are fourteen weeks pregnant, your uterus has expanded above the pelvic rim, so your GP or midwife will also measure the height of the fundus, which is the distance between the top of the dome-shaped uterus and the pubic bone (symphysis pubis). This measurement is given in centimetres and it usually increases by around 1 cm a week until Week 30 of your pregnancy. At fourteen weeks, for example, the symphyseal-fundal height (SFH in your hand-held notes) is about 14 cm and by 21 weeks it will be around 21 cm (with the fundus reaching as far as your belly button, or thereabouts). So, you could say that, at this time, the measurement matches the number of weeks of gestation. If at any stage the SFH is significantly too low or high for your dates, you may be asked to have an ultrasound scan to measure the estimated fetal weight.

You will have another blood test at around 28 weeks to check for anaemia(*see* Chapter 4, p.127). In the third trimester,

---

BLOOD TYPES: RHESUS D POSITIVE AND NEGATIVE

There are four blood groups: O (the most common), A, B and AB (the least common). Within these groups, you can be either Rhesus D (RhD) positive or RhD negative, with the former being more common. If you are RhD positive, you have a substance known as D antigen on the surface of your red blood cells and if you are RhD negative you do not.

The maternal and fetal circulations are usually kept almost totally separate by the placenta, but they can come into contact, sometimes during pregnancy and often at birth (for more on the function of the placenta, *see* Chapter 4, p.92). If you are RhD negative and your partner is RhD positive, your baby could be RhD positive. If this is the case, your system will create antibodies in your blood, which will remain in your system after pregnancy and may react to a subsequent fetus as if it were a foreign body. This can result in severe fetal anaemia, as well as in other complications. Your GP or midwife will test your blood on a regular basis to check you are not already creating antibodies and, if necessary, will offer to administer an 'anti-D' injection between 28 and 34 weeks of pregnancy; you may also be offered one soon after birth to decrease the risk of problems in future pregnancies.

If your partner's blood type is RhD negative like yours, then your baby's will be too, in which case there will be no risk of Rhesus problems to you or your baby. However, all women will have a blood test for antibodies at 28 and 34 weeks, regardless of blood type. If antibodies are found, you may need a referral to a specialist centre for more tests, to make sure the fetus is not adversely affected by their presence.

You will be asked by your GP or midwife to provide a urine sample at every antenatal appointment and it will be tested there and then with a dipstick to check the levels of sugar or protein. These two substances are normally filtered out by the kidneys but, during pregnancy, it is common for small traces to remain and to show up occasionally in the urine. This is especially so during the second and third trimesters, largely because of the increase in blood flow through the body (*see* Chapter 4, p.85).

Glycosuria

Traces of sugar in your urine, a condition known as glycosuria, can be a sign that you may have gestational diabetes (*see* Feature on pp.64–5). This can cause serious problems, so if glycosuria is found at your initial booking appointment, you will probably be given advice about limiting sugary foods and you may be asked to have a random blood sugar test. If it is found later on in your pregnancy, and certainly if it is present at two consecutive antenatal appointments, you will be asked to come back for a glucose tolerance test to confirm whether or not you are developing gestational diabetes. This test is now routinely offered by most hospitals at around 28 weeks, because glucosuria is often symptom-free and is becoming more common.

A glucose tolerance test checks how well the body is processing glucose (sugar). You will be asked not to eat for a certain length of time before the test and to provide a urine sample first thing in the morning. A blood sample is taken, still on an empty stomach, after which you will be given a sugary solution to drink. Further blood and urine samples are taken at regular intervals over the next two to three hours and you will not be able to eat or drink anything else during this time. Results are usually available within a week and if gestational diabetes is diagnosed, you will be given guidance about your diet and your pregnancy will be monitored at the hospital.

Proteinuria

If protein is found in your urine, known as proteinuria, you will be asked to supply another, midstream, urine sample. This ensures that the protein is definitely urinary and not from vaginal secretions. The most common cause of proteinuria in a mid-stream specimen is a urinary tract or kidney infection, which, if left untreated, may lead to an illness that can cause miscarriage or premature labour, as well as to damage to your kidneys. In later pregnancy, proteinuria is also an early warning sign of pre-eclampsia (*see* Complications, p. 289). This is why, protein in your urine is always taken seriously.

and certainly at 36 weeks, as well as doing the above checks, the GP or midwife will palpate your abdomen to determine your baby's position, or lie (*see* Chapter 5, p. 148), as this will provide information about how the birth needs to be managed. Palpation involves gently but firmly pressing with the hands over the abdominal area to feel the baby, and may be a little uncomfortable (but not painful). If the lie cannot be established, you may be referred for an ultrasound scan. Up until about 36 weeks, babies change position frequently; after this, space is often too tight in the uterus for them to do so.

Your baby's presentation (the part of the baby's body that lies closest to the cervix) will also be determined during the last few weeks of pregnancy. From around 36 weeks, and especially if this is your first pregnancy, the presenting part (the head or the bottom) usually starts to 'engage' in the pelvis, meaning that it starts to descend into the pelvic cavity in readiness for birth. The different levels of engagement will be assessed at your antenatal appointments and documented in your notes (*see* Chapter 5, p. 151).

> " I had to have a glucose tolerance test, as my brother is diabetic, which put me at higher risk. The testing was easy enough. I had to have a blood and urine test, then drink a special liquid, wait for a while, then have another blood and urine test. The waiting was the hardest bit: you cannot eat or drink anything for a while and you get very hungry! Thankfully, the results were all normal. " **SARAH**

Diabetes

Diabetes (sometimes known as 'diabetes mellitus', or DM in your antenatal notes) is a metabolic disorder, where either the pancreas produces insufficient amounts of the hormone insulin or produces it too slowly, or the body's cells are resistant to insulin. In pregnancy, diabetes can cause complications both to the mother and to the developing baby.

Normally, when glucose enters the blood stream after eating, the insulin the body produces enables the glucose to be metabolised and taken up either by cells or to be stored in the liver as glycogen and used subsequently to provide energy whenever blood glucose levels fall. When a person has diabetes, the lack of insulin prevents the glucose from being broken down and used, so blood sugar levels remain high, and this can lead to a range of symptoms, in addition to an increased risk of heart and circulatory problems.

What is diabetes?

There are two types of diabetes: type 1, which usually develops in childhood/early adulthood and is controlled by daily insulin injections, and type 2, which develops in adulthood and is controlled, at least initially, by diet (to regulate blood glucose levels) and, if necessary, tablets or insulin injections. There is also a type known as gestational diabetes (written as GDM in your notes), which is the term given to diabetes that arises during pregnancy. When you are pregnant, blood glucose levels increase to cope with the growing fetus, so more insulin is required. If insufficient insulin is produced, blood glucose levels stay high, leading to diabetes. You are at increased risk of developing gestational diabetes if your BMI is 30 or above, you had a previous baby weighing 4,500 g or more, you had gestational diabetes in a previous pregnancy, you have a family history of diabetes or come from certain ethnic backgrounds. Some hospitals screen all pregnant women for the condition, regardless of their apparent risk factors.

About two to five per cent of pregnant women have diabetes, making it one of the most common major pregnancy complications. Of these, the majority have gestational diabetes (which may or may not disappear after the birth), 7.5 per cent have type 1 diabetes and five per cent type 2.

The increased risks to fetal and maternal health for women with pre-existing diabetes include:

- miscarriage
- pre-eclampsia
- premature labour
- Caesarean section
- stillbirth and perinatal mortality
- congenital fetal abnormalities (notably cardiac)
- macrosomia (very large babies, weighing upwards of 4,500 g) – a 20–30 per cent increased risk
- shoulder dystocia during labour (*see* Complications, p. 291) and consequent birth injury
- low blood sugar levels in the baby after birth (requiring admission to the neonatal unit).

For women who develop gestational diabetes, the risks are similar, although there is no increased risk of congenital abnormalities and women are 50 per cent more likely to develop type 2 diabetes within the next ten years.

How your care will be managed

Depending on whether you are already diabetic or whether you develop the condition in pregnancy, your care will need to be altered to ensure that you and your baby remain in the best possible health.

Women with pre-existing diabetes

If you already have diabetes (type 1 or 2), early pre-conception counselling from your GP, at least six months before you plan to conceive, is essential before planning your pregnancy, as it is very important to control your blood sugar levels, especially around the time of conception and during the embryonic period of development (the first ten weeks of pregnancy) in order to reduce the likelihood of congenital abnormalities. You may be advised to stop, change or take certain medication before and during pregnancy and you should start to take a higher dose of folic acid (5 mg) until the end of the first trimester, as well as a daily vitamin D supplement during the entire pregnancy. You should be given advice about diet, exercise and (if relevant) weight control before and during pregnancy to reduce the risks associated with diabetes (*see also* Feature on obesity in Chapter 2, pp.30–1).

As soon as your pregnancy is confirmed, ask your GP to refer you to an obstetrician specialising in diabetes – don't wait until your hospital booking appointment. Ensure that you give birth in a hospital where advanced neonatal resuscitation is available 24 hours a day, because of the risks to your baby during and immediately following delivery.

During your first trimester, you have a higher risk of episodes of hypoglycaemia (low blood sugar levels), so you should avoid being by yourself, always have a snack in your bag and, if the episodes of hypoglycaemia are acute, you should avoid driving. You may also find it harder in general to control your blood sugar levels, which will be made worse if you suffer from nausea or vomiting due to morning sickness. You should be offered immediate contact with a joint diabetes and antenatal clinic. Throughout your pregnancy, you will be asked to measure your blood glucose levels every day and record them in a diary. A midwife should then call you on a regular basis to check the results and discuss ways of improving control if they do not stay within the ideal range.

You will be monitored more often throughout your pregnancy than non-diabetic women. For example, you should be offered a detailed ultrasound scan of the fetal heart at eighteen to twenty weeks of pregnancy to check for cardiac abnormalities. In addition, because placental growth and function are not always as good as they should be due to the variations in blood glucose levels, you should also be offered ultrasound monitoring of fetal growth, amniotic fluid volume and placental growth every four weeks from 28–36 weeks. Towards the end of your pregnancy, it may become harder to maintain your blood glucose levels within the ideal range.

You should be offered induction of labour after 38 completed weeks of gestation, or a Caesarean section if you previously delivered that way, because there is a significantly higher rate of an adverse outcome after 39 weeks. If you need steroids to help mature the fetal lungs, you will need to be admitted to hospital for close monitoring of your blood sugar levels and possibly to receive an intravenous sliding scale insulin infusion if your blood sugar levels increase. This is only necessary if the levels are consistently above a safe level and the increase is caused by the steroids. In this way, the dose of insulin can be adjusted on an hourly basis while your body metabolises the steroids. During labour itself, most diabetic women will need a sliding scale insulin infusion, as blood sugar levels are otherwise difficult to control.

After labour the infusion will continue until you are eating and drinking again and your insulin dose has been reduced to your pre-pregnancy requirement.

Women who develop gestational diabetes

Gestational diabetes usually develops during the second trimester and is mostly symptomless. If antenatal urine testing shows higher than normal levels of sugar (glycosuria – see Box on p.63) or if you are in a high-risk category for gestational diabetes, your carers will suggest you take a glucose tolerance test to assess how well you metabolise

glucose. If the diagnosis is confirmed, you will be given advice on increasing your physical activity to 30 minutes of exercise a day and on adjusting your diet. This will mean eating low-sugar, low-fat foods, including lean protein and plenty of vegetables (not fruit, which contains too much sugar), as these measures are often sufficient to control or eliminate the condition. If your diabetes is not controlled in this way, you may need oral medication in the form of metformin or insulin injections (up to four times a day).

You will also be shown by a specialist midwife how to measure your blood glucose levels at home and what the ideal range should be. You should record these levels on a daily basis in a diary. A midwife will be in regular contact with you to discuss the results. The better you control your blood glucose levels, the more you will reduce the risk of the fetal and maternal complications associated with diabetes. See also Useful Resources for more information on the antenatal care offered.

Your postnatal care

If you have gestational diabetes, your blood glucose levels should return to normal soon after delivery, so you should no longer require medication (if it was prescribed). Your levels will nonetheless be checked before you are discharged from hospital, and you should be offered lifestyle advice, including dietary and exercise recommendations, to reduce the likelihood of developing type 2 diabetes at a later stage, or gestational diabetes in a future pregnancy. You may be offered a subsequent glucose tolerance test six weeks after delivery, as well as an annual screen for diabetes.

If you have pre-existing diabetes, you are at increased risk of hypoglycaemia after the birth, so you will need to monitor your blood glucose levels carefully to establish the correct dose of insulin. This is especially the case if you breastfeed, so make sure you always have a meal or snack available before/during feeds. You are likely to return to your pre-pregnancy treatment for diabetes, but your medical carers will discuss your specific situation with you.

Your baby

Babies are at increased risk of developing hypoglycaemia immediately after birth, so you will be encouraged to breastfeed as soon as possible in order to stabilise your baby's blood glucose levels. Babies of diabetic mothers are closely monitored at birth and soon after, so don't be surprised if yours goes to the neonatal unit, even for a few hours, to ensure that levels are stable. Babies are not usually discharged until at least 24 hours after the birth, once the neonatologist is satisfied that they are feeding well and have stable blood glucose levels.

ULTRASOUND SCANS

An ultrasound scan uses sound waves to 'visualise' babies in the womb. It involves no radiation and is completely safe and painless, and the image that is produced can be used to assess the development of your baby and check that all is well in your pregnancy.

Ultrasound scanning enables many health problems in both the mother and baby to be identified. Although it can be performed by an obstetrician or midwife, it is most likely that your ultrasound scan will be done by a sonographer, a medical professional who specialises in creating and interpreting images of the body. A probe covered in a water-based gel is placed centrally on your abdomen. This probe emits very high-frequency, inaudible sound waves as it is moved over the area. When the waves pass over a solid object in fluid (your baby), they bounce off and create an image on a screen. Various features, such as your baby's anatomy and the site of the placenta, can then be examined.

If yours is a straightforward pregnancy, you should be offered two ultrasound scans. You may have a further one if your BMI is over 35, or if you are found to have a low-lying placenta at the fetal anomaly scan (*see* p.70) or if you had a baby in a previous pregnancy that was smaller than expected. No scan is obligatory, although the majority of women do take up the opportunity to see their developing baby. You may be able to buy a photo of the scan (usually two-dimensional) for a token charge.

Early ultrasound scans

Occasionally, there is a need for an ultrasound scan early in the pregnancy, particularly if you have been bleeding (*see* Chapter 4, p.122). If you have had a previous miscarriage

DID YOU KNOW...?

Keep your scan photo in a dark place to prevent fading, but don't laminate the picture as it will fade with heat. You can ask to take a photo of the screen on your phone.

PAYING FOR ADDITIONAL SCANS

If your pregnancy is going well and there are no causes for concern, you will only have two ultrasound scans as part of your antenatal care under the NHS. However, some women want peace of mind from having additional scans between their routine appointments, which can be obtained privately for a fee. These can be done as early as six weeks into your pregnancy (when they will be done transvaginally – *see* main text) right up to your estimated delivery date, if you wish. Scans may be in colour and four-dimensional, as opposed to the more usual black-and-white, two- or three-dimensional ones you have from your hospital. It should be stressed, however, that although they offer a better *visual* image of your baby, these scans provide no more detailed *medical* information than those offered by the NHS.

or ectopic pregnancy (*see* Complications, p. 285), your GP may arrange for you to have a scan at about six weeks (whether or not you have any vaginal bleeding) to ensure that the fetal sac is growing inside your uterus. However, if there is no medical reason for you to need an early ultrasound scan and you simply want reassurance, you can pay for one privately. Before ten weeks gestation, scans will be done transvaginally (the probe is placed into the vagina), because the fetus is too small to be easily detected by an abdominal probe. This is painless and poses no threat at all to your pregnancy, even if you have a history of first trimester bleeding or miscarriage.

The dating scan

Your first ultrasound scan, at around twelve weeks, is often referred to as the 'dating' scan, because it is used to determine the exact gestational age of your baby. This can be done because, at this stage, all fetuses develop at the same rate, irrespective of their future size. The measurements taken at this scan are used thereafter to ensure that your baby is growing normally. Because the fetus is still very small, you need to have a full bladder so that a clear image can be produced – you will probably have to drink half a litre or more of water beforehand.

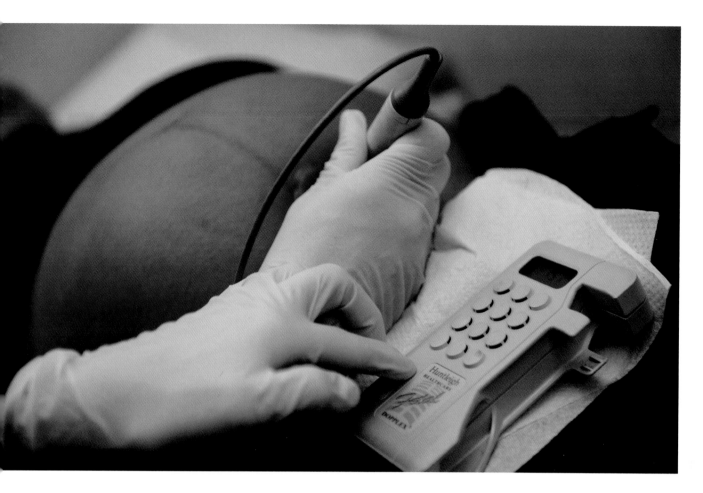

In order to enable the precise gestational age to be calculated, two key measurements of the fetus are taken:

▸ **the crown–rump length (CRL in your notes):** the length from the top of the baby's head to the base of the spine (rump)
▸ **the biparietal diameter (BPD):** the measurement across the two parietal bones, one on each side of the baby's head.

In addition, heart rate will be measured and the position of the placenta checked, although it is still too early to determine the sex of the baby. For most parents, seeing the beating heart on the screen is the first time they can begin to imagine the growing fetus as a real, future person.

Scanning is the most accurate way of dating a pregnancy, particularly if your cycle is irregular or you are unsure of the date of your last period.

The nuchal translucency scan

The nuchal translucency (NT) scan forms part of the combined screening test for Down's syndrome; the other element is a serum (blood) test (*see* pp.72 –3). The scan is usually done between eleven and fourteen weeks, often at the same time as the dating scan. Indeed, by thirteen weeks, the majority of women have had both scans. The NT scan measures the thickness of the skinfold at the back of the fetus' neck (the nuchal translucency). If this measurement is under 2 mm at eleven weeks or under 2.8 mm at fourteen weeks (as is the case in 95 per cent of pregnancies), the fetus is unlikely to be affected by Down's syndrome. If it is greater than 3 mm, there is an increased chance of the fetus having Down's syndrome. However, it is important to note that the nuchal translucency measurement is only one part of the screening test and only indicates probability rather than certainty – having a measurement of over 3 mm does not mean that your baby definitely has Down's syndrome, nor does a measurement of under 2/2.8 mm guarantee that your baby is not affected. The risk factor you are eventually given is calculated using the nuchal translucency measurement, your age and the results from the serum test. See p.73 for more information on how to interpret the risk factor and further considerations regarding diagnostic tests. A 'negative' serum screening result means the probability that your baby has an abnormality is low (usually one in 150 or less). If the result is 'positive', it means the probability is greater than one in 150.

Miscarriage

The loss of a pregnancy before 24 weeks is called a miscarriage. When this loss occurs during the first trimester, it is referred to as an 'early miscarriage'; a 'late miscarriage' refers to a second trimester miscarriage. If you experience three or more miscarriages in a row, which happens to about one per cent of women, this is called a 'recurrent miscarriage'.

Although miscarriage is the most common complication of pregnancy, the exact number per year is unknown. This is because the miscarriage happened so early that the woman did not even realise that she was pregnant, and so it is not recorded in any data. Nevertheless, it is thought that fifteen to twenty per cent of confirmed pregnancies end in miscarriage, mostly before twelve weeks gestation.

Maternal age, diabetes, obesity, smoking, infection and genetic (i.e. chromosomal) factors are amongst the common causes of miscarriage at all stages of pregnancy. In late miscarriages, a weak or incompetent cervix may contribute, although this can be difficult to diagnose antenatally (see Complications, p. 293). However, many miscarriages remain unexplained and more research is still needed before the reasons can be fully understood. In a first trimester miscarriage, hospitals usually offer only chromosomal/serum blood tests to try to determine the cause if yours is a recurrent miscarriage. Tests are available that can sometimes identify why a late miscarriage occurred, but bear in mind that a reason is found in only fifteen per cent of cases. This can be difficult to cope with, as it is normal to want answers as to why such a loss occurred.

Some women only discover when they have a scan (usually at twelve and at twenty weeks) that they have lost the pregnancy. This 'delayed' or missed pregnancy can be particularly upsetting, because they may still 'feel' pregnant and have not yet had any symptoms of a miscarriage.

Early miscarriage of pregnancy

About one in four of all pregnancies end in miscarriage, because many women miscarry before they even realise they are pregnant. However, by the eighth week of pregnancy, the chances of miscarrying have significantly reduced to approximately one in sixteen. About two-thirds of early miscarriages occur because the baby had a chromosomal defect that was incompatible with life. This type of miscarriage is more likely to be an isolated occurrence (unless you and your partner are carriers of a particular genetic abnormality), and most women go on to have successful subsequent pregnancies. See Feature on p.75 for more information on congenital abnormalities.

Miscarriages in the first few weeks of pregnancy resemble a late, slightly heavier period. Towards the end of the first trimester, the bleeding that occurs during a miscarriage may be accompanied by abdominal pain or cramping. Occasionally, women have no symptoms at all.

If you have any bleeding or cramping, you will be referred to your nearest Early Pregnancy Unit for assessment. An ultrasound is often used to confirm whether a miscarriage is taking place. If you are miscarrying spontaneously, your healthcare professionals may advise you to let nature take its course (see below). It can also reveal whether your miscarriage is 'complete', meaning that your uterus has expelled all the pregnancy tissues. If it shows that the baby has died but a miscarriage has not yet begun, or that the miscarriage is 'incomplete' (i.e. some tissues have remained), then you will be advised on the best course of treatment. It is important that all tissues from the pregnancy are removed in order to avoid infection and haemorrhage. In many cases, bleeding will begin naturally in time, but you may be offered a combination of pills and a pessary to open the cervix and start the process. If the tissues have not been completely expelled after three weeks of bleeding (occurring in fifteen per cent of cases), they may need to be removed surgically under general anaesthesia (see below).

Late miscarriage of pregnancy

Miscarriage after twelve weeks is relatively rare, occurring in one to two per cent of pregnancies. Miscarriages at this time are more likely to be caused by blood disorders, a structural problem with the umbilical cord, placenta, uterus or cervix, or can be the result of an infection or severe food poisoning, such as salmonella or listeria (see Chapter 2, pp. 24–5). Losing a baby at this time is very distressing, especially very late in the second trimester and after you had begun to feel your baby moving inside you.

Physical symptoms of late miscarriage can be the same as those of early miscarriage (see above) or, if your pregnancy is more advanced, you may experience a rupture of membranes ('waters breaking') and contractions. As with early miscarriage, there may be no symptoms at all and you may discover that your baby has died only at your next ultrasound scan. This will come as a great shock and may be hard to comprehend. Your obstetrician discuss with you what the next course of action should be, and may advise induction of birth.

Because the date of legal viability is 24 weeks, the death of a baby before this time will not be registered and no death certificate will be issued. Many parents find it very upsetting that this late loss of their baby is referred to as a miscarriage. However, there is nothing stopping you having a ceremony, similar to a funeral, to mark the death of your baby. And creating a memory box for your baby, similar to that created by many parents affected by stillbirth or neonatal death, can also be a good way of remembering the existence of your baby (see Complications, pp. 294–96).

Recurrent miscarriage

Defined as three or more miscarriages in a row, recurrent miscarriages affect one in 100 of couples. You should be offered referral to a specialist recurrent miscarriage clinic so that further investigations can be undertaken, although you should be aware that, even after full tests have been carried out, an explanation is only available in around half of cases. This is understandably frustrating and upsetting.

There are several known causes for recurrent first and second trimester miscarriage. As well as chromosomal abnormalities (which account for around 50 per cent of miscarriages, recurrent or otherwise), uterine or cervical abnormalities are also factors, as are underlying health problems with the mother. But the most important *treatable* cause of recurrent miscarriage, affecting around fifteen per cent of women with recurrent miscarriage, is where they have antiphospholipid syndrome. This is a condition where the blood contains a higher than normal level of an antibody called antiphospholipid, which blocks the blood supply to the fetus and results in a miscarriage. Treatment involves taking a low dose of aspirin plus heparin, and can be very successful.

Couples referred to a specialist clinic undergo highly specialised investigations, including blood testing, blood karyotyping of both you and your partner (to rule out chromosomal issues), pelvic ultrasounds and, where relevant, genetic counselling. However, it has also been shown that supportive care involving regular antenatal appointments and scans at a specialist clinic, even when no actual treatment is involved (e.g. if no cause has been found for the pregnancy losses), can significantly improve the likelihood of having a successful subsequent pregnancy.

Management of your miscarriage

If it is confirmed that you are miscarrying, and depending on how far advanced your pregnancy is, there are several options for you. The first is to let the body deal with the end of the pregnancy naturally. This is often preferable in a first trimester miscarriage. The body will usually 'resorb' (or absorb) the small amounts of tissue associated with the pregnancy, or occasionally you will pass these vaginally. The advantage of letting nature take its course is that no surgery is involved. The disadvantage is that sometimes persistent bleeding occurs, which can increase the risk of infection.

The second option is to deal with it medically: this involves a combination of pills and vaginal pessaries to encourage the body to expel the pregnancy tissue. The advantages and disadvantages are similar to that of the previous option.

The final option is to manage the miscarriage surgically. This involves an operation, often done under general anaesthesia, and is referred to as 'surgical management of miscarriage' (SMM), although many still call it an ERPC (evacuation of retained products of conception). During the operation, the remaining pregnancy-associated tissue is removed gently using a suction tube. Many women opt for this, especially if bleeding has persisted for more than a week, or if there has been no bleeding and pregnancy tissue is still visible on an ultrasound.

Feeling supported

At whatever stage it occurs, miscarriage is always distressing, both for you and your partner, as well as for your wider family and friends. The loss is often no less keenly felt for early miscarriages, because couples have already started to plan their future as parents. It is important that you allow yourselves time to grieve and to work through your loss, perhaps by talking to a specialist counsellor or by contacting one of the support organisations for miscarriage (see Useful Resources). You may also benefit from some of the information in the Feature on Stillbirth and Neonatal Death in Complications, pp. 294–96.

The fetal anomaly scan

Your other routine antenatal scan is performed between eighteen and twenty weeks. It takes about twenty minutes to complete and you won't need to have a full bladder this time, because your baby will be larger and there will be enough amniotic fluid in your uterus to produce a clear image of your baby on the screen.

A series of measurements of the fetus are taken and listed in your notes as millimetres against the gestational age in weeks and days (e.g. biparietal diameter: 20+4/40 = 49.4 mm). These figures are compared to the average to ensure that the baby is growing normally. In addition, some physical features are checked to ensure there are no defects. Sometimes, the position of the fetus makes it difficult to see all the organs, so you may be asked to walk around for a while in the hope that your baby changes position or you may even have to come back later. The following elements will be examined:

▸ **heartbeat and structure of the four heart chambers:** the top two chambers (atria) and the bottom two chambers (ventricles) should be equal in size and the valves should open and close with each heartbeat; only certain major problems can be detected at this scan

▸ **abdominal cavity and wall, structure of the lungs, stomach, intestines, and liver:** all internal organs should now be enclosed behind the abdominal wall and the diaphragm (the muscular shelf separating the chest from the abdominal cavity) should also be complete; the fetus should be swallowing some of the amniotic fluid, seen as a black bubble in the stomach

▸ **kidneys:** the sonographer will check that there are two, and that there is no blockage between the kidneys and the bladder; if it was empty, the bladder should fill up during the time that the ultrasound is being done – your baby has been passing urine every half an hour or so for some weeks now (see Chapter 4, p.93)!

▸ **shape and structure of the brain, skull and spine, size of brain ventricles:** measured along the length and also in cross section, to ensure that all the bones align and the skin covers the spine at the back

▸ **arms, legs, hands, feet:** fingers and toes are looked at, but may not be counted

▸ **structure of the face:** to check for a possible cleft lip; it is hard to see inside the baby's mouth, so a cleft palette is sometimes missed; you may be able to see your baby's face now for the first time

TYPE OF ABNORMALITY	PERCENTAGE IDENTIFIED AT SCAN
Defect of the spinal cord (spina bifida)	90 per cent
Cleft lip	75 per cent
Edward's syndrome or Patau's syndrome (chromosomal abnormalities)	95 per cent
Defect of the abdominal wall (gastroschisis)	98 per cent
Major kidney problems (missing or abnormal kidneys)	84 per cent
Major heart problem (defects of chambers, valves or vessels)	50 per cent

▸ **femoral length, abdominal circumference, head circumference:** these are all measured and listed in your notes as FL, AC, HC respectively
▸ **position of the placenta:** it will either be lying on the anterior (front) or the posterior (back) wall of the uterus, and can be high up (at the fundus) or low-lying (close to or covering the cervix). See Complications, p. 287 for more on what happens if the placenta is low-lying (placenta praevia)
▸ **position and structure of the umbilical cord:** normally, the cord contains three blood vessels, but occasionally there are only two; this does not usually cause a problem, but the baby's growth may be monitored more closely and you may be offered another ultrasound later in the pregnancy
▸ **volume of amniotic fluid:** if there is too little (oligohydramnios) or too much (polyhydramnios), further tests will be required, including another scan a few weeks later. See Complications, pp. 287 and 288 for more information on these conditions
▸ **sex of the fetus:** if you don't want to know, inform the sonographer beforehand (although it may, in the end, become obvious, depending on what position the fetus is lying in).

About fifteen per cent of scans need to be repeated for a variety of reasons, most often because the sonographer has not been able to see everything that needs to be checked. This could be because your baby was not lying in the right position, or because you are overweight, in which case the ultrasound should be repeated at 23 weeks. Some hospitals have a policy of not revealing the sex of a baby, so you will have to pay for a private scan if you wish to find out. Be aware, however, that mistakes can occur: sometimes the penis is hidden and you might be told you are carrying a girl, only to have a shock when you actually give birth!

For most women, the fetal anomaly scan will be a reassurance that everything is progressing well in their pregnancy. However, some conditions are not detectable by scan; nor are scans a cast-iron guarantee that your baby will be free from abnormalities, as some more serious conditions are more difficult to spot than others. The chart above lists of some serious conditions, most of which are very rare, and what the percentage chance is of your sonographer identifying them at the fetal anomaly scan.

If it is suspected that your baby has an abnormality, you will be given a lot of support to help you through this difficult time. Some conditions are treatable through surgery or treatment after birth (*see* Complications, p. 292), and sometimes even while the fetus is in the womb. Knowing in advance that your baby is affected will allow you to make an informed choice about what options are available.

THE INCIDENCE OF FETAL ABNORMALITIES AT BIRTH
The fetal abnormalities listed in the chart are rare and most are detected by antenatal scanning, as indicated. The following statistics show the incidence at birth of some of the fetal abnormalities discussed (kidney and heart problems are too wide-ranging to provide specific statistics):

▸ Cleft lip and/or palate   1:700
▸ Spina bifida   1:1,000
▸ Gastroschisis   1:3,000
▸ Edward's syndrome   1:35,000 births (most miscarry/are terminated)

SERUM SCREENING TESTS

You will be offered a serum (blood) test during your pregnancy to screen for a range of fetal abnormalities, notably Down's syndrome, and neural tube defects such as spina bifida. The screening takes place either at the end of the first trimester, or in the first part of the second.

There are two important things to remember about serum screening: firstly, it is optional; and secondly, it is a screening test and not a diagnostic test. It therefore provides information on the *risk* of the fetus being affected by an abnormality but it does not diagnose and *confirm* an abnormality. The following are the serum screening tests currently offered by the NHS:

- **the combined:** carried out between 11+2 and 14+1 weeks of pregnancy
- **the quadruple:** carried out between 14+2 and 20+0 weeks
- **the triple:** carried out between 14+2 and 20+0 weeks.

If you have your booking visit early enough in your pregnancy, you should be offered the combined test, which involves both a blood test and a nuchal translucency scan to assess the risk for Down's syndrome and other chromosomal abnormalities. If not, you will be offered the triple or the quadruple instead, which involves a blood test only. Alternatively, your hospital may be able to offer you the Harmony prenatal DNA test or you could opt for it to be done privately (*see* Box below).

The combined test has a high detection rate, correctly identifying about 90 per cent of babies with Down's syndrome, and a false positive rate of five per cent. (A false positive is where your baby is thought to have a condition but is later discovered not to.) The quadruple test is similarly effective, whereas the triple test has a detection rate closer to 75 per cent and a false positive rate of 58 per cent. The low false positive rate is important: a false positive could lead you to have a further diagnostic test (*see* p.74) – which has a risk of miscarriage – that you did not need to have. If your hospital only offers the triple test, you may choose to pay privately for either the combined or, if you are being tested later, the quadruple test. See Useful Resources for more information on screening for abnormalities.

THE HARMONY PRENATAL DNA TEST

A new screening test, the Harmony prenatal DNA test, is now available privately (and without the need for GP referral) and also in some NHS hospitals. It measures the very tiny amounts of fetal DNA present in the mother's blood to screen for (not diagnose) the risk of the three most common chromosomal abnormalities: Down's Syndrome (Trisomy 21), Edward's Syndrome (Trisomy 18) and Patau's Syndrome (Trisomy 13). The test can be done from ten weeks of fetal gestation (i.e. twelve weeks of pregnancy), is safe and non-invasive and is suitable for all babies (including IVF babies, except those conceived using donor eggs). The test comprises two elements:

- a scan at twelve weeks (to date your pregnancy accurately)
- a blood test.

The blood sample is sent away to be analysed and results are available within two weeks. It is more accurate than other screening methods and has a low false positive rate:

- **Down's syndrome:** 99 per cent accurate and a 0.1 per cent false positive rate
- **Edward's syndrome:** 97 per cent accurate and a 0.1 per cent false positive rate
- **Patau's syndrome:** 80 per cent accurate and a 0.1 per cent false positive.

However, as the test is not 100 per cent accurate, invasive procedures such as amniocentesis and chorionic villus sampling still remain the only way to *diagnose* whether your baby is affected by the above abnormalities.

What do the serum tests measure?

Serum screening involves measuring the levels of specific substances in your blood. Maternal factors, such as your age, your ethnic background and your weight, as well as the gestational age of the fetus, are among other elements that are then incorporated to work out the risk of the fetus being affected by a range of abnormalities, including Down's syndrome and spina bifida.

The combined test

Two elements – the serum screening and the nuchal translucency scan – form the so-called combined test. The blood sample can be taken from 10+0 weeks and two substances are measured:

▶ a pregnancy-associated protein A (PAPP-A)
▶ beta human chorionic gonadotrophin (BhCG), a hormone produced by the placenta.

The quadruple test

Four substances are measured by the quadruple test:

▶ alpha-fetoprotein (AFP), a protein produced by the fetus
▶ BhCG
▶ unconjugated estriol (uE3), a form of oestrogen produced by the fetus and placenta
▶ inhibin A, a hormone released by the placenta.

The triple test

The triple test measures three substances in the blood:

▶ AFP
▶ BhCG
▶ uE3.

Results are usually available within five working days and the way you receive the information depends on your system of antenatal care and the hospital's chosen method of informing you. For example, you may have to phone up for the result, or you may receive the information by letter or from a midwife.

What do the results mean?

In both the triple and the quadruple tests, low levels of AFP and uE3 and high levels of BhCG (and inhibin A for the quadruple) may indicate Down's syndrome; increased levels of AFP indicate a higher risk of the baby having spina bifida.

The result will say that you have a one in X chance of having a baby affected by an abnormality. This may be, for example, a one in 250 chance of having a Down's syndrome

baby. It is important to realise that a high-risk result does *not* mean that your baby definitely has Down's syndrome; nor, for that matter, does a very low-risk result mean that your baby does not have the condition. If the figure is higher than one in 150 (*see* table below), you will be offered a diagnostic test, which is the only way to know for certain if your baby is affected. You will now be faced with a very personal decision: these tests are invasive and carry a risk of miscarriage. For some people, a one in 250 risk is very small indeed (and may be lower than the chance of miscarrying following a diagnostic test), whereas for others it is unacceptably high and they decide to go ahead with further testing.

Your midwife or obstetrician will be able to discuss the situation with you if you want, and there are support groups that can also help (*see* Useful Resources). Remember also that most women who are in the high-risk group and have a diagnostic test go on to find out that their baby does not have Down's syndrome or another fetal abnormality.

MATERNAL AGE AND DOWN'S SYNDROME
The risk of having a baby affected by Down's syndrome increases with maternal age.

Maternal age	Risk of Down's
25	1:1,350
28	1:1,100
30	1:900
31	1:800
32	1:680
33	1:570
34	1:470
35	1:380
36	1:310
37	1:240
38	1:190
39	1:150
40	1:110
41	1:85
42	1:65
43	1:50
44	1:35
45	1:30
46	1:20
47	1:15
48	1:11

If your baby has a suspected abnormality, you will be offered a diagnostic test, which can confirm or rule out the condition. Knowing for certain whether your baby is affected can help parents to decide upon how to proceed.

If you choose to have a diagnostic test, it is usually for one or more of the following reasons:

▸ the nuchal translucency scan and/or serum tests, or the fetal anomaly scan, has given a high-risk result or revealed a potential abnormality
▸ you and/or your partner have a family history or are carriers of certain specific chromosomal abnormalities or genetic disorders (*see* Feature opposite)
▸ you have had a previous pregnancy affected by an abnormality.

Diagnostic tests allow specific conditions to be confirmed with certainty. This gives parents the opportunity to prepare themselves for caring for a child with a disability or to consider terminating the pregnancy. The three diagnostic tests used are amniocentesis, chorionic villus sampling (CVS) and cordocentesis (*see* pp.76–8), and your obstetrician will suggest which is the most suitable one for you. However, as these are invasive tests, they carry a risk of miscarriage. You therefore need to make sure that you are clear about what each test involves, whether you are prepared to take the risk of miscarrying and what you would do when given the result of the investigation. Allow yourselves sufficient time to think about this before making this very important decision. See Complications, p. 293 for information about termination.

> ❝ We were too late for a nuchal scan, so we had to have a quadrupal test. It came back as high risk for Down's and this was obviously a concern. We saw the specialist, who talked us through our options. We decided against amniocentesis, as we wanted the baby regardless of the outcome. At the fetal anomaly scan, our baby showed no signs of heart defects or limb shortages, so we stayed with our decision – the risk of miscarriage was too big for me, even at one per cent. ❞ **DAWN**

YOUR HEALTH AFTER A DIAGNOSTIC TEST

It is common to feel some mild cramping and to experience some vaginal spotting (light bleeding) after a diagnostic test, but this is not necessarily indicative of a problem. Nevertheless, you should take things easy for the first 48 hours after the procedure. Most miscarriages that occur after a diagnostic test are due to infection, so you should monitor your temperature at home and contact your GP or obstetrician if:

▸ at any stage your temperature rises above 37.3°C
▸ if you feel achy, shivery or generally unwell
▸ if your underwear becomes wet, as this could indicate leakage of amniotic fluid.

These symptoms can arise anytime up to two weeks after the test. If an infection is found, your doctor can treat it with antibiotics in the hope of reducing the risk of miscarriage, but cannot actually prevent one occurring.

Chromosomal and genetic abnormalities

When an abnormality is found in a fetus, it can be the result of an error in the number or structure of chromosomes or a problem with one or more genes, caused by environmental, inherited or other factors. These result in structural differences in the way babies are formed.

Chromosomal abnormalities

Chromosomal abnormalities occur when there are either too few or too many of a specific chromosome. We know of around 300 of these, and most are incompatible with life. This means that the pregnancy ends in miscarriage or (more rarely) that the baby survives for only a short time after birth. Some chromosomal abnormalities result in developmental or behavioural problems with no structural malformations; others cause a child to have profound physical and mental disabilities that require lifelong support. The most common chromosomal abnormality is Down's syndrome (Trisomy 21), where there are three copies of chromosome 21, followed by Patau's syndrome (Trisomy 13) and Edward's syndrome (Trisomy 18). These, together with Turner syndrome (45 X, because one of the X sex chromosomes is missing) make up 98 per cent of all chromosomal abnormalities. See Complications, p. 284 for more on these conditions. Maternal age is known to increase the risk of a baby being affected by a chromosomal abnormality (*see* Box on p.73), as is increased paternal age (although to a much lesser extent).

Genetic abnormalities

Genetic abnormalities occur as a result of having one or more faulty genes. Some are inherited: they can be passed from parent to baby, although the manner in which they do so varies. Genes are either dominant or recessive. If a gene is dominant, only one copy (from one parent) is needed for the fetus to inherit its characteristic. If it is recessive, a copy from each parent is required to ensure the characteristic is dominant. Certain genetically inherited diseases, such as Huntingdon's disease, are carried on a dominant gene, whereas others, such as cystic fibrosis and sickle-cell disease, are recessive genetic diseases (*see* Complications, p.284).

Other diseases are sex-specific: for example, muscular dystrophy and haemophilia are inherited by men, but are caused by a recessive gene on the female X chromosome. Females carry the disease, but are not affected. This is because women have two X chromosomes, while men have one X and one Y chromosome. If a female inherits the abnormal gene from, for example, her mother, she will still have a normal X chromosome from her father and will simply be a carrier of the disease (and can pass it on to future generations) but will not display any symptoms. A male, however, has only one X chromosome, so if he inherits the faulty gene (from his mother), his Y chromosome will not be able to counter it and he will have haemophilia.

Some of these diseases may already have occurred in your extended family, in which case you may be referred for genetic counselling before or in early pregnancy. Tests described in this section, such as amniocentesis or CVS, can then be carried out if you need confirmation as to whether the fetus is affected. In addition, where you know that you have a family history of a certain inherited genetic disease, preimplantation genetic diagnosis (PGD) may now be used for an increasing range of disorders. Here, embryos are created in vitro (in a test tube), in a similar process to IVF, and screened for the presence of that disorder. Only healthy embryos are then implanted into the uterus, so the couple know that the resulting fetus is free from very serious disease.

Amniocentesis

Amniocentesis is most often performed between fourteen and sixteen weeks, but can be carried out as late as 26 weeks. Although the risk of miscarrying following the test is said to be one per cent, if it is carried out by experienced medical staff, the risk can be much lower, at around 0.3 per cent.

Some anaesthetic gel is applied to the skin on your abdomen and a local anaesthetic may be injected into the skin area. Under ultrasound guidance, an experienced obstetrician inserts a very fine needle through the uterine wall and removes a sample of amniotic fluid (about 10–20 ml, or two to four teaspoonfuls), which is transferred to a syringe. This procedure takes about 20–30 minutes. The fetal cells that are present in the fluid are cultured in a laboratory where they divide and multiply, after which an analysis of the chromosomes can be done. Chromosomes 21 (for Down's syndrome), 18 (Edward's syndrome), 13 (Patau's syndrome) and the sex ones will be examined. Results are

99 per cent accurate and are available around two weeks later, although you can ask if they can be sent for more rapid diagnosis using newer, more complex techniques, such as polymerase chain reaction (PCR) or fluorescent in-situ hybridisation (FISH). This may only be possible at a cost, and you should bear in mind that these techniques can only identify certain chromosomal abnormalities. However, the results will be available within two to seven days.

DID YOU KNOW…?

You can ask your hospital for their yearly percentage rate of miscarriage after an amniocentesis. If you feel the rate is too high, you are entitled to ask for a referral elsewhere.

Amniocentesis Guided by an ultrasound probe, a very fine needle is inserted through the uterine wall (the wall of the womb) in order to remove a small amount of amniotic fluid. This contains some fetal cells, which can then be analysed.

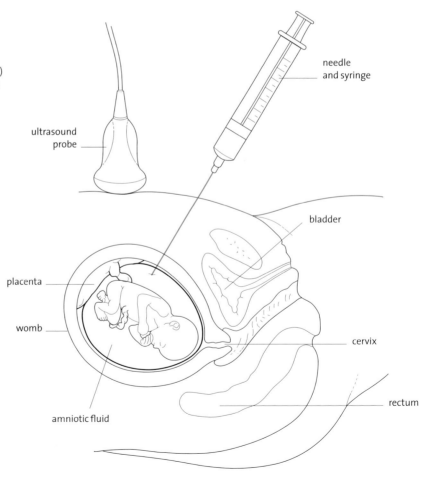

ultrasound probe

needle and syringe

bladder

placenta

womb

cervix

rectum

amniotic fluid

Chorionic villus sampling

Chorionic villus sampling (CVS) is a similar procedure to amniocentesis, but is carried out earlier, at eleven to thirteen weeks. Accessed through the uterine wall, a minute tissue sample is taken directly from the placenta – from the chorionic villi, to be precise – rather than from the amniotic fluid (*see* Chapter 4, p.89). If the placenta is difficult to reach, the procedure may be performed via the cervix using a narrow tube.

Because the cells come from the living placenta, they can be analysed more quickly, giving a provisional result within three days, and a definitive one within seven to ten days (sometimes slightly longer for some genetic disorders). CVS carries a one per cent risk of miscarriage, although, again, the greater the doctor's experience, the lower the likelihood of a miscarriage occurring.

There is a greater chance of inaccuracy with CVS than with amniocentesis, because placental cells may be mixed with those of the chorionic villi. If the fetus is female, it is not then possible to know whether these placental cells are from the mother or the fetus (since both will have the female X chromosomes).

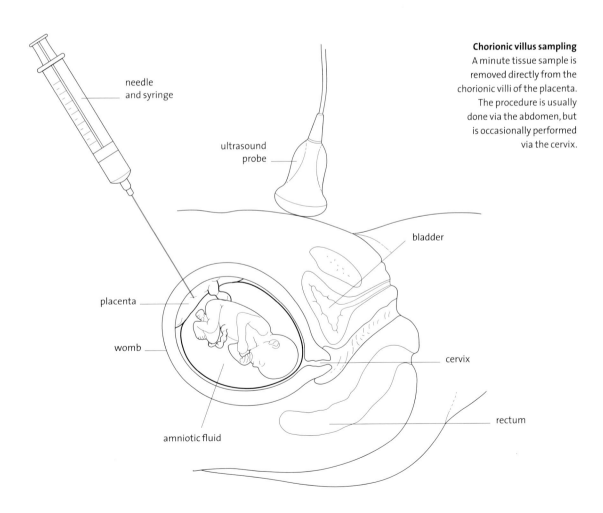

Chorionic villus sampling
A minute tissue sample is removed directly from the chorionic villi of the placenta. The procedure is usually done via the abdomen, but is occasionally performed via the cervix.

needle and syringe

ultrasound probe

bladder

placenta

womb

cervix

rectum

amniotic fluid

Cordocentesis

Cordocentesis is usually carried out when amniocentesis or CVS are unsuccessful in providing a definitive diagnosis of a chromosomal or other fetal abnormality. It can be performed after eighteen weeks and involves removing a small sample of fetal blood directly from the umbilical cord, using advanced ultrasound as a guide. This method of testing can diagnose a chromosomal abnormality within 72 hours, but it does carry a one to two per cent chance of miscarriage. Because of its relative risk, it is invariably performed in a specialist fetal medicine centre.

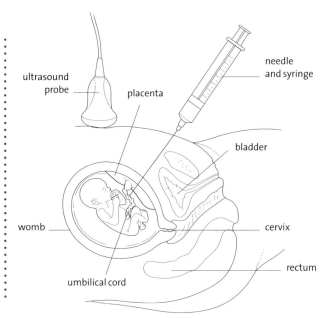

ultrasound probe · placenta · needle and syringe · bladder · cervix · rectum · womb · umbilical cord

Cordocentesis
A small sample of blood is removed directly from the umbilical cord.

SUMMARY OF PRINCIPAL ANTENATAL TESTS

TEST *only offered if medically necessary	WHEN CARRIED OUT
First blood screening test (including blood group, Rhesus factor, anaemia, hepatitis B, rubella immunity, syphilis, HIV)	Ideally by 10 weeks
Dating scan Nuchal translucency (NT) scan	11–14 weeks
Chorionic villus sampling*	11–13 weeks
Second blood screening test, one from:	
▸ combined	From 14+2 to 20+0 weeks, plus NT scan
▸ triple or quadruple	From 14+2 to 20+0 weeks
Amniocentesis*	14–26 weeks
Fetal anomaly scan	18–20 weeks
Cordocentesis*	From 18 weeks
Glucose tolerance test*	26–30 weeks
Further blood test for anaemia	28 weeks
Growth scan if BMI over 35 or baby small at previous scan*	28 weeks

35+ mothers

Increasing numbers of women are giving birth later in life: one in five of all births is now to women over 35, and the numbers of births to women over the age of 40 is at an all-time high, almost doubling in the space of ten years.

The figures highlighting the increasing trend towards older motherhood are very revealing: in 2000, the number of women giving birth in the 35–9 age group was 84,974 and the number of those over 40 was 15,066; by 2010, this had swelled to 115,841 and 27,731 respectively. There are many reasons for this trend, but factors include the availability of safe, reliable contraception, women's desire to pursue further education and a career, and waiting until they are financially secure and in a stable relationship before starting a family.

Fertility after 35

Contraception has given women greater freedom in when to have a baby and many are choosing to wait until they are in their 30s before trying to get pregnant. However, after the age of 35, hormonal changes start to take place as you move towards the pre-menopausal years. These changes affect your menstrual cycle and fertility, often leading to shorter and/or irregular cycles. In addition, as you get older, your ovaries do not always release an egg or, conversely, they release more than one (which is why the older you are, the higher chance you have of conceiving non-identical twins).

Egg quality also deteriorates after the age of 35, so that eggs are either less able to be fertilised or have a greater chance of carrying a genetic or chromosomal defect. This can prevent a pregnancy from taking place or result in miscarriage or a decision to terminate. Some chromosomal abnormalities are not incompatible with life and the most common of these is Down's syndrome, the frequency of whose occurrence is very clearly related to maternal age (see p.73). However, Down's syndrome is also responsible for many miscarriages and neonatal deaths, so it does not therefore always result in a live birth.

When trying to conceive naturally, 75 per cent of women aged 30 will be successful within one year, compared to 66 per cent of women aged 35 and 44 per cent of those aged 40. By the age of 45, the success rate has fallen to one to two per cent.

Pregnancy

Although most pregnancies to older women result in a healthy baby, the chance of developing complications in your pregnancy rises with age, especially after 40. These include hypertension (high blood pressure), pre-eclampsia and gestational diabetes. And the older you are, the greater the likelihood that you are already suffering from conditions, such as diabetes or obesity, that can cause complications during the pregnancy. Miscarriage rates also increase. This is due, in part, to the higher number of embryos carrying abnormalities that are incompatible with life, but also to problems with the mother's endometrium (lining of the uterus), hormones or the placenta. At the age of 25, your risk of miscarriage is approximately fifteen per cent. At the age of 35, the figure rises to twenty per cent, and by 40, your risk has risen to 40 per cent. Maternal age is also associated with an increase in stillbirth, both antenatally and during labour, as well as neonatal mortality. For example, a woman aged 40 has a similar stillbirth risk at 39 weeks of gestation as a 29-year-old woman at 41 weeks. In absolute terms, the stillbirth risk at 41 weeks is 0.75 per 1,000 births for women under 35 and 2.5 per 1,000 for women aged 40 onwards, and higher if this is your first baby (twice as high if you are Afro-Caribbean). It is not clear what the reasons for the increase are, because although placental insufficiency is a factor, it is not the sole cause.

Labour and birth

Women who give birth over the age of 35, especially for the first time, have a higher risk of complications during labour and of needing medical intervention, and this risk increases for those over 40. For example, you are more likely to develop hypertension, heavy bleeding during and/or after labour or a postnatal venous thromboembolism or deep vein thrombosis (especially if you have had a Caesarean section that has limited your mobility after the birth). Your labour will not necessarily be more difficult if you are over 35, but statistically this tends to be the case. As a result, older mothers are more likely to be induced and to require an assisted delivery or a Caesarean section, especially for a first birth. Caesarean rates amongst women below the age of 25 are just below 20 per cent; in women aged 35–9 the rate is nearly 40 per cent and in those over 40 it is 50 per cent. In addition, when you are in your 40s rather than your early 20s, if you do deliver vaginally, you are likely to find labour more tiring and your post-birth recovery, from either labour or a Caesarean, is usually slower.

However, just because you fall into the 35-plus category does not necessarily mean that your labour will be more medicalised – plenty of older women give birth without the need for medical intervention. Similarly, if you are thinking of having a home birth and you are 35–9, your age alone should not rule this out if you are otherwise fit and healthy and your pregnancy is progressing without any problems – especially if this is not your first baby. Nonetheless, if this is your first birth and you are over 35, you do need to know the facts and statistics, some of which are provided in Chapter 1, so that you can make a fully informed decision. And you should be aware that many doctors and midwives will not encourage a home birth if you have not previously had a successful vaginal delivery. Similarly, midwifery units designed for low-risk births may not accept you if you are a first-time mother over the age of 35, unless you have seen an obstetrician and they are satisfied that there are no other medical indications for a hospital delivery. This may seem unreasonable, but your healthcare professionals have to work on the basis of clinical experience and statistical evidence.

Maternal age and the increased risk of medical problems

The older you are, the greater the likelihood of complications in your general health and your ability to conceive, as well as in your pregnancy and labour, especially if this is your first baby. These include:

Gynaecological issues
▸ history of sexually transmitted infections/pelvic inflammatory disease, leading to blocked Fallopian tubes
▸ endometriosis
▸ fibroids
▸ cervical surgery

Other acquired medical problems
▸ hypertension
▸ pregnancy-induced hypertension
▸ diabetes or gestational diabetes
▸ heart disease
▸ obesity

Conception and implantation difficulties
▸ reduced fertility
▸ miscarriage and ectopic pregnancy
▸ chromosomal abnormality or other birth defects
▸ multiple pregnancy (natural/assisted)
▸ increased need for IVF but poorer outcome

Pregnancy outcomes – increased incidence of:
▸ stillbirth and neonatal death
▸ prematurity
▸ pre-eclampsia
▸ intrauterine growth restriction
▸ placenta praevia
▸ induction and Caesarean section rate
▸ maternal morbidity.

The advantages of older motherhood

Even if they risk a more complicated conception, pregnancy and birth, the majority of women over 35 do go on to have a healthy baby. Moreover, although you may not have as much energy as you did when you were young, there are benefits to waiting until you are a little older before having children. You may be in a long-standing relationship and, if this is your first baby, you (and your partner) may be better equipped financially and emotionally for pregnancy and parenthood. A later baby is often a much-wanted one, and you are probably very motivated to do everything you can to have a healthy pregnancy. You may also be more secure in your career and this might enable you, if you wish, to take a longer maternity leave. In addition, you may also be earning more than you were when you first started work or have had time to save, which can help with the costs of bringing up a child.

Once your baby is born, you are likely to bring a greater life experience to motherhood, which will help you in the many decisions you have to make when bringing up a child. Many women also find that, after focusing on their job through their 20s and early 30s, having a baby now gives them a broader perspective: seeing your child in the evening after a day at work helps to diminish the importance of any troubles you might have encountered that day. Furthermore, some women decide that they can afford to step off the career ladder, either partly or entirely, and are all the happier for it, yet would never have wanted or been able to do so if they had had their children earlier in their lives.

There is never an ideal time to have a baby. There is an ideal fertile time, but often that does not coincide with a time in your life where you want or are in a position to have a child. Those women who do have a child after the age of 35 find they never regret their decision.

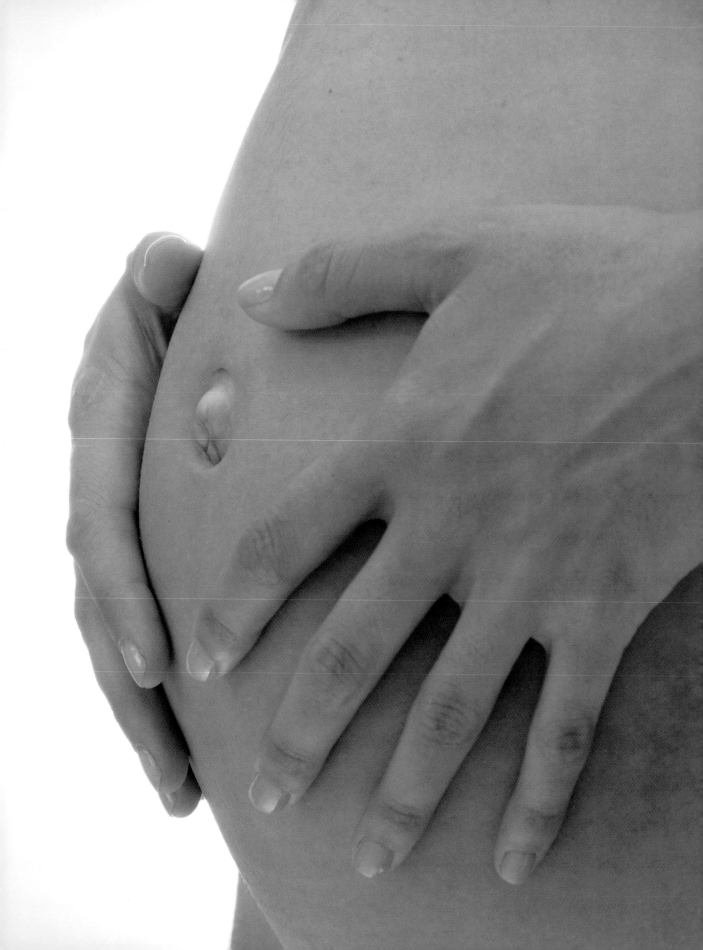

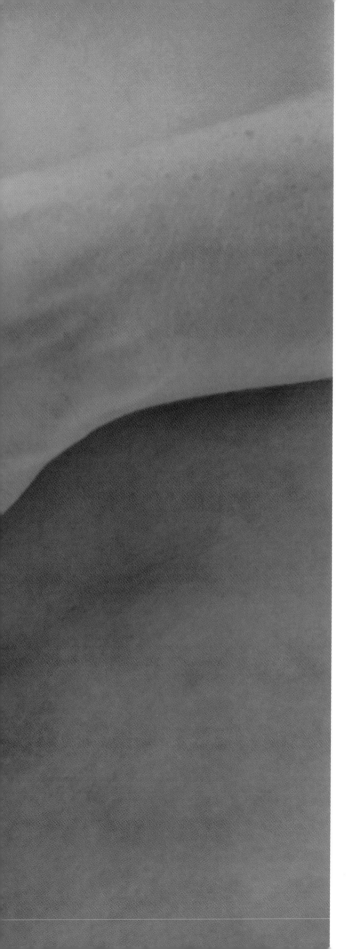

The Three Trimesters

The length of a pregnancy – called gestation – is 40 weeks, although anything between 37 and 41 weeks is considered normal. A pregnancy is divided into three parts, or trimesters, each approximately three months long. From the moment of conception your body undergoes many changes and your baby develops in remarkable and fascinating ways.

FIRST TRIMESTER

The first trimester begins on the first day of your last menstrual period and is considered to finish at the end of the thirteenth week. It is a crucial time in your pregnancy, during which the baby's major organs are formed and external physical features develop.

Your body also undergoes an extraordinary amount of changes, most of which you will not be aware of. Despite this, by the end of Week 13, you probably still do not look pregnant, and the only change that might be noticeable to others is that your breasts have become larger. Initially, your pregnancy is supported by hormones alone until the placenta takes over towards the end of the trimester.

Weeks 1–3

Your baby
Your baby starts to develop as soon as the egg is fertilised by the sperm (see picture), that is, in Week 3 of your pregnancy (see below). Fertilisation is described in detail in Chapter 1, p.10. On its journey towards the uterus, the egg (blastocyst) has been rapidly dividing into more and more cells, which become specialised: the outer, trophoblast cells develop into the placenta, while the inner cells are already programmed to form three different layers, the 'germ' layers, which will grow into the various parts of your baby:

▸ the outer layer, or ectoderm, which will become the skin, hair, nails, the nervous system and the brain
▸ the middle layer, or mesoderm, which develops into the heart, the blood vessels, the skeleton and cartilage
▸ the inner layer, or endoderm, which will form the digestive and respiratory systems, including the bladder and lining of the bowels.

Six days after fertilisation, the blastocyst attaches itself to the endometrium (lining of the uterus). This is called implantation.

While the outer (trophoblast) part embeds further into the lining, the inner cells continue to multiply and form what is now an embryo. By the end of the first week after fertilisation, cells that will become the brain and the central nervous system are already starting to develop.

You
The gestation (length) of your pregnancy is calculated from the first day of your last menstrual period, so for the first two weeks, you are not actually pregnant. However, your body is preparing for ovulation as part of your normal monthly cycle. If an egg is fertilised, on or around Day 14 of your cycle, the levels of pregnancy hormones – notably oestrogen, progesterone and beta human chorionic gonadotrophin (BhCG) – are raised. Even before your period is due and you know you are pregnant, these (and other) hormones are already at work, maintaining the pregnancy until the placenta is sufficiently developed and can take over towards the end of this trimester. See Box opposite for more on the roles these hormones play in your pregnancy. It is not uncommon to experience a small amount of bleeding at this time, caused by implantation. It is much lighter than your normal menstrual bleeding, however, and happens a little earlier than your period would have arrived.

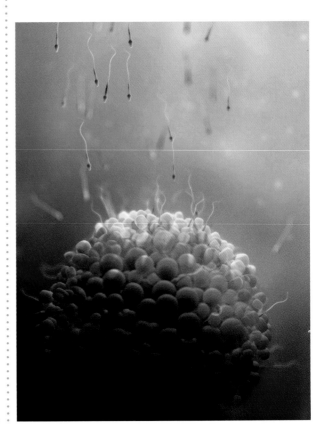

Week 4

Your baby

The embryo is now completely embedded in the endometrium and a primitive circulation has been established. This tiny structure, which can be seen under powerful magnification as a little bump in the surface of the uterus, measures just 2 mm (*see* picture).

You

You are already four weeks pregnant by the time your period would have been due. Other than a missed period, most women do not necessarily have any symptoms of pregnancy at this early stage. Some say, however, that they feel different – this may be a feeling of calmness, fullness or some other, indefinable, sensation – or that they simply 'know' that they are pregnant.

If you have become pregnant following assisted conception, the date that you had your embryo transfer (whether frozen or otherwise) is counted as Day 14 of your pregnancy, and all your pregnancy dates thereafter will be calculated on that basis.

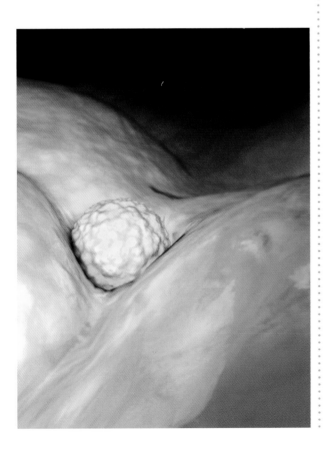

There are three main pregnancy hormones: oestrogen, progesterone and beta human chorionic gonadotrophin (BhCG), each of which has a specific function in maintaining your pregnancy.

The higher oestrogen levels that occur in pregnancy help to thicken the endometrium, ensuring that the developing embryo remains safely embedded and able to obtain all the nutrients it needs to continue to grow. Oestrogen also stimulates the growth of milk glands in your breasts, which usually causes them to feel tender in these early weeks (*see* p.126). This tenderness should disappear by the start of the second trimester.

BhCG is a hormone that occurs almost exclusively during pregnancy. It is secreted by the cells of the implanting egg and later, at a lower level, by the placenta. Like oestrogen, it also helps to keep the embryo embedded in the endometrium. Secretion of the hormone rises sharply in the first few weeks of pregnancy and peaks at around Weeks 8–10.

BhCG also stimulates the thyroid gland to produce a hormone, thyroxine, which speeds up your metabolism by 10–25 per cent during pregnancy. This rise in metabolic rate is needed because many of your organs increase in size during pregnancy and they need more oxygen to function well. In order to meet this need, the volume of plasma (the watery fluid) in your blood increases rapidly. The volume of oxygen-carrying red blood cells also starts to rise during the first trimester, albeit more slowly, and this ensures that the blood does not become too watery. In fact, your overall blood volume increases, from around 3.5 litres at the start of your pregnancy to around 5.4 litres by the end.

Progesterone plays a vital role in regulating these metabolic changes. In order to accommodate the increased blood volume, higher levels of progesterone encourage blood vessels to dilate, which prevents your blood pressure from reaching dangerous levels. Progesterone also thickens the cervical mucus so that a protective plug is formed, which stops any bacteria entering the womb during pregnancy and causing an infection (*see* Chapter 6, p.156).

✓ *Take a pregnancy test*

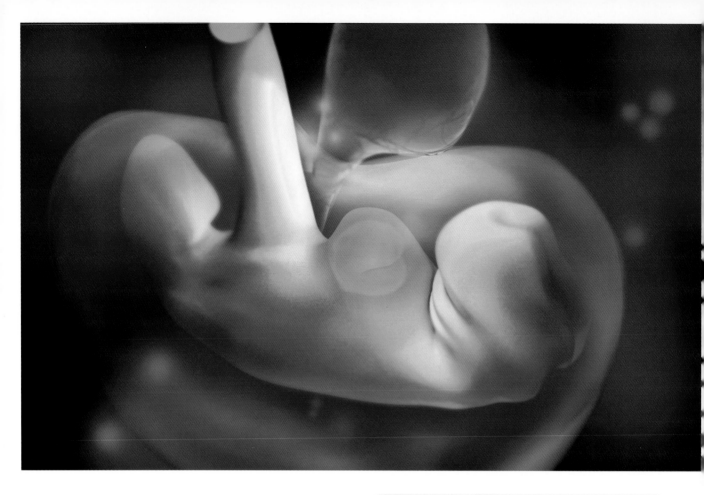

Week 5

Your baby

The embryo is just visible on an ultrasound scan, although it will only look like a small blob of tissue. A thin layer of translucent skin covers the embryo and, inside, the primitive heart starts to form. Although it is just a basic tube-like structure at this stage, blood already circulates through it. The spinal cord is in position and is identifiable as a row of dark cells running down the back of the embryo. Gradually, these cells fold in on themselves lengthwise and become the neural tube. At the top of this row of cells are two large lobes. These are the brain, which is proportionately much larger than the rest of the developing embryo. The early digestive system is also in place as a tube running from the top (and what will become the mouth) to the tail. Eventually, the stomach, liver and other digestive organs will evolve from this tube.

You

If the initial pregnancy test you took was negative, yet your period still has not arrived, try testing again, as more of the pregnancy hormone BhCG that gives you a positive result

> **DID YOU KNOW…?**
> If your job poses a potential risk to your pregnancy, your employer should assess this and provide you with a safer role, if necessary, with no loss of pay.

may now be present. Even this early on, you need to take some simple steps in your lifestyle to make sure you don't put your pregnancy at risk. See Chapter 2 for more information.

✓ *Make sure you know which foods should be avoided in pregnancy and how to prepare meals hygienically*

✓ *Wear protective gloves when emptying cat litter or gardening to minimise the risk of toxoplasmosis*

Week 6

Your baby

The embryo changes shape significantly in this week, becoming a tiny comma shape that resembles a slightly strange-looking prawn (*see* illustration). The head, which is bent over the middle section, has a bulge from which the nasal region and oral cavity will develop. It also has gill-like folds that will become the face and jaw. The heart, which is now starting to divide into four chambers, bulges from the middle section of the embryo and tiny bud-like protuberances are emerging to become the limbs. Finally, the embryo ends in a tail.

The embryo has doubled in size and now measures 5 mm and weighs 1 g. An ultrasound scan done transvaginally at the end of this week of pregnancy would show the fetal pole – this is the term used to refer to the first signs of an embryo inside the amniotic sac. The fluttering heartbeat may also be visible, although the absence of the latter and/or a fetal pole may indicate that the date of fertilisation is not accurate and not necessarily that there is a problem with the pregnancy.

You

Extra blood supply is required by almost every part of your body; the volume directed to the uterus doubles, much of which is needed to form new blood vessels in the developing placenta. When you are not pregnant, your uterus is approximately 8 cm long, but during pregnancy it will expand so much that, by the

SUPPORTING YOUR PREGNANCY

The embryo requires a support system for it to continue to grow (*see* diagram). At this stage, it is attached by a stalk to a yolk sac, which provides the hormones and nutrients required to maintain the pregnancy. Together they float in a fluid-filled bubble, the amniotic sac, which is covered by an outer membrane called the chorion.

end, it will be up to 1,000 times larger in volume and will have increased twenty-fold in weight from about 50 g to 1,000 g. This change starts to happen quickly, so that by now, four weeks after fertilisation, your uterus is already the size of a tennis ball. However, because it is still contained within the pelvic bones, the increase in size is not visible and only a doctor examining you internally would be able to feel the change. The increase in blood to your vulva, vagina and cervix means that these organs have developed a bluish-purple colouration that is unique to pregnancy. In fact, in the days before pregnancy tests were available, this was one of the main methods that doctors used to confirm a pregnancy.

✓ *If you have had a previous ectopic pregnancy (see Complications, p. 285), you should ask for a transvaginal scan at six weeks*

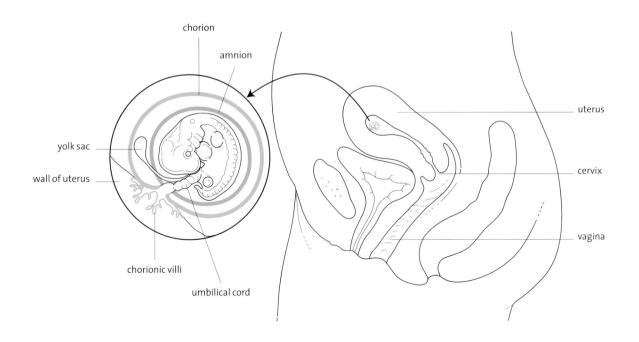

chorion

amnion

yolk sac

wall of uterus

chorionic villi

umbilical cord

uterus

cervix

vagina

Week 7

Your baby

Between Weeks 7 and 10 of pregnancy, the embryo grows so quickly that it will quadruple in size and start to look more like a human being. All babies develop at exactly the same speed in the first trimester, which is why it is possible to date a pregnancy very precisely using ultrasound to measure the embryo (*see* Chapter 3, pp. 66–7).

External and internal changes are occurring rapidly. From Weeks 6–8, the bowel grows faster than the abdominal cavity, so it initially develops outside the body. The limb buds develop paddle-type hands and feet. The brain grows faster than any other part and, consequently, the head is still out of proportion to the rest of the body. The neck and a high forehead start to develop, while primitive bones form the beginnings of facial features such as the nose, eyes, ears and jaw. Because the back of the head grows faster than the front, the head still appears to be bent over the embryo's body.

You

If you haven't already made an appointment to see your GP, do so now, so that they can make sure that you are starting your pregnancy in the best possible way (*see* Chapter 1, p.14). They can also arrange your an appointment with a midwife, who will start to plan your antenatal care (*see* Chapter 3, p.60).

 Ask your GP or midwife for a form that enables you to claim free prescriptions and dental care while pregnant and for the first year after the birth

SUPPORTING YOUR PREGNANCY

The external side of the chorion (the membrane that surrounds the amniotic sac) has developed tiny, finger-like projections called chorionic villi (*see* diagram on p.87), and from Week 7 these start to concentrate around the circular area directly in contact with the endometrium (lining of the uterus). Eventually, this will become the placenta. At the same time, the outer layer on the rest of the chorion gradually smoothes out. Over the next few weeks, the blood vessels from the chorionic villi will burrow ever deeper into the endometrium so that they can access the maternal blood supply.

The umbilical cord forms and blood starts to circulate through it. Most of the nutrients required by the fetus are still being received from the yolk sac, but this will further diminish as the trimester progresses and the placenta develops. The amniotic sac is now made up of an inner membrane, called the amnion, in which the fetus floats, as well as the outer layer (chorion), which contains the villi. The yolk sac is contained in the space between the amnion and the chorion. In the early weeks of the pregnancy, the yolk sac was responsible for producing the embryo's blood cells, but as the trimester progresses, it shrivels away and, by the end of Week 13, the fetal liver has taken over this function. With the disappearance of the yolk sac by the end of the trimester, the space between the chorion and amnion also disappears and the two fuse together.

DID YOU KNOW...?

Most women wait until their pregnancy has reached the second trimester before telling other people, as the risk of miscarriage will have diminished significantly. However, you may choose to tell close family that you are pregnant earlier than this, as they would be the ones to support you should you suffer a miscarriage now. See Chapter 2, pp.47–9 for more on telling other people.

Week 8

Your baby

The face is starting to develop and ten tooth buds, which will develop into milk teeth in early infancy, are present in each jaw. Elbows and shoulders have formed, such is the speed at which the arms develop. The arms are bent at the elbow, wrists are identifiable and the hands are starting to develop basic finger structures (*see* picture). The lower limb buds, which will become the legs and feet, grow at a slower speed, and this pattern of development continues throughout pregnancy and into babyhood: babies are able to hold objects and use their hands far earlier than they are able to crawl and walk. The embryo measures 16 mm and is already 10,000 times larger than the fertilised cell from which it originated.

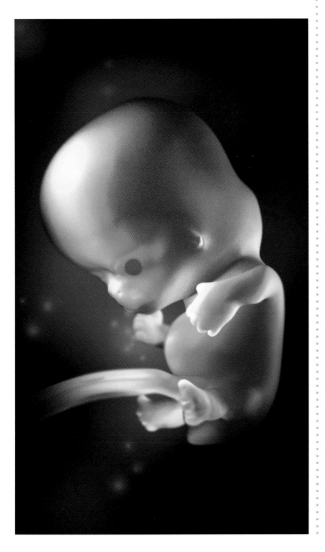

> **DID YOU KNOW...?**
> The ears and eyes are particularly sensitive to the teratogenic (harmful) effects of infections such as rubella, especially when it is caught in the sixth to eighth week of pregnancy (*see* Chapter 2, p.42).

You

Most women will have already started to experience a range of pregnancy symptoms, including breast tenderness, abdominal aches and pains, morning sickness and tiredness (*see* p.122 onwards for more details of these common side effects). However, if you have not, this is not a cause for concern. In all likelihood your pregnancy is developing normally – you are just one of the lucky few! You may also find that you are more susceptible to mood swings (*see* Chapter 9, pp. 264–83). Try not to let your heightened emotional sensitivity affect your relationship with your partner. Keep talking to each other and reassure yourselves that your mood will stabilise as your pregnancy moves into the second trimester.

It is possible that your pregnancy symptoms are putting you off sex; or you may be worried that having sex may harm your developing baby. You should know that, unless you have specific medical issues, sex is safe throughout your entire pregnancy (*see* Box on p.96 for more details).

You may notice that you need to pass urine more frequently. This is partly because your enlarging uterus is starting to press down on your bladder, but also because the blood supply to your kidneys has increased by around 30 per cent, which means they are filtering much more fluid and producing more urine. However, if you experience a stinging sensation when you pass urine, you may have a urinary tract infection, so do consult your GP (*see* p.128).

✓ *Buy some ginger capsules or acupressure wristbands for nausea / morning sickness*

✓ *Remember to rest whenever you can*

✓ *If you are a smoker and haven't already given up, make sure you do so now. See your GP for help if necessary*

Week 9

Your baby

This week sees further neurological changes: the brain is four times the size it was at Week 6, the brain and the spinal cord are now differentiated, and nerve cells are multiplying fast. Special 'glial' cells are also formed within the neural tube, which help to join the nerve cells so that messages can be transmitted from the brain to the body. Eyelids are beginning to form, the tip of the nose is distinct (*see* picture) and primitive toes are visible in the feet. The trunk is elongating and straightening, with the length from crown to rump now measuring 23 mm.

The primitive tube that was the heart at Week 6 has now completed its division into four chambers; two of these, the atria, receive blood, while the other two, the ventricles, pump blood to the lungs and round the body. Valves have developed between the atria and ventricles to ensure blood flow occurs in one direction only. The heart beats at 160 beats per minute, approximately twice as fast as a normal adult heart. See p.114 for more on the fetal heart and circulatory system.

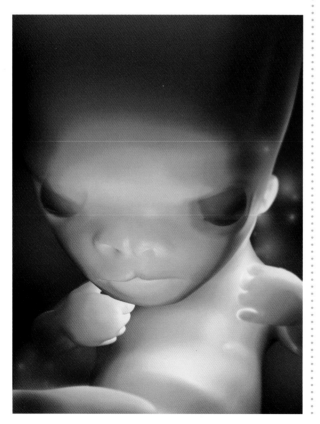

DID YOU KNOW...?
Although your abdomen and waist may have started become a bit thicker, this is more likely to be the result of fluid retention rather than the growing baby, which only weighs a few grams at this point. See Chapter 2, p.52 for a handy tip for how to expand the waistband on your skirts and trousers.

You

You will probably have noticed that your breasts have increased in size, seem heavier and still feel tender to the touch. The nipples and the darker skin surrounding them (the areola) have darkened in colour. The areola has also enlarged and the sweat glands around the nipple, which resemble little pimples and are called Montgomery's tubercles, become more prominent and may have started to secrete a clear fluid. This is all due to oestrogen, progesterone and a hormone called human placental lactogen, which are causing the milk ducts to grow in preparation for breastfeeding. Towards the end of the trimester, you may also have developed an outer ring of lighter pigmentation around the areola and the veins on your breast may become more visible as a result of increased blood flow throughout your body.

✓ Get fitted for a maternity bra

Week 10

Your baby

The crown–rump length (CRL) now measures 32 mm and the fetus weighs 3–5 g, a huge change from Week 6. The webbed hands have developed separate fingers with touch pads at the end. The legs have knees and the feet are developing toes. The external ear is developing, while the middle ear, which is responsible for balance and for hearing, is already formed. Nostrils and an upper lip are now visible. Inside the mouth, a tiny tongue has already developed and taste buds are starting to form.

The digestive system is developing at such a speed that it is now forming loops and protruding through the abdominal wall, although it is not yet able to function. The tail has all but disappeared and, because muscles are beginning to develop, some movement can be seen on an ultrasound scan.

By the end of this week all the major organ formation has taken place, which means that the embryonic phase is complete and your baby is now known as a fetus. These early weeks are critical: this is when the developing baby could be affected by the teratogenic (harmful) effects of certain drugs, viruses or environmental factors (*see* Chapter 2, pp.38 –45). After Week 10, at around the time the placenta is starting to take over support of the pregnancy, it is very rare for the baby to be harmed in this way.

You

The uterine muscles are thickening and, although you still will not be able to see it, your uterus has continued to increase in size. The increased blood flow means that it is now roughly 10 cm in diameter.

Your increased metabolic rate means that you need around fifteen to twenty per cent more oxygen during pregnancy, half of which is used by the growing uterus, placenta and baby. You also exhale more carbon dioxide. Your lungs adapt, thanks to the dilating effects of progesterone, to enable the volume of air you inhale to increase by up to 40 per cent. Some women notice, towards the end of their first trimester, that they feel breathless and even that they are hyperventilating. This is all

DID YOU KNOW…?
Wearing cotton underwear and loose clothing can help prevent the occurrence of thrush.

SUPPORTING YOUR PREGNANCY
The quantities of beta human chorionic gonadotrophin (BhCG), the hormone whose function is to make sure the corpus luteum in the ovaries continues to produce high levels of oestrogen and progesterone, peak at around Week 10. After this time, the placenta takes over the production of these hormones, the corpus luteum shrinks away, and the levels of BhCG fall to a low level until the end of the pregnancy, after which it is no longer secreted.

The fetus floats in a small amount of amniotic fluid (about 30 ml). This fluid, which increases in volume as the pregnancy progresses, serves several purposes, principally creating a safe, sterile environment for the fetus (*see* p.101). It remains at a constant temperature which, at 37.5°C, is slightly warmer than your own body temperature.

normal, but if you have any actual pain on breathing in, you should see your GP or midwife without delay (to exclude a chest infection or pulmonary embolism – *see* Box in Chapter 3, p.60).

The progesterone in your body, which causes your muscles to relax, also makes your intestines more sluggish and this can lead to bloating and constipation (*see* p.124). You may also notice that your vaginal discharge has increased. This discharge, which will remain heavier for the rest of your pregnancy, should be mucus-like, odourless and clear or milky in colour. If it becomes yellow, itchy or starts to smell, you should let your GP or midwife know, as you may have developed a vaginal infection such as candida, commonly known as 'thrush', which is very common in pregnancy (*see* p.127).

✓ *Have first blood test (see Chapter 3, p.62)*

Week 11

Your baby

Development during the fetal period is characterised by the rapid growth, especially in Weeks 11–18, of the body and organs that were formed in the embryonic phase. However, the growth of the head now slows down relative to the rest of the body. In this week, it makes up one half of the total CRL, which measures 42 mm. The shape is much more recognisably human, with a clear neck and jawline now visible. Calcium continues to harden the cartilage and to form bones throughout the fetus' body. This process is called ossification and, although it starts in the first trimester, it will continue after birth and right through to the end of adolescence. The baby's internal sexual organs, the ovaries for girls and testes for boys, are fully formed, and although the external ones – the penis and clitoris – are developing, they are not yet distinguishable.

You

Symptoms such as nausea, vomiting and tiredness will fade and disappear completely in the majority of women as this first trimester comes to a close (and usually by Week 16 at the latest). This is because the placenta has taken over the production of hormones necessary to keep the pregnancy going (see Box). You will probably have your booking visit with your midwife around this time, as well the 'dating' ultrasound scan (see Chapter 3, pp.60 and 66).

HOW DOES THE PLACENTA WORK?

In essence, the placenta allows the fetus to grow, to receive oxygen and to excrete what it does not need. The chorionic villi (see p.88), which have continued to proliferate at great speed on the outer surface of the chorionic membrane, now make up the outer surface of the placenta and adhere to the uterine wall. These villi, which contain fetal blood vessels, float in a lake of maternal blood called the intervillous space. A few longer villi reach down into the decidual lining of the uterus, while the longest reach down even further, as far as the deeper layers of the uterine wall where they can access maternal blood vessels and act as anchors for the placenta (see diagram).

The fetus' blood is present in the villi's very fine blood vessels. Every time your heart beats, blood spurts into the intervillous space and soaks the villi. Oxygen and nutrients are then filtered through the chorionic membrane, before being absorbed by the villi and passed into the fetal circulation through the umbilical cord. Simultaneously, carbon dioxide and other waste products are transferred from the fetus into the maternal circulation via the intervillous space and taken away. Only a small amount of fetal cells 'spill' into the maternal circulation, thanks to the thin, protective chorionic membrane. It is important for the healthy functioning of the placenta that good quantities of oxygenated blood reach the maternal arteries. This is why smoking and disorders such as hypertension (see Complications, p. 286), both of which reduce blood flow to the placenta, can hinder the growth and health of the fetus.

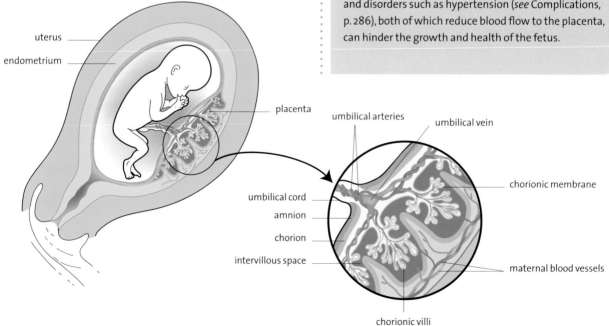

uterus

endometrium

placenta

umbilical cord

amnion

chorion

intervillous space

umbilical arteries

umbilical vein

chorionic membrane

maternal blood vessels

chorionic villi

Week 12

Your baby

The fingers and toes are no longer webbed and tiny fingernails are present. Eyelids meet and adhere and the eyes contain some pigment. The tooth buds for the 32 permanent teeth begin to appear, but at different times over the coming weeks. The fetal skin is still thin, translucent and permeable to amniotic fluid, but it is now covered in a layer of very fine hair. Muscle development continues, and this means that the fetus is starting to show reflex reactions in response to external stimuli. For example, if the fetus' hand brushes against its mouth, the lips might purse in an early sign of the sucking reflex. It will also try to move away from any pressure that is exerted onto it from the abdomen, although it feels nothing.

The abdomen has now enlarged sufficiently for the intestines to continue their development within the abdominal cavity. The digestive system develops further, with the stomach linked to the mouth and the intestines. The kidneys are developing, so that around Weeks 11–14 the fetus is able to ingest the amniotic fluid and excrete it as urine. The CRL measures 54 mm and the weight is 14 g.

You

There is an increase in blood supply to all your major organs. As your early pregnancy symptoms lessen and you start to feel more energetic, you may want to think about your exercise regime. Exercising regularly will help you cope with the physical demands of pregnancy and birth, as well as boosting your mood with the production of endorphins. Make sure, however, that any activities you do are appropriate for pregnancy (*see* Chapter 2, p.32).

✓ *Enrol in pregnancy yoga / Pilates class*

✓ *Wear supportive footwear and a sports bra when exercising*

✓ *Do some research on local hospitals*

Week 13

Your baby

At end of this week – the close of the first trimester – the facial features have developed still further: the eyes are closer to the front of the face, while the ears are now visible and are higher up the side of the head (*see* picture). From Weeks 13–15 taste buds are continuing to develop and the fetus is gradually straightening out.

You

Your uterus is approximately 12 cm in diameter and will have risen to just above your pelvic bone. Your GP or midwife will be able to feel it through your abdominal wall, a technique known as palpation (*see* also Chapter 3, p.63). Particularly if this is your first pregnancy, your abdomen will now start to swell out and you are likely to look pregnant, even though you may still be able to keep this to yourself for a few weeks more with the help of loose clothing. For some women, their breasts will also have filled out quite significantly over the last few weeks, particularly if they were small-chested to begin with. If you have suddenly blossomed in this way, you should know that they don't continue to expand at this rate throughout your entire pregnancy. In fact, your breasts will not increase in size at all during the second trimester, and will only fill out a little more in the final two weeks or so of pregnancy in preparation for your milk coming through.

As you approach the start of the second trimester, you are likely to be feeling much better than in previous weeks, to have renewed energy and appetite and to feel confident that your pregnancy is now well established.

DID YOU KNOW...?

Any scans before Week 14 will measure fetal growth in terms of crown–rump length (CRL) and the distance between the two parietal bones of the skull. Thereafter, measurements focus on abdominal and head circumferences and femoral length. CRLs are given throughout this chapter purely to aid visualisation of the size of the fetus. See Chapter 3, pp.66–71 for more details on the measurements taken at scans.

SUPPORTING YOUR PREGNANCY

In the last three weeks of the trimester the placenta continues to develop rapidly and by Week 13 it is fully functioning, although it will still continue to grow until the end of the pregnancy. The placenta is able to provide all the fetus' needs through your bloodstream. It is now firmly attached to the uterine wall and connected to the fetus via the umbilical cord.

The umbilical cord consists of three intertwined blood vessels: one large vein, which carries oxygen-rich blood and nutrients from the uterus via the placenta to the fetus, and two smaller arteries, which transport waste products and oxygen-depleted blood from the fetus back to the placenta and on to your own blood supply. These three vessels are encased within a thick, tough, gelatinous substance called Wharton's jelly.

SECOND TRIMESTER

Your baby continues to grow fast, from a small fetus at the start of the trimester to a fully formed baby at the end of Week 26. You will start to feel your baby move at around the middle of the trimester and, as the baby increases in size and strength, these movements will become more vigorous and defined.

The second trimester is the time in pregnancy when most women feel at their best. The unpleasant early symptoms, such as tiredness and morning sickness, have usually disappeared; you are starting to look pregnant, but your bump is not so large that it hinders you; and you feel optimistic that your pregnancy is now 'safe', because the placenta rather than just the maternal hormones is now fully supporting the pregnancy.

Week 14

Your baby

Reflex muscular activity is occurring, although you will not yet feel your baby moving. The external genitalia have differentiated into male or female, allowing the sex of the fetus to be determined by ultrasound scan. The fetus starts to produce its own blood cells, rather than using only those supplied by the placenta. The heart still beats at around 110–160 beats per minute (compared to an adult's average of 70 bpm), but this slows down gradually as the pregnancy progresses. (A child's heart rate only reaches that of an adult at about ten years of age.)

Downy, colourless hair, called lanugo, starts to develop and now breaks through the skin on the eyebrows and upper lip. The lower limbs are fully formed and growing fast, and all limbs are more in proportion with the rest of the body. The arms are now long enough for the hands to meet in front of the chest. The central nervous system continues to develop during these early weeks of the second trimester, allowing

SUPPORTING YOUR PREGNANCY

By the start of the second trimester, the structure of the placenta is developed and it is fully functioning, ensuring that the pregnancy continues to thrive. It provides all the oxygen and nutrients, via the umbilical cord, that the fetus requires for continued growth. The placenta also acts as a barrier against many (though not all) infections, as well as reducing the harmful effects of medication, drugs, alcohol and tobacco – although it cannot eliminate them entirely.

The placenta has now taken over the production of the four main hormones: oestrogen, progesterone, human placental lactogen and BhCG. While production of BhCG peaked at Weeks 10–12 and then declined sharply (*see* p.91), the levels of the other three continue to rise throughout this trimester. These hormones are essential for fetal growth and for enabling your body to adapt during pregnancy and to prepare for it birth and breastfeeding.

for an increasingly wide range of movements. These include reflex facial movements, which can be seen on an ultrasound scan, so that it looks as if the fetus is frowning or grinning. Indeed, the face looks more human now, because the eyes are positioned at the front. Although the eyelids are still closed, the retina at the back of the eyes is sensitive to light. The fetus measures 80 mm crown to rump and weighs 45 g.

You

Many women experience a heightened sex drive in pregnancy, and especially in the second trimester when they are feeling at their best. This is possibly due to increased levels of hormones flooding through your body and the greater blood flow to the pelvic region. As your pregnancy progresses, your changing shape will mean that you may need to find alternative positions for sex. See Box on p.96 for more information about sex in pregnancy.

 ✓ *Have screening blood test for Down's syndrome*

Week 15

Your baby

Growth is particularly rapid from now until Week 18. This week sees the fetus making some rudimentary breathing movements. Limb movement is becoming more coordinated, although still cannot be felt. The fetus will even start to suck its thumb if the latter comes into contact with the mouth. This is not a conscious action, but merely an example of muscular activity. The pattern of hair on the scalp is determined, although the hair itself will not be visible until Week 22.

You

Significant changes to your blood and to your circulatory system are taking place over the next few weeks:

▸ The volume of red blood cells rises rapidly in the early weeks of this trimester to catch up with the increase in the blood's water content that took place earlier on in your pregnancy.
▸ The amount of blood being pumped through the heart (your cardiac output) also increases during this time, though less so in the last few weeks of the trimester.
▸ The volume of blood pumped by the heart at every beat (your stroke volume) similarly increases.
▸ The blood vessels dilate (meaning that your 'peripheral resistance' decreases), thanks to the relaxing effect of progesterone. As a result, some women find that their blood pressure is actually lower at this stage than it was before they became pregnant.
▸ The heart increases slightly in size and pumps more powerfully, but not faster.
▸ At the start of the second trimester, 25 per cent of blood flow (five times more than when you are not pregnant) is directed to the uterus to support the growing fetus and placenta.
▸ A greater amount of blood than normal is also directed at your skin and mucous membranes.

IS SEX SAFE?

Some couples worry that sexual intercourse could potentially damage their unborn baby or in some way threaten the pregnancy, especially during the first trimester when the risk of miscarriage is greatest. Babies are well-cushioned by amniotic fluid, and will not be harmed by penetrative sex. Unless you have a history of miscarriage or are experiencing some unexplained first-trimester bleeding, it is perfectly safe to have sex at this time, as there is no link at all between intercourse and an increased chance of miscarriage. Indeed, if yours is a normal pregnancy, it is safe to continue having sex until your membranes rupture (or 'waters break' – *see* Chapter 6, p.157). This is because, until this time, the baby is protected by a cervical plug of mucus, which seals off the uterus from bacteria, and is also cushioned by amniotic fluid.

Fears that intercourse in later pregnancy can trigger premature labour are unfounded. While it is true that semen contains prostaglandins and that artificial prostaglandins are used to ripen the cervix when labour is induced, semen alone cannot trigger labour unless the cervix is ready to start dilating (usually at term). However, you may be advised to avoid sexual intercourse if:

▸ you have had previous premature labours (in case your cervix has already started to dilate)
▸ you have threatened premature labour (*see* Chapter 7, p.222–3)
▸ you are bleeding (until you have seen your obstetrician and been reassured that all is well)
▸ an internal examination has revealed that your cervix is shortened or slightly dilated
▸ you have placenta praevia (*see* Box opposite).

DID YOU KNOW...?

Between Weeks 15 and 30, the height of the fundus (the distance from the pubic bone to the top of the uterus) increases by approximately 1 cm per week, although this can vary slightly from one woman to another.

Week 16

Your baby

The fetal head, although still large, is proportionately less so than in Week 14 and the body has straightened out (see picture). In the male fetus, the penis and scrotum are now more clearly visible, while in the female, the uterus, Fallopian tubes and vagina are beginning to form. Slow eye movement occurs and toenails are just starting to appear. Overall, the fetus now looks more like a baby, even though it still has no fat and red blood vessels and even bones can be seen through the thin, translucent skin. The CRL is 12 cm and the weight is 110 g.

You

Your kidneys are filtering an extra half litre of blood every minute until the end of your pregnancy and their filtering capacity is around 60 per cent higher than normal. This will remain the case until a few weeks before term, when it reduces slightly. Because of this greater workload, your urine may contain small quantities of sugar and protein (see Chapter 3, p.63).

SUPPORTING YOUR PREGNANCY

By Week 16 the placenta has reached a thickness of around 1 cm and a diameter of 7–8 cm, although it will continue to grow for several more weeks until it is almost three times its current size. Up to a third of women discover at their twenty-week fetal anomaly scan (see Chapter 3, p.70) that they have a low-lying placenta (placenta praevia – see Complications, p. 287). This is a problem if this is still the case at the end of the pregnancy, as it may be partially or fully blocking the cervix and therefore will prevent the baby's descent through the vaginal canal at birth. However, for the majority of women, the placenta will move up over the next few weeks. This is not because it has literally shifted its position, but because the lower part of the uterus has expanded so much between Week 20 and Week 37 that the placenta is no longer close to the cervix.

THE FETAL AND MATERNAL CIRCULATIONS

From about Week 16, the placental membrane between mother and fetus thins to allow greater nutrient exchange. By and large, the fetal and maternal circulations do not mix, although a very small number of fetal cells do cross into the mother's bloodstream via minuscule defects in the membrane. These cells generally cause no harm, but this is the reason why women with a Rhesus negative blood group are given an injection of 'anti-D' in order to prevent any further immune response they might have to their baby's Rhesus positive blood group (see Chapter 3, p.62).

The presence of fetal cells in the maternal circulation is becoming clinically useful for non-invasive screening (notably Harmony and FISH – see Chapter 3, pp.72 and 76). These cells are also now known to persist in the maternal circulation for years, if not decades – they have been found up to 27 years after a pregnancy ended – and may have a role in aiding cell repair in maternal tissues.

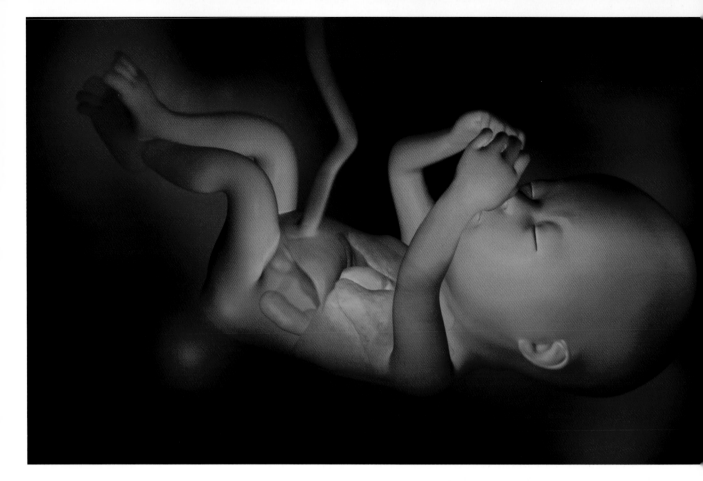

Week 17

Your baby

The digestive system and lungs are developed (*see* picture) and are starting to mature, as is the nervous system. A layer of fat, called myelin, coats the nerves in the spinal cord that link the fetal muscles to the brain. This process, called 'myelination', protects the neurons contained in the fibres and enables messages to move quickly between the brain and other parts of the body , which results in the fetus' ability to move around within the amniotic sac. Myelination is complete by the age of two, but there is some evidence to suggest that further development continues until about the age of twelve. So stimulating and encouraging your baby both physically and mentally from birth will help to develop their skills in their early years. The testes in a male fetus are still inside the abdominal cavity and will not begin to descend until well into the second trimester. Your baby's eyes are now further towards the front of the face and, at this stage of gestation, the head makes up just under a third of the total body length of 15 cm.

SUPPORTING YOUR PREGNANCY

The umbilical cord continues to be the link between the fetus and the placenta (and mother) by providing the fetus with oxygen-rich blood and nutrients via a single large vein, and by excreting back waste products and oxygen-depleted blood to the placenta via two smaller arteries. In about one in 200 pregnancies, the fetus will have only one artery and one vein in the umbilical cord. If this is spotted during one of your routine antenatal ultrasound scans, a further scan may be offered, as this malformation can lead to a slightly increased risk of congenital abnormalities.

You

Hypertension (high blood pressure) sometimes occurs in the second trimester, particularly if you are overweight, over 40 or have diabetes. While hypertension can be problematic for the pregnancy in itself, it is also an indicator, later in pregnancy, of the serious condition of pre-eclampsia. See Complications, p. 289 for more information.

Week 18

Your baby

Ossification continues and bones are clearly visible, with the legs catching up with the development of the arms. The formation of the facial bones is complete and the nose is more prominent. The external ears are in their final position on the side of the head, and the tiny bones of the inner ear have hardened, enabling the fetus to be aware of sounds. Consequently, the face appears increasingly recognisable and the features more delicate. In the female fetus, ovaries have formed. Fetal movements are becoming more extensive (*see* picture). The CRL is 14 cm and the weight is 200 g, almost double what it was two weeks previously.

You

This is the time when the fetal movements (known as 'quickening') can first be felt, although first-time mothers may not be aware of these until Week 20. It may feel like an odd, 'fluttering' sensation deep inside your abdomen, and is often mistaken for wind.

The top of your uterus (called the 'fundus' in your antenatal notes) is midway between your pubic bone and your navel. The increase in blood flow to your skin and mucous membranes means that those blood vessels have become dilated. As a result, you will start to feel hotter and to sweat more, and you may develop a stuffy nose. The greater dilation of blood vessels prevents your blood pressure from increasing, although it does rise slightly in the third trimester. But because your blood vessels are more flexible, varicose veins and haemorrhoids can develop, and you can suffer from nose or gum bleeds and occasionally feel faint. See pp.126 and 129 for more on these common side effects of pregnancy.

The extra blood to your blood vessels also explains why you may start to notice, later on in this trimester, fine red lines on your face, neck, shoulders and chest, called spider naevi, which recede with pressure. These usually disappear after the birth. The blue veins on your breasts are also becoming more noticeable, again as a result of hormonal changes and increased blood flow to breast tissue. New milk ducts are growing and the areolae are larger than usual. Your breasts may start to secrete a clear, yellow-orange fluid called colostrum from the little pimples (Montgomery's tubercles) around the areolae, particularly if you have already had a baby – this is an early type of milk (*see* Chapter 6, p.212).

One of the benefits of the increased blood flow and levels of hormones during pregnancy is that your skin glows and your hair is thicker, shinier and more luxuriant than normal. Indeed, women lose less hair when they are pregnant and it grows faster, although after the birth, they lose what they would have lost during the nine months had they not been pregnant (which is why they sometimes feel that lots of hair is 'falling out').

✓ *Attend the second routine antenatal scan, the fetal anamoly scan (Weeks 18–20)*

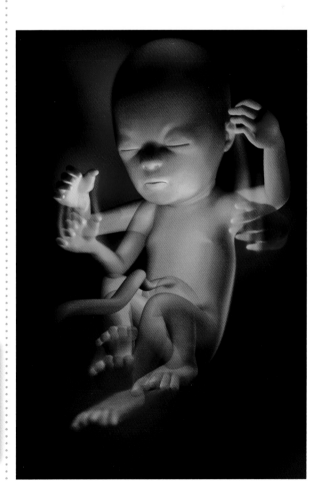

> ### DID YOU KNOW…?
> Whether you get stretch marks (*see* p.129) or not is largely down to inherited genetic factors, although keeping an eye on your weight gain throughout your pregnancy may help to limit their occurrence.

Week 19

Your baby

Growth slows down from now until Week 22, although the CRL still increases by around 50 mm. The legs reach their final length. A thick, white, waxy coating called vernix caseosa starts to be secreted from the sebaceous glands around this time and remains until birth. It serves to protect the fetus' skin from fingernail scratches and, importantly, to prevent the amniotic fluid from penetrating the skin and causing it to become waterlogged.

The fetus begins to develop a thin layer of subcutaneous white fat, while small amounts of insulating brown fat are also formed and deposited at the nape of the neck, around the kidneys and behind the breastbone. This is essential for body warmth, which is why very premature babies, who have insufficient brown fat, find it very difficult to keep themselves warm.

THE BABY'S IMMUNE SYSTEM

The job of the fetal immune system before birth is to enable the baby to *tolerate* everything 'foreign', including its mother; after birth, its function is the opposite: to *fight* everything foreign, including infections. Until now, it was thought that both the fetal and the infant immune systems were immature versions of the adult one. But recent research has shown that at the mid-pregnancy point, the fetal immune system develops from stem cells in the liver, whereas in adults, immune cells form in the bone marrow. Why the immune system switches to the adult version at some stage during the third trimester is not yet understood, but it could have major implications for the treatments of certain conditions and for vaccinations.

You

You probably experienced some minor abdominal aches and pains in the first trimester, as the ligaments in the pelvic area were adjusting to the pregnancy. These can continue throughout the second trimester, but if you experience any sudden pain, contact your GP or midwife. See p.127 for more information about abdominal pain.

 Shop for maternity clothes (see Chapter 2, p.52)

Week 20

Your baby

The development of the sexual organs continues. The uterus in a female fetus is fully formed, her vagina is developing, and the ovaries already contain six to seven million immature eggs, known as oocytes (*see* Box below).

Instead of the rapid growth of the previous weeks, development is concentrated on internal organs, such as the lungs and digestive system, as well as the immune and central nervous systems. Bones are thickening as calcium continues to be deposited on the skeletal structure, and the spinal cord is developing a fibrous sheath around the nerve bundles, which will protect them from any possible future damage. The increasingly complex network of nerves enables the fetal range of movements to become not only more extensive, but also more sophisticated and precise. The development of the nervous system also means that the fetus responds to external pressure – for example, a finger pressing on the abdomen – by moving away inside the uterus, and when exposed to sudden, loud sounds from the outside, its heartbeat will speed up.

The eye's nerve connections have also developed to the extent that, although the eyelids are still closed, the eyeballs can now move from side to side and the retina is increasingly light-sensitive. The tongue can be seen moving in and out of the mouth, and taste buds on it can now tell the difference between sweet and bitter flavours (*see* p.109 for how the facial reflex resulting from the bitter taste occurs). The CRL is 16 cm and the weight is 320 g.

REPRODUCTIVE DEVELOPMENT IN THE FEMALE FETUS

A baby girl is born with all the eggs she will ever produce. Although by the twentieth week of gestation, six to seven million immature eggs (or oocytes) are present in her ovaries, at the time of birth this number has reduced to around 1 million. By puberty, this figure has reduced still further to 3–400,000 and over the course of a woman's reproductive life, only around 400 will ever mature into eggs and be released.

WHAT IS AMNIOTIC FLUID FOR?

Amniotic fluid has several functions, including:

▸ cushioning the fetus against bumps and jolts
▸ allowing fetal movements
▸ preventing the fetus from adhering to the wall of the uterus
▸ helping the development of alveoli in the lungs.

Until the start of the second trimester, amniotic fluid is absorbed through the skin, as well as being ingested and excreted by the developing fetus. By Week 20, the maturing kidneys enable the fetus to excrete the amniotic fluid as urine into the amniotic cavity, thus stimulating the development of the intestines. By Week 20 the amount of amniotic fluid has increased to around 400 ml and the fetus, with its increasingly developed nervous and musculo-skeletal system, can now make the most of the cushioning effects of the fluid to move around safely and exercise its limbs. By the end of the trimester, there is around 700 ml of amniotic fluid, which is being replaced every three hours by the process of ingestion and excretion.

You

You are now halfway through your pregnancy! Your heart is pumping 7 litres per minute round your body and you will almost certainly look pregnant to others by now. While you generally feel very well by this stage, some women are still suffering from morning sickness, while others can develop temporary but painful conditions such as carpal tunnel syndrome (*see* p.131). If you have not already started feeling your baby move, you may do so around this time.

Week 21

Your baby

The CRL measures around 18 cm (about half that of a newborn baby) and the weight is approximately 450 g, although genetic characteristics inherited from you and the father now mean that size and weight will vary a little from one baby to another. If your routine scans ever give cause for concern about your baby's growth, then further measurements will be plotted on a chart that takes account of personal factors such as your own height, weight and ethnicity. See Complications, p. 286 for information about babies that are small for gestational age and intrauterine growth restriction.

You

By this week, the fundus will have just reached your navel. Hormonal changes that occurred from the start of pregnancy can make your skin very dry and itchy, so make sure you use a good moisturiser (it doesn't really matter which one, as long as you apply plenty of it). See p.129 for more on taking care of your skin in pregnancy.

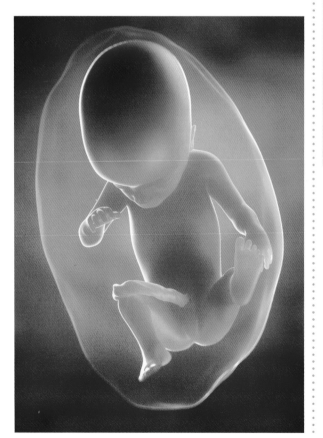

CORD BLOOD BANKING

I am increasingly asked by parents about the possibility of collecting and banking their baby's cord blood after birth, once the umbilical cord has been cut. The blood from the baby's cord and from the placenta contains blood-forming stem cells similar to those found in bone marrow. These can be used as an alternative to a bone marrow transplant for certain life-threatening blood and immune diseases. Unlike bone marrow transplants, cord blood transplants do not require a perfect match between donor and recipient and the cord blood appears less likely to be rejected. On the minus side, the volume of blood is small, so fewer stem cells are available for transplantation than when using bone marrow. In addition, only one transplant from the donor is possible, whereas more than one is possible from the same bone marrow donor.

There is still insufficient evidence to show that, in low-risk families (those with no history of the sorts of diseases that can be helped by cord blood transplant), parents should actively consider collecting and banking their baby's cord blood. Several private companies arrange for collection and storage (the blood is frozen), but I urge you to discuss this with your hospital before making any sort of commitment, because you may incur financial costs just by registering with these companies. Your hospital should, in any case, have a policy in place explaining if and how they are able to support you if you do decide to bank cord blood. See also Useful Resources for further sources of information.

 Collect MAT B1 certificate from now on

Week 22

Your baby

The fetus' face is fully defined and lips and head hair, as well as eyebrows and eyelashes, become visible. The testes in a male fetus start to descend, but they will not emerge from the abdominal cavity until much later in the pregnancy or even after the birth. The fingers and toes are fully formed and the hands will grasp at anything they come into contact with, such as the umbilical cord. The fetus can hear the maternal blood flow and heartbeat, as well as intestinal rumblings and external loud noises.

The outer layer of skin (epidermis) develops the individual finger and toe prints that are unique to each human being (see Box). The fetus is still very thin and the skin is now covered in lanugo, which will remain until around Week 36. This hair helps to keep the fetus warm during the weeks when it has insufficient body fat (it is still visible on premature babies) and also enables the vernix caseosa to adhere to the skin.

You

The pigmentation of your nipples, areolae, genitalia and moles also increases and by this week they have usually darkened; a dark line, called a linea nigra, running down the middle of your abdomen may also be noticeable. That said, if you have archetypal English fair skin with freckles, don't be disappointed or worried if you don't see one: your pregnancy is still fine! The linea nigra is situated where the left and right vertical abdominal muscles meet and, as your growing bump causes them to slowly separate, it darkens, but disappears after the birth. Some women may also notice patches of skin on their face that are different from their normal colour. In fair-skinned women, the patches will be darker, whereas in darker-skinned women, the reverse will be true. These patches, called chloasma, usually appear on the nose, cheeks and chin, and are caused once again by the flood of pregnancy hormones, though they, too, will disappear after the birth.

THE DEVELOPMENT OF FINGERPRINTS IN THE FETUS

Everyone is born with a unique set of fingerprints – even identical twins will have slightly different prints from each other. This is because fingerprints are not solely a genetic characteristic: the developmental environment in the womb is a factor in their formation, too. For example, the rate of growth of the fingers in the first trimester, the amount of blood and nutrients received by the fetus (which depends on the exact length and diameter of the umbilical cord), even how much the fetus moves in the womb, all play a part in creating the final shape of the fingerprints.

Some chromosomal abnormalities affect the development of the ridges on the skin of the fingers and toes. For example, babies with Down's syndrome have distinctive print patterns that can be used to diagnose the condition.

DID YOU KNOW...?

A high degree of colour change in your skin is linked to folic acid deficiency. In addition, exposure to sun will intensify chloasma, so make sure you use a high factor sunscreen and wear a hat.

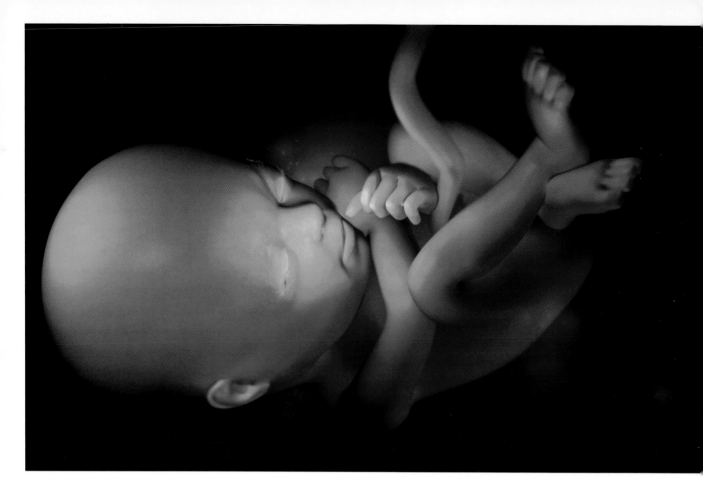

Week 23

Your baby

The next month of gestation sees rapid weight gain, although the body is still lean (*see* picture). The skin is wrinkled and translucent, seeming pinkish red because the blood is visible in the capillaries. Rapid eye movements begin.

As the brain matures, the fetal brainwaves become similar to those of a newborn baby and can be monitored on an EEG (electroencephalogram). Although it does not yet have conscious thoughts, it seems that the fetus can recognise your voice and may even move more rhythmically to it or to music. Whether this affects the baby in a beneficial way after they are born or means that some primitive memory may start to develop at this stage has not been proved one way or the other. However, talking to your baby can help you to visualise and feel closer to them and may mean that you are more used to talking to them after the birth, something which has been shown to improve a baby's acquisition of language.

DID YOU KNOW…?

The tear-forming gland, situated on the outer area above the eyelid, is present at birth, but the tear ducts in the inner corner of each eye are not fully formed until a few weeks afterwards, so a newborn baby is unable to shed tears when crying.

You

If you are feeling fit and well and there are no complications with your pregnancy (which may require you to attend hospital appointments), now is a good time to plan either a short break or longer holiday. It will possibly be the last time for a while that you will be able to indulge in a little 'me time', so enjoy yourself! See Chapter 2, p.46 for more information on travelling while pregnant.

Week 24

Your baby

The fetus is ingesting large amounts of amniotic fluid, which is being filtered through the kidneys and excreted. You can sometimes feel (and see, on an ultrasound scan) the fetus hiccupping. The lungs (*see* picture) are full of amniotic fluid (as they will be until birth), which is helping to form and fill the alveoli, the tiny air sacs that will be required at birth for the transfer of oxygen to take place and for the lungs to expand and function properly. These alveoli continue to increase in number and develop until your child is about eight years of age, after which they simply become larger. This is why many children who have asthma when they are very young find that their symptoms improve or disappear altogether as they get older, simply because their lungs mature.

All the major organs are now developed. The skin is still wrinkly, but as layers of fat continue to be deposited, it gradually becomes less translucent and more reddish in colour over the next few weeks. The eyelids have partially opened, creases on the palms of the hand are forming and the fetal movements can be felt, both by you and by someone else when they place their hand on your abdomen. The fetus can somersault and wriggle around a lot, because space in the uterus is not yet as limited as it will be in the third trimester. There are distinct times of the day when the fetus is either active or resting and these may not coincide with yours – women often feel their babies moving around late at night just as they themselves are trying to get to sleep! The CRL is 21 cm and the weight is around 630 g.

You

You will have been able to feel your baby for a while, although some babies move more than others, and some women feel the movements more than others – if your placenta is at the front of your uterus, it will be harder for you to feel any movements. By this time, however, you will probably start to get a sense of when and how much your baby moves in any given day, and whether the movements increase if, for example, you are lying down or exercising. As your pregnancy progresses, the type and frequency of movements will change because space becomes tighter inside your uterus, especially after 32 weeks. If you have not felt your baby move at all by this stage, contact your midwife without delay, as she will check the baby's heartbeat. If necessary, further ultrasound testing can be arranged.

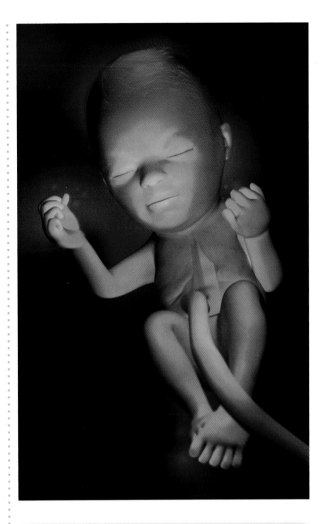

DID YOU KNOW…?

Hypertension (high blood pressure) in pregnancy is often an indicator that you may be at risk of developing chronic hypertension later on in life, as pregnancy reveals what happens to the body when it is put under physical stress. You can, of course, help to reduce this risk by addressing lifestyle issues such as smoking and obesity.

Week 25

Your baby

Your baby's face is becoming ever more defined. A colour 3-D (or 4-D) ultrasound scan towards the end of the second trimester can give a very clear image of your baby's face, but bear in mind that most fetuses look very similar at this point in their gestation, so it will be difficult to pick out any familial characteristics.

You

Back pain can become a problem and you need to take care of your posture when sitting and standing, as well as finding ways to safely bend down and pick things up. See pp.128–9 for more information on why back pain occurs and the Feature in Chapter 2, p.34 for exercises to relieve the symptoms.

✓ *Inform your employer in writing by this date that you are pregnant*

DID YOU KNOW...?

A small number of women go into labour very prematurely (*see* Box). Even though it is still very early days, if you think that you are leaking fluid or your underwear is inexplicably wet at any time in the next few weeks, tell your GP or midwife, because this could indicate your membranes have ruptured and that labour may begin (*see* Chapter 6, p.156).

VERY PREMATURE BIRTH

Around eight per cent of births occur before 37 weeks and are therefore classified as premature. Of those, only six per cent occur between 22 and 27 weeks, and one per cent before 22 weeks, so a very premature birth before the 26th week is rare.

It is still impossible to anticipate whether some women will go into labour very early, although if you have previously had a late miscarriage (defined as delivery before 24 weeks) or a very premature delivery (delivery between 24 and 32 weeks) your pregnancy will be considered high risk and you are likely to be monitored closely by your midwife and obtetrician. This may include being referred to hospital for a swab of your cervix and a scan to measure its length. If appropriate, procedures to help delay the onset of labour may be recommended (*see* Chapter 7, p.224 for more information).

Symptoms that you may be in very premature labour include:

▸ rupture of membranes (leaking of clear fluid)
▸ abdominal tightenings
▸ dull, lower back pain
▸ vaginal bleeding.

Often, women have no warning that they are going into labour and many don't feel any contractions until they are near to delivery. This is what makes it difficult to predict and is the reason why you should always take your antenatal notes with you if you are staying away from home.

Week 26

Your baby

By the end of the second trimester, the fetus measures 23 cm and weighs around 800 g. Fingernails are growing and its body is still lean. The adrenal gland, which is situated just above the kidney, plays a key role in hormone production during gestation and during the third trimester produces large amounts of androgen-like hormones (which, in female fetuses, are converted to oestrogen). As a result, it is disproportionately large: by Week 20, the adrenal gland is as large as the kidney (although it is not always visible on an ultrasound scan) and, by Week 30, has a relative size that is ten to twenty times larger than that of the adult adrenal gland.

The thyroid gland is the first endocrine gland to appear, and it reaches structural maturity by Week 17. From Week 18 to the end of the pregnancy, thyroid function gradually develops and hormone production adjusts until the correct levels are reached for life outside the womb.

SUPPORTING YOUR PREGNANCY

By Week 26 the placenta receives approximately 400 ml of blood per minute from your circulation. This enables the exchange of nutrients, oxygen, gases and waste products to take place between you and your baby. Some, though not all, harmful substances in your bloodstream are also prevented from reaching the baby's circulation.

You

While you will only put on a little weight during the first trimester, in the second trimester you will be gaining about 0.5 kg per week, so that by the end, you will be around 6–6.5 kg heavier. If you have gained much more or much less than this, your GP or midwife may bring this to your attention at your antenatal checks (*see* Box in Chapter 2, p.29 for more on weight gain during pregnancy).

The fundus now measures 26 cm and you are likely to experience indigestion and heartburn because your digestive organs become increasingly compressed (*see* p.124).

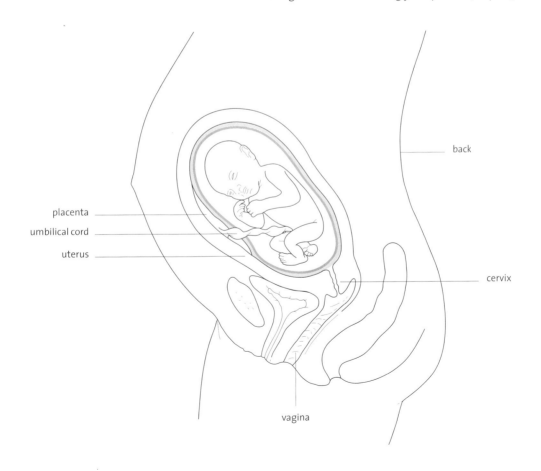

back

placenta

umbilical cord

uterus

cervix

vagina

Reaching the third trimester is a significant milestone in your pregnancy. Now that all the main fetal systems are in place, all that is needed is time for them to mature. In the early weeks of this trimester the placenta continues to grow, though not as fast as the baby.

These last few weeks can be physically demanding: your lungs and other internal organs are becoming more compressed as the baby increases in size; your blood pressure is slightly more raised and any back pain you have been suffering from may increase in intensity. While your increasing size can give you discomfort, you can nevertheless start to look forward to your exciting new arrival.

Week 27

Your baby

The brain is growing fast and, in order for it to fit inside the skull, the brain tissue now folds over itself so that, in cross section, it resembles a walnut. The fatty, protective myelin sheath that covers the nerves in the spinal cord now coats the brain's nerve fibres, which leads to faster nerve impulses from the brain to the rest of the body. This results in fetal movements and reaction times that are much quicker and more sophisticated. Not only is there still sufficient space in the uterus for the fetus to move more (after about Week 30, your baby's movements will gradually diminish as space becomes tighter), but its strong kicks, somersaults and changes of position are felt most strongly in this period. This is because less amniotic fluid is being produced than before, so its cushioning effect is reduced.

DID YOU KNOW…?
It is common for women to have vivid dreams throughout their pregnancy, especially during the last trimester. No one really knows why this is so, but it is thought that dreams are a way to subconsciously deal with your fears and concerns about impending birth and motherhood (*see* Chapter 9, p. 264–6).

You

The birth is still some way off, but you can keep your partner involved in your pregnancy by talking about your antenatal appointments when you have had one. Most partners will want to be present at the birth, but this is not always the case. It is a good idea to have someone to accompany you during labour – they are known as your 'birth partner'. If this is going to be someone other than the person you are in a relationship with, you could start thinking about who this might be, so that they can prepare themselves and attend antenatal classes with you, if necessary. See Chapter 5, p.134 for more information on choosing a birth partner.

 Start researching baby equipment (e.g. prams, cots) and whether there are any items that you could borrow

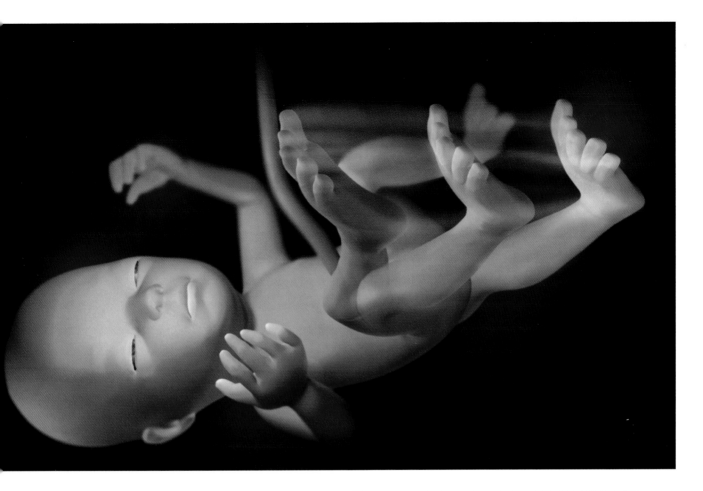

Week 28

Your baby

Skin creases are visible on the hands and the eyes are fully open, blinking and are sufficiently sensitive to light that the fetus will turn away if a strong light is shined at your abdomen. The fetal lungs are maturing fast and lanugo and head hair are well developed. The amount of white fat increases to 3.5 per cent of body weight and smoothes out the wrinkles on the skin. Toenails are visible, lagging behind the fingernail development by four weeks. The CRL is 25 cm and the weight is about 1,000 g.

You

The bottom of the rib cage has started to arch out a little in order to create more space for the increasing size of the uterus. This can cause pain in the lower ribs, especially if you are of relatively small build. Heart palpitations (cardiac arrhythmia) can also arise at some point in the third trimester, which can feel very unpleasant, although they are not usually a sign of anything serious (see p.127).

DID YOU KNOW…?
Between Weeks 28 and 30, the reflexes between the fetal taste buds and the facial muscles are sufficiently developed that if you eat a bitter-tasting substance, this can induce a grimace in the fetus.

If a blood test taken at the start of your pregnancy has shown that you are Rhesus D positive, you will be given an 'anti-D' injection, either now or at any time up to 34 weeks.

✓ *Have another blood test for anaemia and glycosuria*

THIRD TRIMESTER

Week 29

Your baby

From Week 29, the lungs start to produce a substance called surfactant, which coats the alveoli in a very thin film and gives them the elasticity they need to expand and contract with every breath taken and exhaled. It is surfactant that enables a baby to breathe unaided and this why a baby born before Week 34 (approximately) is likely to need help with breathing: its lungs do not yet produce enough surfactant and, as a result, they are too rigid, unable to expand when air is inhaled and liable to collapse when it is exhaled. Every day that the fetus remains in the womb from now on is therefore an extra day in the lung maturation process. See Chapter 7, p. 230 for further information on assisted breathing for premature babies.

The fetal bones are fully developed, although they still need to harden. Bone marrow is now the primary producer of the fetal red blood cells that help to transport oxygen around the blood stream. This is vital in preparation for birth, when the baby will no longer be reliant on the placenta for oxygen and will immediately have to breathe independently.

You

You may notice that your balance is starting to be affected. This is because your growing bump is altering your centre of gravity and hormones are loosening your joints in preparation for the birth. In addition, your increasing inability to see your feet may mean that you stumble more often. While a fall may be unfortunate for you, rest assured that your baby is well protected and is very unlikely to be harmed.

DID YOU KNOW…?
Bored by your pregnancy? With several weeks still to go, it is not uncommon for women to feel they have already had enough of talking about babies and birth. Feel free to change the topic of conversation!

FETAL LUNG DEVELOPMENT
The lungs are developing to enable your baby to breathe at birth (*see* diagrams):

- ▸ **Weeks 7–18:** branching takes place to form terminal bronchioles; no alveoli or respiratory bronchioles yet
- ▸ **Weeks 19–26:** each terminal bronchiole divides into at least two respiratory bronchioles; these then divide into three to six alveolar ducts
- ▸ **Weeks 27–40:** alveoli form and capillaries develop around them; close contact between the two is essential for delivering a sufficient blood supply when the new respiratory system starts working at birth; alveoli continue to develop and increase in number
- ▸ **From birth until eight years of age:** remaining five-sixths (around 83 per cent) of growth in lung size after birth is primarily due to the increase in the number of alveoli and respiratory bronchioles.

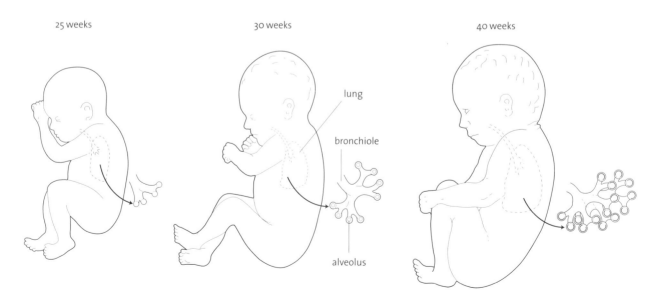

25 weeks

30 weeks

lung

bronchiole

alveolus

40 weeks

Week 30

Your baby

The CRL measures 27 cm and the fetus weighs 1,300 g on average. Billions of neurons are forming daily in the growing fetal brain and their development is helped by a good maternal diet, especially one rich in proteins and in the essential fatty acids found in oily fish, nuts and seeds. Iron is also important, as the fetal bone marrow is now producing all the red blood cells, and stores of iron, as well as calcium, are being laid down in preparation for birth. See Chapter 2, p.22–23 for more on eating well in pregnancy.

You

Your diaphragm is also becoming compressed and, by Week 30, when the fundus is at its maximum height of approximately 30 cm, it is flatter and more stretched out. This makes it less able to expand and contract as you breathe and, together with the compression of your lungs, means that for much of the trimester you will feel short of breath and/or will need to breathe deeply. The decrease in lung efficiency, as well as the increased progesterone levels that dilate your blood vessels, can make you feel light-headed and even faint on occasion (see p.126 on how to deal with the symptoms).

✓ Qualify for Statutory Maternity Pay or Maternity Allowance

✓ Start antenatal classes soon

SUPPORTING YOUR PREGNANCY

By Week 30, the placenta weighs 450 g and receives 500 ml of blood per minute from your circulation. It has had a three-fold rise in weight since Week 20 and will continue to grow and increase in weight until Week 35. The quantity of amniotic fluid is still increasing, and the fetus is excreting around 500 ml a day in urine. The volume of amniotic fluid peaks at about 1 litre by 35 weeks before slowly starting to diminish.

DID YOU KNOW…?

To reduce the likelihood of developing varicose veins, keep your feet raised when sitting down, avoid standing for long periods of time and stay active. Exercise keeps leg muscles working and helps maintain good blood circulation (see Chapter 2, p.32).

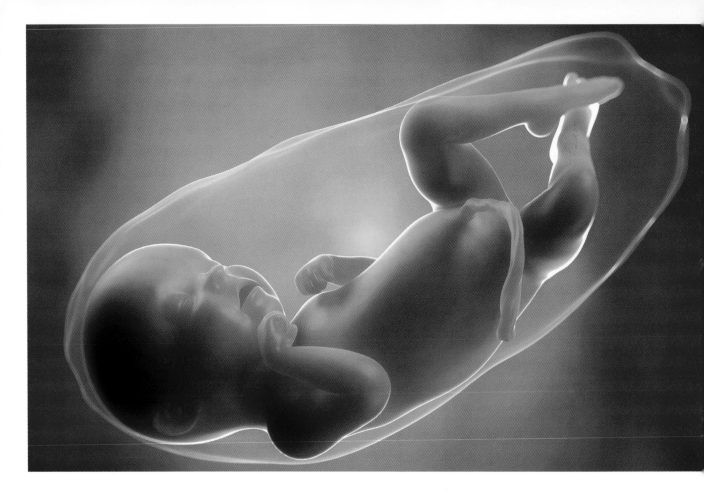

Week 31

Your baby

By Week 31, more white fat is being deposited around the body, with the result that lanugo starts to thin out and may only remain on certain parts (although the fetus will still be covered in a thick layer of vernix caseosa). The hair on the scalp, however, continues to thicken. Between Weeks 28 and 32 the fetus gains around 500 g per week, and gradually looks a little plumper and less wrinkly. The skin is now pinker, because there is more fat to cover the blood vessels. Due to this gain in weight, the fetus is starting to be able to regulate its body heat.

You

You may notice that your breasts continue to grow; on average, women have gained an extra 1 kg of breast tissue by now. If they have not already done so earlier, the breasts often start to leak colostrum, the yellowy-orange clear liquid that is the first milk you produce just after giving birth.

Cramp is a common feature of the third trimester and, although it can be very painful, it is not indicative of anything serious. See p.126 for advice on how to relieve the symptoms.

PATERNITY LEAVE AND PAY FOR PARTNERS
Partners are entitled to paternity leave and pay, although the arrangements are not as extensive as maternity leave (*see* Chapter 2, pp.50 –1). In legal terms, a partner is anyone with responsibility for the child, and same-sex partners have the same legal rights as all parents. However, partners have no legal right to take paid time off to accompany you to antenatal appointments, although many employers make allowances if a sensible notice period is given and arrangements for cover can be made. In order to qualify for Statutory Paternity Pay and up to two weeks' Paternity Leave, your partner must give their employers correct notice. In addition, they, too, have the right to request flexible working, and unpaid Parental Leave is also available for both parents up until the child's fifth birthday (*see* Useful Resources for websites that can give you the latest information).

✓ *Enrol in antenatal aqua aerobics class*

Week 32

Your baby

Between Weeks 32 and 35, the fetal rate of growth slows to about 200 g per week. The eyes are able to focus to a distance of approximately 15–20 cm. In males, the testes continue to descend. By the end of this period, the skin is pink and smooth and the upper and lower limbs are more substantial. The CRL is 28 cm and the weight is around 1,700 g.

Around 25 per cent of babies at this stage are in the breech (bottom down) presentation, but there is still enough room for them to turn completely, so that at term, the percentage of breech babies is much lower (*see* Chapter 5, p.148).

You

Your abdomen has expanded so much that, in some women, their belly button now protrudes and is visible through clothing (*see* p.131). You are likely to tire very easily from now, not helped by the difficulties in finding a comfortable position in which to sleep (*see* Box), so make sure you don't overdo it and take as many opportunities as you can to rest in the final few weeks of your pregnancy, particularly if you are working or looking after other children .

 Order large baby equipment, such as the pram and cot, to make sure it arrives in time

 Start writing your birth plan (see Chapter 5, p.138)

 Wear loose, cotton clothing to keep cool

SUGGESTED SLEEPING POSITIONS IN LATE PREGNANCY

Your increasing size can make it more difficult to find a comfortable position in bed and turning over or shifting position is now a lengthy and complicated manoeuvre. You will no longer be able to sleep on your front and sleeping on your back is inadvisable, as the weight of the uterus presses on the major veins pumping blood back to your heart. A 'V'-shaped pillow can allow you to sleep propped up in bed. If you prefer sleeping on your side, put one or more pillows beside you to support your upper (and bent) leg, or have a pillow between your knees, as well as one under your bump to support its weight. If your abdomen feels very tender, you could lie on a folded-up duvet for extra comfort.

DID YOU KNOW…?

Contrary to the myth of 'eating for two', pregnant women don't need to increase their calorie intake until the last trimester. So now you can have that extra banana a day!

Week 33

Your baby

The brain and nervous systems are fully formed by Week 33 and lung maturation is such that a baby born now may only need minimal assistance in breathing.

You

As your bump puts increasing pressure on your pelvic floor, you may find that you leak a little urine from time to time, especially if you laugh, cough or sneeze. This is called 'stress incontinence' (*see* p.128). If you haven't already developed them, varicose veins and haemorrhoids are an unsightly and sometimes painful accompaniment to the later stage of pregnancy, although they almost always improve or disappear shortly after the birth.

THE FETAL CIRCULATORY SYSTEM
The circulation of blood in a fetus' body differs from that of an adult, as oxygen is obtained from the maternal circulation via the placenta, not from the lungs (*see* diagrams). Fetal blood flow therefore bypasses the lungs and travels straight through an opening in the rear of the heart (called the 'foramen ovale') to the rest of the body. This hole closes after birth, with some changes occurring with the first intake of breath, and others several hours and days later, so that blood can flow to the lungs for oxygenation.

✓ *Keep up the pelvic floor exercises (see Feature in Chapter 2, p.37)*

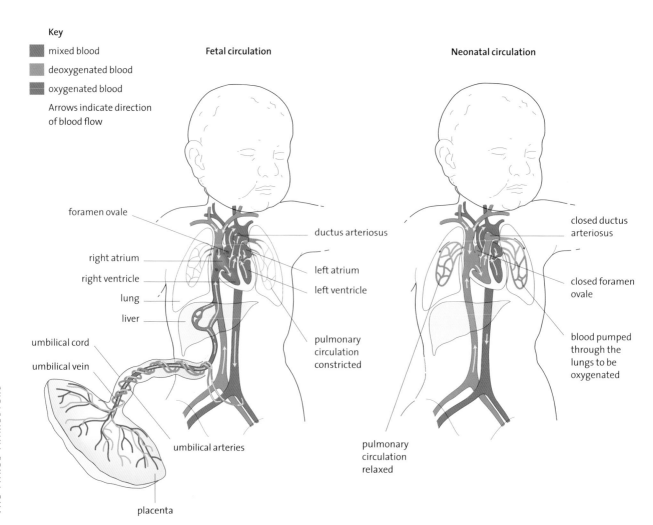

Key
- mixed blood
- deoxygenated blood
- oxygenated blood
- Arrows indicate direction of blood flow

Fetal circulation

Neonatal circulation

foramen ovale

ductus arteriosus

right atrium

left atrium

right ventricle

left ventricle

lung

liver

pulmonary circulation constricted

umbilical cord

umbilical vein

umbilical arteries

placenta

closed ductus arteriosus

closed foramen ovale

blood pumped through the lungs to be oxygenated

pulmonary circulation relaxed

Week 34

Your baby

Fingernails reach the end of the fingers, although this is not yet the case for toenails, which grow more slowly (as they do all through life: six months to grow a new fingernail, eight to twelve months for a toenail). The CRL is 30 cm and the weight is about 2,100 g, still a significant increase from Week 30.

You

As you progress through the final leg of your pregnancy, your body starts to prepare itself for the forthcoming birth. From around Week 34, many women (though by no means all) notice that their uterus hardens several times a day. These tightening sensations are called Braxton Hicks contractions, and they can start as early as the second trimester, although it is more common for them to begin during the third. They are named after John Braxton Hicks, the 19th-century British obstetrician who first noticed and described them. During these contractions, the muscles of the uterus tighten for approximately 30–60 seconds and sometimes for as long as two minutes. Braxton Hicks are sometimes called 'practice contractions' because they prepare the uterus for labour itself. As the due date comes closer, they can sometimes become uncomfortable and difficult to distinguish from real labour, especially if this is your first baby (see Box). However, Braxton Hicks contractions are unlike labour in that they:

▸ are infrequent
▸ are irregular in intensity
▸ are unpredictable
▸ are non-rhythmic
▸ feel uncomfortable rather than painful (although, for some women, Braxton Hicks can feel painful)
▸ do not increase in intensity or frequency
▸ taper off and then disappear altogether.

So, if your contractions are easing up in any way, they are most likely Braxton Hicks.

DID YOU KNOW...?
If the fingernails have not reached the fingertips at birth, this is one of the indicators of prematurity.

COPING WITH BRAXTON HICKS CONTRACTIONS
Although it cannot be predicted exactly when and how frequently Braxton Hicks contractions occur, there are some known triggers:

▸ increased activity (yours or the baby's)
▸ someone touching your abdomen
▸ a full bladder
▸ sex
▸ dehydration.

When you are having strong Braxton Hicks contractions, try moving around or changing position and use any breathing techniques you may have learnt in your antenatal classes to help you relax during labour (see Chapter 6, pp. 186–7), because being tense always increases pain. If you are at home, you could have a warm bath to ease the discomfort. Drink some water, herbal tea or milk to prevent dehydration. If you are not sure whether you are experiencing Braxton Hicks or the early signs of labour (see Chapter 6, p.157), don't hesitate to contact your midwife or maternity unit, especially if your contractions are accompanied by lower back pain or your pain is severe. The midwives will not mind at all, and will be best placed to advise you. If all is well, it is better to be reassured than to sit at home in a panic.

Week 35

Your baby

The body is continuing to round out as fat accumulates under the skin. While this helps the fetus to regulate its body temperature, there is still not enough for a baby to keep warm outside the womb. Babies born now are therefore likely to need to be placed in an incubator.

You

Your blood volume increases again during this last trimester and reaches its maximum of approximately 5.4 litres by Week 35, an increase of over 50 per cent compared to your non-pregnant state. Plasma (the fluid element of blood) accounts for most of the increase, rather than the oxygen-carrying red blood cells – this is why anaemia is common in the third trimester of pregnancy (see p.127). Unlike in previous trimesters, your peripheral resistance does not decrease to make way for this additional blood volume; consequently, your blood pressure will go up a little over the next few weeks. You will also feel hotter and may sweat more than usual, because your peripheral blood vessels are more dilated in

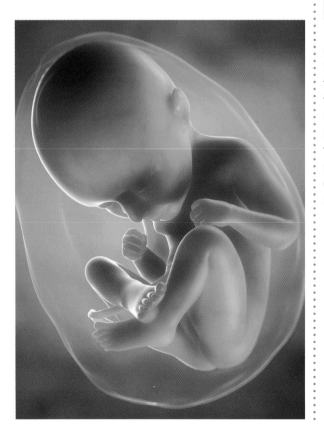

The placenta reaches maturity at Week 35, when it is 2–3 cm thick, measures around 25 cm in diameter and weighs 500–700 g. It is at its most efficient in supplying nutrients and oxygen to the baby, and from this point on it no longer increases in size and weight. As it starts to age, its reserves gradually become depleted. This problem becomes more acute after 42 weeks gestation, and pregnancies are not usually allowed to continue beyond this date, because it is dangerous for the baby.

The levels of amniotic fluid continue to increase from around 500 ml in Week 27 to a maximum of 1 litre in Week 35. After Week 35, levels of amniotic fluid start to decline, and post-mature pregnancies (those that continue beyond 40 weeks gestation) can have as little as 100–200 ml of amniotic fluid remaining. Antenatal scans can reveal if you have too much amniotic fluid (polyhydramnios), which is associated with maternal diabetes or physical problems in the baby, or too little amniotic fluid (oligohydramnios), which can be indicative of a growth-restricted baby or of fetal kidney problems. See Complications, pp. 288 and 287 for more information.

an effort to dissipate the extra heat generated by your increased metabolism. You may also find that, because of the extra blood volume, your fingers, legs and feet look puffier than normal (see p.131) and some simple exercises can help relieve the discomfort of this (see Box in Chapter 2, p.32). However, should you suddenly start to look puffy, or notice that your hands and feet are significantly more swollen, you should contact your doctor immediately, as this could be an early sign of pre-eclampsia (see Complications, p. 289), which is extremely dangerous for you and the baby if left untreated.

✓ *Invest in new maternity/breastfeeding bras*

Week 36

Your baby

This week also marks the stage at which the fetus has developed the full range of sucking movements. Babies born much before this time will have difficulty in sucking and swallowing, so the more premature they are, the longer it can take for them to learn to breastfeed (although, in time, these babies can and do breastfeed very successfully). The heart rate has slowed down further and, although a baby born at this stage would be referred to as premature, nearly all those that are born now do very well, can breathe unaided and rarely need to go to the neonatal unit. This is because the cells lining the airways have developed and large quantities of the hormone cortisol are being produced, which ensure that enough surfactant is lining the lungs for these to function well. See Chapter 7, p.230–1 for more on the common complications of prematurity.

You

If this is your first baby, the head may start to 'engage' from now. This means it starts to move down into your pelvic cavity in anticipation of labour (*see* Chapter 5, p.151). If you are slow to engage and this is your first baby, you will probably be sent for an ultrasound scan to determine what the reason might be. Failure to engage is usually caused by:

▸ a uterine fibroid
▸ placenta praevia (a low-lying placenta)
▸ a breech (bottom down) presentation
▸ your pelvis being too narrow to enable the baby's head to travel down through the birth canal, known as cephalo-pelvic disproportion (CPD) – although it may happen for a large baby, true CPD for an average-sized baby is uncommon.

That said, failure to engage can also be perfectly normal, even with first-time mothers, and engagement sometimes does not occur until labour has actually started. If this is not your first baby, the head is unlikely to become engaged until active labour has begun. The reason engagement happens later, if at all, with second and subsequent babies is that the uterine muscles are looser, so there is less pressure on the baby's head, and it is consequently slower to move down into the pelvic cavity. In addition, any previous labours will have slightly altered the shape of the pelvis, meaning engagement happens more slowly. Failure to engage is rarely a cause for concern, as more than 80 per cent of women who do not have an engaged head at term have a vaginal delivery.

If your baby's head does engage, you will notice that your bump 'drops' (i.e. appears lower than before). As a result, you will also notice that your breathing becomes easier and your appetite and digestion improve a little, because the baby has moved down and enabled the diaphragm, lungs and stomach to expand once more. However, you will probably now need to urinate even more often, because the baby's head is pressing down on the bladder harder than ever.

✓ *Pack a bag for hospital*

✓ *Start stocking up the freezer with ready-meals or batches of home-cooked food*

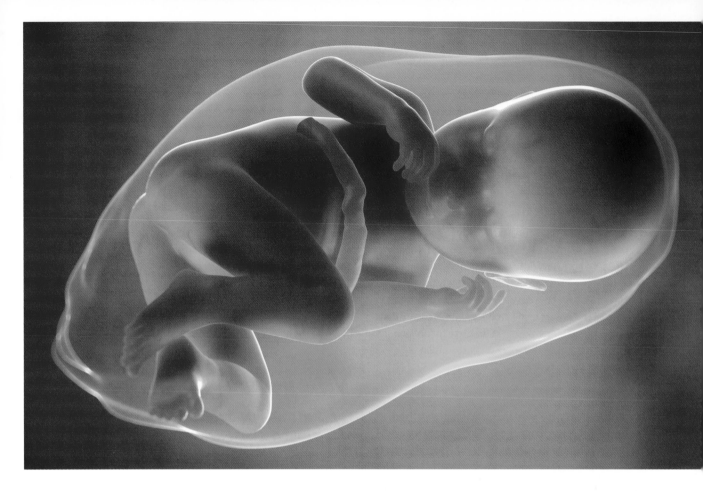

Week 37

Your baby

The fetus has developed a firm grasp and turns its head spontaneously towards a light source. From this week onwards, the fetus' movements are more restricted because space in the uterus is now tight, although there is a slowing in the rate of growth.

A baby born from now on would not, technically, be premature – just early – and would be unlikely to need any time in the neonatal unit unless there was an underlying health problem that had been detected prior to the birth or soon afterwards.

You

Your pregnancy is considered 'at term'. Although you will still notice large movements, you will be less able to feel the smaller ones. If you are finding that making frequent trips to the toilet at night is disturbing your sleep, try drinking plenty throughout the day the keep you hydrated, but drink less in the evenings. You may also find it more comfortable to sleep in an upright position.

> **DID YOU KNOW…?**
> Only five per cent of women give birth on their estimated delivery date (EDD). Approximately 50 per cent do so within one week and 90 per cent within two weeks either side of their EDD.

✓ Create a list of useful telephone numbers (midwife, labour ward, taxi firm)

✓ Put a thick towel or protective undersheet on your mattress in case your waters break during the night

✓ Prop yourself up in bed at night with lots of pillows to aid breathing and comfort

Week 38

Your baby

The toenails have reached the ends of the toes and the limbs are flexed (*see* picture). The abdominal and head circumference are (briefly) equal, before the abdomen overtakes once more. With two weeks to go to full term, the lanugo and layer of vernix caseosa covering the baby has largely disappeared and the testes in a male fetus have usually descended into the scrotum. The skull bones, although fully formed, are not fused and are soft enough to be able to slide over each other when the baby makes its way down the birth canal. Although the fetal lungs are now mature enough to breathe independently if your baby is born now, the alveoli are still primitive, and 95 per cent of the 300 million alveoli present in adult lungs develop after birth. The CRL is 34 cm and the weight is about 3,000 g.

You

The blood flow to the uterus is now five times what it was before you were pregnant. The non-pregnant uterus weighs 50–60 g, whereas at full term of pregnancy it alone weighs 1,000 g. It may have expanded up to 18 cm above to your belly button, making everyday living, and sleeping at night, increasingly difficult. If your baby's head has started to engage, however, your bump will now appear lower and you may find your lung capacity and digestion have slightly improved.

Your pregnancy is mature and your baby may be born any day now. Look out for the signs that labour may be imminent (*see* Chapter 6, p.156), which may include a 'show', the detachment of the mucus plug that seals the uterus. This is sometimes accompanied by light spotting, but if you experience any heavier or prolonged bleeding, contact your maternity unit immediately. For more information, see p.122.

 Discuss with your midwife or obstetrician that you may need to be induced if your pregnancy goes beyond 40+12 weeks (see Chapter 6, p.192)

 Take your hand-held maternity notes with you, even if you are just going out for a short while

If you are still working, consider stopping now!

DID YOU KNOW…?
Although the membranes of the amniotic sac usually rupture ('waters break') at the start of labour or sometime thereafter, occasionally the baby's head emerges from the birth canal with the membranes intact. This is known as being born in a 'caul' and, in many cultures, is taken as a sign of good luck.

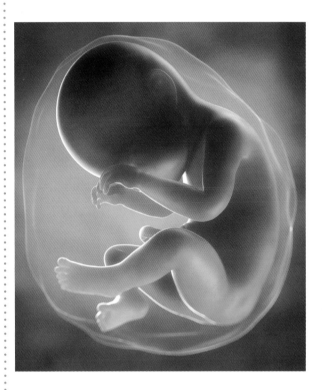

Week 39

Your baby

The fetus has been ingesting the lanugo and vernix caseosa as it has been shed, as well as discarded cells, amniotic fluid, mucus and bile. These substances and secretions form a thick, greeny-black substance, called 'meconium', which is stored in and lines the bowel. Meconium is normally excreted after birth in the first few bowel movements, but if present in amniotic fluid (once your membranes have ruptured), it can be a sign of fetal compromise (*see* Box in Chapter 6, p. 194) .

Most maternal hormones do not cross the placenta, but some placental hormones, notably oestrogen, which triggers milk production in your breasts, can sometimes affect the fetal breast tissue, causing it to swell. This is why some newborns (both boys and girls) have slightly swollen breasts at birth. Baby girls may also have a small vaginal bleed shortly after birth, once the presence of maternal oestrogen in their circulation disappears.

You

Your baby's movements have been more restricted in the latter half of the last trimester and, if you are occupied with other things, you may not notice them much, if at all. Usually, afternoon and evenings are times when fetal movements tend to be felt the most, although there are times during a 24-hour period when babies sleep and therefore are very still. These episodes usually last 20–40 minutes and rarely for more than 90 minutes.

You will probably recognise your baby's movement patterns and know what feels like a 'normal' level and type of activity. Although movement charts for the later stage of pregnancy are in your hand-held maternity notes, I don't recommend them for routine use. Instead, the important thing is that, if you realise there has been a significant change or reduction in the typical pattern of movement of your baby, you should contact your midwife or maternity unit without delay. Don't ignore the issue and decide to go to sleep instead. Changes are not usually indicative of a problem, but they could be a sign that reduced amounts of oxygen are reaching your baby. You may be asked to lie on your left side for two hours and to make a note of fetal movements. If you don't feel at least ten separate movements during that time, you may be asked to go to hospital to be examined and to have your baby's heartbeat checked; you may also be given an ultrasound scan, depending on the situation. In most cases, women who have had an episode of altered fetal movements go on to have a healthy baby.

THE THREE TRIMESTERS

THE UMBILICAL CORD AT BIRTH

The umbilical cord continues to grow in length and breadth throughout the trimester. At birth, it is usually 2 cm in diameter and 60 cm long. Due to its length, it has a tendency to form knots or wrap itself around the fetus, although in most cases this causes no problem. If your baby is breech or lying transverse, a vaginal delivery can lead to a higher chance of a prolapsed cord (*see* Complications, p. 293). See also Chapter 6, p.176 for information on how the cord is cut at birth.

✓ *Stock up on nappies – better still, get somebody to do it for you!*

✓ *Fill the car with petrol*

✓ *Get a hair cut/wax/pedicure!*

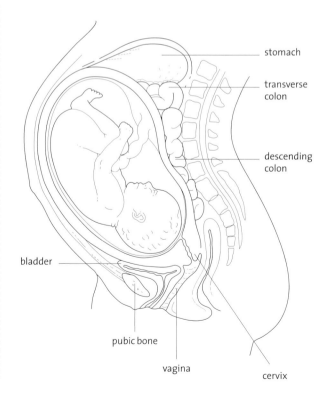

stomach

transverse colon

descending colon

bladder

pubic bone

vagina

cervix

Week 40

Your baby

The fetus measures around 36 cm crown to rump and weighs 3,400 g on average – the fetal brain weighs alone around 390 g at term. The amount of white fat on the body comprises about sixteen per cent of body weight. The total length is, on average, 50 cm. The fingernails have grown beyond the fingertips. The eyes are blue in Caucasians, dark grey or light brown in African and Asians, and can remain like this for several months after birth before they slowly start to take on their final colour. The vast majority of babies (95 per cent) are now head down, in a cephalic presentation. Of the remaining five per cent, four per cent will be breech, and one per cent will be transverse (*see* Chapter 5, p.148).

You

Your skin has been stretched by an extra 75–155cm – an extraordinary figure, considering that, after the birth, your skin will eventually shrink back to its pre-pregnancy state. You are probably feeling very impatient with the 'any day now' scenario, but try to remember that only a tiny percentage of babies arrive actually on their due date. If you are experiencing a strong desire to tidy up the house, the 'nesting' instinct (*see* Chapter 9, p.276), remember not to overdo it! Take the opportunity to rest as much as you can and enjoy what time you have left – soon enough your baby will be here.

> **DID YOU KNOW…?**
> A male fetus is generally slightly longer and weighs a little more at birth than a female one.

OVERDUE PREGNANCY

A pregnancy that goes beyond 40 weeks is described as overdue, or post dates. Being overdue is common (especially in a first pregnancy) and, apart from the discomfort of being heavily pregnant, does not usually pose problems. There is a small but significant increase in stillbirths in pregnancies that continue longer than 42 weeks, although the numbers remain low (*see* Feature in Complications, pp. 294–96), and is also slightly more common in mothers aged 40 and above – it is likely that the placenta becomes less efficient at nutrient and oxygen transfer. If you have not given birth by 40+12 weeks, you will therefore be offered an induction of labour to avoid problems of placental insufficiency (*see* Complications, p. 288).

Discussion about possible induction should take place at about 37–8 weeks. At around 40 weeks your midwife will re-check your estimated delivery date using your dating scan measurements. She may also do an internal examination to ascertain how 'ripe' (ready) the cervix is and may, after discussion with you, do a 'sweep' of the membranes around the baby at the top of the cervix. This means stretching the internal cervical opening with her finger to encourage the release of prostaglandins and uterine tightenings (*see* Box in Chapter 6, p.193). While it is known to reduce the need for induction with drugs, if you prefer not to have the procedure, you will agree a date to start the induction process, usually between 40+10 and 40+12 weeks. You may, of course, decline induction and wait for labour to begin naturally, in which case you will be offered daily monitoring after 42 weeks with CTG (though, again, you are free to decline). Bear in mind, however, that no amount of monitoring can predict whether your placenta might cease to function adequately just a few hours after an assessment, potentially putting your baby in danger. You might prefer to have a Caesarean section rather than an induction, and you should discuss with your obstetrician the pros and cons of this method of delivery, which will depend on factors such as whether you have had a previous vaginal delivery.

COMMON SIDE EFFECTS OF PREGNANCY

As your pregnancy progresses, you are likely to experience a number of side effects that, despite being completely normal, can nevertheless affect your general well-being. Although you should be reassured that they are unlikely to be detrimental to your baby, if you are at all concerned about your symptoms, you should always contact your midwife, GP or obstetrician.

Bleeding

Bleeding in pregnancy should always be investigated, although it does not always threaten the pregnancy or mean that there is a serious cause for concern. Many women are naturally worried that bleeding indicates that they are having a miscarriage. While this can be the case, there are also several non-harmful causes of bleeding. For example, bleeding after sexual intercourse can be indicative of cervicitis, a mild inflammation of the small blood vessels on the surface of the cervix, usually as a result of a simple candidial (yeast) infection, which can easily be treated. Other non-harmful causes of bleeding most commonly occur in early pregnancy; bleeding in later pregnancy tends to indicate more serious problems that may require immediate medical attention.

Bleeding in early pregnancy

Up to one in three women have some bleeding in early pregnancy, yet we do not always know why it occurs. The type of bleeding can range from light spotting through to more heavy loss and even the passing of large clots; the blood itself can also differ in colour, from brown to bright red. I would strongly advise you to contact your GP (or your local hospital, especially at night) so that you can arrange to have an ultrasound scan at your nearest Early Pregnancy Assessment Unit (EPAU), where they can discover whether your pregnancy is still intact. You will be asked to describe the bleeding you have been experiencing when you are examined.

Not all bleeding in early pregnancy indicates a problem. For instance, you may experience bleeding at about three to four weeks, when the fertilised egg implants in the lining of the womb (which is why some women mistake this for a light period and don't realise they are actually pregnant).

Some women have regular bleeding throughout their pregnancy, and this sometimes coincides with the times when their period would have occurred. In many other cases, the actual cause of bleeding is not identified.

Bleeding on its own is not usually a sign that that there is something wrong with the pregnancy. If, however, you are also experiencing abdominal cramping or pain, this may indicate a miscarriage or ectopic pregnancy. An ectopic pregnancy is where the embryo develops outside the uterus, usually in the Fallopian tube (*see* Complications, p. 285). From the fifth to sixth week of pregnancy, a transvaginal ultrasound scan (*see* Chapter 3, p.66) should be able to identify a pregnancy sac in your uterine cavity and even a fetal pole (the first visible sign of a developing embryo) and yolk sac, and this would mean that the chances of an ectopic pregnancy are virtually nil. From the sixth to seventh week, you should also be able to see the fetal heart beating. If you are not able to see the fetal pole or heartbeat, it is not an immediate cause for alarm, as it may be that the actual date of conception is a little later than you thought – at this early stage of pregnancy, a few days makes all the difference between being able to see these developments on an ultrasound.

Although bleeding is always worrying, the risks of having a miscarriage do diminish significantly as the first trimester progresses. By the time you are six weeks pregnant, the risk is down to about fifteen per cent. At eight weeks, it is lower still, and if a scan shows a fetal heart, the risk is as low as three per cent. By the end of this trimester, only one per cent of pregnancies will end in miscarriage. The majority of women who have bleeding in the early weeks do go on to have a successful pregnancy. See Feature in Chapter 3, pp.68–9 for more information on miscarriage.

Bleeding in later pregnancy

Light spotting towards the end of pregnancy sometimes occurs with a 'show': the loss of the mucus plug and associated blood vessels from the cervix that sometimes indicates that labour may be about to start (*see* Chapter 6, p.156). If you experience any other sort of bleeding in the last trimester, particularly if it is prolonged or heavy, call the maternity unit at once so that it can be investigated promptly. This kind of bleeding may also, but not necessarily, be accompanied by abdominal pain. The source of the bleeding could be from the placenta or from the cervix itself and there are several possible causes, including incompetent cervix, placenta praevia, placental abruption or marginal bleeding from the placenta, rather than actual abruption (*see* Complications, pp. 284–93 for more on these conditions). You will be monitored and, if appropriate or necessary, your baby will be delivered early.

Morning sickness

The term 'morning sickness' is misleading, because it can occur at any time of the day and symptoms range from occasional mild nausea through to vomiting, which can become severe and constant. It is impossible to predict who will be affected, or how, and the symptoms can also vary from one pregnancy to another. Furthermore, morning sickness can last from a few days to a few weeks and, although it almost always disappears between the twelfth and fifteenth week of pregnancy, for a few unlucky women it persists for much longer.

Between 70 and 80 per cent of pregnant women suffer from morning sickness, yet it is still not known exactly why. One theory is that it is caused by the high levels of certain hormones, especially BhCG and progesterone. The latter relaxes smooth muscles, including those of the digestive tract, and this results in food taking longer to pass through the stomach and intestines. Another theory is that it tends to occur at the times of the day when women might have low blood sugar and/or are tired, such as first thing in the morning or in the late afternoon. Finally, some people think that it is nature's way of making women avoid certain foods and liquids that could be harmful to the developing fetus at what is a developmentally crucial time. But this, too, cannot be proved, particularly since not all women suffer from morning sickness; and of those that do, there is such a wide range of foods that they go off completely that it is impossible to make any sort of firm link.

There are a several myths surrounding morning sickness, none of which is based on scientific evidence. One is that suffering from morning sickness is a sign of a healthy pregnancy and a healthy fetus. This is absolutely not the case and there is no link at all between a lack of symptoms and a higher rate of miscarriage. Another is that you will have a boy or a girl depending on whether or not you suffer from morning sickness. Again, this is totally without foundation.

DID YOU KNOW...?
A scan can only tell you the status of your pregnancy on the day it is performed – it cannot tell you what will happen tomorrow. With continued bleeding, a repeat scan and blood test (for BhCG) may be necessary.

TIPS FOR ALLIEVATING MORNING SICKNESS
The following advice has come about as a result of dealing with pregnant women over many years who are suffering from morning sickness. They may not work for everyone, but could nonetheless be worth a try:

▸ Eat small amounts every one or two hours to limit the build-up of stomach acid.
▸ Aim for small, easy-to-digest meals, or even tablespoon-sized portions.
▸ Stick to bland, starchy foods, such as toast, plain pasta or plain biscuits.
▸ Place a bland snack (e.g. plain biscuits, oatcakes) by your bedside at night so that you can nibble on it first thing if your nausea is worse in the morning.
▸ Boost your diet with plain, non-sugary cereals, such as cornflakes with skimmed (i.e. non-fat) milk, as many cereals are fortified with vitamins and minerals and the milk contains important calcium.
▸ Avoid rich, fatty or spicy foods.
▸ Avoid acidic drinks, such as fruit juices, and drink water and herbal teas (e.g. peppermint, camomile) instead.
▸ Wear acupressure wrist bands (sold in pharmacies to prevent motion sickness); these should be worn at all times and preferably until you are about sixteen weeks pregnant for best effect.
▸ Take ginger (a known remedy for nausea) in tablet or capsule form (ginger-flavoured biscuits or tea do not have enough concentration to make a difference).
▸ Keep away from kitchen smells and avoid cooking, if possible, until your morning sickness improves.
▸ Rest as much as you can (ask family/friends to help, especially if you have small children).

The tips listed (*see* Box) may help relieve some of the symptoms of morning sickness. If you find that you are either unable to eat and drink much at all over a period of a few days or are vomiting on a regular basis, be reassured that this will not affect your baby's development. Similarly, don't worry if you can only face a limited range of foods. As long as you are still eating and drinking something, your baby will be drawing all the nutrients it needs from your own reserves. Although this is not good for you in the long term (anaemia, bone thinning and a weakened immune system are some of the consequences of a poor diet), you will not be harming yourself or your baby if your diet is less than ideal for a few weeks.

However, if you cannot keep even fluids down over a period of more than 24 hours, call your midwife for advice or go to your local hospital, as you may need intravenous fluids to prevent dehydration. Many hospitals now have facilities to give you fluids during the day and allow you to go home at night.

A few women continue to suffer from morning sickness throughout the second trimester and even right up to the end of their pregnancy. If this is the case for you, please do not worry. Although it is not usual, it is not a sign that there is something wrong with your pregnancy. Ongoing nausea and sickness are often caused by low blood sugar levels, so do try to eat at least a spoonful of food every few hours, even if it is only a glucose sweet.

Hyperemesis gravidarum

If you are unable to keep down any food or fluids, not just for a few days but for a longer period of time, you may be suffering from a rare condition called hyperemesis gravidarum. It is very important that your symptoms are dealt with, as you can become weak and clinically dehydrated, so you must consult your GP or midwife. You may need to be admitted to hospital for a short while so that you can have the necessary fluids, glucose and minerals administered through an intravenous drip; you may also need anti-emetic medication to prevent vomiting. Research shows that relaxation techniques and distraction therapy can help, so these might be worth investigating.

Food cravings

A strong desire for certain foods is very common, especially during the first trimester when morning sickness means your tastes in food and your appetite are often disrupted. Typically, women go off tea, coffee and alcohol, as well as certain foods such as red meat, fish or cheese. Conversely, they often start to crave other, often salty foods (e.g. pickled onions, gherkins). Some also develop a craving for very strange substances or their smell, for example, freshly mown grass or coal – a condition known as a 'pica'. As with morning sickness, doctors still don't know why these cravings occur. There are various theories suggesting that picas may be caused by stress, deficiencies in certain nutrients or the body's need to protect itself against harmful substances. Whatever the reason, having an obsession with a particular food, drink or substance, is unlikely to be harmful in any way to your baby.

Digestive problems

Indigestion, constipation and heartburn are common features of pregnancy. The high level of progesterone relaxes the digestive tract, and this results in food taking longer to pass through your system. Indigestion and heartburn can become more marked in the third trimester, as the growing uterus compresses the intestines and stomach. In general, for all digestive problems try to:

▸ eat little and often
▸ avoid rich, spicy or pickled foods
▸ have your final meal early in the evening, allowing two hours before bedtime to give yourself time to digest.

Constipation

A sluggish digestion can cause constipation, so you need to pay particular attention to your diet and lifestyle:

▸ Drink plenty of fluids: 2–3 litres per day (as a rough guide, aim to drink a glass an hour while you are awake). Water and herbal teas, such as peppermint, ginger, lemongrass and jasmine, are ideal because they are refreshing and help digestion.
▸ Decrease coffee, tea and other diuretic drinks (such as colas).
▸ Eat plenty of fruit, vegetables and wholegrain foods to keep up your intake of fibre. Mango is especially good, as it is both fibrous and oily in texture, although because it is sweet, you should eat it in moderation, especially if you have diabetes.
▸ Keep moving! Try not to become too sedentary and aim for at least twenty minutes of walking per day.

Iron supplements can also make you constipated, so speak to your doctor if you are taking these because of anaemia. If you are not anaemic, consider whether you need to keep taking them and inform your midwife or doctor if you plan to do so. If the above dietary actions do not help to relieve your constipation, your doctor can prescribe a suitable laxative. See Chapter 2, p.22–3 for more information on eating well in pregnancy.

Heartburn

Heartburn occurs when the valve between the oesophagus and the stomach relaxes as a result of the high level of progesterone, allowing acid gastric juices – and sometimes food – to seep back up from the stomach and irritate the oesophagus. The following can help to alleviate the symptoms:

▸ Drink low-fat milk or eat low-fat probiotic natural yoghurt before or after a meal, as they neutralise the acidity in the stomach.
▸ Use an extra pillow at night to raise your head up and reduce acid reflux.
▸ If the heartburn does not improve or is a problem for you, you can take suitable antacid medication. Although several of these are available over the counter (your pharmacist will be able to advise you), if you ask your GP to prescribe one,

it will not cost you anything, because pregnant women do not pay for prescriptions.

Tiredness

Although pregnancy is an entirely normal and natural state, the demands it makes on your body can leave you, at times, feeling very tired. This is a particularly common symptom in the first trimester and one that, once again, no one can truly explain. It may be caused by the flood of hormones through the body, alterations in blood sugar levels or the raised cardiac output, blood volume and oxygen consumption. Whatever the cause, the fact remains that many normally active women are wiped out by the evening or find themselves needing to have a sleep during the day. This is not a sign that there is anything wrong and the best thing to do is listen to what your body is telling you and rest where possible. If that means slowing down, not going to the gym as much (or at all), reducing your social life and trying to get more sleep at night, then so be it.

Acute tiredness usually diminishes in the second trimester, but can arise again in the third, as your growing size means that moving around takes a lot more effort. In addition, as your pregnancy moves into its final few weeks, good-quality sleep can become increasingly difficult: your sleeping positions in bed will be more limited; your baby may be kicking a lot throughout the night; and your decreased bladder size is probably waking you regularly.

To avoid getting progressively more tired as the weeks go by, try to have a nap, either after lunch or later on in the day, as this can do wonders for your energy levels. If this is not possible, then you could practise some simple relaxation techniques for ten to twenty minutes: lie down, close your eyes and name and relax every part of your body, starting with your toes and going right up to your head (or vice versa); or simply picture a pleasant, relaxing scene (e.g. an idyllic beach lapped by the ocean waves). If you can get into the habit of taking a bit of time to rest before the baby is born, you will be more able to continue doing so after the birth, and this will help you to cope with the tiredness caused by looking after a new baby.

Anaemia can also be a possible cause of tiredness, and this will be tested for both at your booking appointment and at 28 weeks (*see* Chapter 3, p.62).

Dizziness

It is common to feel dizzy, faint or light-headed during the first and third trimester. If this happens while you are sitting down, it is probably because you have low blood sugar levels, in which case you should try to eat and drink something as soon as possible. If you find yourself feeling faint or light-headed after a period of standing, or when you suddenly stand up, it may be that blood has pooled in your legs and, because a greater part of your blood supply is now diverted to your uterus, not enough blood is reaching your brain. This can happen, in particular, if you have low blood pressure or in hot weather when your veins are dilated. If you feel dizzy or light-headed, sit down (ideally with your head between your legs) or, better still, lie down to enable blood to flow sufficiently back to your brain. Later in pregnancy, feeling dizzy may be a sign that you are getting too hot or of anaemia, particularly in the first trimester (*see* below and opposite).

Sore breasts

Raised oestrogen and progesterone levels can cause your breasts to feel very heavy and extremely tender to the touch (*see* Box on p.85). Having a good maternity support bra can help, as can wearing a sleep bra at night (*see* Chapter 2, p.52).

Feeling hot and sweaty

Most women find that they feel warmer than usual when they are pregnant. This is caused by increased cardiac volume and subsequent dilatation of blood vessels in your feet and hands to keep your blood pressure within safe limits. To alleviate these symptoms, common sense is the best policy: wear layers so that you can cool down easily and quickly, avoid wearing synthetic fabrics, and try to keep the room you are in well ventilated.

Blocked nose and nose/gum bleeds

A blocked nose and nose and gum bleeds are among the minor side effects of pregnancy and are likely to last until the birth. The result of dilated blood vessels, nasal stuffiness can be relieved by deep steam inhalations. Bleeding from the nose or gums is caused by higher levels of hormones and increased blood flow. Again, there is not much to be done to prevent this, but you can make sure your oral hygiene remains good (by brushing your teeth regularly and flossing on a daily basis) and reduce your sugar intake to protect your teeth and gums.

Cramp

Cramp in the legs, calf or feet is particularly common in the third trimester, often occuring at night. It is not known what causes it, although it could be due to the uterus pressing down on certain nerves in the pelvic area. It is not a cause for concern, although it can be very painful, and will disappear once the baby is born. If the cramp is in your leg, pull the foot towards you and stretch out your leg, while massaging the affected area. If it is in the foot, flex the foot and put your thumb and forefinger over the ball of your foot – or ask your partner to do this – until the cramp eases.

Anaemia

Red blood cells are found in blood plasma (fluid) and give the blood its red colour. Their function is to deliver oxygen, taken from the lungs, to all the cells in our bodies and it is for this that haemoglobin, a protein in the red blood cells, is needed. Iron is required to make haemoglobin and lack of iron leads to a deficiency in the red blood cells, a condition called anaemia. As a result, less oxygen is delivered around the body.

During pregnancy, blood volume increases by approximately 50 per cent, but the volume of plasma increases more than that of red blood cells. This means that the proportion of haemoglobin and iron in the blood is lower than in a non-pregnant state. In addition, the demand for iron increases because of the growing fetus and the placenta's own requirements.

As a consequence of these changes, anaemia is a common side effect of pregnancy and symptoms usually include unusual levels of tiredness and pallor. More rarely, they may also include heart palpitations (*see* below), dizziness or headaches. Your blood is tested for anaemia at least twice during your pregnancy, once at your booking appointment, and once at around 28 weeks when the concentration of haemoglobin is at its lowest, but speak to your GP or midwife if you suspect you may be developing symptoms of anaemia at any other time. See also Chapter 2, p.22 for examples of iron-rich foods and how to treat iron deficiency.

Heart palpitations

Up to 50 per cent of women experience heart palpitations (cardiac arrhythmia) during pregnancy, particularly during the third trimester. Episodes can last for a few seconds or a few minutes, but although they can be frightening, they are rarely dangerous or indicative of a more serious condition. While palpitations can be a symptom of anaemia (*see* above), they are usually a result of the heart having to work much harder during pregnancy. Occasionally, they can be caused by excessive anxiety and stress, and can even be a sign of a panic attack.

However, if the palpitations are accompanied by a tightness in the chest and/or dizziness, seek the advice of your GP.

Abdominal pain

Discomfort or mild to moderate pain in the abdominal area can occur throughout all stages of pregnancy and is caused by a number of different factors. In the first trimester, minor abdominal twinges and aches are very common and, like bleeding, they can be very worrying. However, they are invariably caused by the ligaments and muscles in the pelvic area adapting to the enlarging uterus and are therefore not serious. As your pregnancy progresses through the second and third trimesters, the muscles stretch and the ligaments loosen even further, especially in the pelvic and lower spine areas. The pain does not usually last long and is nothing to worry about. However, if it becomes intense or your abdomen becomes tender to the touch, you should see the doctor at once, as it could be a sign of placental abruption (*see* Complications, p. 288) or premature labour (*see* p.106).

If at any point in your pregnancy the pain is more severe, on one side only, constant or feels like cramping, it could be a sign of:

▸ a uterine fibroid (*see* Complications, p. 285)
▸ appendicitis (*see* Chapter 2, p.43)
▸ a urinary tract infection (*see* below)
▸ ectopic pregnancy (especially if you are between six and ten weeks pregnant – *see* Complications, p. 285).

You should always contact your GP, EPAU or, if your pregnancy is advanced, the maternity unit immediately in the event of severe abdominal pain, so that you can be assessed as quickly as possible and, if necessary, have an urgent ultrasound scan.

Vaginal infections

Vaginal secretions are less acidic during pregnancy and this can cause the yeast-like fungus candida albicans, which is present in the vagina and gut, to multiply, resulting in an infection commonly known as 'thrush'. Typical symptoms are an itchy vagina and a thicker vaginal discharge, which is creamy or curd-like in appearance. Over-the-counter medication in the form of pessaries and topical cream can clear up the infection, but it is preferable to speak to your GP or midwife first so they can take a vaginal swab to check that candida is in fact the cause of the itching.

If your vaginal discharge changes from its normal milky colour and becomes yellow-green, if it develops a strong smell or your genital or anal region becomes red and painful, speak to your GP, as you may have developed a different sort of vaginal infection. This will require treatment, as it can trigger premature labour (*see* Chapter 7, p.222).

Urinary tract infections

The pregnancy hormones that relax the muscles and ligaments in the body also cause the urinary tract to dilate, allowing bacteria to travel up it more easily and cause an infection. Symptoms often include lower abdominal or back pain and you may – though not always – have some pain when urinating or even pass blood. It is important to treat urinary infections (UTIs) quickly so that they do not develop into kidney infections, which can take longer to clear up. UTIs can also trigger threatened premature labour, because they can cause the uterus to contract, although once treated, these contractions tend to cease. If you are given antibiotics to treat the infection, make sure you finish the full course, even if your symptoms have disappeared, as failure to do so may result in the infection coming back even more strongly than before and in your body becoming increasingly immune to the antibiotics.

Frequent urination and stress incontinence

In early pregnancy, the need to urinate more frequently is caused by the increase in blood supply to kidneys. In late pregnancy, the weight of the uterus presses down on the bladder and causes the sensation of wanting to go to the toilet, even though you may not pass much urine each time. This compression is compounded once the baby's head has engaged (*see* Chapter 5, p.151). Frequent trips to the toilet can be quite disruptive, especially during the night or when you are out and about. In order to limit the number of times you need to go, steer clear of diuretic drinks (e.g. caffeinated coffee, tea and colas) and drink more water instead. Don't be tempted to cut down on your fluid intake, as this could lead to dehydration. If, however, you are passing only very small amounts of urine – and especially if you notice a stinging sensation or blood – see your GP as soon as possible, as you may be suffering from a urinary tract infection (*see* above).

As well as needing to urinate more frequently, you may find that you leak small quantities of urine, particularly when you laugh, cough or sneeze. This is called 'stress incontinence' and it often happens during the third trimester because the growing uterus is putting strain on the pelvic floor muscles. This is why it is important to strengthen these muscles by doing exercises (*see* Feature in Chapter 2, p.37) from the start of pregnancy, as labour will stretch them even further.

Bladder function should return to normal within three months of delivery if you do regular pelvic floor exercises and lose your pre-pregnancy weight. If you are still experiencing symptoms after this time, your GP can rule out more straightforward problems, such as mild infections, and refer you to a gynaecologist if necessary. See also Complications, p. 288 for information on postnatal incontinence.

Back pain

Many women find that they start to experience back pain towards the end of the second trimester. As your uterus expands and your baby increases in size, this can cause problems for your posture, particularly in your lower back. Sometimes, the pain becomes more localised, which can be caused by a number of different physical issues.

Sciatica

Sharp, constant or intermittent pain in the lower back, buttocks and one/both legs can indicate sciatica. This occurs when the sciatic nerve, which runs from the spinal cord through to the back of the legs, is compressed, usually by the baby's head, and this results in shooting pains and/or a sensation of tingling, weakness or numbness in one or both legs. The baby's head may change position and this should alleviate symptoms, but you can also try the following:

▸ improving your posture
▸ wearing low-heeled/flat shoes and walking barefoot at home
▸ lying on a firm mattress
▸ stretching exercises and pelvic tilts
▸ yoga (pregnancy yoga classes are specifically tailored to help with this).

See also Feature in Chapter 2, pp.34 for exercises that can help relieve back pain. If your pain is not relieved by simple analgesia or any of the above methods, consult your GP. Although pain of this sort is often caused by the sciatic nerve, there may also be a problem with a disc in your spine, which should be investigated before you do any more exercise.

Coccygeal pain

The coccyx (tailbone) can become displaced from the sacrum (the large triangular bone at the base of your spine) either as a result of looser ligaments during pregnancy or by a previous fall or injury in the pelvic area. It can also be caused by the descent of the baby's head through the birth canal during labour. This can make sitting, in particular, extremely painful until the area heals. In the meantime, only rest will ease the discomfort, although some women find that an ice pack, hot compress or massage can relieve symptoms. You may also have to take paracetamol for the pain.

Sacroiliac pain

The sacroiliac joints are where the sacrum meets the pelvis and these can be made unstable by the loosening of the ligaments by the pregnancy hormones. As a result, some women develop severe lower back pain when walking or standing. A physiotherapist or osteopath who is experienced in treating pregnant women can help relieve the symptoms, as can maintaining a good posture and wearing low-heeled or flat shoes (but not ballet pumps, which give no support).

Pubic symphysis dysfunction

The symphysis pubis is the point where the pelvic bones meet at the front of the pelvis. Again, the ligaments around this joint can loosen, resulting in extreme pain when you walk (because the pelvic bones are, in effect, rubbing together). Knee-squeezing exercises and pelvic tilts can help relieve the symptoms of pubic symphysis dysfunction, as can wearing a good support belt to relieve the pressure. Rarely, the pubic bones actually separate, causing very severe pain when you move. This condition, known as diastasis of the symphysis pubis, usually leads to bed rest and very limited mobility until the birth. However, midwives are trained in delivering babies in a variety of positions, so if you develop this problem, a vaginal delivery is still perfectly possible.

Itchy skin

Your skin often becomes very dry during pregnancy and, because you may be sweating more, you can also suffer from rashes in the folds of the skin, particularly if you are overweight. Try to keep hydrated by drinking plenty of fluids and make sure your skin is well moisturised. Ignore the marketing of specific pregnancy creams: a good aqueous cream (fragrance-free, to reduce the irritation that can accompany dry skin) applied plentifully and regularly is all you need, along with some non-perfumed emollient bath or shower cream. If necessary, use calamine lotion to calm any inflammation and relieve itchiness. Very occasionally, more severe itching all over your body that is not accompanied by a rash can be a symptom of a liver condition called obstetric cholestasis (see Complications, p. 287), so always speak to your GP or midwife if you develop itchy skin, because a simple liver function test can quickly establish if this is the problem.

Stretch marks

Stretch marks are thought to be caused by the tearing of the collagen beneath your skin and by insufficient collagen in the body and elasticity in your skin. In fact, they are associated with skin growth and stretching – many teenage girls will see stretch marks developing over their thighs and breasts during puberty, although these soon fade. Most women do develop some stretch marks in pregnancy, although if your weight gain is gradual and you stay fit, you may be able to limit their appearance and number. However, much depends on genes, skin type and probably your age. At first, stretch marks are pinkish or reddish in appearance (and they can become itchy, too, as the skin over your abdomen stretches), but with time they will fade to a silvery white colour and will be much less noticeable. As with itchy skin problems (see above), I don't believe that applying anti-stretch mark creams and oils makes any difference, because they cannot affect the collagen beneath the skin. By all means keep your skin hydrated and supple, but don't think these products will prevent you from developing stretch marks. Just use the same basic moisturiser you normally use, but apply it more often.

Varicose veins

Varicose veins are one of the most common side effects of pregnancy and they usually occur in the last trimester. These are veins that have become dilated because of the extra blood volume and the reduction in the peripheral resistance of your blood vessels during pregnancy. They usually develop in the legs or the anal region (when they are called 'haemorrhoids' – see p. 131). Varicose veins usually improve – if not disappear completely – after the birth, although this is not always the case and some women need subsequent treatment. During pregnancy, the following can be helpful to relieve or improve the problem:

▶ Wear support tights, preferably specific pregnancy support tights. Ideally, put them on before you get out of bed in the morning, so that your veins will not become dilated as a result of your standing up.
▶ Raise your feet as high as possible when you are sitting down (this helps the draining of blood).
▶ Avoid standing, especially standing still, for long periods of time. Move your feet around or shift from one leg to another.
▶ Exercise on a daily basis to improve circulation.
▶ Avoid excessive weight gain, as this can exacerbate varicose veins.

In about ten per cent of pregnancies, generally in second or subsequent ones, varicose veins can appear in the vulva. They will not interfere with delivery, although they can cause more blood loss during labour if a vein tears or they are cut during an episiotomy (see Chapter 6, p.174). They will disappear after the birth, but if you have any concerns, don't be embarrassed about consulting your GP, as they will have seen many cases before and can reassure you.

Haemorrhoids (piles)

Haemorrhoids, commonly known as 'piles', are varicose veins inside or outside the anus. They are common towards the end of pregnancy when the baby's weight presses down on the pelvis, making it harder for blood to flow back to the heart. Haemorrhoids can be itchy or can cause throbbing pain, but they can also result in some bleeding from the rectal area. Unfortunately, there is nothing much you can do to get rid of them, but once the baby is born they should disappear on their own. In the meantime, there are various ways of alleviating the symptoms:

▸ Apply haemorrhoid cream or ointment (sold over the counter), which contain a lubricant and a light anaesthetic.
▸ Avoid constipation by drinking plenty of water and eating a fibre-rich diet (straining when you have a bowel movement aggravates the problem).
▸ Practise pelvic floor exercises regularly (*see* p. 37) – another good reason to do them!
▸ Apply a small ice pack (wrapped in some fabric) for five to ten minutes to reduce the swelling.
▸ Avoid lifting heavy weights (including small children).

If you ever find that they are protruding outside of the anus and you cannot push them back inside without sharp pain, get them checked out by your GP. Very occasionally, women need to stay in hospital to be given pain control, applications of ice and bed rest.

Protruding belly button

By halfway through the final trimester, some women notice that their belly button now sticks out and may even be visible through clothing. A protruding belly button is entirely normal, and it will return to its usual form after the birth, although in rare instances, it will need minor corrective surgery to return it to its previous state. However, if you have a pierced belly button, you should take care not to snag it on clothing – better to take it out for the duration of your pregnancy.

Fluid retention (oedema)

Your body retains fluid as a natural part of the physical processes that take place during pregnancy. As a result, your hands, feet or ankles may start to swell up, a condition known as oedema. Your midwife will check you at every antenatal appointment to ensure that any puffiness is within the normal limits. Any sudden or significant swelling, however, should be examined promptly by your GP or obstetrician, as this can be an early sign that you are developing pre-eclampsia (*see* Complications, p. 289).

Carpal tunnel syndrome

Some women develop a sensation of pins and needles in their fingers or hands and even a feeling of numbness. Under the effect of increased oestrogen, the protective carpal tunnel, which wraps around the nerves as they pass from your arm to your hand, narrows and compresses the ligaments and nerves contained within it. As a result, you start to lose sensation in your fingers and hands. Many women find it helpful to hang their arm down by the side of the bed at night or, conversely, to raise it up on a pillow. A wrist splint may help to relieve the pressure during your pregnancy, and the symptoms usually disappear soon after delivery.

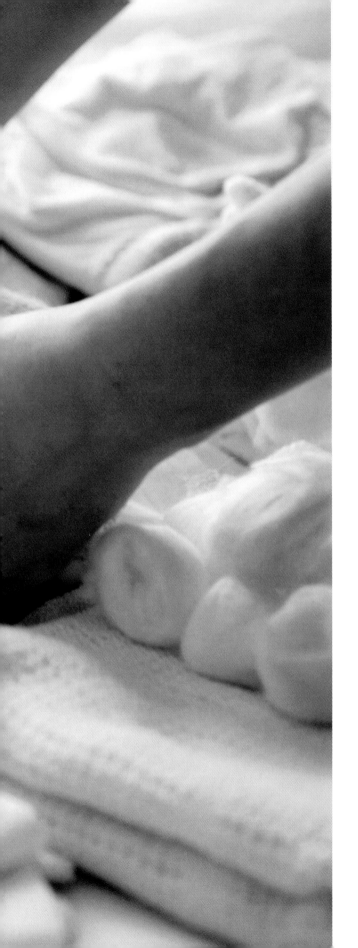

5

Preparing for the birth

The last few weeks of your pregnancy are invariably very exciting, because you can enjoy preparing for the arrival of your baby. You may want to choose a birth partner, write a birth plan and make sure that you have all you need for the birth and for the first few weeks afterwards. Your baby is making preparations, too, by getting into position ready to enter the world.

YOUR BIRTH PARTNER

Most women choose to have someone to accompany them when they give birth, who is known as their 'birth partner'. While your needs in childbirth will be taken care of by a midwife, it is a good idea to have someone else there to provide more personal emotional and practical support. Indeed, there is medical evidence that a woman labours more effectively and calmly if she is never left alone.

For many, the birth partner will be the person you are in a relationship with, for others, their own mother or a close friend. Society now expects partners to attend the birth, yet I believe very strongly that you should do what seems right for you as a couple, and no one should feel obliged to be a birth partner if they really don't want to be. If your partner prefers not to be there for whatever reason, then that is entirely up to you and them. That said, they invariably remember the birth of their child as one of the most powerful moments of their life, and one that creates a unique bond between you as a couple.

Seeing someone that you care for in pain is always difficult for a birth partner. Whoever you choose, they will usually cope much better with this if, firstly, they know what is happening and, secondly, they can take steps to help you. Your birth partner should therefore inform themselves about birth by reading up on labour, Caesarean sections, the different types of pain relief and some of the potential complications, so that they feel confident about discussing any issues with the medical staff. They should also read your birth plan, if you have one, so that they know what it contains (see p. 138–9). If possible, they should also attend antenatal classes (there is usually a specific, one-off session for partners if they are unable to attend the entire course) and tour the labour ward in advance so that they know what to expect. If you are having a home birth, your birth partner should know where things are kept in your house and what the arrangements will be on the day. It is important, however, that anyone who is planning to be with you during labour understands that you can change your mind at any stage, and should not feel offended if, in the end, you decide to give birth without them being present.

The essential role a birth partner has is to act as your advocate when dealing with medical staff. During a labour that is progressing normally, you may be left unattended for short periods of time. If you become concerned that something is happening to you or your baby, your partner can ask for the help of the midwife or obstetrician, insisting if necessary, without being confrontational. You may not be thinking very clearly due to pain or fatigue, whereas they can ask questions for you about the situation and seek clarification if it is needed.

FOR THE BIRTH PARTNER'S EYES: YOUR ROLE ON THE DAY

In order to support the mother-to-be during the birth, you should:

- encourage her, tell her how well she is doing and remind her to focus on her breathing in order to cope with the pain
- maintain eye contact as much as possible, to enhance her feeling of security
- be sensitive to her needs, which may change from one minute to the next
- help her in practical ways: ensure she has a water bottle to hand, that her pillows are comfortable, that she is not too hot
- accept that, although it can be minimised, pain is part of the birth process: you will not be able to take it away
- maintain an atmosphere of calm and quiet wherever possible
- stay fed and watered, but in a discreet way, and take regular, short breaks
- keep your sense of humour, at least in the early stages
- try not to let fear/distress/panic show: remain outwardly confident, positive and encouraging
- be prepared to seek medical help if you think it is needed
- be assertive – but not aggressive – with the medical staff
- seek further information or a second opinion when necessary
- provide clear information and reassurance for her, and explain what the medical staff have told you.

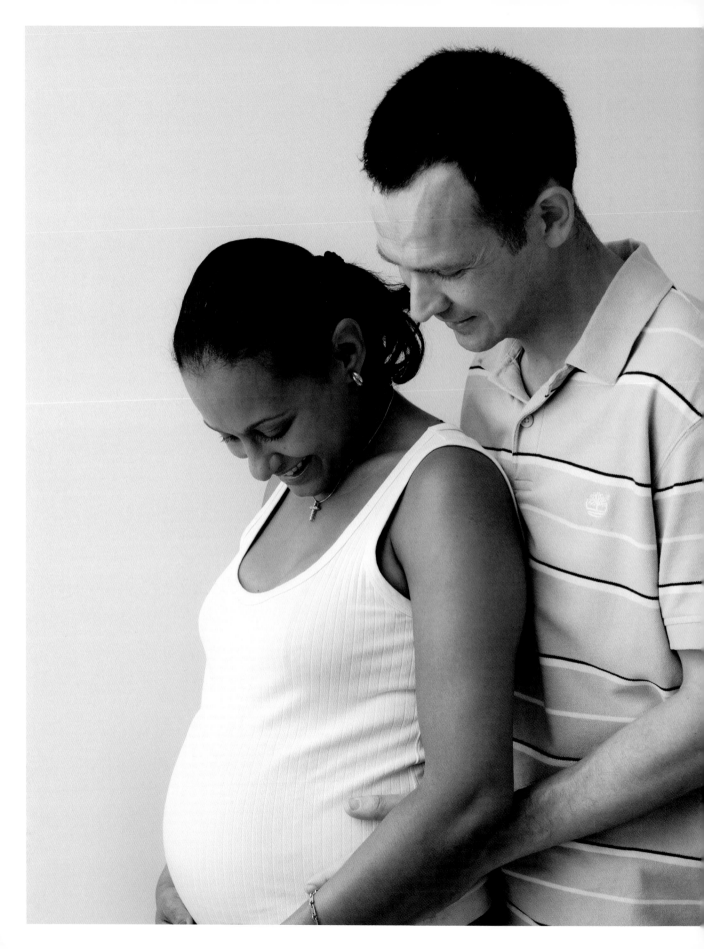

The word 'doula' comes from the Greek word for woman servant or caregiver, and it now refers to a woman who can be hired to offer support, advice and practical help to a woman in childbirth and the period after (and also to her partner, if required). In effect, a doula 'mothers' the mother. Increasingly, in an age where women often do not have close family and friends living nearby, doulas are stepping in and filling the need for support during this important and emotional stage of a woman's life.

Doulas don't perform a clinical or medical role during pregnancy and labour, but they have had some training, have good knowledge of a woman's physiology and are experienced in childbirth and the postpartum period. (Although it is not an essential qualification, most have given birth themselves.) While they are there to support both parents, they can also be your sole birth partner if you so choose. It is best to recruit a doula via an agency (see Useful Resources), which can perform background checks and act as a mediator if there are any problems – this is important, as this is (as yet) an unregulated profession.

You should meet your doula sometime during your pregnancy – by the time you are 36 weeks pregnant, at the latest – so that you can discuss the help you think you would like and to make sure that you are going to get on. During labour, a doula can offer advice on breathing and relaxation and different positions to help you cope with the pain, encourage and reassure you and help to explain any medical situation that arises. She encourages – though never pressurises – the partner to be involved and will remain sensitive at all times to what you both feel comfortable with. Her aim is to help you feel supported in what is happening, so that the labour is something you look back on positively.

A doula can also be hired for the period after the birth – indeed, some women prefer them to be involved only once they have returned from the hospital. The length and type of involvement depends entirely on the specific arrangement between you but, generally speaking, the doula's role will involve being of practical and emotional help to you as new parents. This means helping around the house, providing advice on breastfeeding and offering guidance and reassurance on all aspects of babycare. This could be a particularly valuable source of support if you are a single parent or don't have a network of female relatives and friends on hand. As a result of the doula's help, many women find that they are better able to recover from labour and bond with their baby and that the postnatal period becomes more relaxing and enjoyable for both parents. See also Chapter 8, p. 238 for more on managing life when you are back at home.

In addition to being your advocate, your birth partner can see to your personal needs and provide emotional support. For example, you may want physical reassurance by having your back massaged or your hand held (it is important that your birth partner learns how to massage you *in advance*, and doesn't leave experimenting with different techniques until the day). Some women don't like to be touched during labour and prefer verbal reassurance and encouragement instead; conversely, you may not want to talk at all or prefer to focus on some background music. While you can, to some extent, talk this part of the role through beforehand, it is impossible to know in advance how you will feel, so your birth partner will need to listen to you carefully at the time in order to be able to respond effectively. They should be aware that your needs may change from one moment to the next: it is common for women to want their birth partners close to them for some of the labour and to push them away, verbally and/or physically, later on. It is important that your birth partner is prepared for this, to avoid any surprises and unintentional hurt.

Other birth partners

Some women also wish to be attended during the birth by an alternative medicine practitioner, such as an acupuncturist, a doula (see Box) or another family member. While all maternity units allow you to have one other person with you, many cannot accommodate more than this, so check in advance what your hospital's policy is. If you have hired an independent midwife for a home birth (see Chapter 1, p. 15) and have had to transfer to hospital because of complications, she may not manage the actual delivery herself, but will be allowed to support the hospital midwives and manage practical issues, as well as reassure and encourage you.

WRITING A BIRTH PLAN

Many women choose to draw up a 'wish list' for labour and birth, called a birth plan, and there is a page for this in your maternity notes. You don't have to have a birth plan – plenty of women give birth successfully without one: they simply use their voice (as does their birth partner) to express a preference or to seek clarification for why a procedure might need to take place.

However, making a birth plan can be useful for getting you to consider why certain preferences are important to you and for helping your healthcare professionals to make the birth as close as possible to what you would like. Specifically, writing one in advance can:

- ▸ give you the opportunity to discuss your wishes with your healthcare professionals, so that you can discover if any of your choices are incompatible with hospital policy, are unsafe or simply unrealistic
- ▸ help you to feel more relaxed on the day, because you know that you, your birth partner and the hospital are clear about what sort of labour you would like.

However, there are a number of disadvantages to having a birth plan, too:

- ▸ It may raise your expectations as to what should happen in labour, even though, in reality, you have no idea what circumstances will occur.
- ▸ You may end up more stressed, due to the level of detail in the document.
- ▸ If things don't go to plan, you may feel very disappointed, if not distressed.
- ▸ You may have feelings of inadequacy after the delivery, because you may think you have 'failed' or 'lost control' of your labour.

The key thing is to expect the unexpected in childbirth and it is much better to be prepared for all eventualities. Furthermore, there is no 'right' way to give birth, other than aiming for the safe delivery of a healthy baby. Remember also that every birth is different: what works for one woman may not work for you and, even if you have given birth before, what happened to you last time may not happen this time. So, rather than thinking of your document as a 'plan', consider it an open-minded and flexible list of what you would *prefer* to happen.

Before writing your birth plan, read as much as possible about labour and birth. If you can, watch a documentary-style delivery on TV. (There is even a great episode of *ER* – Season 1, Episode 19 – that includes nearly all the major labour complications and which doctors now use for training!) You should also find out about Caesarean sections (which make up around 25–30 per cent of births in Great Britain), so that you can understand why they are necessary and what the procedure entails. This will help you to remain calm if a decision to perform one needs to be made quickly. Equally, it will be reassuring to know that the expression 'emergency Caesarean' does not always mean a life-or-death situation, but rather an operation that is not planned and does not have a pre-designated start time (*see* Chapter 6, p. 204). Even if you

THE ROLE OF YOUR HEALTHCARE PROFESSIONALS IN THE BIRTH

Sometimes, in planning the perfect birth – just as in planning the perfect party or wedding – the reason behind your preparations can get forgotten or lost among the detail. It is important to remember that the aim of the medical professionals is to ensure that you and your baby are safe and healthy throughout the labour, delivery and afterwards. So, although your midwife and obstetrician will try to adhere to your birth plan as much as possible, sometimes a medical situation arises that needs a quick decision to be made. While this could lead you to feel that you have no control over what is happening, bear in mind that they are acting with your and your baby's best interests at heart. Nonetheless, it is your right to seek and to receive an explanation – even after the event – for why a certain decision was taken and medical staff will always try to offer this before you even need to ask. When time allows you to be involved in decisions, you should listen to professional advice, even if this goes against the preferences listed in your birth plan.

have chosen to have a home birth, you still need to inform yourself about this in case you develop any complications.

You can start to discuss your birth preferences with your healthcare professionals from about the 30th week of your pregnancy. The list can cover anything you like, but remember: the longer the plan, the less likely it is that your expectations will be met (as staff will simply get lost in the detail), so try to limit yourself to a page of bullet points at most. Elements you could consider for your birth plan include:

- outlining who your birth partner(s) is and what they will be doing to support you
- what you like to be called
- what atmosphere you want in the room (e.g. quiet with minimal disturbances, background music, dim lighting)
- pain relief preferences (e.g. you want to try to labour without pharmacalogical methods but have not ruled out an epidural)
- if you are happy for your obstetrician or midwife to suggest artificial rupture of the membranes if your labour is taking a while to progress (*see* Chapter 6, p. 193)
- whether you have strong feelings about an episiotomy or a tear (*see* Chapter 6, p. 174)
- whether your partner wants to cut the umbilical cord (many partners change their mind when they see blood!)
- whether you want to receive an oxytocin injection to speed up the delivery of the placenta.

Depending on what else you decide to include in your birth plan, you may also need to find out hospital policy on, for example, breech birth, birthing pools (specifically, whether the midwives prefer you to get out of the pool to deliver), permitted or preferred positions for delivery, pain relief (e.g. whether there is a 24-hour epidural service), eating and drinking during labour and wearing your own clothes. See also Chapter 1, p. 19 for questions to ask when choosing your hospital. Your birth partner should also familiarise themselves with your birth plan, or even help you draft it, so that they are aware of what it contains and can try to ensure that it is followed whenever possible.

> **I decided that, rather than have a birth plan, I would just go with how I felt at the time. You just don't know what's going to happen and I didn't want to set myself up for disappointment, although I did request that Finn was put straight onto me at birth if all was OK.** TRACY

Whether you are planning a home or a hospital birth, you will need to gather together some equipment for use during labour, as well as things for the baby when it is born. If you organise yourself at home in advance of your due date, you will be prepared for birth whenever it may occur.

Packing a bag

If you are having a hospital birth, you will need to pack a bag of personal items and baby things to take with you. In fact, I suggest taking two separate bags or having a larger bag that is divided into two sections: one for before and the other for after the birth. If you are planning a home birth, I would still advise you to pack a bag in case you need a hospital transfer, as trying to think what you may need at that point could be stressful. Make sure that your bag(s) is packed by 36 weeks at the latest, in case you go into labour earlier than expected.

Check in advance what the hospital will supply in terms of towels, pillows and other necessities. Try not to worry that you may have forgotten something, as your partner, family or friends can always bring it in later. The following list is not exhaustive but is intended to be a useful guide:

Labour bag
- an old nightdress/large T-shirt
- dressing gown, slippers, socks (feet often get cold in labour)
- lip salve, face spray, flannel
- water bottle, juice cartons with straws (easier to drink from)
- snacks (for energy)
- reading matter/MP3 player/anything to help pass the time
- massage oil, TENS machine (if using)
- specialist equipment, such as a birthing ball or stool (if desired and not provided by the hospital)
- camera/camcorder
- music to play as you labour (hospitals prefer you to use their music systems unless yours is battery-operated or wi-fi)

Bag for after the birth
- nightwear (front-opening if you are planning to breastfeed)
- toiletries, hairbrush
- maternity bra and breast pads (if breastfeeding)
- extra-absorbent sanitary towels and disposable knickers

- ear plugs, eye mask (labour wards are bright, noisy places)
- loose fitting/maternity clothes to wear when you leave hospital
- make-up!
- baby clothes: two sleepsuits and vests, plus a hat (essential for immediately after birth to help regulate temperature)
- small pack of newborn-size disposable nappies
- zinc or other barrier cream for the baby's bottom
- cotton wool (for cleaning your baby)
- outdoor suit or shawl/baby blanket for going home.

Avoid wearing your best clothes in case of leaks and remember that hospitals can be very warm, so you probably won't need cardigans or jumpers for either you or the baby. However, when you take the baby home, they are likely to need an outdoor suit or shawl/blanket, a hat and mittens. If you are travelling by car, you must use a baby seat (required by law – see p. 142), but it may be easier to have your partner fetch this afterwards rather than take it in to the labour ward with you.

Preparing for a home birth

One of the advantages of giving birth at home is that you can move from room to room during labour as your mood and needs change. However, it is a good idea to choose one place in which to deliver and, if it is practical, to prepare this in advance. A room that is near to a bathroom is best, and it should be warm, so that your baby doesn't get cold when they first emerge into the outside world. If you have pets, make sure the space is clean and that they can be kept out of the room.

If you are planning to use your bed, check that the midwife can have easy access to you from all sides. Your mattress (and bedding, if applicable) should be protected with plenty of plastic sheeting, as should the floor and whatever you are going to sit on (chairs, stools and so on) – your midwife will provide large, disposable mats when you deliver, which will absorb any fluids. A bucket or bowl in case you are sick might be useful. There should be a hard surface somewhere in the room (the floor will do) on which the midwife can resuscitate the baby, should it be necessary. This should be near an electric socket to enable a bright light source (e.g. a desk lamp) and the endotracheal suction catheter to be plugged in. If this lamp is easily moveable, the midwife can also use it to examine you during labour and to do any stitching following the birth. A stool or chair for her to use is also a good idea, but it should be at the same level as your bed.

YOUR OTHER CHILDREN

If you have other children, you will need to decide whether you want them to be present at the birth, waiting nearby in another room or taken care of elsewhere. Young children may be upset or frightened at the sight and sound of labour, particularly if they see you in pain. If they remain at home but in another room, you might find that they want to see you or your birth partner at a time that is not convenient and this could be distressing for them and may distract you during the birthing process. So, it makes sense to have another adult in the house to take care of them.

If you are hiring a birthing pool, make sure you do this well in advance of the due date and check that it can fit in your car, otherwise you will have to pay for delivery. Check that the room it will be placed in is large enough: it will be surrounded by plastic sheeting and there should also be plenty of space around the pool for you, your midwife and your birthing partner to move around. If it is to be placed upstairs, you may want to consider whether your floorboards can support the weight of the pool once it contains water and occupants. Bear in mind that pools often take a considerable time to fill – and to empty! – so allow for this when your labour begins.

Have plenty of pillows or cushions available – large floor cushions, a bean bag or a birthing ball can be very comfortable to use while labour progresses. The clothes and personal items that you may require during and after labour, both for you and your baby, are listed opposite. If you gather everything together in one or two bags in advance of your due date, as you would if you were having your baby in hospital, you won't have to round it all up once labour has actually started. And if you do need to be transferred to hospital at any point, you will already have everything organised.

Finally, if your labour begins at night, leave any outside lights on and gates unlocked to allow the midwife easy access.

What your midwife will provide

At around 36 weeks, your midwife will visit your home and may bring some basics for the birth. These vary from one midwife to another, but could include anything from sterile pads and incontinence bed mats to vitamin K to keep in the fridge. Once you are actually in labour, the midwife will bring all other essential medical equipment and instruments, as well as certain pain-relieving drugs. However, she will not have any form of electronic fetal monitoring (EFM) or be able to administer an epidural.

Final tasks

As your due date approaches, it makes sense to put in place some measures that will help things go smoothly. First and foremost, you should ensure that you and your birth partner have programmed the numbers of your GP and midwife (and doula, if you have hired one) into your phones and, if you are having a hospital birth, the number of the maternity unit (usually displayed on the front of your hand-held notes). In addition, you need to make a written list of these and other useful telephone numbers and ensure that this is always to hand (and that your partner has this list as well) – this is in case you need someone else to ring them and you don't have your own phone handy. These may include the numbers of a taxi firm, your partner's various contact details and those of family and friends, so that you can notify them about the birth and/or arrange for them to help (e.g. look after your other children). Your hospital notes should also be with you at all times when you go out, as you could go into labour at any time.

Secondly, make sure you know where to go in the hospital and, importantly, where the night entrance is, to avoid having to work this out when in labour. Plan your route to the hospital and how long this is likely to take, bearing in mind rush-hour traffic, if relevant. Find out whether you can be driven up to the main entrance to get dropped off, where you can park (if being driven) and whether you will need change for ticket machines.

Finally, stock the freezer and store cupboard with food so that you don't have go shopping as soon as you get home! Even if you never normally use them, ready-meals are a godsend for the first few weeks after the birth and there are several companies that will deliver healthy frozen meals, too (see Useful Resources). An economical way to fill your freezer is to cook double the amount at each meal for a couple of weeks before your due date and freeze half for later use. Also, if you have never done so before, set up internet grocery shopping so that everything can be delivered to save time and effort both now and after the baby is born.

DID YOU KNOW…?

To save being swamped by clothes for your newborn, ask anyone who would like to give a gift to contribute towards home delivery of ready-meals – worth their weight in gold!

EQUIPMENT FOR YOUR BABY

There is a huge range of equipment for babies, as well as a vast array of tempting products aimed at parents. However, much of it is expensive and far from essential, but you can get some idea of the most useful things by talking to other people who have had babies. Borrow some of the more short-lived items if you can, as the newborn phase is surprisingly short and, before you know it, you will have to invest in more equipment for your growing baby.

Car seats

It is illegal (not to mention dangerous) to carry a baby in your arms in a car or taxi, so you will need a rear-facing infant car seat if you ever travel this way. These are best bought new, but if you have been given one that has been used before, check that it has not been damaged (e.g. in an accident) and that all the straps are fully functional. Rear-facing car seats usually have a handle to allow you to carry your baby in and out of the car, which is useful if they have fallen asleep. They can also double-up as a baby chair for when you are out or at home – but make sure the harness is fastened at all times. Check that the model you have selected fits in your car and complies to current safety standards. Infant car seats must not be placed in the front passenger seat if an airbag is enabled, as a baby can be seriously injured if it inflates.

Prams, pushchairs and buggies

A pram, pushchair or buggy will be one of your main purchases – and one you may use for a couple of years – so it is worth investing some time into researching this. Understanding the difference between them is one of your first tasks, but even within these categories you may need an expert to explain the different types of design. If this is your first baby, you may want to consider a model that converts into one that can accommodate two infants.

Put some thought into what is going to best suit your budget and lifestyle: for example, consider whether you will primarily be walking about (in which case a sturdy model with plenty of storage for your changing bag and shopping might

be best) or taking the car or public transport (when a lighter, easy-to-collapse one will be easier to use). Before you commit to buying, try to speak to as many people as you can, so that they can tell you about the pros and cons of the type they have. Even if you eventually plan to purchase online, it is worth visiting a specialist shop or department store so that you

SUGGESTED EQUIPMENT

The following items are ones you may need in the first few weeks of your baby's life and many of these will last you for the first year and beyond:

- rear-facing infant car seat
- pram/pushchair/buggy with rain hood (and parasol, if a spring/summer baby)
- outdoor blanket
- Moses basket/crib/carrycot (optional)
- cot
- two top sheets, two bottom sheets, two cellular blankets (all cotton) for each size of mattress
- baby sleeping bag (optional)
- changing mat
- plastic bin or bucket with lid (for used nappies) or nappy disposal system (some have in-built deodorisers)
- nappies (cloth or disposable)
- nappy-changing bag
- several muslin cloths
- bottles and slow-flow teats (2–4 if breastfeeding, at least 6 if bottle-feeding)
- sterilising equipment
- feeding cushion (optional)
- baby bath
- bath support (optional)
- bath thermometer (optional)
- baby carrier/sling
- baby chair
- baby monitor
- baby thermometer

See Chapter 8, pp. 244–5 and p. 250 for more information on the equipment for feeding and bathing.

can understand how your chosen pram, pushchair or buggy works (including how you activate the brake). Wherever and whatever you buy, ensure that you and your partner have *personally* erected and collapsed it several times rather than just watching the sales assistant do it – you would be surprised at how many people cannot remember how to do theirs just when they need to put their newborn baby in it. You should aim to be able to erect/collapse it and put it into the car with one hand, as your other is usually holding the baby. Furthermore, if yours is a winter birth, look for a system that can keep your baby protected in bad weather.

Prams

A pram is a chassis supporting a carrycot that can be removed entirely and is deep enough to accommodate a mattress. Some models, known as 'travel systems', also come with infant car seats that attach to the chassis. Your baby needs to be able to lie completely flat for the first few months, even when being taken for a walk, so a pram with an integral carrycot is both good for your baby and practical – it can be used for night-time sleeping, so is useful if you are limited for space at home (it will take up less room than a separate crib and pushchair). Prams are sturdier than pushchairs and buggies but can, as a result, be very expensive. However, they are suitable from birth onwards and, because they usually convert into a pushchair to allow the baby to sit up, will last well into the toddler years.

Pushchairs

A pushchair has a soft, padded body that usually cannot be removed from the wheels and is forward-facing. The movable back allows your baby to lie down or, when they are older, to sit up. While your baby can lie more or less flat, a pushchair is not suitable for night-time sleeping because it cannot accommodate a mattress. They are lighter to manoeuvre than prams and are more substantial and comfortable than buggies, and are suitable from birth through the toddler years.

Buggies

Designs for buggies (also called strollers) are constantly evolving, and many are now marketed as suitable for newborns. Babies can lie almost flat, but are lower to the ground and less shielded from the elements. Lighter and less sturdy than a pram or pushchair, a buggy is easier to push around, but may not be as durable. Buggies have a simple 'umbrella' mechanism for folding away and are useful if space in your home or car is tight. They take up less room in shops, cafes and restaurants (where they are particularly useful in allowing your baby/toddler to drift off while you enjoy your meal). However, generally speaking, they are usually better from six months onwards when your baby can almost sit up.

" We didn't see much point in spending a lot of money on things that only get used for a few weeks or months, and we're lucky to have several friends with children just a couple of years older than ours who could pass things on to us. " DIANE

143

Moses baskets/cribs, carrycots and cots

The decision as to whether to buy a Moses basket or crib, use a pram carrycot or go straight to a full-size cot is a personal one. A Moses basket will only be suitable for the first three months (potentially less if yours is a big baby) and cribs and carrycots for up to six, but they can be carried around easily, which can be useful in the early days when you want to keep an eye on your baby. A cot will last at least a couple of years, until your baby is in a proper bed. Whatever you decide to use, the mattress must fit snugly to the sides without any gaps; if you have been given a second-hand basket, crib or cot, you should invest in a new mattress so that you know it is free from dust or damp (which can increase the risk of Sudden Infant Death Syndrome, or 'cot death' – *see* Chapter 8, p. 255) and to give your baby the best spine support (a used one might be moulded to a previous baby's shape). If you use a cot bumper to protect your baby from banging against the bars, make sure it is firmly attached and does not have any bows or objects that could be detached or become a strangulation hazard when they are a little older.

Bedding and baby sleeping bags

Use only cotton bedding: this is breathable, warm and will not irritate a baby's very sensitive skin in the way that wool can do. Many parents swear by sleeping bags made specially for babies. Made out of breathable cotton, they ensure that the babies cannot wriggle out of their bedclothes in the middle of the night, get cold and wake up. If you decide to use one, choose the right size for your baby and the appropriate tog for the season.

Nappies and nappy-changing

You should face the fact that changing nappies is going to be a large part of your life from now on and so the quicker and easier you can do this the better – in the first few months, a baby's nappy needs changing up to ten times a day. Your principal decision will be whether to use cloth nappies (also called 'reusable' or 'real' nappies) or disposable ones, and the debate about which system is the best and the most environmentally friendly rages on (*see* Useful Resources for more information).

There is no doubt that disposable nappies are convenient, but they are expensive, particularly as you will need them for two to three years. And even if they are biodegradable, they do contribute significantly to landfill. All the different brands are broadly similar and make a range of sizes to fit babies as they grow (some even market different types for boys and girls). You will also need nappy sacks to seal used nappies in to contain the odour.

> **DID YOU KNOW…?**
> Muslin cloths are a parent's best friend: they can be used as anything from a bib, a mop cloth, a privacy shield when you are breastfeeding in public, an emergency nappy – the list is endless!

Investing in a cloth system (i.e. waterproof outer cover, liners and at least twenty shaped cloths) will require significant outlay at the start (although traditional towelling squares are cheaper), but will last you through one baby and often another as well. Using cloth nappies may well endear you to your local council, but does require more work: they tend to be more prone to leaks, the cloth is less absorbent than disposables and so they need changing more frequently and, of course, they must be washed (energy, detergent and water use will also impact upon the environment). While there are nappy-laundering companies that will deliver clean nappies and take away the dirty ones, this is not a cheap option and you will need somewhere to store the soiled nappies (odourlessly!) until they are collected. If you cannot decide which system to use, you could buy a few of each sort and see which suits you best or opt to use a combination of the two: cloth nappies at home and disposables as a back-up and when you are out and about or on holiday.

Creating a changing station

Having a designated space with all the things you need to change your baby's nappy – in other words, a 'changing station' – will help speed up the routine. You don't need a special changing table. All that is really necessary is a wipeable changing mat and a plastic bin or bucket with a lid for storing the dirty nappies until you are ready to wash them (in the case of cloth nappies) or empty disposables into the outside bin. Keep cotton wool, nappies and barrier cream stocked up and to hand, as well as a couple of spare changes of clothes for your baby in case of leaks.

Nappy-changing bag

A nappy-changing bag will be your constant companion when you go out. It doesn't have to be a specially constructed changing bag, which can sometimes be bought to match your pram or travel system, but the advantage of these is that they have different compartments for storing items such as bottles, creams and spare clothes, and small changing mats are incorporated in them.

Baby carriers and slings/papooses

Baby carriers and slings (or papooses) can be a very good way of carrying a baby, both outdoors and in the home, as they leave you with both hands free. Baby carriers are designed to fit on the front of your body, with straps over both shoulders and round your waist (those that you wear on your back are only suitable for older babies who can support themselves). To start with, the baby can face inwards towards your body, but can be positioned outwards when they have more head control. Ensure that the one you choose has good head support for your baby and wide straps that don't dig in to your shoulders.

A baby sling or papoose is a piece of fabric that is worn across the body, generally over one shoulder, to form a pouch for the baby – make sure you know how to carry your baby safely inside it in order to protect their spine. Slings/papooses can be useful for supporting the baby while breastfeeding (and can act as a privacy screen when doing so in public), but you may find them cumbersome to use when your baby grows bigger.

Baby chairs

A baby chair provides a place of safety for your baby, which also allows them to see what is going on around them and to interact/play with you. Broadly speaking, a chair can either be a swing/rocker, suitable up to 11 kg, or a bouncing seat, which can be used until your baby can sit up at around six months and is more portable. Their swinging/bouncing motion can help to soothe and settle a baby, and some play music, too. Most are suitable from soon after birth, although you should not leave your baby in them for long periods of time.

Baby monitors

A baby monitor is, essentially, an electronic device that enables you to hear your baby's sounds when you are not in the same room. However, designs are becoming ever more sophisticated, with some models offering webcams and two-way talk back so that you can see and speak to your baby, too. Consequently there is a wide range of prices, so ask a specialist shop for advice and/or research on the internet.

BABY CLOTHES

There is no doubt that buying baby clothes is one of the great pleasures of being pregnant. There are so many thoroughly cute and appealing outfits out there that it is extremely difficult not to succumb and buy enough to fill a whole wardrobe. However, try your best to resist buying too many, firstly, because you will be given lots of outfits as presents, and, secondly, because babies grow out of their clothes astonishingly fast and may not even get a chance to wear some of them. In fact, some newborns are already too large even at birth to fit into the smallest-size of baby clothing.

Make sure that whatever you do buy is fully machine-washable and, preferably, can be put in the tumble dryer. Use only natural fabrics, ideally cotton, particularly for any item of clothing that is in direct contact with your baby's skin (because it is very sensitive) and avoid anything that is fiddly to put on or fasten. The following items are the essentials:

▸ 4–6 vests
▸ 4–6 all-in-one sleepsuits (babygros)
▸ 2 pairs of socks/booties
▸ 2 pairs of scratch mittens
▸ cardigan
▸ outer jacket or coat
▸ hat (fleece for colder days, cotton sunhat in summer)
▸ all-in-one coat with hood and booties (if a winter baby)
▸ gloves (if a winter baby)

Baby thermometer

A special baby thermometer is worth buying in advance of the birth, so that you don't have to rush out to get one the first time your baby is unwell. The simplest to use are ones that can be placed in your baby's ear or against their forehead to give a digital reading of your baby's temperature.

❝ **The best piece of equipment I bought was a baby monitor with a camera so that I could see my baby. It's extremely reassuring to see him in his cot and know that everything is OK.** ❞ SARAH

As term approaches, your baby will start to move into position ready for birth. From around 30 weeks, your GP or midwife will usually assess this by palpating your abdomen. This information, which is written in your antenatal notes, can indicate the approximate timing of the birth and, possibly, the method of delivery.

There are three elements to take into consideration when your baby's position is assessed:

▸ **'lie'**: whether the baby is longitudinal (vertical), transverse (horizontal) or oblique (diagonal) in your uterus
▸ **presentation**: which part of the baby lies closest to the cervix and therefore the birth canal (as this will be the part that 'presents' itself first during the birth)
▸ **engagement**: when the head or bottom starts to descend, or 'engage', inside the pelvic cavity.

Lie

At term, 99 per cent of babies lie longitudinally in the uterus, with either their head or their bottom near to the cervix. The remaining one per cent are lying either horizontally (transverse) or diagonally (oblique). All non-longitudinal labours should take place in hospital and, unless the baby turns at the last minute, are highly likely to be delivered by Caesarean section.

Presentation

There are two presentations in a longitudinal lie: cephalic (where the baby is head down), which accounts for 95 per cent of presentations at term, and breech (where the baby is bottom down), which accounts for 4 per cent; in a non-longitudinal lie there will be no presenting part. However, the exact position in a cephalic presentation is an important factor, because certain ones may make labour slower. In pregnancy, the term 'position' refers to how the baby's spine and the occiput are placed relative to the inner wall of the uterus – 'occiput' is the anatomical term for the posterior (back) portion of the head or skull. There are several different positions and your baby may take up all of these during the last week of pregnancy and in early labour:

▸ **anterior (in front):** the baby's spine is lying against your abdomen, and the baby is, in effect, looking backwards
▸ **posterior (to the back):** the baby's spine is lying against yours, and your baby is facing the front of your abdomen, looking forwards
▸ **lateral (to the side):** the baby's spine is to one side or the other, the most common position.

In anterior (occiput-anterior, or OA) and posterior positions (occiput-posterior, or OP), the baby is usually facing a little to the right or to the left; it is rare for them to be facing directly towards the back (direct anterior) or front (direct posterior). All lateral descriptions refer to the mother's left or right.

The anterior position is ideal for a cephalic labour, and this, together with a lateral position, is considered normal. When a baby is in a posterior position, with its back towards yours, a first labour may be slower: this is because the presenting part is the widest part of the head, not the occiput (which would be preferable), and the cervix tends to dilate more slowly as the fetal head does not fit so closely. This position is also associated with a slower descent through the birth canal. See Chapter 6, p. 196 for more information on prolonged labour. Most babies do, nevertheless, rotate and are born face backwards, although this often takes longer in a first labour. However, it is still possible for the baby to be born face forwards. See p. 150 for diagrams to illustrate the various positions in a cephalic presentation.

Around 30 per cent of premature babies (those born before 37 weeks) are breech, but even if a baby is breech at 36 weeks, they can still turn to a cephalic presentation, even though space is tighter during the last few weeks of pregnancy. Second and subsequent babies are more likely to be breech, because there is usually more room inside the uterus (as the muscles have stretched once already), which enables them

DID YOU KNOW...?

Human beings are the only mammals to deliver their babies in the OA position (facing backwards). All other mammals deliver their babies in the OP position (facing forwards) so that the babies can climb up onto the abdomen unaided.

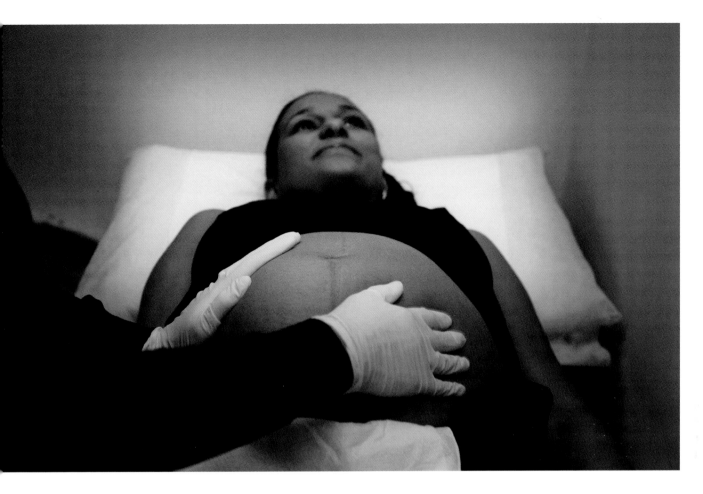

to keep changing position right through to the end of the pregnancy. Breech presentation is also more common in women with fibroids and in those carrying very large or very small babies. See Chapter 6, p. 202 for further information on the types of breech presentation and vaginal delivery of breech.

By the last month of pregnancy, you will be having antenatal visits every two weeks, and at each one, your baby's head will be palpated to assess how far it is engaged. Usually, an external abdominal examination is enough to note this progress but, occasionally, an internal examination or an ultrasound scan will be required if there is any doubt about whether the head or the bottom are presenting. Even if it is confirmed that your baby's head is engaged, this does not mean that you are about to go into labour, especially if this is your first baby and you are still in the 36th week. It simply means that your baby is moving into position ready for birth.

YOUR BABY'S HEAD

Although your baby's head at term is smaller relative to the rest of the body than it was earlier in the pregnancy, its circumference is as large as the abdomen and it still is one of the largest parts of the baby's body. In order for the head to be able to pass safely down the birth canal during labour, it needs to mould firstly to the shape of your pelvis and then to the birth canal and vagina. This is possible because the skull bones of a baby's head are quite soft at this stage and also do not fuse together until a baby is much older. The bones are therefore able to overlap as the baby's head gradually descends through the pelvic cavity and the birth canal. Variations in shape at birth will invariably return to the typical oval within a relatively short space of time.

Positions in a cephalic presentation

Below are the most common positions in a cephalic (head down) presentation, together with their rate of occurrence. It is rare for a baby to face directly backwards or forwards.

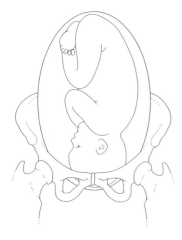

Left occipito-lateral: 40 per cent
The baby's back and occiput are on the left side of your uterus, with the spine at a right-angle to yours.

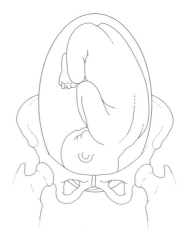

Left occipito-anterior: 12 per cent
The baby's back is nearer the front of your abdomen, but is still on the left side of your uterus.

Left occipito-posterior: 3 per cent
The baby's back and occiput are towards your spine and on the left of the uterus.

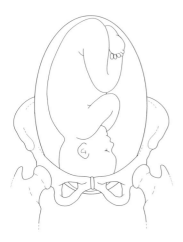

Right occipito-lateral: 25 per cent
The baby's back and occiput are on the right side of your uterus, with the spine at a right-angle to yours.

Right occipito-anterior: 10 per cent
The baby's back and occiput are towards the front and right of your uterus.

Right occipito-posterior: 10 per cent
The baby's back and occiput are towards your spine and on the right of the uterus.

Engagement

Engagement is the term used to describe the baby's descent into the pelvic cavity. In first pregnancies, this tends to start at around 36 weeks, whereas in subsequent pregnancies, engagement is usually later and may not even occur until the onset of labour itself. Early engagement in a first pregnancy happens because the uterine muscles are tighter and exert greater downward-pressure on the baby. There are several levels of engagement, and these will be noted in your medical notes (*see* Box).

Not engaged More than half the presenting baby's head is above the pelvis brim, so it is 'not engaged'.

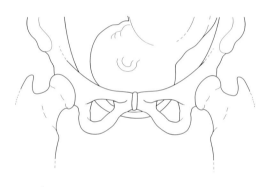

Engaged When more than half the presenting baby's head has descended into the pelvic cavity, the baby is 'engaged'.

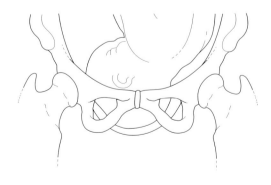

YOUR NOTES EXPLAINED

You may be intrigued by the many abbreviations used in your hand-held antenatal notes. The ones relating to your baby's position in the uterus and level of engagement are:

Lie
- ► **L/Long:** longitudinal
- ► **T/Tr:** transverse
- ► **Obl:** oblique

Presentation
- ► **C/Ceph:** cephalic
- ► **B/Br:** breech

Position
- ► **LOL:** left occipito-lateral
- ► **ROL:** right occipito-lateral
- ► **LOA:** left occipito-anterior
- ► **ROA:** right occipito-anterior
- ► **ROP:** right occipito-posterior
- ► **LOP:** left occipito-posterior

Engagement
- ► **Free or ⁵/s:** can move baby's head/breech
- ► **³/s:** not engaged
- ► **²/s:** engaged

Being familiar with your hospital and its equipment will help you feel reassured when you arrive to give birth, even if you have already had a tour of your particular birth setting. If you have planned a home birth, you may need to transfer to hospital for greater medical support, so it is still useful to know what to expect.

The midwifery unit

Birthing rooms in midwifery units (*see* Chapter 1, p. 18) are furnished with the aim of helping women feel relaxed and comfortable while they are labouring and after the birth. They often contain a birthing pool, soft mats, a birthing ball to sit/lean on during labour and at least one comfortable chair. Many have en suite bathroom facilities and they may have double beds to allow you and your partner to stay together as a family. As gas and air is the only pain relief available, the room does not contain the usual medical equipment seen in a hospital delivery suite.

The obstetric unit

All obstetric units have delivery rooms, one per labouring woman, which each contain the items listed below. Also in the unit are operating theatres in case a Caesarean section is required (see opposite).

The delivery bed

The height of the delivery bed is adjustable and the end can be removed for delivery, if necessary. Slots for inserting leg rests are visible on the side. These are required for more detailed internal examinations, for assisted deliveries and stitching of episiotomies and perineal tears (*see* Chapter 6, pp. 198 and 174).

Sphygmomanometer

A sphygmomanometer is an instrument that measures your blood pressure and it will be used every fifteen minutes if you have an epidural. It can be wall-mounted or attached to a trolley so that it can be moved from room to room.

Cardiotocograph

The strength, frequency and duration of your contractions are measured by a cardiotocograph (CTG); this machine also records your baby's heart rate by providing detailed electronic fetal monitoring (EFM). The information is then visible both in the form of a paper print-out and flashing red numbers on the front of the machine. Although it can be used in pregnancy if there is some concern about the baby's well-being, a CTG is mostly required in labour and the majority of women have some form of EFM.

There are two sorts of EFM, external and internal. External EFM is frequently used at some stages during labour. Two fabric-type bands are secured around your abdomen, and a device is attached to each of these bands. One picks up contractions, one the fetal heart rate. Continuous fetal monitoring is avoided, if possible, because this can restrict your movements, which is known to increase the need for epidural pain relief in labour. That said, many hospitals now have remote-controlled CTG monitors (a form of EFM) that enable you to walk around.

Internal EFM is used less often, in situations where, for example, it is difficult to get an accurate reading of a baby's heart rate. This can happen with a very active fetus or if a mother is overweight. Internal monitoring does require the membranes to have ruptured and the cervix to be sufficiently dilated in order for a small electrode, connected at one end to the CTG machine, to be clipped to the baby's head (or bottom, if breech). This will be painless for mother and baby, although the baby may be left with a small scratch mark on their head/bottom, which will disappear within a few days of the birth.

Piped gas and air

At the head of the bed in all delivery rooms is a mix of oxygen and nitrous oxide, commonly called 'gas and air', delivered via a mouthpiece to give pain relief (*see* Chapter 6, p. 181).

Mobile drip stand

Fluids or drugs might be administered intravenously via a drip during or after labour. A saline solution is used to maintain hydration and to optimise blood pressure, particularly if you have opted for an epidural. If your labour is being induced or augmented, syntocinon will be given via a drip to start or strengthen contractions (*see* Chapter 6, p. 193).

Baby resuscitation trolley

A mobile trolley with an overhead heater containing items such as piped oxygen is always ready for use in a delivery room to provide immediate and short-term assistance for the baby,

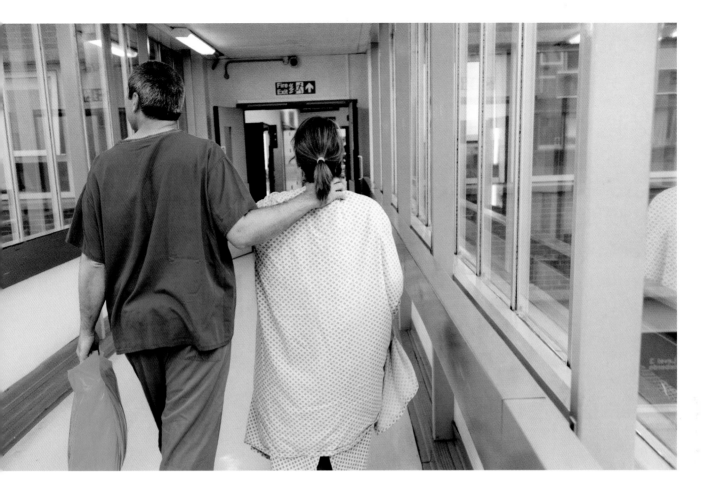

in the event that the newborn takes time to breathe alone or needs to be warmed up. Although these procedures can sound alarming, they are performed routinely and mean that your baby remains in sight within the room. See Chapter 6, p. 172 for what happens if your baby doesn't breathe at birth.

Baby cot
A mobile cot can be used for your baby when they are not in your arms.

The operating theatre
Caesarean sections and some assisted deliveries are performed in an operating theatre and some of the equipment found in obstetric units, such as a baby resuscitation trolley, are also to be seen here. If you are having a Caesarean section, there will be a trolley carrying a tray of instruments needed for the operation; if yours is an assisted delivery, the trolley will contain a ventouse machine and forceps. There will also be a stool for your partner to sit on by your side (at the head end!).

Operating table
All operating tables can tilt. This enables you to lie on your back for the delivery without compressing the inferior vena cava, the large vein that carries blood from the lower half of the body back to the heart, which can decrease oxygen flow to the placenta and compromise the baby. If you have arrived at the theatre on a wheeled bed, medical staff will work together to lift and transfer you to the table.

Anaesthetic machine
The anaesthetic machine records your blood pressure, your heart rate and rhythm, and your oxygen saturation (how much oxygen the blood is carrying). It can produce print-outs of these readings to be added to your records. An anaesthetist will be in charge of checking this machine and monitoring you during your time in theatre.

Intravenous pumps
There are different pumps to administer intravenous drugs both during and after delivery. These include, for example, insulin pumps for diabetic patients; syntocinon, if used to help contractions; and syntocinon infusion (containing a higher concentration of the drug), to encourage rapid and sustained contractions after delivery. In some cases, women are given a patient-controlled analgesia (PCA) pump to control their pain relief themselves in the immediate post-surgery period.

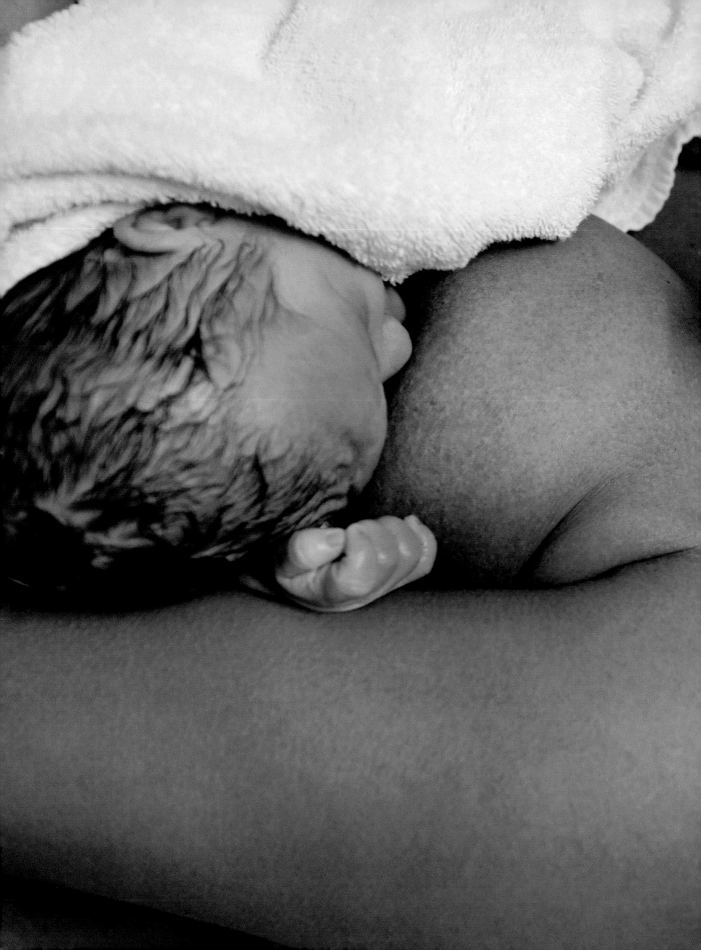

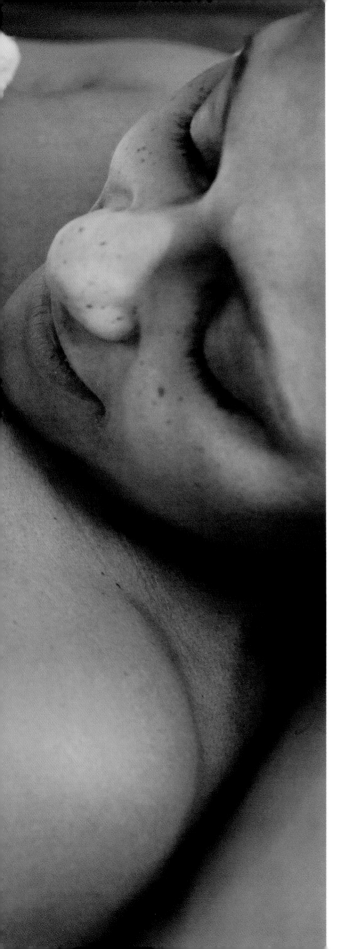

Birth

The birth can be the most exciting but also, for many women, the most daunting part of pregnancy. Even for women who have previously had a baby, no two births are the same. This is why I believe it is important to be as informed as possible in advance, and to understand that anything can happen, because that will help you to cope with the unpredictability of giving birth.

PREPARING FOR LABOUR

It is entirely natural to feel concerned or even fearful about labour, even when this is not your first baby. But learning how to recognise the signs of labour and how it normally progresses – as well has what happens when it doesn't go to plan – can help you approach it with confidence.

The three stages of labour

Labour is divided, medically speaking, into three stages. The first stage lasts from when contractions begin to when it is time to push the baby out. This stage is further divided into three phases:

▸ **early (latent) phase:** when the cervix effaces (softens and thins out) before starting to dilate (open) and contractions are first felt; continues until the cervix is 2–3 cm dilated (see p.160)
▸ **active/established phase:** when contractions are regular (every five minutes) and increasingly strong; lasts from the end of the early phase to when the cervix is fully dilated to 10 cm (see p.162)
▸ **transition phase:** often occurs between full dilation and the need to push the baby out; can last a few minutes or up to an hour, contractions continuing strongly and frequently (see p.163).

The second stage is characterised by strong, regular contractions that push the baby down the birth canal and out through the vaginal opening (see pp.166–7). This stage, which ends with the delivery of the baby, usually lasts between one and two hours, particularly with first deliveries, but it can be as short as ten minutes, especially in subsequent pregnancies.

The third stage is when the placenta is delivered (see p.176), usually lasting between a few minutes and an hour.

> **DID YOU KNOW…?**
> During a contraction, the uterus, which is like a giant muscle, becomes compressed, so that the baby gradually gets pushed down through the birth canal.

Signs that labour is imminent

We still do not know what actually triggers labour, and so it is not possible to predict accurately when it will begin. However, there are certain physical signs that indicate that labour *might* be imminent and these are listed below. It is worth clarifying three things, nonetheless. Firstly, that while one or more of these physical indications can occur, there is no particular order in which they might do so. Secondly, that experiencing one of these does not guarantee that labour is about to begin. Thirdly, some women do not get any of these signs before their actual contractions start.

Furthermore, if this is not your first pregnancy, remember that each labour can follow a different pattern from the others. The fact that your waters broke last time just before the start of your contractions, for example, will have no relevance as to what might happen this time round. As ever, labour is unpredictable. For information about your emotional preparations for motherhood, in particular the 'nesting' instinct, see Chapter 9, p.276.

Increase in Braxton Hicks contractions

Towards the onset of labour, Braxton Hicks contractions (see Chapter 4, p.115) become much more frequent and more noticeable – indeed, it can be difficult for first-time mothers to know the difference between these and the mild contractions of early labour. However, Braxton Hicks contractions occur only occasionally (no more than about twice an hour), do not escalate in strength and fade gradually; proper labour contractions occur regularly and build up in intensity before fading quickly. So, keep an eye on the nature of your contractions: a rule of thumb is that if you can talk through a contraction, you are not yet in labour.

Having a 'show'

Throughout your pregnancy, a thick plug of mucus, located at the lower end of the cervix, has prevented any bacteria from reaching the uterus. As term approaches, the cervix begins to change shape in preparation for effacement and dilation, which often causes the plug to become dislodged. This mucus, known as the 'show', is often a little blood-stained (either with fresh, bright red blood, or brownish, older blood), because it was attached to small blood vessels. Its appearance is not, however, a guarantee that labour is about to begin – it might still be a few days, if not weeks, away! – but it indicates that things are moving in that direction.

Rupture of the membranes

When the amniotic fluid contained inside the membranes in your uterus begins to leak out from your cervix, this is termed a rupture of the membranes or, in common speech, your 'waters breaking'. Usually, it is the pressure of the baby's head on the dilating cervix that causes the membranes to rupture, but in about fifteen per cent of pregnancies they do so before contractions have started to dilate the cervix (although it is not known why).

What to do if your membranes rupture

It is not always obvious, particularly if this is your first labour, if your waters have broken. There may be quite a large amount of liquid, in which case you will know at once; more often than not, however, it is just a trickle of fluid, which could be mistaken for a leak of urine (which often happens in the last trimester – see Chapter 4, p.128). If you are in doubt, put on a sanitary towel: if the liquid is clear or pale in colour and is odourless, it is amniotic fluid. In addition, the leakage will continue steadily, particularly every time you move, irrespective of whether you try to control it, whereas if you were leaking urine, the flow would eventually stop.

If you think your membranes have ruptured, you will need to be examined by a midwife, particularly if the amniotic fluid has a greenish or black tinge, as this can indicate that your baby is secreting meconium (a substance present in their digestive system) and may need to be delivered (see Box on p.194 for more information). If you are having a home birth, your midwife will visit you there to make an assessment of the membranes, but if meconium is discovered, you will need to transfer to hospital. If you are having a hospital birth, phone ahead to say that you are on your way for an examination. Have a drink and a snack before you leave in case you are there for a while, and remember to take your hand-held maternity notes with you (your birth partner can bring your hospital bag in later if you are admitted).

If, after seeing your midwife, you have been advised to stay at home or return from the hospital to await events, you need to take a few hygiene precautions, as the membranes protecting your baby in sterile amniotic fluid have now been broken and bacteria could enter your uterus, causing harm to your baby. So, if you want to have a wash, take a shower rather than a bath and when you go to the toilet, particularly if you have a bowel movement, make sure that you wipe yourself away from your vagina, because fecal contamination is one of the most common causes of vaginal infection.

Although 83 per cent of women whose membranes rupture spontaneously do go into labour within 24 hours, most obstetricians and midwives advise those whose contractions have not begun by then to have their labour induced (provided the pregnancy has progressed to at least 34 weeks) in order to minimise the risk of infection. See p.192 for more information on induction.

How do I know if I am in labour?

This is the key question! Labour is usually slower to establish in first pregnancies and recognising that it has begun is not always straightforward. Ultimately, the real sign that you are in labour is if you are experiencing defined, regular contractions, each of which increases in intensity before quickly dying away; you may also experience pain or discomfort in your lower back (rather than lower abdomen, as with Braxton Hicks) and feel the need to empty your bowels. The other sign is that the cervix is dilating, although you would need an internal examination to determine this (see p.158).

If you think your contractions are beginning, time them so that you can work out how often they are occurring and how long they are lasting for each time (see Box). Bear in mind that, particularly in the early stage of labour, the strength and frequency of contractions can vary: they may appear to be getting stronger and more frequent, only to calm down again for a while.

TIMING CONTRACTIONS

If you think you may be in labour, you (or, preferably, your birth partner) need to time both the length and the frequency of your contractions.

Using a stopwatch or watch with a second hand, jot down the times that a contraction begins and ends and then subtract one from the other in order to calculate the length. To determine the frequency, note the time one contraction starts, ending the timing when the next one begins and follow the same procedure. You don't need to monitor every single contraction – record them for a while until you notice a pattern, then start timing them again when that pattern changes. If you are feeling too distracted to make these calculations yourself, there are apps/programs for your phone/computer that are specifically designed to do this for you.

When to call your midwife or hospital

If you have any concerns or need advice and reassurance, don't hesitate to call your midwife or the hospital – that is what they are there for. It is better to speak to an experienced midwife than to worry at home on your own. If you are having a hospital birth, it is possible you will be asked to come in so that you can be examined, and most units have a triage (assessment) service for women who are unsure whether their labour has started or not. Be prepared for the fact that you may get sent home again if it is confirmed that labour is not yet established. You should always contact your midwife or hospital if:

▸ your contractions are occurring at least every five minutes
▸ your contractions are getting stronger and/or longer
▸ the pain is getting difficult for you to bear and you would like some analgesia
▸ you think your membranes have ruptured, especially if fluid is not clear
▸ there has been a change in your baby's movements or they appear to have stopped
▸ you live relatively far away from hospital or it is difficult for you to come in quickly
▸ you are showing signs of early labour and you have not yet reached 37 weeks
▸ you are passing blood, particularly if it is bright red in colour. **Call the hospital at once, as this could potentially be very serious.**

Once you think you are in labour, if you are due to give birth in hospital, try to call them in advance to let them know that you are planning to come in. This will give them time to organise a bed for you, so that you don't have to wait once you arrive. It will also allow you to discuss your symptoms with the midwife, so that you can make sure that it really is the right time for you to be admitted: there is no point in coming in too early when you could be staying comfortably at home for a little while longer.

What happens at the hospital

Once you arrive at the labour ward with your bag and your notes, you will be met and introduced to your midwife. If you have hired an independent midwife, she will probably have met you at your home in order to accompany you to hospital. Your doctor or midwife will read through your notes, then check your blood pressure, pulse and temperature. Your urine will be checked for signs of protein and glucose, your abdomen will be palpated to confirm the presentation of your baby, and the fetal heartbeat will be listened to using a Pinard's stethoscope or a Doppler monitor. A cardiotocograph (CTG) may also be used (see Chapter 5, p.152). You may be examined internally, usually with a speculum if you think your membranes have ruptured, or digitally (with fingers) if they are still intact, in order to assess whether the cervix has started to dilate. You should also be asked if you would like some pain relief and be able to discuss your birth plan, if you have one.

Your cervix needs to be more than 2 cm dilated with regular contractions every five minutes for you to be in established labour. Prior to that, even if you are experiencing regular contractions, you would be in the early phase of the first stage (see pp.160–1). If this is the case and you wish to stay in hospital, depending on the sort of maternity unit you are in, you may be shown to a bed on the ward where you can rest and wait for your labour to progress further. Alternatively, you may be able to go home for a while, especially if you live nearby. Your doctor or midwife will discuss the various options with you so that you can express your preferences and make an informed choice.

Once you are admitted, if appropriate, you can familiarise yourself with the labour ward before being shown to a room where, if you want, you can get changed into the nightdress or T-shirt that you would like to give birth in. You will be given a bracelet to wear, with details of your name, date of birth and hospital number. See p.161 for how you feel and how to manage contractions in the early phase of labour.

SUDDEN DELIVERIES (PRECIPITATE LABOUR)

Very occasionally, labour takes less than an hour between the first stage and the delivery of the baby. This is known as a 'precipitate labour'. Because it happens so quickly, a woman may have to deliver her baby either on her own or with the help of someone who has no medical training. Such occurrences are rare, and I can reassure you that in the vast majority of cases, everything turns out fine, as help (in the form of ambulance paramedics) invariably arrives just as the baby is being born, or very soon after. Nonetheless, below are a few key pieces of advice on what to do, should you find yourself in this situation:

1   If you think you don't have time to get to the hospital, it is better to stay at home than to set off, only to have to give birth in the back of a car.

2   Call 999, explain what is happening and ask for an ambulance to attend at once – the emergency services and ambulance crews are very experienced at handling such a situation. If necessary, an emergency services operator will talk you through, step-by-step, how to deliver your baby safely.

3   Wash your hands and your vaginal area, if possible, and fetch two clean towels, one to lie on and one to wrap around the baby.

4   An empty bath is a safe, contained place in which to give birth: you will be in a comfortably supported, semi-recumbent position, any mess can easily be cleaned up, and the baby won't drop onto the floor.

5   If you feel the urge to push, try to delay this by lying down to take the pressure off the cervix, and use short, pant-like breaths.

6   If the baby's head starts to emerge despite this, panting in this way will mean that it does so more slowly. Once the head is delivered, check the umbilical cord is not wound round the neck. If it is, gently hook your fingers under it and loop it back over the baby's head.

7   The first, upper shoulder should emerge from under the pubic bone in the next contraction. Gently sweep the head and first shoulder upwards, and the second shoulder should then have room to emerge during the next few contractions. After this is done, the rest of the body will slip out easily.

8   After the delivery, put your baby on your chest, skin to skin. Place a towel over them, so that they don't get cold.

9   Once the umbilical cord is out, keep it elevated so that blood is able to flow towards your baby.

10 Don't pull on the umbilical cord but allow the placenta to detach and be delivered naturally (which should be over the course of the next fifteen to twenty minutes).

It is highly unlikely that you will have to go through more than a few of these steps (if any) before help actually arrives. The main thing is to try to keep calm – easier said than done, I know – and to keep your baby warm if the birth takes place before specialist help can reach you.

“ I spent a lot of time mentally planning for my birth. Despite the horror stories I was told, I kept a positive mindset about what my experience was going to be like. I knew all the facts to help me deal with what might happen and wrote a birth plan, so that if I got to a point where I couldn't speak, my husband and midwife would know my plans. We were all on the same page. ” HEATHER

The first stage of labour describes the time when the cervix dilates. It is usually the longest stage, although there is no precise amount of time that it takes. If this is your first labour, it generally takes about twelve hours for your cervix to dilate from 2 to 10 cm; in a subsequent birth it will probably be somewhat shorter.

The early phase

The early phase of the first stage of labour is when uterine contractions begin. This phase can last for anything from a few hours to as many as 24–48 hours in a first labour; in subsequent labours, progress is usually considerably faster. At this point, contractions are mild and irregular, occurring every fifteen minutes or so, and often produce lower back pain similar to period pains. In fact, if you've ever had painful periods, the sensation is similar to the most severe one you've experienced! That said, they are usually bearable, although this can vary from one woman to another and from one

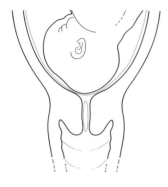

Before labour Before contractions begin, the cervix is closed, thick and around 2 cm long.

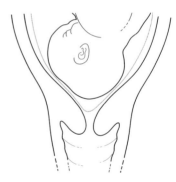

Early effacement During the early phase of labour, the cervix becomes thinner, shorter and softer.

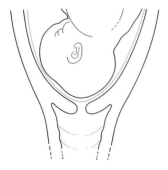

Complete effacement Once the cervix has fully effaced, it begins to dilate. The active phase of labour begins after you are 2–3 cm dilated.

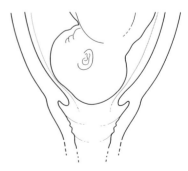

Complete dilation When the cervix is fully dilated to 10 cm, the transition phase of labour begins, followed by the second stage, when you are ready to push.

labour to another. You may also find that, at this point, your membranes rupture.

During this time, you may start to feel tired and/or nauseous, so it is important to rest as much as possible. Try to eat and stay hydrated whenever you can, as you need to keep your strength up for the rest of labour. If possible, move around so that gravity can help your labour to progress (*see* Box on p.163). If the contractions are getting uncomfortable, you could have a warm bath (unless your membranes have ruptured), as this can help alleviate the pain, and you could use other methods of non-pharmacological pain relief at this stage, such as asking your birth partner to massage your lower back, using a TENS machine or breathing deeply while listening to some soothing music to take your mind off what is happening (*see* pp.186 –8). A glass or two of wine is probably *not* a good idea, however tempting it might be!

Your contractions will eventually become stronger, more regular and less spaced out. These have the effect of softening the cervix, in a process called 'effacement'. During effacement, the cervix also begins to change shape, from being thick and around 2 cm long to being thinner, shorter and softer. (Your cervix has actually been shortening and softening over the last two weeks, but you have probably not been aware that the occasional pressure sensations you may have been experiencing were due to the cervix changing.) Once the cervix has fully softened, it can start to dilate to allow for the eventual passage of the baby's body. See diagrams opposite for how effacement and dilation progresses in labour.

PARTOGRAMS EXPLAINED

During labour, most hospitals use a chart known as a partogram to keep a visual and written record of your progress. The partogram has separate graphs showing the fetal heart rate, the rate of cervical dilation and descent of your baby through the pelvic cavity, the number and strength of your contractions per ten minutes, and your blood pressure, pulse and temperature. The partogram will also include information such as your personal details and whether any pain relief or drugs have been administered during labour. As a result, it is easy for medical staff to know at a glance what is happening in your labour – this is particularly important when there has been a change of shift – and if there are any problems that might need some level of intervention.

ARTIFICIAL RUPTURE OF MEMBRANES (ARM)

When the membranes surrounding your baby rupture and the head is no longer cushioned by the amniotic fluid, the cervix can dilate faster and prostaglandins are released into the bloodstream, which speed up uterine contractions. Rupture of the membranes usually happens spontaneously at some stage during the early phase of labour, because of the pressure that the baby's head is exerting on the cervix. However, there are some circumstances where it may be appropriate do this manually, in a procedure called artificial rupture of membranes (ARM). For example, the decision could be made to perform ARM if:

- ▸ your labour is progressing slowly, because it increases the release of prostaglandins that are involved in initiating the labour process
- ▸ there are concerns that your baby's heart rate may indicate the possibility that they have passed meconium (i.e. your baby is compromised – *see* Box on p.194) and performing an ARM allows the obstetrician to diagnose one way or the other
- ▸ you need internal electronic fetal monitoring (*see* Chapter 5, p.152)
- ▸ your labour has reached the second stage and you are ready to push.

You will always be asked whether you agree to ARM and it is your choice as to whether or not to go ahead. The procedure itself is a little uncomfortable, but no more so than having a cervical smear. See p.193 for further details of the procedure and information about the use of ARM for induction of labour.

Depending on the type of labour and birth, you will be attended by one or more of the following medical staff:

Midwife

If you have a straightforward labour and non-assisted delivery (requiring no instrumental assistance), and you do not require regional anaesthesia (e.g. an epidural), you will be attended only by a midwife and are unlikely to see a doctor at all. Most women, and especially first-time mothers (for whom labour tends to be longer than average), see more than one midwife during labour, because the first midwife's shift often ends before you have delivered your baby.

Anaesthetist

If at any stage you require regional anaesthesia (e.g. an epidural) for pain relief, an anaesthetist will be called to administer it.

Obstetrician

An obstetrician will oversee your labour if you are induced or require an assisted delivery using ventouse or forceps.

Paediatrician

A paediatrician will be present if your baby is premature or has shown any signs of compromise (*see* Box on p.194) during labour.

Medical student/student midwife

You may be asked if a medical student or student midwife can be present during some of your labour and help with some of the tasks such as observations of blood pressure and pulse. This gives them valuable experience, as all doctors and midwives need to be competent in delivering a baby by the end of their training. However, you are within your rights to say you would prefer they did not attend.

The active phase of labour

Once your cervix has dilated to 2–3 cm, you are in the active phase of the first stage of labour. This is not to say that you will be aware of this change of phase – in fact, you are unlikely to notice any difference at all! Over time, however, your contractions will progressively become stronger and longer, with the gaps between each one becoming shorter. At first, they will be every fifteen minutes or so, but as the active phase progresses, they will be coming every ten, then every five and eventually, by the end of the active phase, every two minutes, with little time in between. It is important to realise that your contractions may not always be uniform in length and frequency, so don't be disheartened if things slow down for a while.

The tightening feeling that, earlier on, was confined to the lower abdomen/back during each contraction now starts at the top of the uterus and spreads downwards, making you feel as if you are being gripped by a very strong band. This sensation is a result of the constriction of the blood vessels in the uterine wall, which become short of oxygen and, as a consequence, release chemical substances that trigger pain. The reduced blood flow also affects the placenta and the umbilical cord, often causing the baby's heart rate to drop a little during the strongest part of each contraction. This is entirely normal, but will nonetheless be monitored by your midwife to ensure that the fetal heart pattern remains within an acceptable range (*see* Box on fetal distress/compromise on p.194).

The pain at this stage is likely to increase in intensity and the key thing is to keep calm and to try to stay as relaxed as you can. Women often describe a contraction as a wave, which starts slowly and builds up to a crest before ebbing away again. Use the breathing techniques you have learned in your antenatal classes (your midwife can instruct you if you have not) to ride this wave, focusing only on the contraction you are experiencing rather than thinking about how many more there are to come. Repeating a familiar phrase or a line from a song or poem, either out loud or to yourself, can help increase your focus. Inhaling gas and air (*see* p.181) for pain relief at this stage of labour can aid deep and rhythmic breathing, and you can, of course, use any non-pharmacological methods, too. If, however, you are finding the pain too much to bear, you should discuss other options with your midwife. See also Box on p.164 for further tips on pain management.

In a first labour, the cervix dilates 1 cm per one to two hours on average; in subsequent labours, this usually happens significantly faster. However, the rate at which dilation occurs is often not regular: typically, it takes much longer to dilate to 4 cm than from 4–10 cm. The descent of the baby's head and shoulders through the birth canal can also take one to two hours. This is why your midwife or doctor will monitor you every two to four hours, by palpating your abdomen and examining you internally, so that they can assess the situation. Dilation can only be calculated by a vaginal examination.

POSITIONS FOR THE FIRST STAGE OF LABOUR

Downward pressure of the baby's head helps to dilate the cervix and to keep the baby moving down the birth canal, so the more upright you can be, the more you can use gravity to magnify that force and help labour progress. The chances are that you will instinctively find positions that work for you, but you may find the following suggestions helpful:

► kneeling on all fours
► kneeling and leaning forwards on some pillows
► squatting (most women can only squat for two minutes or so at a time)
► sitting, leaning forwards and being supported by your birth partner
► sitting on a birthing ball and gently rotating your hips
► standing up, leaning forwards against a wall.

These positions all have the added advantage that your partner can massage your lower back at the same time, something that you might find beneficial for relaxation and reassurance. If you are able to do so, walking around will increase the effect of gravity and being mobile may help you to better manage the pain of contractions.

How many times you are examined depends on the way your labour is progressing. Similarly, to determine how far the baby's head is engaged, in other words, how far down it has descended through the pelvis, an internal examination is necessary.

Descent of the fetal head is calculated relative to how many centimetres it is above or below the ischial spines, which form the narrowest part of the pelvis (*see* diagram). The centimetre measurements are referred to as 'stations' in your notes. If the head is, say, 3 cm above, it is said to be at '-3', when it is level with the ischial spines, it is at '0', and if it has descended, say, 2 cm below, it is at '+2'. Most women will feel the need to push once the baby's head has passed below the ischial spines.

The transition phase

The transition phase of the first stage of labour, which does not occur for everyone, is when you are fully dilated to 10 cm but not yet ready to push the baby out. It can last anything from a few minutes up to an hour and the contractions come thick and fast. You may, by now, have been in labour for many hours (if not a day or two), so unsurprisingly many women find this is when they feel most exhausted. You may also feel cold, shivery and/or nauseous, and it is not uncommon to be sick at this point. In the heat of the moment, it can be hard to feel positive about the situation, but try to remember that the second stage will soon begin, which means the end of labour and the birth of your baby is now not far away.

Sometimes, women experience an urge to push even though they are not fully dilated. Your midwife will ensure that you refrain from pushing during the contractions to avoid your cervix becoming swollen, which can lengthen your labour. The most helpful thing in this situation is for you to have adequate pain control, so don't be afraid to request it. You will also be asked to take short, shallow breaths, like panting, rather than the deeper ones that you would take if you were pushing. You might also need to change position so that pressure on your cervix from your baby's head is reduced. Once you are fully dilated and your baby's head is felt to be at the ischial spines or below, your midwife or doctor will encourage you to push.

The ischial spines The distance between the ischial spines represents the narrowest part of the mother's pelvis and marks the point by which the descent of your baby's head is measured.

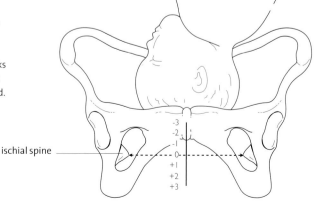

ischial spine

-3
-2
-1
0
+1
+2
+3

TIPS ON HOW TO MANAGE YOUR PAIN

You will probably be given advice about how to manage pain in labour, either by friends and family or in your antenatal classes, but here are some of my own. Note down any you feel might be useful and keep the information to hand in your hospital bag so that you can refer to them if necessary. You might think that you will remember on the day, only to find that your mind is not as clear as you thought it would be!

1 First and foremost, don't be heroic – the aim, after all, is to deliver a baby safely, not to win a gold medal for suffering.

2 View your labour as you would a flight of steps: you need to climb each step so that you can get to the top.

3 Each step is a contraction, and your aim is simply to manage the next one.

4 Don't think beyond this next step/contraction. Focus on this one only by breathing correctly and staying as relaxed as possible.

5 Don't think about how much further you might have to go until the top – the end of labour – because you might be tempted to stop. And anyway, no one knows how much further it is, so there is little point in worrying about it.

6 Don't ask yourself if you can cope with the pain in a few contractions' time. You must only focus on the next one.

7 Stay hydrated by taking little sips of drink and keep your energy levels up by having small snacks, particularly in the early stages.

8 Try to distract yourself so that you are able to think of things other than pain, such as focusing on some music or repeating song lyrics to yourself.

9 Find different positions that help ease the pain (*see* Boxes on pp.163 and 168).

10 Last, but not least, if you are finding the pain too difficult to cope with, don't hesitate to ask for pain relief, or additional pain relief, and don't leave it too late to do so.

BIRTH

164

You are now 10 cm dilated and about to meet your baby! The second stage of labour is characterised by an unmistakeable urge to bear down and push, and typically lasts one to two hours for a first birth and fifteen to twenty minutes for a subsequent one.

The speed of the second stage depends on a variety of factors, including:

▶ whether this is your first labour
▶ the station (position) of the baby in relation to the ischial spines when you are fully dilated
▶ how effectively you are able to push and whether you are pushing in the right place (i.e. your bottom)
▶ the strength of your contractions and whether you can feel them (you may have had regional anaesthesia)
▶ the size and position of the baby's head.

Pushing the baby out

Your midwife may call a colleague to help her when the second stage seems imminent (probably at 9 cm in a first labour, at 7 cm in a second or subsequent one). Your contractions are now two to five minutes apart (they are sometimes less frequent when you are ready to push) and last 60–90 seconds each. It is vital during this second stage that you work together with your midwives as a team and listen very closely to what they ask you to do, breathing as instructed and pushing when necessary. For many women, the pain from contractions at this stage of labour is more bearable than during the first stage – I think this is because now there is something physical to concentrate on. If you have had an epidural or CSE (combined spinal block and epidural), you will not be able to feel your contractions nor experience an urge to push, so a midwife will keep a hand on your abdomen so that they can tell when each contraction begins and ends.

Although you will have been given advice on how to push if you attended antenatal classes, a reminder from the midwife is always welcome at this point. The main thing is to push only when she tells you, so that you don't waste energy by doing so when you don't have a contraction.

Take a deep breath, close your throat, steady yourself (if you are standing or squatting) and bear down, focusing on pushing into your bottom as if you were severely constipated.

Many women use up a lot of energy pushing into their abdomen because they feel embarrassed to be pushing into their bottom, but this is the part of your body that you need to target. Trying to visualise your baby's descent specifically through the birth canal can help.

You should have time, in a 60–90 second contraction, to take around three good breaths, each followed by strong, effective pushing. This is better than holding your breath for one very long push, because you can sometimes become a bit light-headed if your breathing pattern is disrupted in this way.

As the second stage progresses, your contractions will cause the baby's head to move further and further down the birth canal. Some women find that they now experience pain in the rectal area, as the increasing pressure the head exerts on the rectum causes the anus to bulge out. The pain can also radiate down the legs as a result of nerve pressure in your sacral area. At this stage you can involuntarily excrete some fecal matter, because any stools still in the bowel are pushed down ahead of the descending baby's head. This is so common that midwives and doctors are entirely used to this situation, so please don't even think of being embarrassed.

If you are still pushing after 90 minutes, your midwife may examine you if birth doesn't seem imminent. She may then suggest that an obstetrician reviews the progress of your labour. This is to ensure that the cervix is not swollen, the baby's head is low down in the pelvis and that your contractions are coming frequently and are effective. Any time limit on how long you are allowed to push for before an intervention is discussed with you is simply due to the risk of the baby becoming tired, leading to changes in their heart rate or the effect that pushing for a long time can have on the muscles and nerves of your pelvic floor, particularly if they have already been affected by an epidural.

Eventually, the baby's hair will become visible, although it will slip slightly back as each contraction subsides. This bit is so exciting, particularly for your birth partner, and you should be prepared for them to be swept up in the moment and move where they can see the baby emerging. Your midwife will press on your perineum with her hand (and, possibly, a gauze swab) to reduce the risk of tearing. Finally, the head will 'crown', which means that it has arrived at the vaginal opening. This is painful, and you might feel a burning or stinging sensation, similar to that felt if you are severely constipated, only worse! This is a critical time in the birth process and your midwife will tell you when to stop pushing and simply breathe with shorter,

POSITIONS DURING THE SECOND STAGE OF LABOUR

When it comes to a suitable position for pushing, my main advice is to make sure you are comfortable and to let gravity do as much of the work for you as possible. This means finding a position that is reasonably upright. For example:

- ▶ sitting on a bed or birthing chair with lots of cushions and pillows behind you
- ▶ squatting (hard to sustain for more than two minutes)
- ▶ kneeling on all fours, or being supported by your birth partner, with your hips lower than your shoulders.

In the end, as long as you can find a position that allows you to push effectively and doesn't prevent your midwife from assisting you, this should benefit the progress of your labour. You may find that you want to change position several times during the course of the second stage and this, too, is fine.

pant-like breaths to allow your vaginal tissues to stretch and the baby's head to emerge. This lessens the chance of your suffering a vaginal tear. If your midwife thinks that your perineal tissues are likely to suffer a significant tear, she will offer you an episiotomy (*see* p.174).

Once the head has properly crowned, only one or two contractions are usually required for the head to be delivered – in an anterior presentation, the baby will be born with the head facing downwards (*see* Chapter 5, p.148). As soon as the head is free, the midwife will ensure that the umbilical cord is not wrapped around the baby's neck. If it is, she will gently loop it over the head so that it does not become compressed (although the head is out, your baby is still receiving its oxygen supply via the umbilical cord). The midwife continues to exert pressure on your perineum. Once the head is delivered, the baby's neck is free to straighten out and this has the effect of causing the baby to rotate either left or right. This then enables the first, upper (anterior) shoulder to be delivered. Usually, only one contraction is necessary for this to happen. The second (posterior) shoulder then quickly follows, with the rest of the body slipping out soon after, followed by amniotic fluid. Although you may feel exhausted, this is an unforgettable moment.

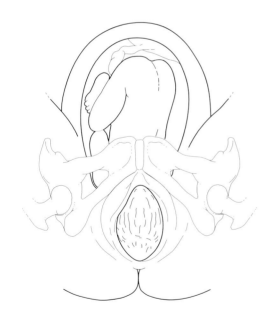

Crowning The head is said to have crowned when it has arrived at the vaginal opening. It is then usually delivered after one or two contractions.

Delivery Most babies are born with their head facing downwards, in an anterior position. The body is delivered with the next contraction.

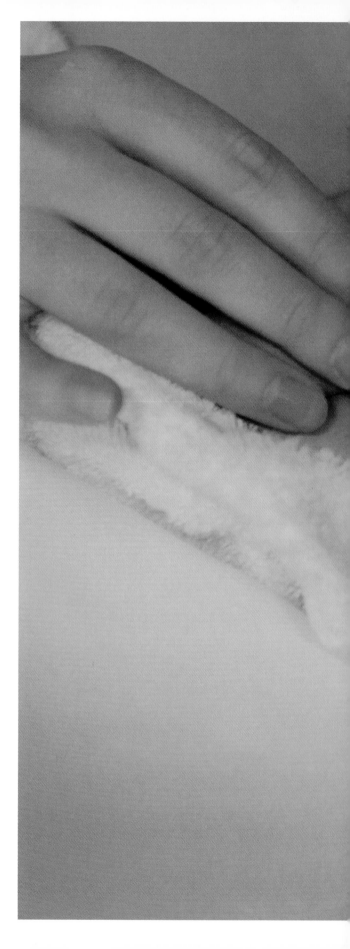

" My contractions started in the night. I paced around for a while, had a bath and then woke my husband at 5am. After arriving at the maternity unit, my midwife examined me and was surprised to discover I was already 6 cm dilated. I still felt relaxed, able to listen to the radio and chat. When the pains picked up, I became more focused in order to manage them, but around the time of transition, I really wanted an epidural. The midwife said I probably didn't need it and was very encouraging, suggesting different positions to help me cope with the pain and push my son out. It was a euphoric moment, as I'd secretly wanted a boy! " MAGGIE

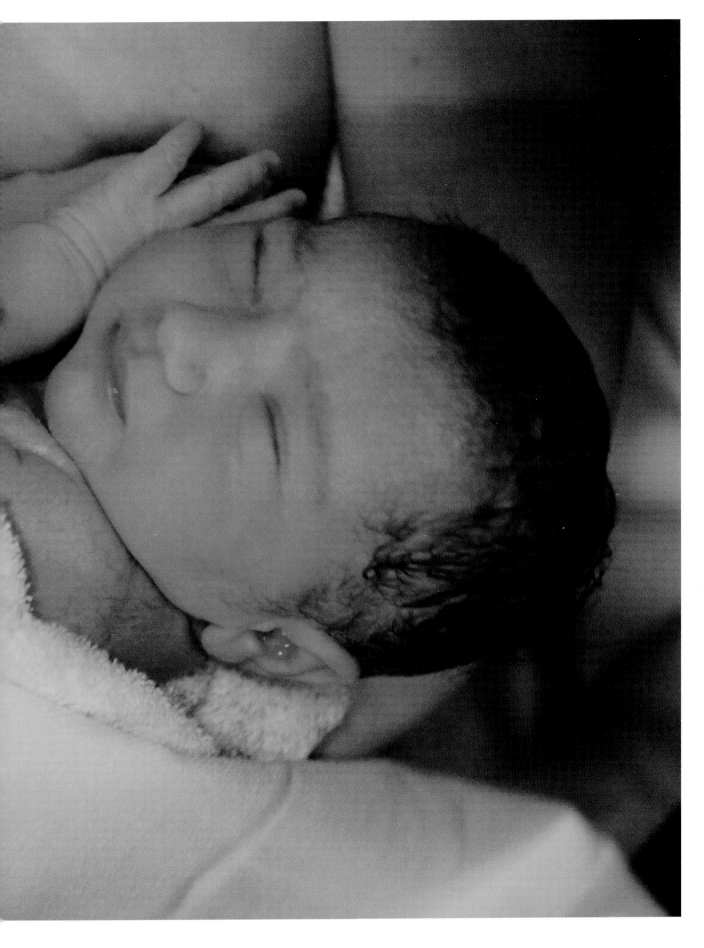

APGAR SCORE	2	1	0
Heart rate/pulse	More than 100 bpm	Less than 100 bpm	Absent
Breathing	Regular, strong breathing	Irregular, shallow breathing	Absent
Muscle tone	Active	Some tone/activity	Limp
Response to stimulus	Strong crying/grimacing	Some reaction/grimace	None
Skin colour	Pink all over	Pink body, blue extremities	Pale/blue all over

The birth of your baby

Assuming all is well, your baby will utter their first cry and take their first breath. They will be placed straight onto your chest so that you can both have immediate skin-to-skin contact, although to preserve warmth, your baby will be covered in a sterile blue blanket. The body will be slippery, as it is covered in vernix caseosa, blood and amniotic fluid and don't be alarmed if the face is a little squashed, red or puffy – this is just the result of their journey down the birth canal and it will settle down very soon (see p.212 for more information on how your baby looks in the first 24 hours after birth).

After this, the midwife will give your baby a quick wipe and the umbilical cord will be cut (see p.176). At one minute and five minutes after the birth, the midwife or paediatrician will perform a series of five straightforward assessments to which they will give a score, known as the Apgar score after the American doctor, Virginia Apgar, who devised this classification. Points are given (0–2) for each of the five elements, and a baby can have a maximum total score of ten (see Chart).

An Apgar score totalling seven or over after one minute indicates that the baby is in good condition; between four and six may mean that the baby needs help with breathing; three or under gives cause for concern and life-saving equipment may be required. At five minutes, the observations are repeated (even if the score was ten) and, once again, a score below seven means that care or monitoring is needed. Apgar scores only provide information on the baby's condition immediately after birth, so please don't worry if your baby's score is not a perfect ten at this stage, as this is no indication of long-term health. A low initial score invariably improves by the five-minute assessment or soon after. Conversely, some babies may have an initial high Apgar score and develop problems later, which is why all babies continue to be observed in the hours that follow the birth.

If there has been any cause for concern during your labour regarding the fetal heart rate, blood samples from the umbilical cord may be taken immediately after delivery to confirm that the oxygen levels in the fetal circulation are within the normal range. Results are available within a few minutes and are helpful in indicating whether or not your baby needs neonatal monitoring.

If everything is fine, your baby will be weighed then wrapped in a blanket to prevent loss of body heat. The midwife or paediatrician will check for any obvious physical abnormalities and will attach an identification bracelet to your baby's wrist and ankle. This will show your surname, the baby's weight and hospital number, and the time and date of birth. You will be given a bracelet with the same information as your baby's, to wear in addition to your own one. Later on, your baby's cot will also display these details. Finally, the midwife will ask you if she can give your baby a dose of vitamin K (you will have discussed this with your midwife antenatally). This helps your baby's blood to clot (rarely, babies develop vitamin K deficiency bleeding, or haemorrhagic disease) and can be given by injection into the thigh muscle. Some parents prefer oral drops to be given: this is done in two doses, one at birth and one within the first week at the GP surgery. For breastfed babies, a third dose is recommended within the first month.

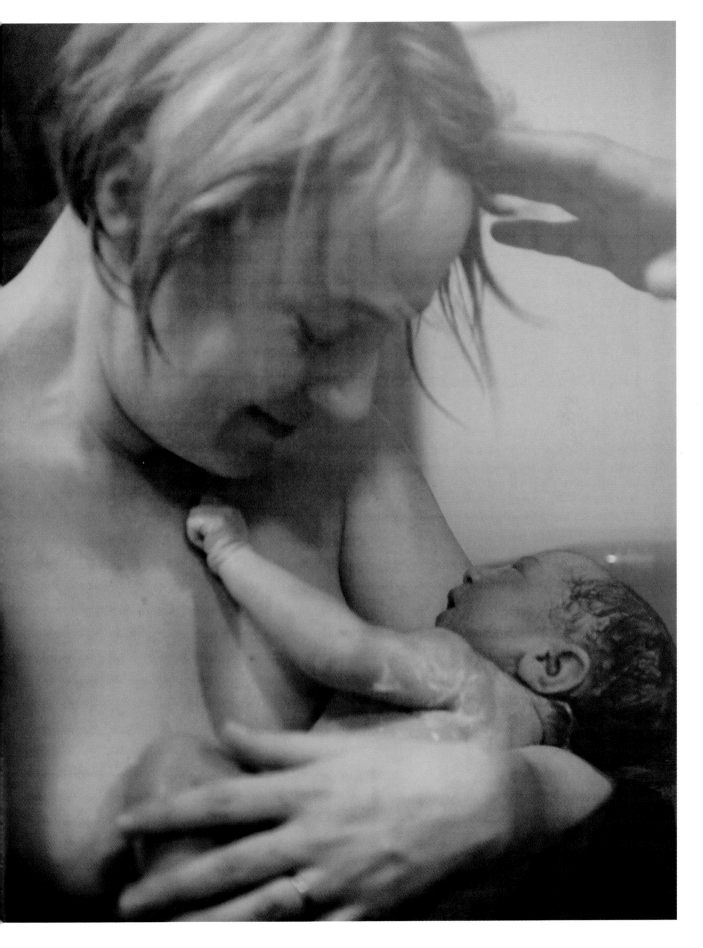

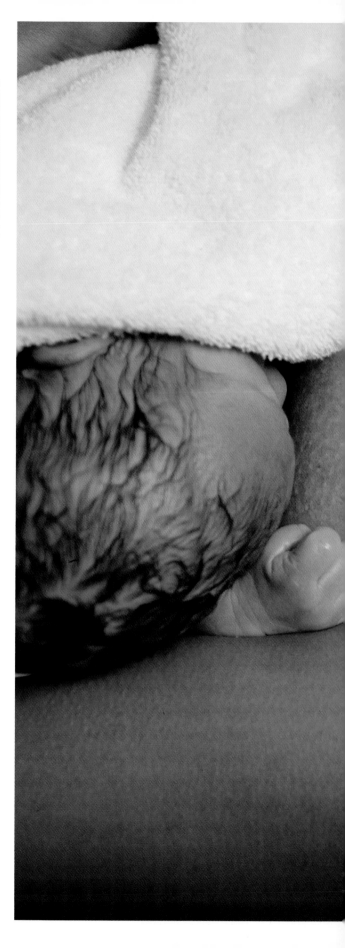

How you feel

Many women have strong physical reactions at the moment of delivery, especially if the first and second stages have been long: you can feel cold and shivery, or even find yourself shaking uncontrollably, with teeth chattering. If you have been given a syntometrine injection to aid the delivery of the placenta (*see* p.176), you may also feel nauseous and be sick, as this one of the side effects of the drug.

At the same time, it is common to experience a strange mixture of emotions, from a feeling of elation to bewilderment and disbelief that labour is finally over and your baby has actually been born! You may also be wondering, 'What now? Help! This is my baby, and I am responsible for them!' If your labour has been prolonged or difficult, you may only feel like resting and not paying your baby much attention. Try not to be too concerned about this: you will have plenty of time to bond and, as long as your baby is placed skin-to-skin, they will already be getting the benefits of being close to you. See also Box in Chapter 9, p.278 for more information about bonding with your baby after birth.

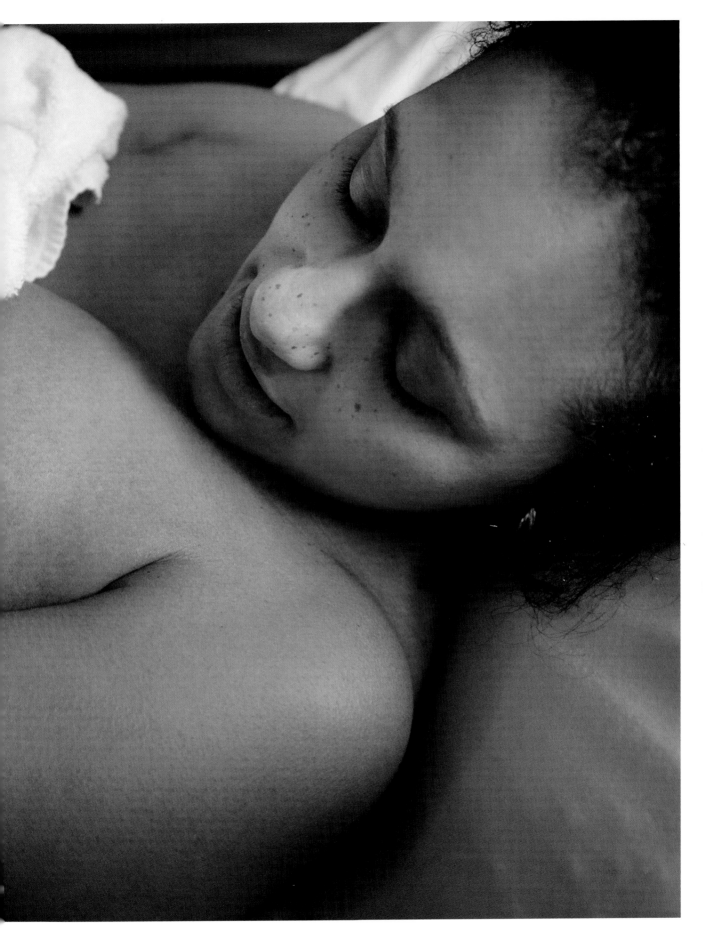

Episiotomies

An episiotomy is a small cut to the perineum (the entrance to the vagina), made in order allow the safe delivery of the baby's head. Around 25 per cent of vaginal deliveries require an episiotomy, and in first births, that figure rises to nearly 40 per cent. You cannot predict in advance, or even as labour progresses, if you are going to need one, but some of the reasons for performing an episiotomy are:

▸ when vaginal/perineal tissue is not stretching sufficiently and risks a larger tear
▸ to facilitate an assisted delivery using forceps (*see* p.200),
▸ when a speedy delivery is essential
▸ when you have suffered a previous third-degree tear
▸ if there is any difficulty in delivering the shoulders
▸ when yours is a breech birth (*see* pp. 202–3).

Understandably, women want to know what an episiotomy actually entails and many are unsure whether it really is necessary or whether it is preferable to let the body tear naturally. It is impossible to answer this latter question, as it depends on the individual and varies from one labour to another. In general, it is common to have minor tears during labour and these tend to heal quickly and easily. However, more severe tearing would affect the anal sphincter and surrounding tissue, leading to long-term difficulties in passing stools, and so it is better to avoid this if possible (*see* below for more detail on the degrees of tearing).

If your midwife or obstetrician offers you an episiotomy, it is usually because they think you could be about to tear quite severely or because the baby now needs delivering quickly as there are signs of fetal compromise (*see* Box on p.194). My own view is that, now episiotomies are no longer routinely performed on women (contrary to popular perception), it is better and safer to take the advice of an experienced practitioner. I must stress that they will consult you and will require your permission in order to carry out the procedure, having first explained why they believe it to be necessary. This is irrespective of whether you have already expressed a preference – or even a strong view – in your birth plan about episiotomies (*see* Chapter 5, p.139). In this way, you are able to reconsider at the time and change your mind if necessary. If you are adamant that you do not want an episiotomy under any circumstances, then please feel free to decline.

Before the episiotomy, your midwife will then inject the perineum with a local anaesthetic (this will not be necessary if you have had regional anaesthesia – *see* p.182). The incision will be made with episiotomy scissors and there is very little bleeding because your perineum is usually fully stretched at this point. There is only one type of episiotomy cut performed nowadays: the medio-lateral cut, which is angled down and away from the vagina and perineum (at '8 o'clock') into the muscle, so that it avoids the anus (*see* diagram opposite).

The suturing (stitching) will usually be done within an hour of the end of the delivery of the baby and of the placenta (which marks the end of the third stage of labour). In order to do this, your midwife will probably ask you to move to the end of the bed and to put your legs into leg rests so that she can see more clearly. If necessary, a further dose of local anaesthetic will be offered so that you do not feel pain. The suturing is done with great care and in three layers, using stitches that eventually dissolve (so they will not need to be removed later). First, the internal vaginal tissue is stitched, then the muscle and, lastly, the perineal skin (the external skin surrounding the vagina and rectum). Remember this is a very small area: most women have a perineum that is 4 cm long, so you will not require more than a few stitches.

Vaginal tearing

Sometimes, particularly if you have had a very rapid labour, tears are unavoidable. There are four degrees of perineal tearing:

▸ **first degree:** like a minor graze to the skin, which heals well without the need for stitching
▸ **second degree:** as well as minor tears to the skin, includes deeper tears to the muscle layers surrounding the vagina and perineal areas (but not the rectal area)
▸ **third degree:** in addition to the above, the anal sphincter muscles are torn
▸ **fourth degree:** as well as the anal sphincter muscles, the mucous lining of the rectum is torn.

Second-degree tears require suturing, which can be done in the delivery room. Third- and fourth-degree tears occur in only one to two per cent of births, and careful suturing must be done by a senior doctor to realign the muscles, so that there is no permanent damage to the rectum. The suturing of third-degree tears are done under epidural, usually in the operating theatre; this is not because your tear is very serious, but simply because the light is much stronger. Great skill is required to repair a fourth-degree tear, which is done under general anaesthetic. The consequences of this sort of tearing not being detected and repaired can lead to long-term problems and possibly to subsequent surgery. Rarely, these tears occur despite an episiotomy having been done. See Chapter 8, p.234 for how to look after yourself after you have had stitches.

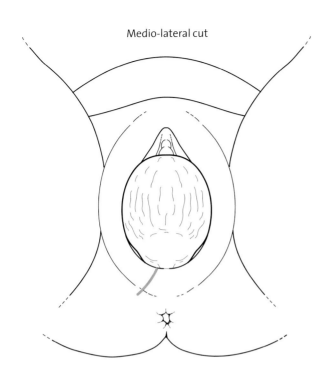

Medio-lateral cut

Episiotomy The medio-lateral cut is angled away from the vagina, perineum and anus. Very little bleeding occurs, as the vaginal tissue is fully stretched while the baby's head is crowning.

"" The second stage of my labour took a long time. I was aware that there were several doctors hovering at the door, waiting to take me to theatre if my baby didn't appear some time soon. My midwife was very firm with them and insisted that I was given a few more minutes. Suddenly, things got more serious as she realised that the cord was wrapped around my baby's neck, so she swiftly performed an episiotomy and my baby was delivered in an instant. I didn't feel the cut particularly, even though there was no time to be given an anaesthetic, but I did experience an intense stinging sensation as my son came through. I'm relieved that my midwife was so experienced, though, as it saved me from having a Caesarean, and my healing has been fine. "" **BECCA**

THE THIRD STAGE OF LABOUR

Once your baby has been born, the umbilical cord will be cut and the placenta is delivered, which comprises the third stage of labour. This can last from ten minutes to about an hour and you may not even be aware that much is happening as you meet your baby for the first time.

Cutting the cord

Immediately after the birth, the umbilical cord will still be pulsating, providing oxygen and blood to your baby. Babies have a relatively low blood volume, so receiving additional blood from the placenta for a short time after the birth can be beneficial, which is why it is common to wait two to three minutes before cutting the cord. The midwife will place two clamps close together approximately half way along the cord, so that blood from the baby does not drain back to the placenta. The cord can then be safely cut. If your birth partner plans to do this, try to let the midwife know in advance. However, don't be disappointed if, on the day, they feel that this is suddenly not such an attractive proposition (many are a bit squeamish when the moment comes). As an alternative, your partner can always trim the cord a bit shorter after the initial cut has been made by the midwife.

Sometime before leaving the delivery room (if you are in hospital), the cord will be cut once more, so that only a short stump remains, and a plastic clip is placed near the base of it. Eventually, this remaining stump dries up and, after a few days, falls off, leaving your baby with a little belly button. Before that, you will need to ensure that it doesn't become infected. See Chapter 8, p.253 for information on caring for the cord.

Delivering the placenta

Once your baby is born, the placenta will be delivered. Your uterus continues to have mild contractions, which you may not even be aware of, so that the placenta can detach itself from the uterine wall. The placenta needs to be delivered in one piece and fairly quickly after birth – failure to do this increases the chances of heavy bleeding from the placental site (postpartum haemorrhage – see Complications, p. 289). A full bladder can make delivery of the placenta more difficult, so if there is a delay, a catheter may be introduced to drain your bladder of urine (after discussion with you).

'Active' management of the third stage

As soon as your baby's head and first shoulder have been delivered, unless you have specified to the contrary in your birth plan or in earlier discussions, your midwife will proceed to the 'active' management of the third stage of labour by giving you an injection of a drug called syntometrine in your thigh. This is a combination of ergometrine, which prolongs contractions, and syntocinon (the synthetic version of oxytocin), which helps the uterus to shrink more rapidly, down to approximately the size of a grapefruit. Both actions enable the placenta to be expelled intact and efficiently. Some hospitals may just use a syntocinon injection.

Your midwife will know when your uterus has contracted firmly and your placenta has detached from the uterine wall – this usually happens faster in an active third stage than when you wait for this to take place in a traditionally managed way (see below) – and she may ask you to give a final push. At the same time, she will place a hand on your lower abdomen to keep the uterus in place and ask you to push while she gently pulls on the umbilical cord. This procedure, called 'controlled cord traction', usually ensures that the placenta and membranes are delivered soon after the birth. If your baby is very premature, the umbilical cord may be fragile and can break, so your obstetrician will be very careful when carrying out this procedure.

Active management of the third stage reduces the risk of a heavy bleed or postpartum haemorrhage. Some bleeding does still occur when the placenta separates from the blood vessels in the uterine wall. However, the speed with which the womb shrinks, together with the rapid formation of blood clots on the ends of these blood vessels, limits further haemorrhaging from taking place. The disadvantages of active management are that it involves an intramuscular injection and that the drugs used can cause your blood pressure to rise and can, occasionally, result in nausea.

'Traditional' management of the third stage

While it is the usual method of delivering the placenta, you don't have to agree to active management. If you prefer, you can opt for 'traditional' management, when the placenta and membranes separate with no assistance from syntometrine. The midwife will not attempt to deliver the placenta until it is clear that it has fully separated from the uterine wall – usually because there is a gush of blood, as well as a series of contractions and an urge to push on your part. It will also

BIRTH

176

help if your baby is able to suckle a little at your breast, as this releases oxytocin, the hormone that causes uterine contractions and therefore helps the placenta to separate quickly. Just as with active management of this stage, the midwife will then place her hand on your lower abdomen and gently ease the placenta and membranes out. She will also massage your uterus regularly over the next hour or so to encourage it to continue contracting, as this reduces blood loss. When the third stage is managed traditionally and all goes well, you should expect the placenta and membranes to be expelled after around twenty minutes.

Although traditional management avoids an injection and the use of drugs, it carries an increased risk of postpartum haemorrhage, especially if the placenta has not been delivered within half an hour; if this occurs, you will be given the drug used to encourage separation and you may have to have the placenta removed in theatre under regional anaesthesia.

Retained placenta

In around one per cent of births, the placenta (or part of it) has not been expelled an hour after the delivery of the baby. If this problem is not addressed speedily it can lead to postpartum haemorrhage, so you will be moved to an operating theatre where you will be given either a general or regional anaesthetic, and an obstetrician will reach up into your uterus and remove your placenta by hand in the manner of a vet!

What happens after the delivery of the placenta?

Once the placenta and membranes are delivered, and once your midwife is happy that you are not bleeding and your blood pressure is normal (and your birth partner is not on the floor!), she will examine the placenta. She will first of all check that it is complete and looks healthy. It should be bright vermilion in colour and roughly the size of a discus: it is 2–3 cm thick, measures around 25 cm in diameter and weighs 500–700 g. The smooth side (the one not attached to the uterine wall) will have the umbilical cord emanating from its centre, with various thick blood vessels radiating from it. Unless you want to take it home with you, or in the unlikely event that it needs further examination because its appearance gives cause for concern (e.g. it may be incomplete), the placenta will simply be disposed of in hospital.

If you need stitching as a result of an episiotomy or tearing, this will be done by your midwife or doctor once the placenta is delivered. After this, you will be helped to wash yourself, then you and your birth partner will be left alone for a little while to quietly spend time with your long-awaited new arrival and have some well-earned tea and toast!

SECOND AND SUBSEQUENT LABOURS

It is often the case that second and subsequent labours are easier and quicker than first ones, on average lasting around eight hours in total. The speed of subsequent deliveries is why, occasionally, women who had intended to give birth in hospital find themselves doing so at home or on their way to the maternity unit! It does appear that the body finds it easier to give birth if it has already done so, and this is especially so where the pregnancies are reasonably close together:

► The cervix effaces more quickly and dilates at a greater rate than 1 cm per hour.
► The uterine muscles contract more efficiently, leading to a shorter first stage: in a first labour, the early (latent) phase alone can last up to 48 hours; subsequently, the whole of the first stage often lasts just six to eight hours.
► More efficient contractions, together with knowledge of the pushing technique, also mean that the second stage can be over in fifteen to twenty minutes (compared to one to two hours in a first labour).
► Just over ten per cent of women require an episiotomy for second and subsequent births, compared to over 35 per cent of first-time mothers. This is because the vaginal and perineal muscles have been stretched before.

That said, the longer the gap between one pregnancy and another, the harder it appears to be for the body to 'remember' what to do in labour and the more likely it is that it has to 'relearn' how to give birth.

If the baby's position is straightforward, there is a higher chance that the second stage will be faster and that you will require less pain relief. Not only is this due to labour being speedier (it becomes easier to tolerate pain when you know it isn't going to last very long), but is also an indication that women who have given birth before are often more relaxed because they know what to expect. In any event, the statistics show that in second or subsequent labours, the need for epidurals is lower (less than twenty per cent of women, compared with over 40 per cent in first labours), and the numbers of women giving birth with no pain relief at all increases from around 3.5 per cent with first-time births to almost ten per cent for those who have already had a baby. See Chart on p.181 for more information on the numbers of women using different methods of pain relief in labour.

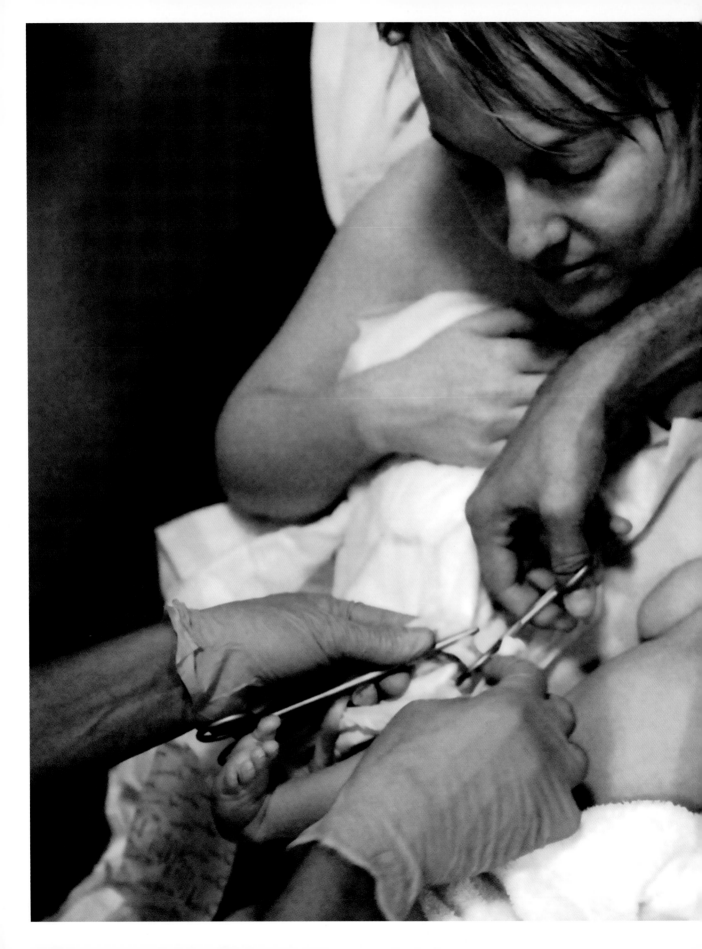

" My husband has a science background and, while for our first birth, he was too absorbed in the arrival of the baby to pay much attention to the medical side of things, for the birth of our second child, he took the opportunity to fill the gap in his knowledge. He wasn't interested in cutting the cord, but he did go off to examine the placenta with the midwife. I, on the other hand, had no desire to see the placenta whatsoever! " **ANNE**

PAIN RELIEF

One of the great benefits of modern medicine is that women can choose what, if any, pain relief they need during childbirth. This can range from simple methods, such as massage or breathing techniques, through to regional anaesthesia.

First of all, the truth: I have never, in twenty years of doing my job, heard anyone say that labour was not painful, at least to some degree. The issue of pain relief in labour is a contentious one, because the arguments surrounding it tend to polarise people. My view is that I don't see why women should feel guilty or, worse, that they are a failure if they wish to have a pain-free experience during part or all of their labour – after all, no one bats an eyelid if we require pain relief for a sprained ankle or a tooth extraction. Nor do I see why so-called 'natural' methods of pain relief seem to be more acceptable to some than pharmacological ones. Conversely, if women want to have a birthing experience that includes pain, they should be free to make that choice.

Pain, however, is unpleasant. It causes tension in the body and can, in the worst cases, exhaust you and prevent you from thinking clearly and managing your labour in a way that helps it to progress. In addition, giving birth while in severe pain can be a traumatising experience, one that does not help you to recover either physically or psychologically. That, to me, is unfortunate, because birth is an extraordinary process and should be experienced positively. Aside from these issues, pain suffered by the mother may not be good for the baby, because the release of stress hormones increases the maternal heart rate and, as a consequence, that of the baby as well. I feel very strongly, therefore, that labour is not an exam that you pass or fail according to whether you gave birth with or without pain relief (or, for that matter, whether you gave birth vaginally or not – see p.204 for the issues surrounding Caesarean section).

It is your choice which method of pain relief, if any, you wish to have. In the end, because no one has any idea what their body is going to do during labour, nor how they will react to pain, it may come down to 'whatever works' for you on the day and you should therefore not be influenced by whatever others might have advised you beforehand to do. Consequently, I believe that in order to make the right choices for you and your baby, it is best to be as well informed as possible about what the various options are.

Broadly speaking, there are two types of pain relief: medical, which uses drugs to relieve or eliminate the sensation of pain, and non-pharmalogical (including natural methods), which focuses on reducing pain or making it more tolerable. There are three main forms of drug-assisted pain relief:

- ▸ analgesia: relieves the sensation of pain (e.g. gas and air, which is inhaled; pethidine, which is injected)
- ▸ regional anaesthesia: numbs a specific part of the body (e.g. epidural, spinal block, pudendal block)
- ▸ general anaesthesia: makes you unconscious and therefore unable to feel pain.

Most methods of non-pharmalogical pain relief employ natural techniques or alternative/complementary therapies and include:

- ▸ breathing
- ▸ water (either in a bath or birthing pool)
- ▸ TENS
- ▸ massage/aromatherapy
- ▸ herbal and homeopathic remedies
- ▸ acupuncture/reflexology
- ▸ hypnobirthing.

The reality is that first labours are generally longer and more painful than second or subsequent births. And whether this is their first time or not, the vast majority of women use at least one form of pain relief during labour, with many using several different methods, depending on the stage they are at. The most common form of pain relief is gas and air, used by over 80 per cent of women, followed by pethidine or similar opiate injection, used by almost one-third. Epidurals are used by 30 per cent, although with first-time mothers this figure rises to over 40 per cent. When it comes to non-pharmacological pain relief, natural methods, such as massage and specific breathing techniques, are employed by nearly half of women at some point in their labour. More than one in five use a TENS machine and over one in ten use water in some shape or form,

DID YOU KNOW…?
Only 6.5 per cent of women use no pain relief at all. This figure is higher – nearly ten per cent – for second and subsequent births, compared to 3.5 per cent for first births.

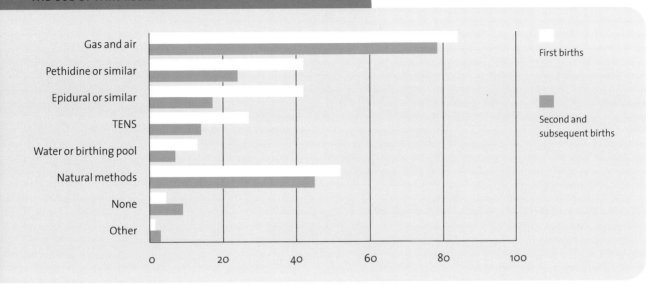

First births

Second and subsequent births

for example taking a warm bath or using a birthing pool, with five per cent giving birth in water. The table above breaks these figures down further between first labours and second or subsequent labours.

Analgesia

Analgesia works by dulling the pain messages sent by the nervous system to receptors in the brain. The two analgesics most commonly used for pain relief in labour are gas and air and pethidine.

Gas and air

The 50:50 mixture of nitrous oxide and oxygen, called 'gas and air', is the most commonly used form of pain relief in labour. In the UK it is often referred to by its tradename, Entonox. Gas and air is very safe to use and, while it does not eliminate pain entirely, it can be very effective in reducing pain. Antenatal clinics or classes often have a cylinder so that you can try it out in advance of labour.

At the start of a contraction, you inhale slowly and deeply through a mouthpiece connected to a tube that leads from a pressurised cylinder (*see* Chapter 5, p.152). Gas and air does not provide instant pain relief, so the effect will only be felt by the time the contraction peaks. You can keep taking deep breaths of gas and air during a contraction, but there is no point in inhaling it in between, because the drug is eliminated quickly from your system and will not therefore reduce the pain of the next one. It is not possible to overdose on gas and air and, although the drug does cross the placenta, it does not affect your baby.

Many women find gas and air a useful form of pain relief, particularly in the early stages of labour. Breathing deeply and strongly through the mouthpiece helps you to relax and to focus on your breathing technique in order to manage the pain: you are the one deciding when and how often to inhale, so you feel in control of the situation. Women often end up biting on the mouthpiece when the contraction is at its strongest, which is an added benefit!

On the downside, gas and air can make you feel light-headed and 'out of it' or distanced from proceedings. Nausea is a common side effect and some women are even sick. Others find that is does not help dull the pain of their contractions very much at all.

Pethidine

Pethidine is a synthetic opiate, from the same family as morphine and heroin. It works on endorphin receptors in the brain and spinal cord in order to dull the pain messages sent by the nervous system. Pethidine is administered by an injection into the thigh muscle. Its effects can be felt within fifteen to twenty minutes and additional doses can be given every three or four hours. Midwives are allowed to prescribe it, so you can have the drug if you are giving birth at home or in a midwifery unit. You may also be offered meptazinol or diamorphine as an alternative to pethidine. Broadly speaking, all three analgesic drugs have the same effects on you and your baby, and are very safe to use.

Pethidine is popular with women who don't want or cannot have regional anaesthesia or whose labour is straightforward and midwife-led. However, it can cause nausea, vomiting, blurred vision, excessive drowsiness and a sense of being 'out of it'. In addition, any opiate quickly crosses the placenta and can make the baby drowsy, particularly if it is given less than two hours before birth. This can then depress the baby's breathing and affect the ability to respond fully after delivery, leading to lower Apgar scores (see p.170). A paediatrician is often called to check the baby in these instances and may give the baby an injection of a drug called naloxone to counteract the effect of the pethidine. For this reason, pethidine is not often suggested as a first choice in advanced labour.

Regional anaesthesia

There are three different sorts of regional anaesthesia: epidural, spinal block and pudendal block, with epidurals being the most common. In addition, a combination of a spinal block and epidural is now routinely given (see Box on p.186). In each case, the purpose of is to numb a specific part of the body by blocking the nerve fibres. There are different medical reasons for using each procedure.

Epidural anaesthesia

Epidurals have been available since the early 1970s and aim to completely block out the pain in your abdomen. The most common reason that women have an epidural is when contractions become too painful. They may also be offered for the following situations:

▸ Caesarean sections, both elective and emergency
▸ breech deliveries
▸ assisted deliveries (ventouse or forceps)
▸ premature deliveries
▸ prolonged labour
▸ extensive suturing following episiotomy or perineal tearing
▸ removal of a retained placenta.

The spinal cord is encased in a thick, protective membrane called the 'dura' and between this and the vertebrae is the epidural space (see Box opposite). Nerve fibres come out of your spinal cord, pass through the dura and the epidural space and, after passing between the vertebrae, reach into your abdomen. When you have contractions, it is these nerve fibres that send messages to your brain that you are in pain. When an anaesthetic drug is injected into the epidural space in your spinal column, the nerve fibres are no longer able to emit pain messages to your brain and the abdomen feels numb (see Box for more details). If given in high doses, the drug also affects the nerve fibres controlling sensation in your legs and bladder, which is why feeling in these areas may decrease.

Nowadays, most women are given what is called a 'mobile epidural'. These deliver a slightly different and 'lighter' combination of anaesthetic drugs, which numb your abdomen but still enable you to feel and put weight on your legs. You can also sense when you need the toilet and are therefore less likely to need a catheter. Aside from leaving you freer to walk around and change position during labour, mobile epidurals can be topped up in lower, more frequent doses. In this way, it is easier to adjust the anaesthesia so that, by the time you are in the second stage of labour and ready to push, you can feel your contractions but still have adequate pain relief.

Epidural anaesthesia is not available for births at home or in a midwifery unit, as it can only be carried out by an anaesthetist (most obstetric units provide 24-hour access to an obstetric anaesthetist). Once your verbal consent has been obtained, epidurals take 20–40 minutes to set up and a further 20–30 minutes to be completely effective. Equally, even if you think at this stage that you plan *not* to have one, remember that, in first labours, over 40 per cent of women do have an epidural, so do remain open-minded about it.

Spinal block

Spinal blocks function in a very similar way to epidurals in that they numb the abdomen by blocking the nerve fibres in the pelvic area. The main difference is that, instead of entering the epidural space, the needle goes through the dura membrane and delivers the anaesthetic into the fluid that surrounds the spinal cord. The other difference is that spinal blocks take effect almost at once. For this reason, they are increasingly popular for Caesarean sections and emergency interventions. On the other hand, a spinal block can only be administered once, and lasts between one and, at most, two hours. They are therefore not suitable for relieving pain during labour. When they perform spinal anaesthesia, anaesthetists sometimes put in place an epidural catheter at the same time, so that pain relief can be administered post-operatively if necessary.

Pudendal block

To administer a pudendal block, a local anaesthetic is injected with a small needle high up in the vaginal tissue surrounding the pudendal nerves on the left and right of the cervix. This procedure is quick to administer and needs five to ten minutes to take effect. A pudendal block significantly reduces vaginal and perineal pain during the second stage, so it is a good method of pain relief when a straightforward assisted delivery is necessary, or if suturing is required following perineal tearing or an episiotomy. It does not, however, reduce the pain from uterine contractions. It does not need to be administered by an anaesthetist, so can be done by an obstetrician.

In order to administer the epidural you will be asked to lie very still on your left side with your legs bent up, or to sit up leaning forwards on the edge of the bed, with your hands holding the side or a table in front of you in order to steady yourself. The reason you lie on your left rather than on your right side is to avoid the weight of the uterus pressing down on the major arteries in the pelvis, as this can make you light-headed and lead to a reduction of blood flow to your baby.

Your lower back will be thoroughly cleaned with antiseptic solution and covered with sterile sheeting to prevent infection. A small amount of anaesthetic will be injected into your lower spine so that you do not feel the insertion of the epidural needle. This is usually the most uncomfortable part, as once the anaesthetic is working, you will feel only pressure, not pain. A dextrose-saline (sugar- and salt-based) solution will be inserted via a drip into your non-writing arm. This prevents your blood pressure dropping once the anaesthetic begins to work.

Once the local anaesthetic has taken effect, a fine, curved, hollow needle is carefully passed between the vertebrae in the lower back and into the epidural space. The anaesthetist will stop what they are doing every time you have a contraction, so don't worry that you will either be unable to move or that you

might endanger the procedure by doing so. Initially, a small amount of anaesthetic is injected to check that it is numbing your abdomen as it should. Very quickly, you should feel it starting to work: you will experience a cold sensation moving down your abdomen as it slowly becomes completely numb. If this is the case, a thin, hollow plastic tube (catheter) is inserted through the hollow needle and the full amount of anaesthetic is administered into the epidural space. The needle is then removed, leaving the catheter in place. The long length is taped securely to your back and over your shoulder to keep it secure, and a filter valve, which protects against bacteria, is fitted to the end of the catheter, together with an attachment for a syringe. This means that top-up doses of anaesthetic can be given throughout your labour.

If you are not already being monitored, an external continuous CTG will be placed around your abdomen to measure your contractions and the baby's heart rate. Your blood pressure will be checked immediately, then every ten minutes for the next half hour, and thereafter on a regular basis. This is because a drop in your blood pressure can reduce the amount of blood flowing through the placenta, which reduces the oxygen supply to your baby.

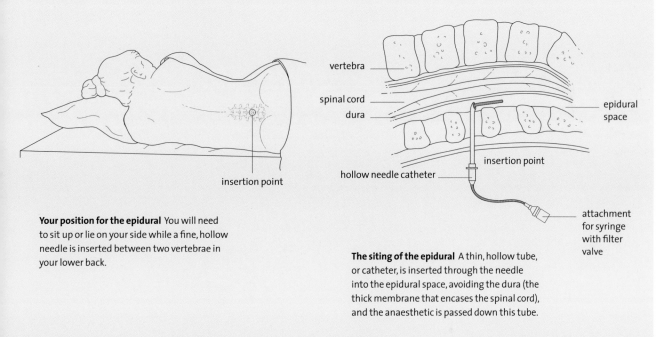

Your position for the epidural You will need to sit up or lie on your side while a fine, hollow needle is inserted between two vertebrae in your lower back.

insertion point

vertebra

spinal cord

dura

epidural space

insertion point

hollow needle catheter

attachment for syringe with filter valve

The siting of the epidural A thin, hollow tube, or catheter, is inserted through the needle into the epidural space, avoiding the dura (the thick membrane that encases the spinal cord), and the anaesthetic is passed down this tube.

The ten most frequently asked questions about epidurals

The idea of epidural anaesthesia understandably worries many women. This is partly because few relish the thought of a needle being inserted into their back so close to their spinal cord, and partly because they may have heard or read stories that are alarming. Below is a list of questions I am most often asked regarding the safety and possible side effects of epidurals. I hope that by answering them in detail, you are reassured about what an epidural involves.

1 Can I ask for an epidural even if I said in my birth plan that I didn't want one?
Yes, you can change your mind once you are in hospital and fully in labour. No one will mind – in fact, this happens quite a lot!

2 How late in my labour can I request an epidural?
You can have an epidural at any point in the first stage of labour – the only limiting factor is your ability to keep still while it is being administered, so this is why it needs to take place before the second (pushing) stage begins. An epidural can take up to an hour to set up and become effective, so if you are progressing quickly through the first stage, you could find that by the time you really feel like you need pain relief, your labour is almost over. In addition, apart from the time it takes to set up, your epidural could be delayed if another woman requests one at the same time. For these reasons, it is a good idea, if you are starting to struggle with the pain from your contractions, to say sooner rather than later that you may require an epidural.

3 Will I be put under pressure to have an epidural?
The short answer is 'no'. However, you may be offered one if you are planning a vaginal breech delivery (*see* p.202) or your baby is in a posterior position, because these labours are usually longer and/or more complicated. Similarly, if you are being induced with a syntocinon infusion (*see* p.193), you will also be offered an epidural, sometimes before the start of the procedure, because the contractions can be very powerful from the start. And if this is your first labour, you may be offered the chance to consider an epidural at some point. This is simply because the medical staff, who are highly experienced, have recognised that you are already having trouble managing the contractions and there may still be quite a long way to go in the first stage. They are therefore informing you that it might be a good time to think about an epidural before you miss the opportunity and it is too late. However, it goes without saying that the final decision is always up to you.

4 What are the risks of damage to my spine?
Spinal damage caused by an epidural remains one of the greatest fears. Fortunately, the latest research shows unequivocally that epidurals are extremely safe (*see* Useful Resources). The study looked at all groups of patients given this sort of anaesthesia, ranging from women in labour through children to frail, elderly patients (who often have epidurals because general anaesthesia is too risky for them). It concluded that in every (rare) case where death or injury occurred, the complications were the result of the patient's condition, rather than mistakes by the medical team and, in most cases, the patient was elderly.

If you are worried about moving during a contraction while the needle is being threaded into the epidural space, you can rest assured that anaesthetists are extremely used to this and stop what they are doing at the start of every contraction and only continue once it has fully subsided. Furthermore, it is extremely rare for the catheter to move inside your spine and if it did, the medical team would realise this at once because the area of numbness would change. Indeed, it is virtually impossible for an epidural to injure or paralyse you.

5 Will the epidural hurt?
Not as much as the contractions! The only thing you will feel is the small injection of local anaesthetic in your lower back to numb the skin in preparation for the insertion of the epidural needle. The process itself only causes mild discomfort, although it is true that some women do tense up considerably in anticipation of the procedure.

6 Does the epidural sometimes fail to block the pain?
Occasionally, a part of your abdomen or thigh remains

unaffected by the anaesthetic; very rarely, one half of your abdomen is not effectively blocked. This is because everyone has a slightly different nerve pathway distribution, which is usually asymmetrical. You will notice this uneven feeling immediately, and the anaesthetist will gently move the tube in your back or ask you to change position so that the drug can reach all the nerves required to anaesthetise you completely. Very rarely, the catheter needs to be taken out and repositioned completely, but this only takes a few minutes. I also want to stress that, if you are having a Caesarean section (see p.204) and have had an epidural, CSE or spinal block (see main text), you will be checked extensively by the anaesthetist before the operation takes place to ensure you are fully anaesthetised. Often, they will 'pinch' the skin over your abdomen to reassure you that, even though you feel some pressure, you will not sense pain.

7 Can I still push my baby out?

Contrary to what many people believe, you can still push during the second stage even if you are completely numb and cannot feel your contractions. Your midwife can tell when each contraction is about to start, because she will be interpreting the information on the CTG and will also have a hand on your abdomen, so will be able to feel when it is tightening up. She can then let you know when you should push. If possible, your epidural (or any top-up) will be timed so that it has worn off a little prior to the second stage. In this way, you can feel your abdomen tensing up at the start of each contraction but are not in any pain. It is true that you may push less effectively if you are completely anaesthetised, but it is certainly still possible to push sufficiently well to get your baby out.

8 Am I more likely to have an assisted (instrumental) delivery or a Caesarean section if I have an epidural?

Studies indicate that having an epidural in the early stages prolongs labour and increases the chance of further medical intervention such as an instrumental delivery by 40 per cent, but not of a Caesarean section. This is because if it is your first labour and you cannot feel contractions, it is difficult for you to push effectively.

9 Is there a risk of backache after the birth?

A lot of research has been carried out to see if epidurals lead to a higher incidence of postnatal backache. The conclusions of some studies indicate that this might be the case, whereas others contradict these findings and state that back problems are more likely to stem from a long, difficult labour or an assisted or Caesarean delivery than from the procedure itself. Postnatal back pain can also be caused by the fact that, during the latter part of the pregnancy, the lumbar region, spine and pelvic areas (including the sacroiliac joints at the base of the spine) were under considerable strain as a result of the increasingly heavy uterus. Weakened back and abdominal muscles, as well as tendons and ligaments that have been softened in preparation for the birth, are also a contributory factor (not to mention poor posture when lifting the baby or carrying the baby on one hip, manoeuvring the pushchair, slumping when breast-/formula feeding and general exhaustion…)

10 Are there other side effects of an epidural?

A small percentage of women suffer from headaches following an epidural. Usually, this happens because the needle has accidentally punctured the dura, the membrane surrounding the spinal cord. The pain is caused by a small amount of spinal fluid leaking out and is usually relieved by lying down. Some women also find that they have a slight tingling or numbness in one of their limbs. I would like to stress that all these symptoms are temporary and, although they sound alarming, they are nothing to worry about and will usually disappear within a few days or, in rare cases, within a few weeks. Your anaesthetist will see you the day after your delivery to make sure you have none of the above problems. Should you have a persistent headache at home, you should always mention this to your midwife or call the maternity unit, as you may need to come back for a further consultation.

General anaesthesia

Epidurals and spinal blocks are now such popular and safe
methods of anaesthesia during a Caesarean section that
general anaesthesia (GA) is rarely performed. Some women
do ask to have a GA because they don't want to be awake
during a Caesarean section, but this would only be agreed
once the pros and cons have been discussed and you are clear
that this is less safe for you than regional anaesthesia. There
are, however, certain circumstances for which it is still the
best, or indeed, only option:

▸ in extreme emergencies (e.g. severe placental abruption,
  cord prolapse) where your or the baby's life is at risk and
  it is imperative to deliver the baby immediately
▸ severe bleeding (to allow the anaesthetist to stabilise your
  blood pressure and cardiovascular system)
▸ if you have had a problem with your blood coagulation
  following an infection, haemorrhage or pre-eclampsia;
  if you have been taking large doses of anticoagulant
  drugs because you have suffered from thrombosis during
  pregnancy; or if you have an inherited or acquired bleeding
  disorder.

You will be awake when you are admitted to the operating
theatre and your birth partner should be able to accompany
you. However, before preparations get under way to
anaesthetise you, your partner will be asked to leave.

You will first of all be asked to lie on the operating table,
which is then slightly tilted to your left, and to breathe from
an oxygen mask for a few minutes to increase the oxygen
levels in your blood. After this, you will inhale the drugs that,
in a matter of seconds, will render you unconscious. Intravenous
drugs to relax your abdomen will be administered and an
endotracheal tube will be inserted down your throat so that
you continue to receive oxygen and do not choke on any food
or fluids that might come up from your stomach. Your blood
pressure will be checked every five minutes. The operation to
deliver your baby will then take place. In total, you should be
unconscious for 45–60 minutes.

You will be taken to a recovery room, where nurses will
continue to check your blood pressure at five-minute intervals.
You should start to regain consciousness within minutes of
the end of the operation, but it will be a little while longer
before you feel more alert. Your baby will stay with you in
recovery, where your midwife will help you to breastfeed,
and you will normally go up to the postnatal ward within
one to two hours.

Non-pharmacological pain relief

When we are in pain, it is a natural reflex to tense up. But
this action releases stress hormones, which make it harder to
cope with the pain and, consequently, our perception of pain
increases. We also know that, if we are able to relax or focus on
other things, pain can become more bearable and its intensity
can even decrease. This is especially true during early labour
and the first stage, so I believe it is worth trying some
non-pharmacological methods of pain relief.

The list of methods below is not exhaustive – it simply
covers the most popular ones. Whether or not they have been
scientifically proven to work is another matter. My own view
is that, provided you are sensible and realistic, none can do
you any harm and you may find some positively useful. I would
also recommend that, if you have never tried them before,
you should test them out in advance – don't assume that
just because a particular method worked for a friend of yours,
it will be of benefit to you as well.

It goes without saying that pain relief methods such as
acupuncture, reflexology or hypnotherapy should only be
carried out by a qualified practitioner (if possible, one that
has been recommended to you). If the practitioner needs to
be present during labour and you are giving birth in hospital,
check in advance with the unit if this is going to be possible
(*see* Chapter 5, p.137).

Breathing
Controlled breathing will help to keep your muscles relaxed
and maintain the flow of oxygen to all parts of your body.
You will feel calmer and reassured by the steady pattern
of breathing and, by focusing on inhaling and exhaling, you
will divert your attention away from the pain of contractions.

If you attended antenatal classes, the correct breathing
techniques for the different stages of labour will have

Increasing numbers of women are making use of birthing pools for labour and birth and most obstetric and maternity units have at least one. Being in warm water reduces pain, particularly during early labour, by relieving tension and enabling your muscles to relax. In addition, the buoyancy offered by water helps support you in your preferred labouring position and reduces the feeling of pressure on your cervix from the baby's head.

If you are giving birth at home, you will need to hire your own birthing pool and you may be able to choose from rigid, inflatable or heated models. Bear in mind that the pool will take a while to fill, so you should think about starting this when you are still in the early phase of labour. Your midwife will probably ask you not to get into the birthing pool until she has arrived, even if labour appears to be well underway, because she will want to examine you internally before giving you the go-ahead to get into the water.

Birthing pools are wonderful for easing the pain of early labour. If you need additional pain relief during this time, you will only be able to have gas and air while you are still in the water. If you want an epidural (and are at hospital) or pethidine, you will need to leave the pool. So, although you may start off in the pool for your labour, don't be disappointed if, in the end, you need to get out because you need greater pain relief.

The temperature of the water in the pool needs to be carefully monitored – your hired pool will come with a thermometer – and should never rise above 37°C (i.e. body temperature). If you remain in the water for a prolonged period of time, your midwife will check your temperature regularly to ensure that you are not getting too hot, as this could cause the baby's temperature to rise, leading to a decrease in oxygen levels, and your blood pressure to fall. If necessary, she will ask you to get out of the water, at least until you have cooled down. For this reason, the room you are in should be kept at a suitable temperature to prevent you from getting cold. Your midwife can still monitor the baby's heartbeat using a waterproof Doppler, but if she has any concerns that need further examination, you will need to leave the pool.

It is perfectly safe for your baby to be born in water, provided they are brought to the surface quickly once fully delivered and the umbilical cord is not clamped until this is done. In this way, the baby will continue to receive oxygen via the cord and will not inhale water. The benefit for you is that the water softens the perineum and reduces the likelihood of tearing. However, you will probably be asked to get out of the pool for the third stage of labour (the delivery of the placenta – see p.176), as it will be easier for the midwife to check the amount of blood loss.

Water births may not be recommended for women with a chronic health condition or pregnancy complications.

hopefully been explained and demonstrated to you. You should keep practising these regularly so that, by the time you are in labour, they are second nature. If you are able, make sure that your birth partner also knows about the techniques, so that they can remind you what you should be doing and can encourage and support you.

During the early stages of labour, the aim is to keep breathing in and out deeply in a slow, regular fashion through each contraction – it can be helpful for you and your birth partner to do this together. Inhale through your nostrils to the count of five, and exhale through your mouth for a further five. As labour progresses and contractions get longer and stronger, you may need to increase this cycle to two or three breaths per contraction. As you breathe, try to imagine yourself in an idyllic and relaxing setting. With the inhalation, feel the air reaching the furthest parts of your body; with the exhalation, visualise letting go of all the pain of the contraction, staying in your idyllic place as you do so. As labour progresses and

contractions get stronger, you will find your breathing naturally becomes stronger and more prolonged. This more purposeful breathing should help you to manage the pain, but I should emphasise that these breathing techniques work better for some women than for others.

TENS (Transcutaneous Electronic Nerve Stimulation)
A TENS machine is a small, battery-operated device with four electrodes that can be attached to your back using adhesive pads. The machine produces tiny electrical currents, which interfere with the pain messages sent by the nerves in your spinal column to your brain and stimulate the production of endorphins, the body's natural painkillers. The machine is portable, which leaves you free to move, although you cannot have a bath or use a birthing pool while wearing it. The effects of TENS can be felt immediately, so it can be used as soon as a contraction begins, and the current does not affect the baby in any way, so it is entirely safe.

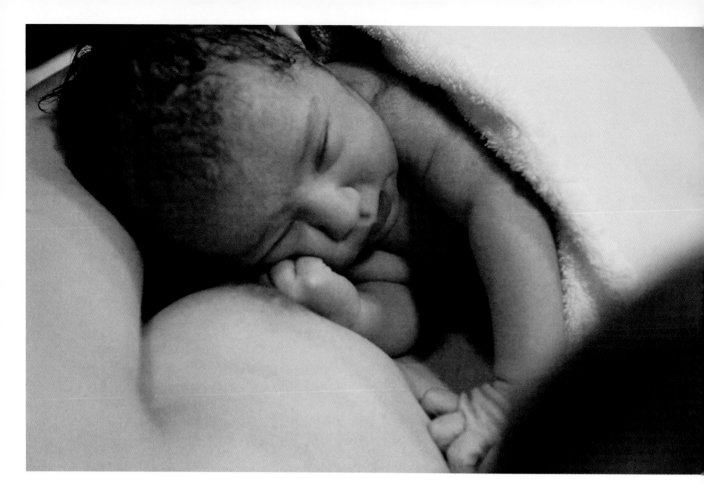

Many women like TENS because they can control the intensity of the current and the frequency at which it is delivered at the push of a button on the handset. Others, however, find it doesn't relieve their pain much at all. The level of pain relief TENS delivers is most suited to the early stages of labour, as it is often less beneficial as labour progresses. It is one of the methods of pain relief you can have for a home birth, and using it can also help you to stay in the comfort of your own home a little longer if you plan to deliver in hospital.

Machines can be bought or hired easily from specialist companies (*see* Useful Resources). Hospitals don't usually have any for use on the day, although you may be able to hire one in advance from them. I would advise you to obtain one from around 37 weeks (if you hire, you will be charged according to how long you keep it for), so that you can make sure you know how it works, including how to attach the electrodes to your back. You will need the help of someone else to do this, so it is a good idea to practise beforehand with your birth partner.

Massage

Massage can relieve tension and lower back pain and may help with the progress of labour. This is because it can stimulate the production of endorphins, the body's natural pain-relieving

hormones. You can use a simple oil or cream for the massage, although aromatherapy oils bring additional benefits (*see* below). Your birth partner should remove any jewellery and warm their hands. Once you are in a position that is comfortable for you, they can begin by massaging you with their fingers on the area of tension or pain, using either stroking or circular movements. This should gradually become firmer, using the palm of the hand as well. They will need to listen to your instructions in order to adjust what they are doing. Having your upper back, shoulders, neck and even temples massaged can often be very soothing, too, as it helps to reduce overall tension in your body.

Aromatherapy

Aromatherapy is the practice of using essential oils (extracts) from plants and flowers to enhance physical and mental well-being. These oils relax the body and calm the mind either by being absorbed through the skin in carrier oils (during massage or by adding them to bath water) or by being inhaled through vaporisers. Each essential oil has specific properties and characteristics, so some are particularly recommended during pregnancy and labour, while others are to be avoided. Essential oils that are recommended are chamomile, citrus, geranium, lavender, neroli, rose and sandalwood. Those that should be avoided include basil, bay, camphor, clary sage, hyssop, juniper berry, marjoram, myrrh, pennyroyal, pine, rosemary, sage, savoury, thuja, thyme and wintergreen.

Herbalism and homeopathy

There is a range of herbal and homeopathic remedies that can be taken during labour, but it is important that, rather than choosing one on your own, you consult a qualified practitioner in order to be given the correct remedy and dosage. Do also let your midwife know which remedy you are taking or planning to take, just to ensure that it is not contraindicated when taken in conjunction with any drugs you might be given during labour. As I have already said, just because the remedy is natural does not necessarily mean it is safe to use in all circumstances. See Chapter 2, p.40 for more information.

Acupuncture

Acupuncture is a traditional system of medicine, based on the Chinese concept of the life force, 'chi'. Ailments and pain occur when there is an imbalance in the way the life force flows through the body. To remedy this, very fine needles are inserted into specific areas to allow chi to flow freely once more, thus restoring balance and promoting healing.

Many women use acupuncture during pregnancy to treat symptoms like morning sickness and back pain, and it can be helpful during labour as well. However, if you do want to make use of it at this stage, you will need to ensure that your acupuncturist is experienced in treating women in labour and, equally importantly, is willing to come to your home and/or to the hospital. You must also check that your hospital is happy to have an acupuncturist attending to you during your labour.

Reflexology

Reflexology is a non-invasive therapy based on the theory that different points on the feet, lower legs, hands and ears correspond with different areas of the body. When pressure or massage is applied to specific points on the foot/leg/hand/ear, this promotes the natural function of the related part and so can be used to aid healing and provide pain relief. As with acupuncture, some women find that reflexology can help

alleviate pregnancy symptoms such as backache and other general pains, as well as – when used in conjunction with traditional medicine – gestational diabetes and hypertension. It can also be effective in labour. You and your partner can learn to massage and apply pressure on your feet in the correct way so that you do not need the reflexologist to be present. However, in order to do this, you will need to have several sessions with a qualified practitioner in advance.

Hypnobirthing

Hypnotherapy during birth is called hypnobirthing. It is becoming increasingly popular in labour. Hypnosis in this setting involves reaching a state of deep relaxation with the aid of specific techniques, which you have learnt beforehand with a teacher. These self-hypnosis exercises work by allowing you to feel complete calm because you are in control of your pain and what is happening to your body. Personally recommended practitioners are preferable, as this is an unregulated therapy. Books on the subject may also be helpful, as well as online information on deep relaxation techniques.

> " I visited a homeopath before my due date and was given different remedies for use in labour and postnatally. I read the instructions beforehand, which were quite detailed, so that I would know how to use them when the time came. I found the remedies very useful for helping with my symptoms, boosting my energy and addressing the emotional aspects of birth. " ANNE

METHODS OF PAIN RELIEF: KEY ELEMENTS TO CONSIDER

	BREATHING	TENS	MASSAGE, AROMATHERAPY	HERBALISM, HOMEOPATHY
EFFECT	Relaxes muscles. Focus on breathing takes mind off pain, so reduces awareness of it	Small electric currents reduce pain messages sent to brain and stimulate production of endorphins	Calm mind and relax muscles, so reduce pain	Plant extracts relieve pain and stress
HOW QUICKLY DOES IT WORK?	Fast, if done properly	Fast	Fast if done well	Fast
HOW LONG DOES IT LAST?	As long as you keep up breathing exercises	For duration of each contraction	A while if done well	Depends on therapy and individual
WHAT OTHER PAIN RELIEF CAN I USE IT WITH?	All methods	All except water and epidurals	All methods	Need to check with midwife
CAN I USE THROUGH LABOUR?	Yes	Yes, though mostly used in early labour	Yes, though mostly used in early labour	Yes, unless not compatible with some drugs; mostly used in early labour
CAN IT BE USED AT HOME OR HOSPITAL?	Both	Yes, though often have to hire and take into hospital	Both	Yes

ACUPUNCTURE, REFLEXOLOGY, HYPNOBIRTHING	GAS AND AIR	PETHIDINE	EPIDURAL, SPINAL BLOCK
Relax body, stimulate body's natural healing response (not hypno), so relieve pain	Reduces contraction pain; can make you feel nauseous, sick, light-headed	Reduces pain by dulling pain messages received by the brain; can make the baby sleepy	Numbs abdomen and (unless mobile epidural) legs and bladder; no pain felt
Within 15–30 mins	Fast	10–20 mins	30–45 mins
Depends on therapy and individual	For duration of each contraction	Up to 3 hours	Depends with epidural, but can be topped up regularly; spinal block lasts 1 hour and cannot be topped up; pudendal blocks are one-shot pain relief at end of labour
All methods	All methods	All methods	No need for other pain relief
Yes, though mostly used in early labour	Yes	Yes	Yes for epidurals; no for others
Both, though check therapist can be with you in hospital	Yes	Yes	Only in hospital obstetric units

INDUCTION

Although most women go into labour spontaneously, not all do so. There are a number of reasons why your labour may need to be started artificially, a process known as induction. Your midwife or obstetrician will discuss this with you by 38 weeks, so that you can be clear about why it might become necessary. You may, of course, decline induction, but be aware that medical professionals do not advise it without good reason.

Overall – and I must stress there is considerable variation from one hospital to another – around 25 per cent of labours may require induction. Of those, around 75 per cent result in a vaginal birth, although the rate of assisted deliveries (using ventouse or forceps) does increase a little, with almost one in five births requiring assistance, compared with one in six of non-induced labours. Induction also increases the risk of having a Caesarean section, although whether this happens depends, to some extent, on the reasons for induction in the first place. The best chance of having a vaginal delivery following induction is if the cervix is ripe, you have had a previous vaginal delivery, the baby and your pelvis are of average size and the head is already engaged. Labour may be induced for various reasons:

- Your baby is overdue. Most hospitals will offer women an induction if they have not gone into labour within twelve days of their estimated delivery date (see Chapter 4, p. 121). Induction for post-maturity does not significantly increase the Caesarean rate.
- Your baby's growth has slowed down or stopped. This can be seen on a scan and you may also have noticed that your baby's movements have reduced in number and strength. On balance it may be better for the health of your baby to deliver sooner.
- Your baby has a medical condition that requires prompt surgery after birth (it may be better to deliver during working hours, so that the specialists will be there). That said, doctors will take into account the risks attached to prematurity before deciding how early to induce a preterm baby.
- Your waters have broken but you have not gone into labour.

Doctors usually allow 24 hours before inducing (although you may request induction sooner) because after this time, the risk of developing a uterine infection increases and this could be dangerous for your baby.

- You are suffering from a medical condition, such as diabetes or pre-eclampsia. Doctors may decide that it is safer for you to deliver now, rather than wait for you to go into labour spontaneously.
- You have a significant personal reason for wanting to give birth now (e.g. your partner is being posted abroad). In rare cases, it might be agreed that you can be induced.

Your midwife or obstetrician will discuss induction of labour and the reasons why it might be necessary with you at your 38-week antenatal appointment. These include the risk of placental insufficiency (see Complications, p. 288) and of increasing rates of stillbirth (see Feature in Complications, pp. 294–96). Alternatively, if your membranes have already ruptured and labour has not begun after 24 hours, they will outline the benefits of induction. The methods used and the risks associated with induction will also be explained (see below), as well as what differences in your labour you can expect. For example, your labour could be longer and/or more intense and so you may need stronger pain relief, such as an epidural. You will also be made aware of the other courses of action available to you, should you decline induction. You can at this point ask for a sweep of your membranes to be performed (see Box opposite), in the hope that this will encourage your labour to begin without need for pharmacological intervention.

If, following your 40- and 41-week antenatal appointments, you have not yet gone into labour, you should be offered a membrane sweep and you can ask for additional sweeps if labour still doesn't begin – two or three a week can be done, even from 38 weeks, if requested, as there is no evidence to show what the ideal number of sweeps should be. Your medical carers will be keen to make sure that your baby is born before 42 weeks of gestation, so if labour has not started at 40+12 and you agree to it, they will book you into hospital to begin the process of induction.

The risks of induction

While the aim of induction is to minimise risk to the baby and the mother of a continuing pregnancy, it is associated with an increased chance of assisted (instrumental) delivery and a longer first stage of labour. It may also lead to a slight increase in the likelihood of hyperstimulation of the uterus, which may require medical intervention. However, it should be noted that this can also occur in spontaneous labour.

SWEEPING THE MEMBRANES

When a pregnancy is overdue, your midwife or doctor may offer to sweep the membranes of your cervix (known as a cervical sweep) in the hope that this triggers labour, thus avoiding the need for induction. The procedure is entirely safe for you and your baby and can be done up to three times a week in the period leading up to your agreed induction date.

A cervical sweep takes around ten minutes and can be a little uncomfortable, although it should not be painful (the breathing techniques used for early labour can be helpful). Using one or two fingers, your midwife or doctor will gently 'sweep' around the cervical os, with the aim of detaching the membranes (amniotic sac) from the cervix and thereby releasing prostaglandins. These are chemicals that cause the cervix to ripen, which then triggers contractions. If the cervix is tightly closed (because this is your first baby), your midwife or doctor may instead run their finger around the cervix in a circular motion, as this can also release prostaglandins.

You will be allowed home after the procedure and will be advised to take a warm bath and paracetamol if you experience any discomfort or contractions. Sweeping the membranes may also result in a little light bleeding, or a 'show' (see p.156). Thereafter, it can take a couple of days for anything to happen, but call the maternity unit if you have any heavier bleeding or regular pains or if you think your waters have broken.

How labour is induced

There are three methods of induction: prostaglandin gel/tablet/pessary; syntocinon via a drip; and artificial rupture of membranes (ARM). The decision to use one method rather than another depends on different factors and circumstances. It is not uncommon for two or even all methods to be used, because doctors may start with the least interventionist (prostoglandins) and, if that fails to bring on contractions, move on to using the other methods. Induction is not usually available at home, although more and more hospitals do allow you home once they are sure your baby is comfortable and the vaginal pessary is correctly placed.

Prostaglandin gel/tablets/pessary

A synthetic version of prostaglandins, the chemicals found naturally inside your uterus that stimulate contractions, can be administered in the form of a gel, tablet or controlled-release pessary. Gels/tablets can be given every six to eight hours (usually only two doses), with the aim that your cervix will ripen and contractions begin. Some hospitals now offer a single-dose, slow-release pessary that gently softens the cervix over 24 hours. After each dose, your baby's heart rate will be monitored for about half an hour. For the rest of the time, CTG monitoring is unlikely to be necessary until contractions start to occur.

Syntocinon drip

Syntocinon is a synthetic version of the hormone oxytocin, which is produced by the pituitary gland at the base of your brain and causes your uterus to contract. When used for induction, syntocinon is combined with a sterile dextrose-saline solution and is usually administered intravenously into your hand or arm via a drip. The initial dose is usually low, but this can be adjusted by a special infusion pump, according to how quickly contractions become established. The fetal heart rate will be monitored continuously using a CTG and your heart rate will be checked by a midwife every 30 minutes. This is because induction using this method invariably causes stronger, more regular contractions from the outset, which means that changes in the fetal heart rate are more likely to occur, as the baby has not had time to adjust by becoming used to the weaker contractions characteristic of the early phase of labour.

Artificial rupture of membranes (ARM)

Artificial rupture of membranes (ARM), sometimes called 'amniotomy', is performed for a variety of reasons (see Box on p.161), including (occasionally) as a first step in order to begin induction. However, ARM on its own would only be done if there is a reason for you *not* to have prostaglandins or if there is a concern regarding the frequency of your contractions or your baby's heart rate.

In a first labour, the cervix has to be 1–2 cm dilated for ARM to take place and this will be established by internal examination. (It can be done without dilation if you have had a previous vaginal birth, as the cervix never fully closes again.) The midwife or doctor will then insert a long, thin, plastic amniotomy hook into your vagina, guided by one finger of their hand in order to protect the internal tissues of your vagina. This is always directed towards their hand rather than towards your body, so it will not be painful while it is being inserted. It will then be rotated so that the sharper side of the hook is facing the membranes. Your midwife or obstetrician will sweep the hook against the membranes – this is often enough for them to break and, in so doing, they release prostaglandins that can stimulate contractions. While the hook can look a little alarming, the procedure itself is not painful and feels a little like having an elastic band pinging briefly inside you.

What happens when I am admitted for induction?

Once you have been admitted to the antenatal ward/induction area, your midwife or doctor will check your blood pressure and temperature. Your baby's heart rate may be monitored for around 30 minutes using a CTG. You will have an internal examination so that the ripeness of your cervix can be assessed and your abdomen will be palpated to determine the level of engagement of your baby's head, assuming it is cephalic (it would be highly unusual to induce a breech baby). A special chart, called a Bishop's score table, is used to note down the results in order to provide a baseline at the start of your induction.

Once all the checks have been done, a prostaglandin gel/tablet or pessary will be inserted into your vagina. If the six-hour version is used, the fetal heart will be listened to, you will be encouraged to walk about to help contractions to begin and you will be reassessed after six hours. If nothing has happened, the whole procedure will be repeated once or twice more. If the 24-hour method is used, your baby's heart rate will be listened to and you will simply wait for 24 hours. Some

hospitals will allow you to go home and come back the next day, but you may need to return earlier than that if your membranes have ruptured spontaneously, your contractions have begun or you are bleeding. Either way, you should not expect to deliver before at least 36 hours after insertion of prostaglandin, if this is your first baby. Bring reading material, music and anything else you need to pass the time if your hospital prefers you to stay in, and bring your own clothes as well, as you don't need to be in bed.

If the prostaglandin is effective, then your uterus will start to contract or your membranes will rupture. The fetal heartbeat will be checked again when contractions begin to occur regularly and you should be offered pain relief. Once your labour is fully established you will be moved to a delivery suite, and you can expect to proceed through the first, second and third stages, just like a spontaneous labour. See Box opposite for a summary of induction and what happens if it fails to stimulate the onset of labour.

Is an induced labour longer and more painful?

In general, an induced labour is longer than one that begins spontaneously, especially if it is a first labour, the head is not engaged or the cervix not ripe. In effect, induction leapfrogs some of the processes that would normally occur during the early phase of a normal labour. For example, the cervix can take around seven to ten days to ripen naturally (without your being aware of it), whereas, although induction tries to speed this up as part of the process of kick-starting contractions, it is not unusual for the cervix still to take up to 48 hours to really begin to change. This can make the early phase of an induced labour rather long, and it may feel particularly so when you are sitting around in hospital waiting for this to happen rather than carrying on with your life at home.

With a syntocinon-induced labour, contractions are often more regular from the start and feel stronger. You may find that, without the slow build-up to established labour, you feel less able to manage the level of pain and that there are fewer opportunities to rest. For this reason, most women who are induced make use of epidural pain relief (see p.182). You may, of course, prefer to see how you get on without regional anaesthesia, knowing that, if a syntocinon infusion is being used, it can be slowed down or stopped for a period of time while waiting for the epidural to be sited. Aside from the pain relief it offers, the other advantage of having an epidural is that there will be no need to arrange further anaesthesia (other than a possible top-up), should the need for an assisted delivery or a Caesarean arise (which saves time in the event of a medical emergency).

38-week antenatal appointment

You will discuss possible induction of labour with your midwife or obstetrician at 38 weeks. Alternatively, if suspected rupture of membranes is not followed by labour after 24 hours, the benefits of induction will be explained to you. Discussion usually includes:

▸ the reasons why induction may be recommended
▸ risks of induction in general (e.g. potential hyperstimulation, labour not becoming established) and solutions for these potential issues
▸ what to expect differently with an induced labour (e.g. could be longer and thus may need stronger analgesia, small increase in chance of instrumental delivery)
▸ what your options are if you decline induction.

40- and 41-week antenatal appointments

You should be offered a sweep of your membranes (or from 38 weeks, after discussion with your obstetrician) at 40 and 41 weeks to try to stimulate the onset of labour. You can ask for additional sweeps if labour still does not occur; two or three can be done and there is no evidence showing a limit to how many times the procedure can be performed.

40+12 weeks

If labour has not started by 40+12 weeks, induction will begin (with your consent). Your midwife or obstetrician will examine your cervix and listen to the fetal heartbeat before administering prostaglandin vaginally. This works either over six hours (gel or tablets) or 24 hours (slow-release pessary).

If the six-hour type of pessary is used, the following procedures will occur once the prostaglandin has been administered:

▸ the fetal heartbeat will be listened to again
▸ you will be encouraged to walk about to encourage contractions to begin
▸ you will be reassessed after six hours
▸ the whole procedure will be repeated once or twice more.

If nothing happens, there are four options, which will be discussed with you:

▸ stop for 24 hours to see if anything happens
▸ artificial rupture of membranes (ARM)
▸ a syntocinon infusion via a drip
▸ a Caesarean section.

If the 24-hour pessary is used, once the prostaglandin has been administered:

▸ the fetal heartbeat will be listened to
▸ you will wait 24 hours (some hospitals allow you to go home)
▸ the fetal heartbeat is checked again when contractions begin to occur regularly

If you do not go into labour, you may be offered:

▸ a syntocinon infusion via a drip
▸ a Caesarean section.

Augmentation of labour

Occasionally, a labour starts spontaneously and appears to be progressing, only for cervical dilation or contractions to slow down (which becomes evident from the partogram – see Box on p.161). Doctors may recommend that labour is accelerated, or 'augmented'. If the membranes are intact, ARM will be performed – this can often be enough to start contractions off again. If the membranes have already ruptured, a low-dose syntocinon drip will be offered until contractions become established and strong once more. You will be monitored regularly using a CTG to check for fetal compromise and, after a couple of hours, your labour should be showing clear signs of progression; if not, the strength of the syntocinon infusion will be increased. However, if progress is still not satisfactory after another two hours, your doctor may review your situation and recommend that your cervix be reassessed. The potential reasons for labour not progressing would then be addressed.

> **DID YOU KNOW…?**
> Women aged over 35 are 30 per cent more likely to have a prolonged labour (over twelve hours) and require a syntocinon infusion.

INDUCTION

Prolonged labour

If it takes longer than twelve hours of regular contractions for you to progress from 4 to 10 cm dilated, it is defined as a prolonged labour. In around five to eight per cent of labours – usually first labours – the cervix either fails to dilate sufficiently or the baby does not descend through the birth canal, which means that labour either doesn't progress or takes much longer than usual. There are several reasons for this, which include:

▸ occipito-posterior or breech presentation (*see* Chapter 5, p.148)
▸ inefficient contractions
▸ obstructed labour (e.g. uterine fibroid, fetal abnormality).

Around ten per cent of babies are in the occipito-posterior (OP) presentation at the start of labour. Although the majority rotate to the occipito-anterior (OA) presentation as labour progresses, not all do so. OP presentation is less straightforward than OA and tends to make labour longer and more difficult (and therefore more painful). Staying as upright and mobile as much as possible throughout can relieve the pressure of the baby's back on your sacrum (as can getting on your hands and knees) and will also encourage the baby to rotate. Lower back massage can also be helpful. An epidural is often given to enable you to manage the contractions, and augmentation of labour may also be necessary so that you and your baby do not become fatigued by the length of the labour.

Underactive contractions usually mean that the cervix does not dilate. A partogram will normally identify this sort of uterine activity and a syntocinon infusion may be offered to help increase the strength of the contractions. If the cervix still fails to dilate more than 2 cm over the next four hours, a Caesarean section may be offered to avoid the increasing risks posed by maternal and fetal exhaustion.

Obstructed labour is a rare occurrence nowadays, thanks to the availability of ultrasound scanning. Antenatal monitoring with ultrasound scans invariably identifies in advance of the birth any potential problem, such as a uterine mass (most commonly a fibroid – *see* Complications, p. 285) or a fetal abnormality (e.g. hydrocephalus), that may impede the progress of labour.

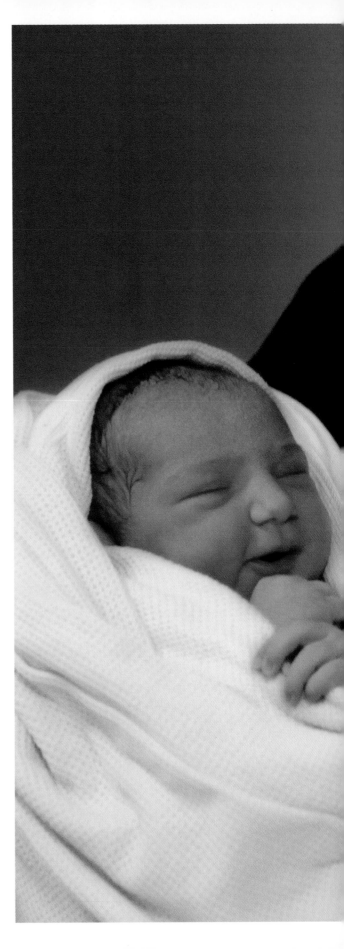

ASSISTED DELIVERY

Around fifteen per cent of vaginal births are assisted during the second (pushing) stage by using either ventouse or forceps to guide the baby down through the birth canal. This is sometimes referred to as an instrumental delivery.

One of two methods is used to assist the delivery of the baby, depending on your circumstances. A ventouse (a suction cap attached to the crown of the baby's head) is used in around two-thirds of assisted deliveries, while forceps (long metal spoons that fit around the head) are used in the remaining third. Although obstetricians are usually responsible for deciding whether this sort of delivery is required and will carry out the procedure themselves, some senior midwives are now trained to be able to perform ventouse and low, lift-out forceps deliveries. Both methods have their advantages and drawbacks. In the end, the best one is one that is carried out by a skilled obstetrician or midwife and is appropriate to that particular labour. The reasons why you might need an assisted delivery include:

▸ the baby is in the occipito-transverse or occipito-posterior position (*see* Chapter 5, p.148)
▸ the fetus is showing signs of compromise (*see* Box on p.194) and a quick delivery is required
▸ the baby is not descending through the birth canal, despite the cervix being fully dilated
▸ your sensation and ability to push is diminished by epidural pain relief.

Women are usually given pain relief when they have an assisted delivery. Many have an epidural and this may have already been set up to offer pain relief earlier on in their labour. If it is too late in your labour for an epidural, or if low lift-out forceps are used, you will be given a faster form of pain relief: a spinal block or a pudendal block. See p.182 for information on regional anaesthesia.

Your legs will be supported by leg rests so that your doctor or midwife will have the best visibility and access to your baby throughout the procedure. You will not automatically have an episiotomy (*see* p.174) if a ventouse or low, lift-out forceps are used, although this is much more likely with the other types of forceps (*see* p.200).

Ventouse (vacuum extraction)

A ventouse (sometimes called 'vacuum extraction') uses suction to aid the birth of the baby. It is a relatively recent invention, popularised in the 1950s and 1960s as an alternative to forceps. A rigid metallic or plastic cup fits over the top of the baby's head and is attached to a tube. This is connected to external apparatus that is used to gradually create a vacuum in the cup, allowing it to be gently suctioned onto the baby's scalp. A chain or handle also attached to the cap allows the doctor or midwife to apply gentle traction. The use of ventouse has become increasingly common and, in many units, has become the main method of assisted delivery. It can only be used if the cervix is fully dilated and the baby's head is already quite far down the birth canal. You remain very involved in the delivery of your baby: I would say that 70 per cent is down to your efforts, 30 per cent to that of your healthcare professional.

Attaching the ventouse to the baby's head usually takes around two minutes, which often corresponds to the amount of time between second stage contractions. After the doctor or midwife has checked that no maternal tissue has inadvertently been trapped under the suction cup, you can continue to push the baby out during the next few contractions. By holding onto the chain or handle, the doctor or midwife can help to guide the baby's head down the birth canal. Once the baby's head has crowned, usually within three or four good contractions, the suction cup is released, and the delivery continues without assistance. If it takes longer than this for the head to be delivered, or if the ventouse cup has been in place for longer than around fifteen minutes, forceps or a Caesarean section may be necessary. If there is any doubt about whether a ventouse delivery is possible, you may be transferred to the operating theatre to have a 'trial' vaginal delivery, so that you are already in the right place should a Caesarean be necessary.

After the birth, there is usually a swelling (known as a 'chignon') on the baby's scalp where the suction has occurred. This can be more prominent if a metal cap is used, or if the cap became dislodged at any stage during the delivery and suction had to be reapplied. The swelling invariably subsides after a few days, although in just over ten per cent of cases, superficial scalp injuries do occur that take a little longer to heal. Usually, these injuries involve an element of bruising, but in around half of these cases, blood collects beneath the top layer of the skull bones and takes up to a couple of weeks to disappear. Very occasionally, if the bruising is severe, it can cause jaundice (*see* Complications, p. 287). Intracranial bleeding (bleeding into the head) is rare (less than 0.3 per cent of ventouse deliveries) and no more common than in babies delivered by forceps or Caesarean section, so the cause is likely to be labour itself rather than the method of delivery. Maternal complications from ventouse extraction are rare, and tend to involve problems with healing after an episiotomy, if it was necessary (*see* below).

There are certain advantages to ventouse over forceps delivery. Firstly, the diameter needed to deliver the fetal head does not need to be wider, in the way that it can do when forceps cradle the head on either side. This means that some women will not need to have an episiotomy. There is also less risk of damage to the perineum. In addition, the baby's head is still free to rotate down the birth canal in a way that it is not when forceps are used. Lastly, if the baby is not in the ideal occipito-anterior position to begin with, the ventouse can be used to encourage rotation. However, compared to using forceps, a ventouse delivery can be slower, because it takes a little while to set up the equipment, and success is dependent on the mother's continued ability to push. It is also not suitable for premature babies born before 37 weeks.

DID YOU KNOW…?
A baby's skull is designed to withstand the considerable pressure of descent down the birth canal, so any bruising from an assisted delivery soon disappears and it is rare for there to be any lasting damage.

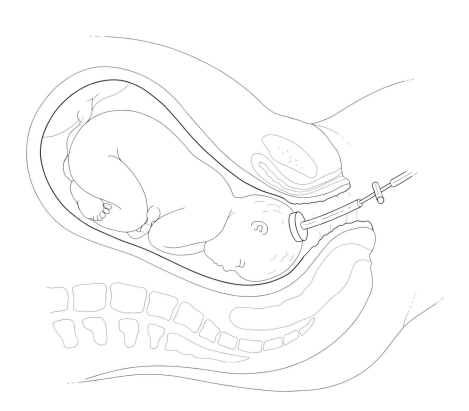

Assisted delivery using a ventouse
A suction cup is attached to the baby's head and gentle traction is used, working with your contractions, to draw the baby out.

Forceps

Forceps are thought to have first been invented in the early seventeenth century by a French doctor living in England and used to be the main method of assisted delivery. However, as the popularity of ventouse has grown, and as the rate and safety of Caesarean delivery has also increased, the use of forceps has decreased. It remains, however, an invaluable method of delivery for some women.

There are three types of forceps: low, lift-out forceps; straight traction forceps; and rotational forceps (Kielland's) forceps. In each case, the curved blades of the forceps are inserted one at a time and cradled around the baby's head. The obstetrician then guides the baby out, using traction. Nowadays, forceps are invariably used once the baby's head has descended into the pelvis, otherwise a Caesarean section is the preferred method of delivery.

Low, lift-out forceps are used when the baby's head is close to being delivered but needs a little help in the final stages, sometimes because the baby is showing signs of fatigue. Straight traction forceps are used when the baby's head has engaged and descended part of the way down the birth canal. Once the forceps are placed on either side of the head, traction is applied so that, within three or so good contractions, the head can usually be delivered. If progress down the birth canal is not made with the first or second contraction, a Caesarean section will usually be performed.

Rotational (Kielland's) forceps are occasionally used by experienced obstetricians. These forceps reach up midway up the birth canal to turn a baby's head from a transverse or occipito-posterior presentation to an occipito-anterior one. After that, they guide the baby down the birth canal in the same way as straight traction forceps. This sort of delivery is usually done in an operating theatre so that a Caesarean section can be done very quickly if the forceps delivery does not succeed.

The principal advantage of forceps is that they can be employed more quickly and in a greater variety of circumstances than a ventouse. For example, they don't depend on the woman's ability to push, so they can be used when an epidural has been administered. After birth, the sides of the baby's head may at first look bruised where pressure from the blades occurred, but this should disappear within the first few days. The vaginal opening needs to be enlarged before forceps can be used and so women are likely to have an episiotomy, which may reduce the chance of an extended perineal tear. However, the circumstances in which forceps are usually needed may, in any case, have resulted in an episiotomy or perineal tearing (e.g. if your baby is very big).

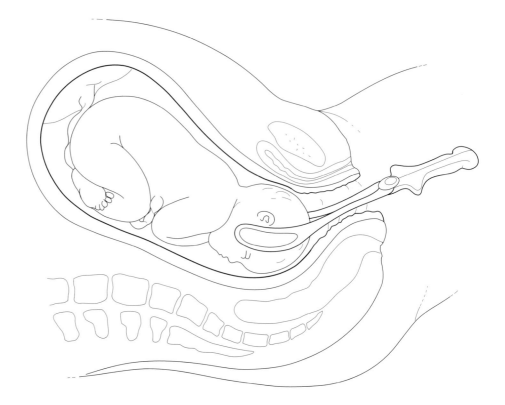

Assisted delivery using forceps Forceps are placed on either side of the head to help guide the baby out. An episiotomy may be required to allow both the head and the forceps to pass through the vaginal opening.

BREECH BIRTH

The breech presentation poses specific difficulties for vaginal birth. As a result, almost 90 per cent of breech babies are born by Caesarean section. Nevertheless, it is possible to deliver a breech baby vaginally, although you are very unlikely to do so at home or in a midwifery unit, as the risks of complications are too high.

There are three types of breech presentation (*see* diagrams):

▸ **frank**: the baby's buttocks are the presenting part and the legs are stretched up in front of the baby
▸ **complete or flexed breech**: the buttocks are the presenting part and the knees are bent in front of the baby
▸ **footling breech**: the legs are beneath the baby and one of the feet is the presenting part (in which case vaginal deliveries are very rarely attempted).

With a breech presentation, the pressure exerted on the cervix is not as great as it is when the head is the presenting part (cephalic presentation – *see* p.148). This means that the cervix is likely to dilate more slowly, making labour longer and leading to a higher chance of fetal compromise. This is one of the reasons why Caesarean sections often become necessary

EXTERNAL CEPHALIC VERSION (ECV)

If your baby is found to be in a breech presentation at 36 weeks, your obstetrician will offer to turn the baby manually using a technique called external cephalic version (ECV). Gentle external pressure is applied manually to your abdomen in an effort to get the baby to turn to the cephalic (head down) presentation in the uterus. The procedure is done after 37 weeks to minimise the chance of the baby turning back again, either in the maternity unit or in a special day care centre at your hospital. You will be asked not to eat anything for six hours before the procedure. There is a small risk that ECV will cause the baby's heart rate to drop – if it doesn't quickly return to normal, an emergency Caesarean section will be required. As ECV can be uncomfortable, you will be offered terbutaline, a tocolytic drug (*see* Chapter 7, p.223) that relaxes the uterine muscle. If at any stage the procedure is painful, the obstetrician will stop. ECV has a 50 per cent success rate in first pregnancies, 60–70 per cent in second and subsequent pregnancies.

during the first stage of a breech labour. There is also an increased risk of a prolapsed umbilical cord (*see* Complications, p. 293), especially if your membranes rupture before your contractions start. Again, this is because the baby's bottom (or foot) fits less tightly inside the pelvis, giving the cord space to slip through the cervix. If the cord becomes exposed to air, it constricts, leading to oxygen deprivation during the birth

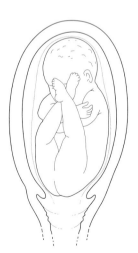

Frank breech

Complete (or flexed) breech

Footling breech

and acute fetal compromise. Finally, in a breech delivery the smaller part of the baby (the bottom) is delivered first, which may mean that the cervix may not be fully dilated when the largest part (the head) is delivered – the bottom can pass through when the cervix is only 8–9 cm dilated, whereas the head needs 10 cm. This can be particularly problematic if you have never had a vaginal delivery before.

Almost four per cent of babies are breech at term, and most are identified at 36–7 weeks. Extensive studies have shown repeatedly that delivering a breech baby via Caesarean section is safer than doing so vaginally. However, a large, more recent global study of breech births found that, although breech babies born vaginally were three times more likely to need a short stay in the neonatal unit than babies who were born head first, at one year, they were performing as well as the cephalic babies (*see* Useful Resources for further details). Nevertheless, you should discuss your delivery options with your obstetrician, who will explain to you the pluses and minuses of each method, and many women still prefer for their babies not to spend their first week or so in hospital.

All women with breech presentations at 36 weeks are offered external cephalic version (ECV – *see* Box), provided it is not contraindicated (e.g. you have a previous uterine scar). This attempts to turn the baby to a cephalic presentation and enable a more straightforward vaginal delivery. If ECV is contraindicated, unsuccessful or you prefer not to undergo it, you may still proceed with a vaginal delivery, once the possible complications have been explained to you, or opt for a Caesarean section. You can, of course, decide upon a Caesarean section from the outset (in which case ECV is unnecessary)

and, in fact, the clear majority of breech presentations are delivered by elective Caesarean section at 39 weeks. This slightly earlier delivery is in case you go into labour spontaneously before your estimated delivery date.

Delivering the baby

Breech births are most successful when your baby is in the frank breech presentation. Throughout your labour, you will be under the close supervision of a senior obstetrician and midwife and have continuous monitoring with a CTG. You will be advised to have an epidural anaesthetic, not only because breech labours are often more painful, but also because of the increased likelihood of an assisted or emergency Caesarean delivery. Your labour will always be considered a 'trial', with recourse to medical intervention should any problems occur.

If labour progresses to the second stage, you may be asked to put your legs in leg rests for ease of access to the baby in the second stage of labour. The bottom is delivered first, followed by one leg, then the other. No pulling takes place. Once the baby's abdomen and arms have passed through the birth canal, the head is the last to deliver. The obstetrician does not touch the baby until the legs are out, so as not to interfere with the gentle descent down the birth canal. The worst scenario – although rare – is when it becomes apparent that the head is not going to be able to fit through the cervix and will become stuck: this leads to an emergency procedure at a very far advanced stage of labour. This is traumatic for parents and also for staff. So if there is any doubt that the head is going to be able to be delivered vaginally, a Caesarean section will be performed earlier.

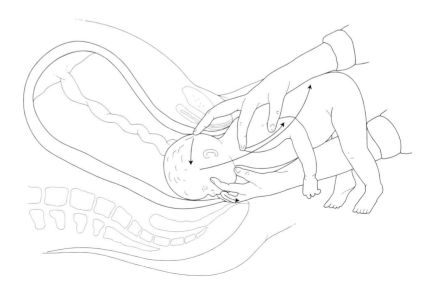

Assisted breech delivery The head is the largest part of the baby to deliver. The doctor will carefully observe the delivery of your baby's body and will wait until they see the nape of the baby's neck. Then, supporting the baby's body over one hand and arm, the doctor will place the first and third finger of this hand on either side of the baby's nose. The other hand is placed just below the occiput (back of the baby's head), with the middle finger placed on the occiput to aid flexion of the head towards the chest. The position of both hands then allows for delivery of the baby's head.

CAESAREAN SECTION

A Caesarean section is an abdominal operation to deliver a baby and is carried out when you and/or your baby are at risk. Around 25–30 per cent of births in Britain are now by Caesarean section (one in three for women over 35), so it is vital that you read about it as carefully as you do about vaginal delivery.

Caesarean sections (sometimes abbreviated to Caesar, C-section or CS) are another much-debated area of pregnancy and childbirth and one on which many people have an opinion. Some people feel strongly that too many Caesareans are now done without justification and, in many cases, a vaginal birth could have taken place if the mother or the healthcare professionals had really wanted it to. Other people feel that the advantages of delivering a baby by Caesarean section almost always outweigh any reasons why that procedure could and should have been avoided. If you have the facts, however, it is easier to decide for yourself what you think.

Much of the hostility towards Caesarean sections stems from the belief that a vaginal delivery is the 'right' way to give birth. Because they have envisaged a 'natural' vaginal birth, and preferably one that uses as little pain relief as possible, women can feel bitterly disappointed when things don't go to plan. Yet I cannot stress enough how important it is to see a Caesarean birth simply as a different sort of birth, rather than as a 'failed' one. Some women have problem-free labours, others do not. You do not 'end up' having a Caesarean, as if it is the last resort and a sign of not giving birth as you should. You have one because, without it, you and your baby would have been at significant risk. After all, there is nothing 'natural' about the high mortality rates of mothers and babies, both throughout history and in many parts of the world today due to inadequate medical care.

Caesarean sections have saved the lives of countless women and babies. It is decided upon with your full agreement – and you can, of course, decline. I hope that the safe delivery of a baby that you have carried inside you for all those months is, in the end, something that you feel is the priority. In short, I strongly believe that there is no 'right' way to give birth, but there is a safe way. If that involves having a Caesarean section, then that should be welcomed as much as a vaginal delivery.

Why the increase in Caesareans?

The Caesarean section delivery rate has increased significantly in the space of a generation and there are many reasons why this is so. One of the principal ones is that the operation is now much safer. This is largely because it is carried out, in most instances, under regional anaesthesia – either with an epidural, a combined spinal block and epidural (CSE) or a spinal block – rather than under general anaesthesia, which always carries an element of risk (general anaesthesia is now used in less than two per cent of Caesarean sections). In addition, antenatal care, including the use of ultrasound and other diagnostic equipment/tests, can identify problems during pregnancy so that, where necessary, a Caesarean can be decided upon in advance. Another change in medical procedure is that rotational forceps (see p.200) are now used less frequently as a method of delivery, because of the risk of damage to mother and baby – a Caesarean section is nearly always performed instead.

Some of the factors that play a part in the increase are social ones. There has been a steady rise in the number of women over the age of 35 giving birth, especially to their first babies, and older mothers are more likely to experience complications in pregnancy and/or labour (see Feature in Chapter 3, pp.80 –1). In addition, the increasing availability of IVF not only swells the ranks of older mothers, but of multiple births, too, which are more likely to be delivered by Caesarean; moreover, women who have conceived through IVF tend to be more anxious about their pregnancy and often prefer the near-certainty of a safe delivery that a Caesarean section brings. The enormous increase in maternal diabetes and obesity (almost one in five women are now clinically obese at the start of pregnancy – see Chapter 2, pp.30 –1) has led

DID YOU KNOW...?
You are now entitled to ask for a Caesarean section, even if you don't have a medical reason for one. Your obstetrician will offer you a counselling appointment to fully explore your reasons for declining a vaginal delivery and, if you still feel very strongly that you would prefer a Caesarean, then in most cases it will be offered.

to a higher proportion of deliveries by Caesarean section. The number of premature births has also increased, in part because of these rises in maternal age and obesity (two of the risk factors associated with prematurity) – premature babies are more likely to be delivered by Caesarean section, as they tire more easily in labour.

Elective and emergency Caesareans

A Caesarean section can either be 'elective', in which case it is planned in advance, or 'emergency', which means that it is an unscheduled operation that is needed because a medical problem has arisen. There are around 50 per cent more emergency Caesareans than elective ones. See Box on p.206 for more information on how the urgency of a Caesarean section is classified.

Elective Caesareans

You may discuss the advantages and disadvantages of the types of delivery with your medical carers and decide that, given your circumstances, a planned Caesarean is the better, safer, choice. In some cases, your situation is such that a Caesarean section is the only option to deliver a baby safely. The following are some of reasons for having an elective Caesarean section:

▸ The placenta is either lying close to the inner opening of the cervix or over it, thus preventing the baby's head from descending into the birth canal (placenta praevia – *see* Complications, p. 287). This occurs in 0.5 per cent of pregnancies at term and will have been diagnosed beforehand. An elective Caesarean is the only way to deliver your baby.
▸ Your baby is in the breech or transverse presentation, cannot be turned and you don't want a trial vaginal birth. Almost 90 per cent of breech babies are now delivered by Caesarean section.
▸ You have had a previous Caesarean section and you don't want a trial vaginal delivery.
▸ Your baby is premature and needs to be delivered before labour starts spontaneously.
▸ Your baby requires an operation just after the birth. It is better to plan a Caesarean, so that the necessary medical staff can be on hand at the right time.

Emergency Caesareans

Sometimes, problems arise, either shortly before or during labour, that mean that it is best to deliver the baby soon by Caesarean section. An unscheduled procedure is termed an 'emergency' Caesarean. An emergency Caesarean only rarely means that the baby has to be delivered in the next few minutes in order to ensure a safe outcome. More commonly, you have 30–60 minutes before you or your baby may be at risk. On other occasions, there are indications before your labour starts that a Caesarean may be required, but you and your healthcare professionals have decided to proceed with a trial of labour, in the knowledge that a Caesarean can be performed if a vaginal delivery does not succeed – this is still referred to as an 'emergency' Caesarean. The following are some of medical reasons why an emergency Caesarean may be necessary:

▸ The umbilical cord has prolapsed, meaning it has slipped out from underneath the baby and is now outside the vagina (*see* Complications, p. 293). This is a particular risk with breech births.
▸ An abnormal fetal heart rate has been detected. This can be caused by a variety of reasons, but your midwife or obstetrician will identify it either as a result of fetal monitoring or because they notice that the baby has started to produce meconium. These are signs of fetal 'compromise' (*see* Box on p.194).
▸ Your labour has failed to progress, either because the cervix is slow to or fails to dilate, or because the contractions are inadequate. This increases the risk of fetal compromise and of maternal fatigue.
▸ You are experiencing significant and on-going bleeding from the placenta during the third trimester of pregnancy. This could indicate antepartum haemorrhage or placental abruption (*see* Complications, pp. 289 and 288), both of which are potentially extremely serious. It is likely your baby will need to be delivered as a matter of urgency.

DID YOU KNOW...?

Any non-scheduled Caesarean section will always be described as an 'emergency', even though there is usually no *immediate* danger to you or your baby. Please be reassured that, except in extreme circumstances, all this means is that delivery can take place within the next half an hour and still result in the safe delivery of a healthy baby.

All doctors work to a classification system (1–4) that enables them to identify more clearly which category of urgency a Caesarean section belongs to, based on the presence or absence of maternal/fetal compromise:

Urgency	Definition	Category
Maternal or fetal compromise	Immediate threat to life of woman or baby	1
	No immediate threat to life of woman or baby	2
	Requires early delivery	3
No maternal or fetal compromise	Delivery at a time to suit the woman and maternity services	4

If your baby is to be delivered by Caesarean section, your obstetrician will be able to inform you of your category of urgency. The classification shows that, while some babies may need delivering within 30 minutes (cat.1), others are at no immediate risk and may be delivered some time later the same day (cat.3). In other words, there is a 'continuum of urgency' that applies to Caesarean sections, rather than black-and-white categories of urgent versus non-urgent.

Risks of Caesarean versus vaginal delivery

It is difficult to compare precisely the benefits of one type of delivery against those of another. A Caesarean delivery is done because your circumstances are such that it is safer for you and/or the baby; or because it is the *only* option to ensure your well-being and and that of your baby. Complications from the procedure usually occur because there is an underlying medical cause, for example, the mother is a smoker, has a known risk of venous thromboembolism (*see* Box in Chapter 3, p.60), is clinically obese or is suffering from pre-eclampsia (*see* Complications, p. 289). Similarly, the baby may be very premature, in need of immediate surgery or known to be at risk for other reasons.

Studies over the years have shown that the risk of postnatal maternal problems, such as urinary or endometrial infection, postpartum haemorrhage or pain during intercourse up to three months after delivery is minimal following a Caesarean section compared to a vaginal birth. All women are now given prophylactic antibiotics immediately prior to the operation to reduce the risk of infection. One in 100 babies receive a cut on the face, head or bottom, which usually leaves no lasting mark, and some have short-term respiratory problems because they have not had their lungs squeezed through the birth canal.

It is true that you will probably stay in hospital for longer following a Caesarean section – usually around three days, compared to about 24 hours following a straightforward vaginal birth – but you can also go home after 24 hours if you wish. If you have an elective Caesarean and do not therefore go into labour, it can take a little longer for your breasts to start producing colostrum (the early nutrient-rich liquid that precedes milk production) and milk. But if you can put your baby to your breast straight after delivery, this will begin the stimulation of your milk ducts. Your midwife and obstetrician will encourage you to do this, and will also offer to give you the baby straight after delivery to have the benefits of skin-to-skin contact, just as they would if you had delivered vaginally.

A Caesarean section is, however, a major abdominal operation and so, inevitably, recovery from this will take longer than if you have a vaginal delivery. This can be difficult when you also have a new baby to look after, have restricted mobility and are taking strong painkillers, so if you are having an elective Caesarean, you may want to think about organising some help at home while you regain your strength. You will have to be careful for a while about lifting heavy objects, and even about driving until you feel comfortable to do so. There is also a slightly increased risk that you will need to be admitted to an intensive care unit or need further surgery in the event of primary postpartum haemorrhage (*see* Complications, p. 289). Longer term, you will be left with a scar (although this will be below your bikini line and will be unobtrusive) and a slight bulge just above. See Chapter 8, p.234–6 for more on recovering from a Caesarean section.

Vaginal deliveries also carry risks. You have a higher chance of developing uterovaginal prolapse in later life as a result of damage to your perineal muscles, although some of this effect is actually due to gravity and the weight of the uterus and baby against your cervix and bladder for nine months (this is a 'design flaw' in humans, now that we walk on two legs, not four!). You also have a higher risk of urinary incontinence: one in three post-menopausal women suffer from this problem to some degree, and this is often caused or exacerbated by a difficult or long vaginal delivery. If you have an episiotomy (around one in four women), there can be problems caused by scarring and infected stitches.

I believe that the risks and benefits attached to Caesarean and vaginal deliveries even out in the end. Remember, the best way of giving birth is, ultimately, the one that is safest for you and your baby and that the birth itself is usually just one day in the whole life of your child.

What to expect in the operating theatre

If you require a Caesarean section, your baby will be delivered in an operating theatre on an operating table. There will be a baby resuscitation trolley in the theatre, various pumps for intravenous medicines, a CTG monitoring machine and, at the head end of the operating table, the anaesthetic machine. A fabric screen will be placed in front of you at chest level so that you do not actually see the operation taking place, although there is nothing preventing your partner from watching. If you would like, and all is well, the screen can be lowered so that you can see the baby emerge. During the operation itself, you can have the radio on or bring your own music if you want. See Chapter 5, p.152 for more information on understanding the hospital setting.

Be prepared for noise in theatre, including high-pitch beeps from the anaesthetic machine and doctors' bleeps, as well as the ringing of the operating theatre telephone. There are bright spotlights above the operating table to enable the obstetrician to see clearly and to ensure the safety of all staff in the theatre. Before starting the operation, you will also hear the theatre staff reading through a safe-surgery checklist. This guarantees that all staff are clear about the nature of the operation and about any possible complications that may be anticipated.

In total, it usually takes less than five minutes to actually deliver a baby by Caesarean section, However, the procedure takes around an hour from start to finish, with most of that

ONCE A CAESAREAN, ALWAYS A CAESAREAN?

In the past, once you had had one Caesarean delivery, it was likely that all further babies you had would also be delivered in this way. It is true that the risk of needing a Caesarean in subsequent pregnancies remains higher if you have had one previously, especially if your labour is induced. However, unless there are clear medical contraindications, there is no reason why you cannot have a trial labour. Nationally, nearly three quarters of women whose previous delivery was by Caesarean section now go on to have a successful vaginal delivery.

Similarly, women used to be advised not to have more than two Caesarean sections, but these days it is possible to have more than this, as long as your particular medical and health circumstances are taken into account, you are carefully monitored throughout pregnancy and birth and you are fully aware of the risks. These include placenta accreta, where the placenta fails to separate from the uterus after birth (*see* Complications, p. 287).

time spent setting up the anaesthetic and preparing you beforehand, then stitching up your uterus, muscle layers and skin after the operation.

What happens during a Caesarean section?

If you are having the operation using regional anaesthesia – either with an epidural, CSE or a spinal block – you will be conscious throughout the delivery (*see* p.186 for information on having the operation under general anaesthesia). Unless time is of the essence, you will be asked to remove nail varnish, make-up and jewellery before going to theatre. Removing nail varnish is necessary because the oxygen saturation monitor that is placed on your finger is impeded by nail varnish, making the anaesthetists' job harder, and jewellery may interfere with the diathermy operating equipment, which uses an electric current to seal small blood vessels.

You will need to be in a hospital gown for the operation, only so that it can easily be lifted up above the operating site and to accommodate the lines from the drip (*see* p.208). You will be given surgical stockings to wear from now until you are discharged from hospital to reduce the risk of developing postpartum blood clots, which could lead to venous thromboembolism (VTE – *see* Box, p.214). If your partner is attending, they will be asked to change into scrubs (and they may be reluctant to change back out of them, deciding that

CAESAREAN SECTION

207

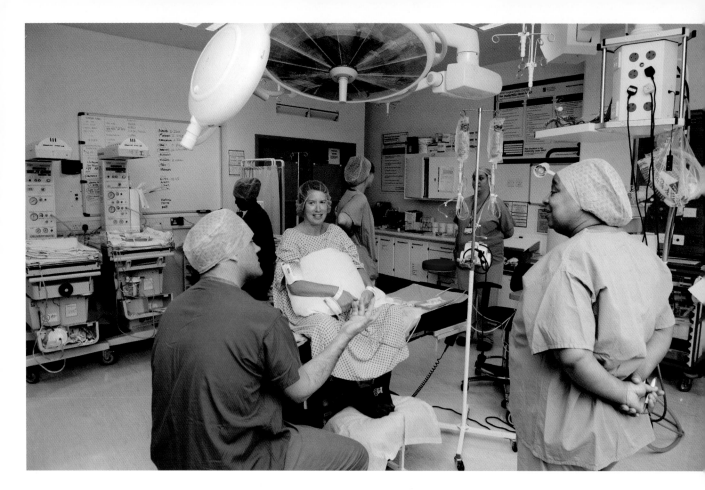

they look like George Clooney!). If you are having an elective procedure, you will be able to walk to theatre, but if yours is an emergency Caesarean, you will be wheeled there on the delivery bed before being transferred to the operating table.

Administering the anaesthetic

Depending on your circumstances, an epidural, CSE or spinal block will be set up (*see* pp.182 and 186 for more information) and a dextrose-saline solution (which is almost identical to the body's own vascular fluid) will be inserted via a drip into your arm to counteract any drop in blood pressure that may occur during the operation. Some women become quite anxious at this stage, either at the thought of the operation or at the idea of a needle about to be inserted into their spine. The anaesthetist will be accustomed to this and, if you start to hyperventilate, shake or feel sick or light-headed, you can let them know and you will be given oxygen through a mask to relieve these symptoms.

Once the anaesthesia has been set up, the anaesthetist will run a series of tests on your abdomen and legs – usually by spraying them with a cold spray – to make absolutely sure that you cannot feel this cold sensation over the operating area. Fear that the anaesthesia will not work is common among

women, but you can be safe in the knowledge that the medical staff will proceed to the next stage only when they are fully satisfied that you are not in pain when they are touching your abdomen. You will still be able to feel the sensation of pushing and pulling as your baby is delivered, but it should not be painful. If you do have any concerns about the sensations you are experiencing, make sure you speak to the anaesthetist – they are hugely experienced at talking to their patients during the operation and fully explaining events in a calm fashion.

Preparing you for the operation

You will have a catheter tube inserted through your urethra to drain your bladder during the operation (this is a completely painless procedure) and this will be left in place for approximately twelve hours. The catheter prevents your bladder from filling and extending into the operating area. It also avoids your having to get up to use the toilet after the operation, something that is difficult to do so soon after abdominal surgery. (Catheters tend to be removed when you are confident you can get to the bathroom alone.) The final step will be to clip your pubic hair just below the line of incision (shaving is no longer necessary), and then to swab your abdomen in antiseptic solution.

Your legs and upper abdomen will be covered with sterile sheeting, so that only the area around the incision will be uncovered and visible. A screen will be created by hooking the sheeting to the drip stands either side of the operating table. This prevents you from seeing what is going on, although if you want to watch the baby emerging, you should tell the medical staff to lower the screen.

The birth of your baby

The operation can now begin. The obstetrician makes a straight or slightly curved horizontal incision approximately 15 cm long, two finger-breadths above the symphysis pubis (pubic bone). This is just below the top of your pubic hair, so that when it grows back, the scar will barely be visible. Layers of fat and of fibrous muscle tissue will be divided before an incision is then made in the lower part of the uterus. If your membranes have not ruptured, the obstetrician will do this now. If your baby is cephalic, the obstetrician will first check the exact position of the baby's head, then gently withdraw it from inside the pelvic brim and lift it out through the incision. If the presentation is non-cephalic, whatever part of the body is below the incision will be delivered first. It can sometimes be a bit of a squeeze for the baby's head to pass through, especially if it is not in a straightforward position. The obstetrician may use forceps, and the assistant obstetrician will lend a hand by applying downward pressure on the uterus.

The baby's head has now emerged and this is often when your baby utters their first cry. The shoulders, trunk and legs are delivered soon after. Throughout the delivery, you will be aware of the obstetrician 'rummaging' around in your abdomen, a strange and, some find, amusing feeling that is often described as someone doing the washing up inside you.

WHO WILL BE THERE DURING A CAESAREAN SECTION?

There will be quite a number of people present in the operating theatre when you are having a Caesarean section, each of whom has a different role to play.

Obstetrician

The obstetrician is in charge of the theatre and will perform the operation to deliver the baby.

Assistant obstetrician

There will be another obstetrician to assist with the operation, whose duties include holding instruments, trimming sutures, helping with the delivery of the baby and taking the umbilical cord samples.

Anaesthetist

The anaesthetist is responsible for administering regional anaesthesia in the form of an epidural, CSE or spinal block. They will be present throughout, to monitor you during the operation and to administer general anaesthesia, if it becomes necessary.

Assistant anaesthetist or operating department assistant

Another member of the medical team will help with positioning you on the operating table, passing equipment to the anaesthetist and, in the case of a general anaesthesia, positioning your airway.

Theatre nurses

The senior theatre nurse checks that all the equipment needed for the operation is present, passes the requisite instruments to the obstetricians during the operation and ensures that the swab and instrument count is correct at the beginning and the end of surgery. The second theatre nurse, often called a 'runner', may be asked to obtain additional equipment as required.

Midwife

Your midwife will assist once your baby is delivered, either to take the baby to the resuscitation trolley if help with breathing is required, or, if all is well, to ensure your baby remains warm while skin-to-skin contact takes place. They will also offer your partner the opportunity to trim the cord. Thereafter they will weigh the baby, carry out the immediate post-birth checks, and so on.

Paediatrician

A paediatrician specialises in the care of children. After the birth, the obstetrician may hand your baby to a paediatrician if assistance with initial care is required. They will perform some basic checks as well as noting the Apgar score (see Chart on p.170 for more information). If the Caesarean section is elective and there are no complications, there may be no paediatrician in attendance.

When your baby has been delivered, the cord is clamped and cut in the same way as if you had delivered vaginally (*see* p.176). You will be given the option of having the baby handed straight to you or cleaned up first. A midwife or paediatrician will place the baby on a special resuscitation trolley so that the vernix and any blood or fluid can be cleaned off, and all the necessary checks can be made and the Apgar score recorded (*see* p.170). After that, your baby will be wrapped in a clean towel and handed back to you to cuddle properly and perhaps put to your breast briefly. If your baby needs to be taken to the neonatal unit, you may not get a chance to see them for more than a brief moment after the birth, as they will be swiftly placed in an incubator and looked after by the paediatric team of doctors and nurses.

Meanwhile, the anaesthetist will give you a syntometrine/syntocinon injection and the third stage of the birth will be actively managed in much the same way as it would be if you had delivered vaginally, except that the placenta and membranes will be taken out through the incision. Once the placenta has been delivered, the surgeon will check that the uterus is empty and the midwife will ensure that the placenta is complete before the obstetrician commences the suturing. This can take a bit of time, as each layer is stitched separately. First, the uterus is repaired with two layers of soluble stitches. Next, the muscles of your abdominal wall and their fibrous sheaths are rejoined with soluble stitches. Finally, stitches, staples or glue will be used to bring the skin edges together.

WHEN IS A VERTICAL INCISION MADE?

A 'classical' incision, that is, a vertical cut in the muscles of the uterus' upper segment, is rarely performed these days, although there are a few circumstances for which it is still used. This type of incision is made if the baby is very premature (before 30 weeks), because at this stage of gestation, the lower part of the uterus is not yet very developed, so it could be difficult to deliver the baby. Similarly, if the baby is transverse and the membranes have ruptured, emptying the womb of amniotic fluid, it may be difficult to manoeuvre the baby through the lower part of the uterus. Finally, large uterine fibroids (*see* Complications, p. 285) or a placenta sited where the horizontal incision would be might mean a vertical incision was inevitable. In such a situation, because the risk of uterine rupture is higher in a subsequent labour, you would be strongly advised to have a Caesarean section for any future deliveries.

If the stitches are not soluble (indicated by a small white bead at each end of the wound), they will be removed after four to five days, as will staples. If glue is used, it dissolves on its own. Small steristrips (used in addition to stitches or glue) usually come off in the shower after a few days.

> " I was very overdue, so was going to the hospital daily for monitoring. There was a major dip in my baby's heart rate and suddenly the CTG machine was surrounded. A midwife started prepping me for theatre, as she knew that a Caesarean was likely, and the anaesthetist came to talk me very quickly through the procedure. When I told her that it all seemed such a rush, she laughed and said, 'If it was a real emergency, I would be running along pushing your bed!' Happily, my son was born fighting fit. In fact, he screamed so loudly that all the midwives gathered outside the theatre to see who this noisy baby was! " ANNE

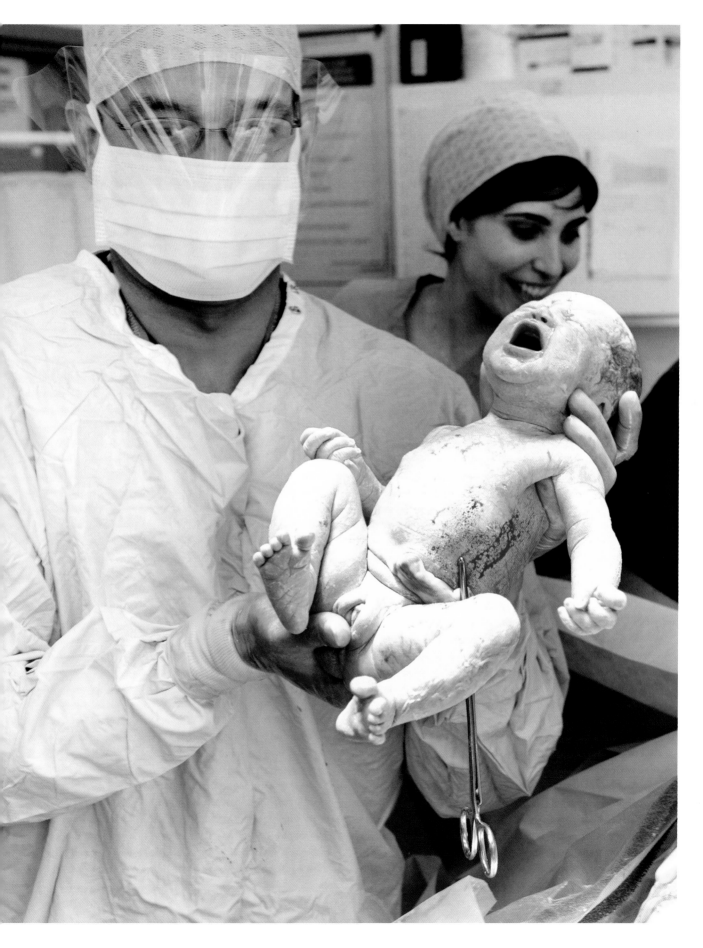

Your baby is finally here! Your first few hours together, whether at home or in the hospital, will be very special, as you and your baby start to get to know each other. You will both need time to recover from the birth, and will be checked over before the midwife decides that you and your baby are doing well.

How your baby looks

First-time parents can be surprised at the appearance of their newborn baby in the hours following the birth. Many babies have puffy eyelids as a result of pressure in the birth canal. Your baby's skin may be wrinkly, blotchy or have some bruising or marks, especially if they were delivered using a ventouse or forceps. Some babies may still be covered, to a greater or lesser degree, in vernix caseosa, the thick white coating that helped protect their skin and keep them warm in the womb. Others may still have some very fine downy hair (lanugo) covering some of their body, particularly if they are premature. This is usually almost invisible to the eye, although may be quite apparent in darker-haired babies; lanugo rubs off within two weeks of the birth.

A baby's genitals are often enlarged or swollen, as are the breasts (in both sexes). This is caused by the high levels of pregnancy hormones they have received from you. In the 48 hours after the birth, their breasts occasionally secrete a little bit of milk, while some girls have a small amount of vaginal discharge (which can contain some blood). Some boys' testes may not be fully descended (especially if they are premature), but they usually descend in the weeks following the birth.

Your baby's eyes will be blue – they will not acquire their final pigmentation for at least six months after the birth, if not more. Initially, babies cannot focus further than 20 cm from their face, but this distance will gradually increase in the weeks following the birth.

Your baby's head

Vaginally delivered babies may have an elongated or cone-shaped head, especially following a slow labour, because the skull bones overlapped as the baby descended the birth canal. The head shape should return to normal within a week. A ventouse delivery is likely to leave a temporary swelling, called a chignon, on your baby's head as a result of the suction cap (see p.198). If you had internal fetal monitoring during labour (see Chapter 5, p.152), the scalp clip may have left a little scratch on your baby's head. This can take as little as a few hours or up to two weeks to disappear, but will leave no permanent marks. At the top of the skull there is a small, soft area, called the anterior fontanelle, where the bones have not yet fused. The fontanelle will not disappear until your baby is eighteen months old, when the bones at the top of the skull have fully knitted together. Your baby's head is a lot more resilient than you think and, while you should take care not to put undue pressure on the area, it cannot be damaged by normal, everyday handling.

The first feeds

Babies are usually quite sleepy during the first 24 hours after birth (and even more so if you have had pethidine or a similar drug for pain relief during labour) and, unless they are premature, they are born with sufficient reserves not to require much feeding during this time. However, if you are planning to breastfeed, it is best to get this underway as soon as possible. Make sure you have guidance so that you get off on the right foot: if the midwives on the ward are very busy, maternity support staff can be helpful and many hospitals have an infant feeding specialist, specially trained lactation consultants who are there to advise and support mothers who wish to breastfeed.

Try to put your baby to the breast every two to four hours, as this encourages the production of oxytocin and prolactin hormones. Oxytocin helps the uterus to contract, while prolactin is essential for the production of milk. Don't worry if your baby does not seem to be suckling much during the first 24 hours – just keep regularly offering the breast. If your baby is able to suckle, they will be able to obtain the nutrient-rich, clear, yellow colostrum that is produced before your milk comes in three to five days after birth. Because colostrum is very rich and high in protein, a teaspoonful per feed is enough to satisfy your baby. See Chapter 8, p.242 for more information on breastfeeding.

If you are not breastfeeding, you will need to provide slightly larger feeds of formula for your baby. When you give birth in hospital, these first few bottles are provided for you. If your baby is premature and cannot suckle, a small amount of expressed breast milk or formula will probably be given, either from a bottle or via a naso-gastric tube (see Chapter 7, p.230).

Your first few hours

As well as being elated about your new arrival, the chances are you will be feeling tired and sore, particularly if your labour was a long one. Despite the excitement of having given birth, try to get some rest while your baby is sleeping. This may not be easy (especially on busy postnatal wards), so avoid having other visitors, other than very close family members, until a day or so after the birth.

You may also find that you rediscover your appetite and suddenly feel ravenously hungry. This is not surprising, given than you may not have eaten or drunk much at all during the last day or two. Make sure you also drink plenty of water too, particularly if you are breastfeeding. Additionally, most hospitals will want you to pass urine twice before you go home and will measure the amount to check that all is functioning well after the birth.

Problems with incontinence, either of the bowels or of the bladder, are common in the first few days following the birth and you should discuss this with your midwife before you leave hospital (*see* Complications, p 288 for more information). Don't panic, though, because 80 per cent of women, regardless of the type of delivery, will find their bladder and bowel return to normal before very long – but remember, the sooner you start your pelvic floor exercises (*see* Chapter 2, p.37), the sooner this is likely to be the case.

It is common to experience abdominal aches similar to period pains for the first few hours and days after the birth, known as 'afterpains', which occur because your uterus is beginning to contract. Afterpains are more powerful when you are breastfeeding, because the oxytocin you secrete every time your nipples are stimulated by your suckling baby helps to contract your womb – you may need to take painkillers if the pains are particularly uncomfortable (anything you are offered will be safe if you are breastfeeding).

POSTNATAL VENOUS THROMBOEMBOLISM
Venous thromboembolism (VTE) can affect women not only during pregnancy (*see* Chapter 3, p.60), but also in the period after the birth. The same risk factors apply, but also include having a Caesarean section or a labour lasting over 24 hours, and being bed-bound/immobile for more than 24 hours. A postnatal VTE risk assessment will be made for all women, and those at intermediate or high risk will be given prophylactic medication for seven days to six weeks after the birth.

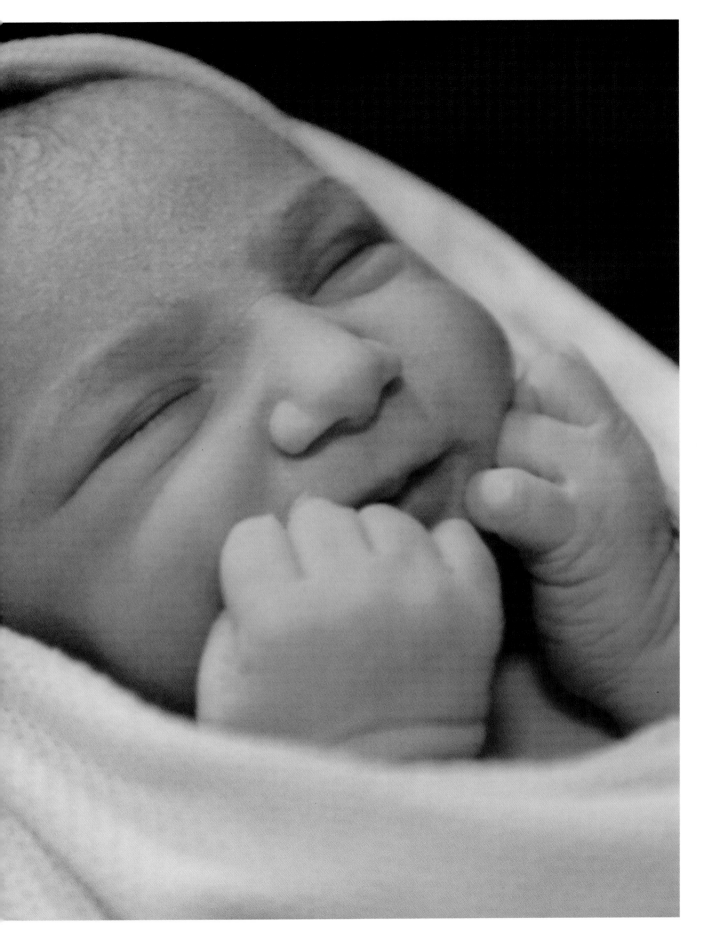

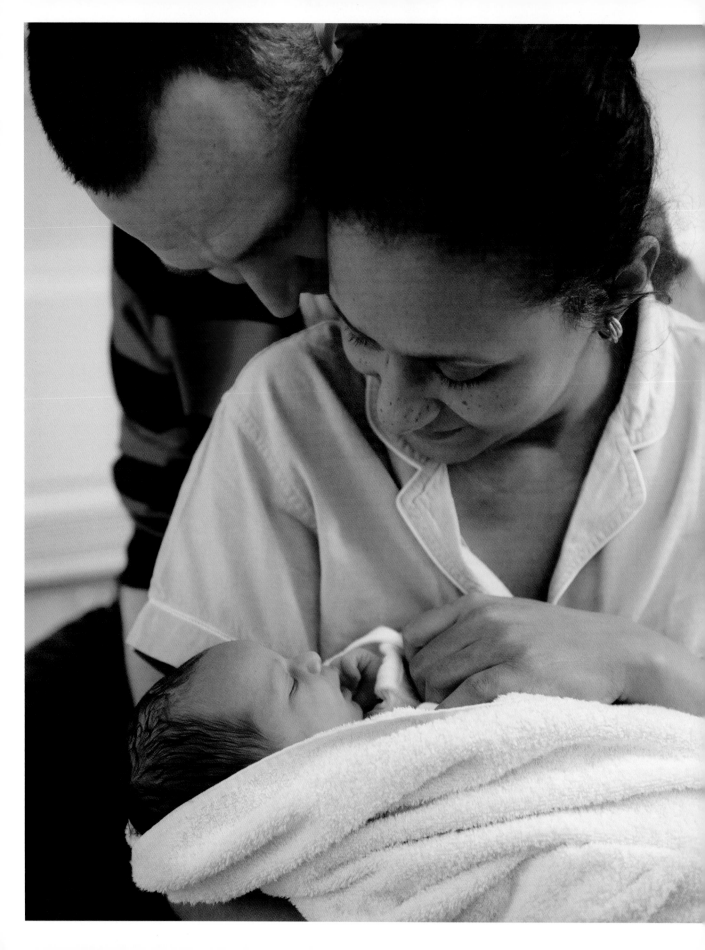

How you feel after a Caesarean section

Once the regional anaesthetic has worn off, you will be given regular analgesia to help reduce the pain caused by the incision. This may be morphine, given orally or via injection, or you may be supplied with a patient-controlled analgesia (PCA) pump, which you can activate yourself to provide pain relief (usually an opioid) intravenously when you need it – the amount is controlled so that you cannot overdose. Some women find that the drugs used in the epidural, spinal block or CSE make their skin itchy, but you can ask for medication to relieve this. After about 24 hours, you can request a non-steroidal analgesic (NSAID), such as ibuprofen, naproxen or diclofenac, which can be given either orally or rectally (the latter is more effective, especially with diclofenac). Similarly, paracetamol can be taken intravenously, orally or rectally. All these forms of analgesia are safe to take if you are breastfeeding. Effective pain relief is an important part of your recovery, so never worry about telling the midwives that you are in pain or need more medication.

You should be able to start feeling your legs within one hour of leaving theatre. The drip will be removed within one to four hours of the operation, the catheter within twelve. You will be offered food and drink when you feel ready. Many hospitals permit partners to stay the first night with you, and this can be really helpful at a time when you are at your least

DID YOU KNOW…?
If it is painful when you breathe in, see your GP or midwife without delay (to exclude pulmonary embolism – *see* Box in Chapter 3, p.60).

mobile (your partner can hand you your baby for feeding and can change nappies). Fortunately, babies themselves are quite sleepy for the first 24 hours, and this allows you to get some rest.

You will be expected to get out of bed within 24 hours of giving birth to reduce the risk of VTE and, depending on your risk factors, you may also be given an injection of heparin. Your abdomen will be very sore at first and you may find it difficult to move around. It is important you take things slowly, but try as much as possible to maintain an upright position. However, do not suffer in silence and, if you need help to pick up your baby because you are unable to bend over or twist round, do ask someone to help you – either a midwife or a nearby mother who is more mobile than you (or your partner if he has been able to stay overnight on the postnatal ward). When you are resting in bed, keep your circulation going by rotating your ankles and wiggling your feet. You may wish to support the abdominal area with your hand or a pillow when you laugh, cough or sneeze. For information on the care of your incision wound, see Chapter 8, p.234.

Care after a home birth

If you have delivered your baby at home, your midwife will perform the same initial checks on you and your baby as she would had you given birth vaginally in hospital (*see* p.170). Together with her assistant midwife, she will clear up any sheets and absorbent pads and take away the placenta for disposal, unless you express a wish to the contrary. Your midwife is likely to remain with you for at least two hours, so that she can be sure that all is well, after which you can enjoy relaxing and recovering in the comfort of your own home.

LOCHIA

The heavy vaginal discharge that you will have following the birth is known as 'lochia'. It consists of a mixture of blood, mucus and tissue from the uterine lining and, for the first few days after the birth, your lochia will be abundant, like a heavy menstrual period, and bright red in colour. For this reason, I would advise you to wear very absorbent sanitary towels and disposable knickers (in case of leaks) during this time. Occasionally, especially if you have been sitting or lying down for a time, you will pass a blood clot or feel a small gush of blood coming out. This is completely normal, particularly in the early days following delivery. If you had a Caesarean delivery, your lochia may be lighter than if you had a vaginal birth, because some of the blood, mucus and debris from the uterine lining will have been removed during the operation. Lochia starts to reduce after about four days and will slowly diminish over the next month until there is no further discharge.

Leaving hospital

Many women go home within 24 hours of a non-assisted vaginal birth (especially if this is not their first baby); for an assisted birth, a hospital stay of one to two days is common, while after a Caesarean section, you may go home any time after 24 hours, although many women stay a couple of days longer, especially for a first birth. Before you are discharged, you and your baby will be assessed to determine whether you are both well enough to go home.

Your baby's neonatal checks

A paediatrician or experienced midwife will examine your baby before discharge. They will see, for example, if there are any physical abnormalities, and will check your baby's heart beat and breathing and that the hips are not dislocated (*see* Complications, p. 286). Newborn babies have certain reflexes at birth (*see* Box) and these will be checked for as well. If you go home less than six hours after the birth, you can choose to see your GP the next day or to come back to the hospital for a paediatric check-up. Similarly, if you deliver in a midwifery unit, you will need to choose one of these options, because these units have no paediatrician.

Your postnatal checks

A midwife will also check your health before allowing you to go home. She will ask you about your lochia, whether you have opened your bowels yet and if you are experiencing any

YOUR BABY'S REFLEXES

Newborn babies are born with certain reflexes that gradually disappear over the next few weeks. These are checked for before your baby is discharged from hospital. The reflexes are:

- **the startle (or Moro) reflex:** the arms and legs are flung out, as if your baby has been startled, when their head is allowed to flop backwards; this is an instinctive response to their sense that they are falling
- **the grasp reflex:** a baby's grasp can be strong enough to support their entire body weight
- **the rooting reflex:** the head will instinctively turn in the direction of something (e.g. a finger) that brushes against a baby's cheek and the mouth will open in a bid to locate the nipple for feeding
- **the stepping reflex:** if held upright under the armpits on a flat surface, a baby performs what appears to be a stepping motion.

difficulties in passing urine. Finally – and incongruously for many women – your midwife will enquire about your plans for contraception. After you have finished laughing (sex probably seems a distant prospect at this stage), you should nonetheless begin to think about the issue!

Before you leave hospital, make sure that you have been shown properly how to bathe and change your baby and to clean the umbilical cord stump. If possible, have a go yourself. If you are breastfeeding, try to ensure you have seen the unit's breastfeeding specialist. These tasks often seem daunting for first-time parents, but you will soon become very adept at them. And you can reassure yourself that babies, even tiny newborns, are much more resilient than they appear to be.

> " My recovery from the Caesarean couldn't have gone any better. I was in bed for most of the day, but I'm a very independent and determined person, so I was keen to get back on my feet as soon as possible. Once the spinal block wore off and I could move my legs, I went for a walk down the ward and even had a shower that evening. It was very painful and uncomfortable, but I had to get on with it: I'm a single mum, so I needed to get up and about, as I had mummy duties! " SARAH

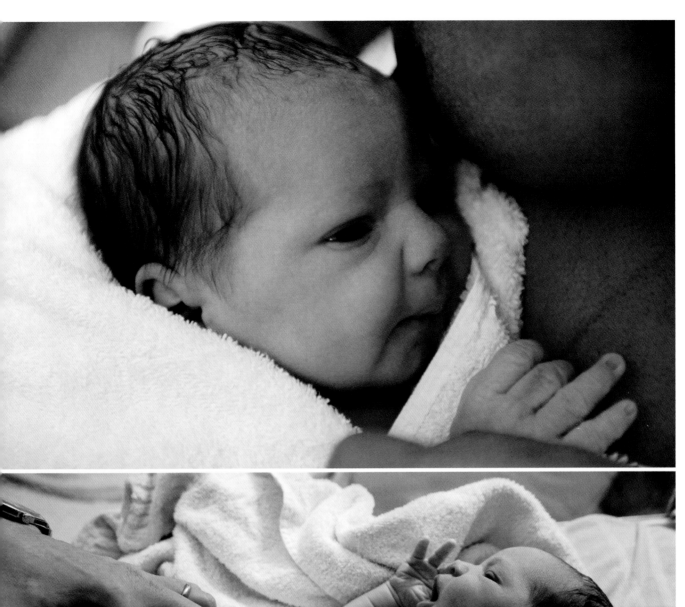
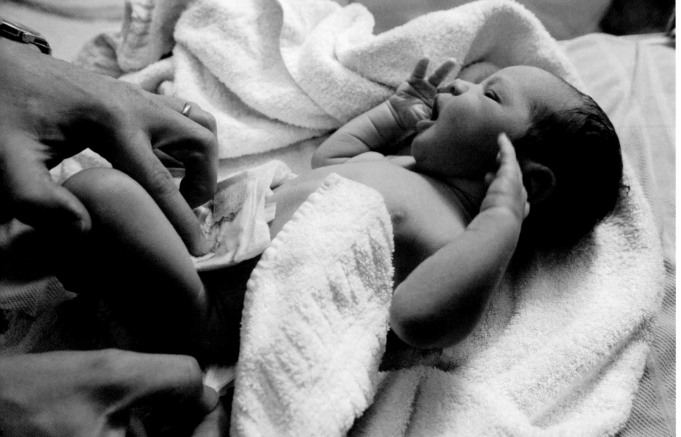

Premature birth

One in thirteen live births takes place before the end of the 37th week of pregnancy and is therefore classified as premature. The advances in medical care over the last twenty years mean that increasing numbers of premature babies now survive, but a premature birth invariably remains a stressful event for parents and is a different start to their baby's life than they had anticipated.

Length of gestation and birthweight are decisive factors in the long-term health of a premature baby. In addition, some of those born prematurely have an underlying problem, identifiable before birth or soon after, that affects their chances of survival or future health.

There are three categories of prematurity:

▸ late preterm: babies born at 32–7 weeks
▸ very preterm: those born at 28–32 weeks
▸ extremely preterm: those born before 28 weeks.

A baby born after 37 weeks but before full term (40 weeks) is not deemed premature, just 'early'. The chances of survival and of a life with minimal or no health problems are helped if a premature baby is of good weight for gestational age at birth. See p.231 for more on birthweight.

There is a marked difference in the short- and long-term health needs of a baby born, for example, at 36 weeks and one born extremely preterm, before 28 weeks. Indeed, although survival rates have improved over the last twenty years, the long-term health outcome for those born extremely early, especially before 26 weeks, remains largely the same. Recent research shows that although 90 –5 per cent of babies born at 28 weeks and 78 per cent of those born at 26 weeks survive, the figure drops to 42 per cent for babies born at 24 weeks, and survival before 23 weeks remains very rare. Furthermore, around a quarter of those born at 25 weeks and one in five of those born at 26 weeks have a severe or moderate disability at the age of three. See Useful Resources for further information on the outcomes for premature babies.

DID YOU KNOW...?
▸ 1 in 13 live births occurs before 37 weeks
▸ 6 per cent of singleton live births are premature
▸ 93 per cent of premature births occur after 28 weeks, 6 per cent at 22–7 weeks and 1 per cent before 22 weeks.

Causes of premature birth

About 40 per cent of premature births are spontaneous and unexplained, although it is thought that most are caused by maternal infection (vaginal, uterine or kidney – see Chapter 4, pp.127–8). A further twenty per cent are triggered by the premature rupture of membranes but, again, infection may be the underlying cause of a significant percentage of these. Of the rest, about 25 per cent of cases involve medical conditions, such as maternal diabetes, placental abruption, placenta praevia, placental insufficiency, fetal growth restriction or fetal abnormality.

In most cases, it is impossible to identify in advance which women will give birth prematurely, especially in a first pregnancy. However, there are certain factors that are known to increase your risk of premature delivery:

▸ previous premature delivery: one in five women who have given birth prematurely before will do so again in their next pregnancy
▸ being over the age of 35
▸ having a pre-pregnancy BMI of over 30.

Older or overweight women have an increased risk of premature birth, because they are more likely to suffer pregnancy complications that lead to an early delivery.

Can anything be done to predict or prevent premature delivery?

Certain tests and steps can now be taken to try to anticipate the occurrence or reduce the chances of premature labour. If you have given birth prematurely in a previous pregnancy, you will be closely monitored so that your chances of doing so again can be minimised, where possible.

Fibronectin test

Fetal fibronectin (fFN) is a protein that acts as a 'glue' between the membranes surrounding the baby and the inside of the uterus. It should only be detectable at the start of the pregnancy and after the 35th week, when it starts to break down naturally, but if fibronectin cells are detected before then, it can be a sign of impending labour. Women who test positive for fibronectin at 23–35 weeks are at increased risk of going into labour within the next two weeks.

The test itself is simple and non-invasive and involves taking a swab during an internal examination. A negative result gives

a more than 95 per cent accurate likelihood of labour *not* starting in the following two weeks. A positive result, on the other hand, is not so clear-cut: it indicates that labour may start during that time, but it could also be some weeks later. For women at risk of premature labour, however, the test is a useful way of assessing their chances of an early delivery and enables doctors to monitor them and, if possible, allow them to go home, thus avoiding unnecessary hospital stays.

Cervical scans and cerclage

If you have a history of second trimester miscarriage or very/extremely preterm delivery, or if you had a procedure to remove abnormal cells from your cervix, you should be offered a cervical length scan at between sixteen and eighteen weeks. If your cervix is seen to be less than 25 mm long and/or the os (the internal part) of the cervix is funnelling (beginning to open), your doctor may discuss with you the option of having a cervical suture (stitch) put in at this stage of your pregnancy. This procedure, known as cervical cerclage, has been found to reduce the risk of premature birth. The suture is usually removed at 36 weeks to enable a normal vaginal delivery.

Cervical cerclage is generally carried out with epidural analgesia, either as a day case or with an overnight stay.

The risks carried by the procedure are low, but include rupture of the membranes, leading to a late miscarriage or premature delivery; there is also the potential risk of developing an infection in the amniotic fluid. Indeed, the procedure is not recommended if there are already signs of infection.

Tocolysis

In certain circumstances, if uterine contractions have begun, tocolytic drugs may be given for up to 48 hours. These slow down muscular activity and, while they can stop contractions completely, they are not primarily given with that aim. They are only used to allow time for steroids to be given, as these will help to mature the baby's lungs and improve the outcome.

DID YOU KNOW...?

Evidence shows that an injection of steroids is advisable if you are going into labour before 34 weeks; many obstetricians will also recommend steroids if you are having a Caesarean section before 39 weeks.

Delaying the labour

If tests or symptoms indicate that you may be about to deliver prematurely, your doctors will try to delay the onset of labour (*see* above), unless there is a medical emergency. Delaying the birth has two main advantages. First, keeping the baby in the womb for longer enables the lungs to keep maturing. A baby born after 35 weeks is often able to breathe unaided, but 24 hours can make all the difference to how much assistance with breathing, if any, a premature baby needs at birth, and also to how long it will be required. The second advantage is that this allows doctors time to transfer you, if necessary, to a hospital with suitable obstetric/neonatal facilities, ensuring that both you and your baby receive the best possible care.

If your membranes rupture after 34 weeks but you don't go into labour, your obstetrician will probably offer induction after 24 hours to limit the chances of infection (*see* Chapter 6, p.192). If, however, your pregnancy has not reached 34 weeks, you will be admitted to hospital, given antibiotics and monitored for signs of infection. The aim would be to keep the baby in the uterus for as long as possible, ideally until 34 weeks.

If you are going to deliver your baby early, you will be given an injection of steroids to speed up the production of surfactant, the substance that coats the tiny alveoli in the lungs. This makes them 'elastic' enough to expand and contract with every breath, and maximises the amount of oxygen that can pass into the blood stream (*see* Chapter 4, p.110).

What happens during premature labour?

The signs that you are going into labour prematurely are often the same as when you are at full term: your membranes may rupture, you may start to experience low back pain, or you may have a 'show' (*see* Chapter 6, p.156). Sometimes, in very premature labour, you may not notice any pain until the labour is quite advanced. If you have any of these symptoms, are starting to have contractions or if you have abdominal pain or bleeding of any sort, then contact your midwife at once, because you will need to be examined as soon as possible.

You will be asked to come into hospital and will be monitored to see how often the contractions are occurring and examined internally to see if you have started to dilate. If appropriate, tocolytic drugs and steroids may be given for up to 48 hours. If this succeeds in stopping contractions altogether, you will be allowed home (after a further period of monitoring) and advised to take things easy until the birth.

If, despite attempts to slow or stop them, your contractions become established, then there is little else that can be done to stop you going into labour. Your baby's lie and presentation will be assessed (*see* Chapter 5, p.148) and an obstetrician will discuss with you whether to perform a Caesarean section or proceed with a vaginal delivery. If a vaginal delivery is attempted, premature labour is likely to proceed in a similar way to full-term labour, although it is often quicker. This is because the baby is smaller, leading to a faster second stage (*see* Chapter 6, p.166).

IS VAGINAL DELIVERY SAFE FOR A PREMATURE BIRTH?

Unless you or your baby are very unwell and urgent delivery is required, your obstetrician will discuss with you whether you wish to have a vaginal delivery or an elective Caesarean section. Recent research found that where birth takes place before 32 weeks, there is no clear evidence that the health of a premature baby is improved by being delivered by Caesarean section rather than vaginally.

The report noted that babies were as likely to survive when born vaginally as when delivered by Caesarean section, as long as they were in the cephalic (head down) presentation. Nearly 80 per cent of women with a cephalic presentation attempted a vaginal delivery, and 84 per cent of these were successful, with the others delivering by Caesarean section. However, for breech pregnancies, about 30 per cent of women attempted a vaginal delivery, and only 17–28 per cent of these were successful (the range varied, because it depended on the length of gestation).

The baby's head will not be engaged before 32 weeks, but this is not, in itself, a reason for performing an elective Caesarean section. However, low, lift-out forceps rather than a ventouse may be used if an assisted delivery is required (*see* Chapter 6, p.200), because a premature baby's skull is softer and more vulnerable than that of a full-term baby.

However, many premature babies are delivered by Caesarean section because of medical considerations. If the baby is breech, for example, or the fetal heart rate is showing any signs of compromise (*see* Box in Chapter 6, p.194), a Caesarean delivery may be suggested; similarly, if you have any antepartum bleeding, have problems caused by diabetes or are suffering from very high blood pressure or pre-eclampsia, you would be offered a Caesarean section rather than an induction, as induction, even at term, carries risks for you and your baby (*see* Chapter 6, p.192).

THE NEONATAL UNIT

A neonatal unit offers specialist care for newborn babies, whether premature or not. It is staffed by highly trained neonatologists and neonatal nurses and the ratio of nurses to babies is very high, so that each baby is kept under extremely close observation.

Whether your baby is delivered vaginally or by Caesarean section, an obstetrician and a neonatal paediatrician (neonatologist) will be present at the birth to ensure that both you and your baby get the best care. Babies born prematurely are at risk of suffering from a range of health complications (*see* pp.230–1), and very and extremely premature babies might encounter further problems during their time in the neonatal unit (NNU), simply because they are vulnerable to infections or to developing neonatal respiratory distress syndrome (NRDS – *see* Complications, p. 290).

After the birth, as long as your baby is stable, most neonatologists will encourage either a quick cuddle or holding hands before transferring the baby to the NNU, and will often invite your partner to accompany them. If you cannot go to see your baby, a photograph will be taken soon after your baby arrives in the unit and will be given to you. If your baby has to go straight to the NNU before you have had the chance of a cuddle, the medical staff will be very aware that this will be a stressful and upsetting time for you and will do their best to reassure you, to explain what is going on and why, and to answer any immediate concerns you might have.

Life in the neonatal unit

As soon as you have recovered from the birth, you will be able to visit your baby and to spend as much time as you wish with them, as there are no restrictions on visiting hours. Usually, only the baby's parents are allowed to visit, to reduce the risk of infection. Hygiene is very important on the ward and all visitors need to disinfect their hands when they enter and leave the unit and often have to wear protective clothes or an apron.

The first time you visit the NNU is likely to be a shock, as nothing quite prepares you for seeing your tiny baby in a cot

CATEGORIES OF CARE IN THE NEONATAL UNIT

There are three levels of neonatal care, but not every neonatal unit (NNU) is equipped to offer them all. This means that some premature babies need to be transferred to units with more appropriate levels of care, depending on their health at birth and how prematurely they were born. Be aware that these NNUs may be in hospitals that are many miles away from where you had your antenatal care/birth and from where you live. See Useful Resources for the location of the different levels of care offered by NNUs in England, Wales and Scotland.

Special care (formerly Level 1)

Special care refers to a level of care beyond that which can normally be provided for a baby by the mother at home. It is used routinely for babies born at 34+0 and more, full-term babies of low birthweight (i.e. below 2,000 g) and those with moderate health problems that cannot be treated on the postnatal ward. For example, Special Care Baby Units (SCBUs) provide assistance with breathing, monitor the baby's heart rate, treat jaundice and provide tube-feeding.

High-dependency care (formerly Level 2)

High-dependency care (HDC) is for babies who need continuous monitoring and includes those born at 28–33+6 weeks and/or those with short-term complex care needs. For example, these babies may need help with breathing via continuous positive airway pressure (CPAP), intravenous feeding or they may weigh less than 1,000 g.

Intensive care (formerly Level 3)

Neonatal Intensive Care Units (NICUs) look after babies born before 28 weeks and those with the most complex and/or long-term health problems. These babies require constant supervision and monitoring and (usually) mechanical ventilation. A specialist doctor should always be available in the NICU, as a baby's condition can deteriorate rapidly.

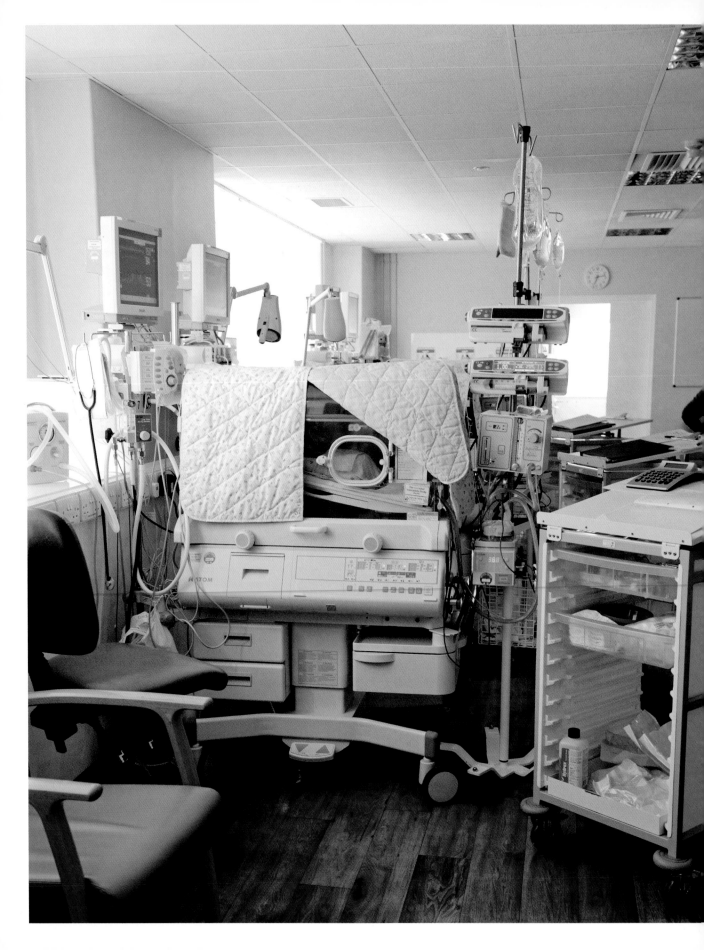

or incubator, possibly surrounded by various machines and wires. If this is your first baby, the situation might be a very long way from how you imagined motherhood to be and that can be very upsetting. It is also easy to feel guilty that you were not able to carry your baby to term or to think that you did something 'wrong'. Bear in mind that a premature birth is usually unforeseen and it is most unlikely that you did anything to cause it.

Nursing and medical staff have the utmost patience and understanding when it comes to reassuring anxious parents and explaining any queries you might have. One of the advantages of the high staff-to-baby ratio is that they do have time for you, and you are always made to feel welcome and part of the unit's life. Indeed, right from the start of your baby's stay in the NNU, you will be encouraged to get as involved as possible with the care of your baby, including nappy changing, washing and feeding. Even if your baby has to remain in an incubator, you will still be able to touch, stroke and talk to them, as there are special portholes on the side to enable you to do this. Most units have special times when no medical procedures take place to allow babies to be stroked and massaged, as this has been shown to benefit their well-being. As soon your baby's health permits, you will be able to cuddle them outside the incubator. 'Kangaroo care' is encouraged as early as possible: this involves holding your baby against your chest to facilitate skin-to-skin contact (often within your clothes to prevent heat loss). This enables your baby to smell and feel your skin against theirs and to hear the sound of your voice and your heartbeat, all of which have a calming influence on them and help them to grow. Kangaroo care also helps with your own milk production and the let-down reflex (see Box in Chapter 8, p.245). However, it is important to know that there is no evidence whatsoever that, just because you are not spending all day and night with your baby, the bond between you will be any less strong than between mothers and babies who leave hospital together.

Occasionally, your baby may need to be moved to another neonatal unit, for example, to have surgery or for a specific medical procedure. Don't think it is because your baby is very sick; it is simply that the other hospital is more specialised and experienced in treating babies with this particular health problem. Your baby may then need to stay there for a while until they can be transferred back to a hospital that is closer to home. Medical staff will do all they can throughout the process to make the transfer as smooth as possible and to keep you informed and reassured.

Generally speaking, babies leave the NNU at around or a little before the time of their estimated delivery date. For example, a baby born at 34 weeks, who simply needed help with breathing and feeding, would typically spend three to four weeks in the SCBU, bringing their gestational age up to 37 or 38 weeks.

Feeding in the neonatal unit

Feeding your baby in the neonatal unit presents special challenges (see p.230), but you will be encouraged to provide breast milk from the start, as this has many important benefits for premature babies:

▸ It is more easily digested by an underdeveloped gut.
▸ The antibodies it contains help to protect vulnerable babies from infections you are immune to and other illnesses.
▸ Colostrum (the first milk you produce) is particularly nutrient-rich.

However, premature babies lack the sucking reflex needed to feed directly from the breast and may also be attached to equipment that makes this impossible. They can, however, be fed your breast milk via a tube and you will be encouraged and shown how to express as soon as possible after the birth

SUPPORT FOR PARENTS OF PREMATURE BABIES
Giving birth to a baby prematurely demands major adjustments from parents, as they come to terms with a situation that is very different from the start to parenthood that they imagined. The experience can be traumatic, with some parents suffering a type of grief for the loss of the birth they had expected or planned. However, in addition to the help provided by staff in the NNU, there are charitable organisations that can offer information and support to parents through this distressing time (see Useful Resources) and, if you feel you may need professional counselling, you can always contact your GP for a referral.

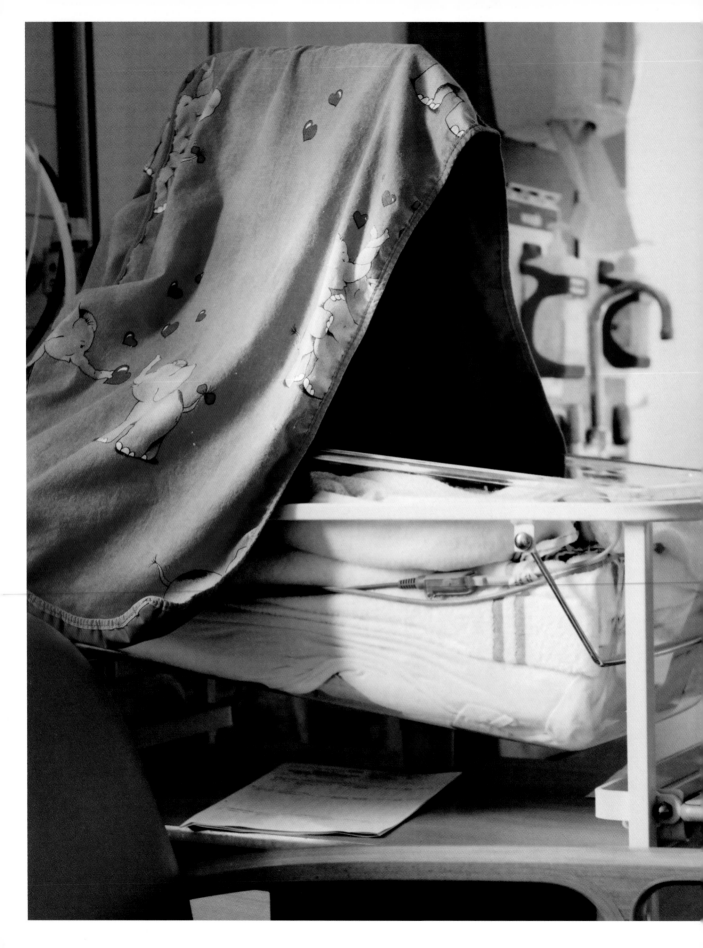

(*see* Chapter 8, p.245). Your milk will take longer to come through if you have given birth prematurely, especially by Caesarean section, so don't worry if things are slow to start. And even if you only supply colostrum for a few days before switching to formula, this will still be an enormous benefit to your baby's immune system.

If you want to continue breastfeeding, you will need the help of a specialist breastfeeding counsellor (all NNUs provide this service). They should come and find you soon after the birth, but if not, do ensure you ask to see them as soon as possible. There is no doubt that 'teaching' a premature baby to breastfeed – especially if you are a first-time mother – requires patience, because these tiny babies don't have the strength or instinct to latch on in the way that a full-term baby does. Aside from the health benefits, the advantage of breastfeeding when your baby is premature is that, because they need smaller but more frequent feeds, you are able to feed little and often much more conveniently than if you were having to prepare formula. The drawback is that only you can do the feeding initially, as giving expressed milk from a bottle is something that is best done only once breastfeeding is established after a few weeks. See Chapter 8, p.242 for more information on the practicalities and health benefits of breastfeeding.

If you are not breastfeeding, formula that has been specially adapted for the needs of premature babies will be given instead. Don't feel that you have 'failed' at the first hurdle of parenthood or that your baby has to 'settle' for formula – you both have a lot to cope with at the moment. Not providing breast milk is *not* a sign of future bad parenting. And you will have plenty of things to feel guilty about as a parent in years to come, so don't make this one of them!

Leaving your baby in the NNU

Returning from the hospital alone is difficult for many parents, but try to remember that everything is being done to enable your baby to join you at home as soon as possible. The best thing you can do while your baby is in the NNU is to recover your strength by resting whenever you can. That way, you will be better able to look after your baby once they do come home. At home, try to delegate as much as possible – easier said than done, I know. For example, ask a willing friend or relative to do some of the domestic tasks while you are resting or visiting your baby. And, if possible, try to spend a little time with your partner as a couple, not just as new parents, because you have just gone through a stressful time together. Women who give birth prematurely are often unprepared for the arrival of their baby and this adds another level of anxiety and stress. If you don't have any baby clothes or equipment, provide a list of what you need so that someone can get this for you (but avoid buying much in size 0 – for the baby, not you! – because it will only last for a short time).

In addition, you may not have started your maternity leave at the time you gave birth but, hopefully, colleagues or clients will be understanding and will work things out for themselves, helped by a small amount of debriefing on your part. Do this by phone or via the internet, so that you avoid getting sucked back into the minutiae of work – others will undoubtedly survive without you!

Your other children

If you have other children, you will need to explain the situation to them. In some cases, they may be so young themselves and your baby so early that you had not yet got round to telling them you were pregnant. Even if they knew you were having a baby, the premature birth is likely to have caught them as much by surprise as you. This, together with the fact that you are spending so much time at the hospital, can be difficult for them, so it is vital to reassure them that you will always have time for them and that they will be loved by you as much as ever.

Initially, you could take a photo of your new baby (when off ventilation) to show them, though try to make sure the baby is in a cot, so that their first sighting is not of you cuddling this new arrival. Suggest that your children provide a gift for their new sibling and give them one on your baby's behalf. These measures help to establish a bond directly between the children and the new baby. See Chapter 8, p.241 for more on introducing older children to their new sibling.

Bringing your baby home

The day will come when your baby is well enough to come home. Just before your baby is discharged, you and your partner will be able to spend a night in the hospital to make sure you feel confident about looking after your newborn on your own. This is often referred to as 'rooming in'. Once home, don't feel as if you have to wrap your baby in cotton wool – they are no more delicate and fragile than a full-term newborn. Try to treat them as you would any other baby. You may not have had the start to parenthood that you anticipated, but you can now look forwards to and start to enjoy your future together as a family.

COMMON COMPLICATIONS OF PREMATURITY

Premature babies are vulnerable to a range of problems. Many are not serious, but simply need monitoring and suitable treatment in the NNU until your baby is well enough to come home.

Among the issues that premature babies face is the difficulty of maintaining body temperature, because they have less body fat than full-term babies. An incubator provides a warm, controlled environment for your baby until they can regulate their own body temperature. Jaundice develops in the majority of premature babies (*see* Complications, p. 287), but is easily treated and rarely indicative of a serious problem.

Your baby is likely to need follow-up appointments with the neonatologists for a year – maybe more, depending on how premature the birth was – so you will have plenty of chances to discuss your baby's progress with medical staff over the coming weeks and months. You don't therefore need to find out everything about your baby's condition before you come home together. Listed below are other common problems that affect premature babies. See also Complications, p. 290 for information on more serious conditions associated with prematurity.

Breathing

Inability to breathe without assistance is the commonest problem of prematurity. The lungs of a premature baby are underdeveloped and too rigid (owing to insufficient surfactant). As a result, they cannot inflate adequately and they overly collapse when air is expelled. This can lead to babies developing neonatal respiratory distress syndrome (NRDS), which affects around half of those born before 32 weeks. To aid their breathing, a baby will be put on a ventilator, a special machine that helps the lungs to fill with oxygen and to exhale without collapsing. There are different ways of ventilating babies, depending on how much help the baby needs (e.g. continuous positive airways pressure, or CPAP). Sometimes, artificial surfactant may be administered directly into the baby's lungs via a small tube in order to increase their elasticity. By 35 weeks, many babies can breathe unaided, but may still have little tubes inserted into their nostrils to ensure enough oxygen reaches the lungs. Oxygen levels are measured on a regular basis by the nursing staff and once they are sufficient, the tubes will be removed.

Infection

Premature babies have an even more immature immune system than full-term babies. They are therefore at greater risk of developing an infection (bacterial, fungal or viral), which can particularly affect their respiratory system and this is why hygiene considerations are paramount in all NNUs. Babies are regularly monitored for any sign of infection and it will be quickly treated where necessary. If you or your partner develop an infection, however mild, it may be better for you to stay away until you are better.

Hypoglycaemia

Premature babies have a very small stomach capacity and cannot take in large quantities of milk at a time. This can lead to hypoglycaemia (low blood sugar levels). As a result, this is tested for by medical staff in the NNU on a regular basis. If hypoglycaemia is detected, your baby will be given small doses of glucose intravenously and/or very small, regular amounts of milk until levels return to normal.

Feeding

A baby's sucking reflex develops in the womb during the last few weeks of pregnancy and is not fully in place until 37 weeks of gestation. In addition, the digestive system is also underdeveloped before this time: it leaks and is unable to cope with anything other than tiny quantities of liquid. Babies born before about 36 weeks therefore cannot feed independently, so have to be fed artificially and very regularly, usually via a naso-gastric tube, which is inserted through their nose and descends into their stomach.

Gradually, your baby will learn to suckle and will no longer need the tube, so you will be able to breastfeed or bottle-feed them (with breast milk or formula). Once your baby can take in the equivalent of 50 ml of milk/formula at one feed, and

---

DID YOU KNOW...?

If you are not breastfeeding, but would like your baby to receive breast milk, many hospitals operate a 'milk bank' of breast milk donated by other mothers. Conversely, if you are breastfeeding and your supply is good, you can donate to the bank yourself.

assuming there are no other health issues that require on-going hospital care, you will be able to take your baby home with you.

Occasionally, very premature babies develop necrotising enterocolitis (*see* Complications, p. 290) and a very small number may need surgery, although the chances of this occurring are reduced when they are fed breast milk, which is one of the reasons why doctors are so keen for you to express milk when your baby is premature.

Weight

Babies who are below 2,000 g, whether premature or not, will be cared for in the NNU until they reach a weight considered acceptable by the medical staff. Babies born before 34 weeks are often below 2,000 g and, in a very small percentage of cases, some non-premature babies are small for gestational age as well, though this is often because they have other underlying medical problems that need addressing at birth. 'Small for gestational age' means that a baby's birthweight is less than what is expected for a baby at that particular week of gestation (this can also be referred to as 'small for dates'). This may or may not be linked to problems with growth in the womb (intrauterine growth restriction, or IUGR – *see* Complications, p. 286 for more on this condition.

THE DEVELOPMENT OF PREMATURE BABIES

Premature birth can affect the way a baby develops. However, unless there are on-going health issues, premature babies catch up developmentally with their peers by the time they reach their second birthday. The normal developmental stages that all babies are expected to reach will be calculated from the date your baby was due, not the date on which they were actually born. So, if your baby was born, for example, eight weeks early (i.e. at 32 weeks), they will be approximately two months behind full-term babies in reaching milestones such as smiling, grasping, rolling over and sitting up. Your baby will therefore not start to smile until about fourteen weeks old, rather than at six weeks for a full-term baby; similarly, your baby will not be sitting up until they are about eight to ten months old, rather than six to eight months.

" Natasha was born by emergency Caesarean section at 34 weeks (weighing 2,100 g) after I developed placental abruption. Initially, she needed ventilation and was taken to Special Care minutes after the birth, but within a few days she was breathing independently. I expressed milk from the beginning – spending hours on the hospital's electric breast pumps! – and she was fed by naso-gastric tube until she learnt to breastfeed shortly before she went home three weeks later. Once I was discharged, I spent the days with her in hospital, but was able to recover from the operation by getting uninterrupted sleep back at home. Despite a worrying start, Natasha has continued to thrive, and my bond with her is as strong as it is with her older brother. " CLAIRE

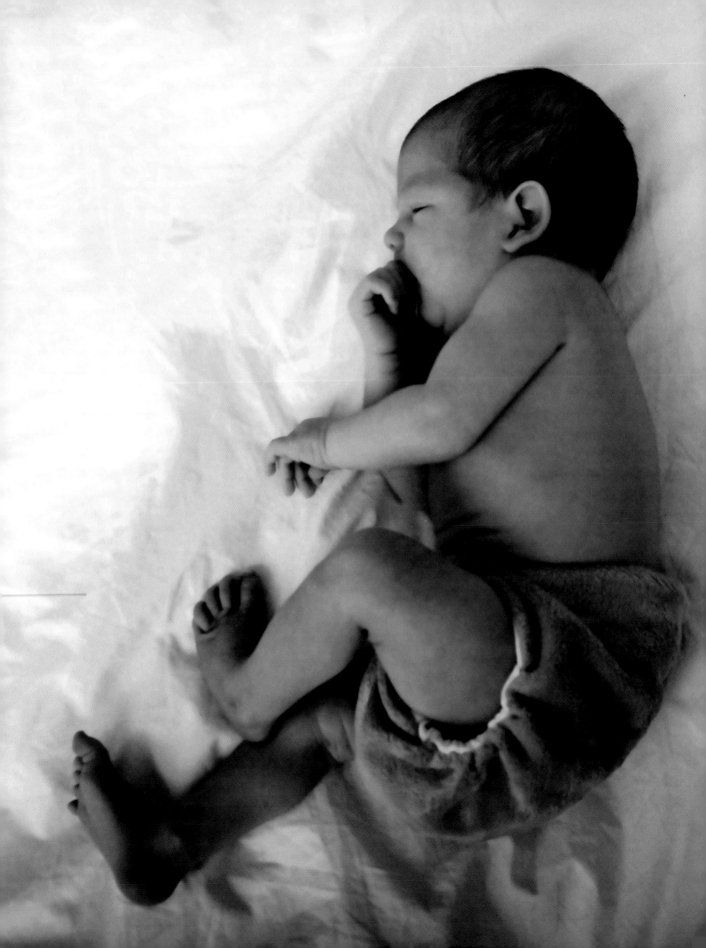

The first six weeks

You now have a tiny newborn baby!
This is both an exciting and a daunting
prospect, especially if you are a first-time
parent. Although you may initially feel
uncertain in your ability to look after
such a fragile-looking infant, you will
soon learn what to do and how best to
care for your baby. However, you will also
need to look after yourself over the next
few weeks and months so that you can
recover from pregnancy and birth, adjust
to your new life and enjoy being a parent.

It is important as a new mother that you rest and let others help you as much as possible, particularly during the early weeks. There is no set length of time after which you should be back to normal – it can take months before you fully catch up on sleep and recover your old energy levels – but you will know as soon as you begin to feel more like your old self.

Your midwife will contact your GP and the community midwife when you are discharged from hospital (or after your baby was born, if you had a home birth), and they will oversee your care once you are back home. Initially, a community midwife will visit you on the first and second day and will then assess how often they need to see you afterwards. They will monitor your physical recovery, particularly if you have had an episiotomy, perineal tear or a Caesarean section. Your emotional welfare is important to them, too, but it will help if those close to you also keep an eye on how you are feeling or if you yourself are aware of the symptoms for the 'baby blues' and postnatal depression (*see* Chapter 9, pp. 278 and 281).

Episiotomies and perineal tears

The area around the episiotomy or perineal tear will feel tight and sore for a while, especially on the second and third day after the birth. This is because the tissue surrounding the cut/tear swells up as part of the healing process, as this helps blood flow to the wounded area. A flexible ice pack or a bag of frozen peas wrapped in a towel or piece of material and pressed against the perineum will help reduce pain and swelling. Topical anaesthetic cream can also be helpful for pain relief. Massaging the area with emollient cream or oil keeps the scar tissue supple and there are also specific creams aimed at helping scar tissue to heal. If sitting is uncomfortable, sit on an inflated rubber ring, so that you take the pressure off the wound. The blood supply to the vagina is plentiful, so the tissues should have repaired after two weeks, and stitches will dissolve in due course. Your GP will check your perineum at your six-week check (*see* p. 237) to make sure it has healed.

In the meantime it is important that you keep the wound as clean and dry as possible. This means changing your sanitary towel every two or three hours when awake, as there will be significant lochia (*see* Chapter 6, p. 217) in the 48 hours following the birth. Avoid scented bath oils, soaps or shower gels until the wound has healed, and take showers rather than baths in the first few days, firstly, because they are more hygienic and, secondly, because it is easier to get in and out of a shower than a bath. Thereafter, take frequent warm baths and pat, rather than rub, the area dry with a soft towel. If it is too painful to touch the perineum at all, you can use a hairdryer on a cool setting to dry the area after washing.

Passing urine can burn and sting in the first few days after the birth, so you may find it necessary to adapt how you do so. Crouching over the toilet with your legs as wide apart as possible or passing urine in water (in a bidet or while taking a shower) ensures that the urine doesn't sting as it passes over the wound. The first time you open your bowels, you may want to press against the scar with some toilet tissue, just to give you the confidence that you can bear down. That said, as long as you don't strain unduly, it is highly unlikely you will encounter any problems with your stitches (e.g. 'bursting open'). In any event, it takes many women three or four days before they have their first bowel movement and, by this time, the tissues will be firmly adhered to each other and the scar will be well on the way to healing. It is important, however, to stay fully hydrated and to eat food that contains fibre, to keep your stools soft and reduce the risk of constipation (*see* Chapter 4, p. 124). Prunes and dried figs are excellent because they have the added advantage of not making you feel bloated, as is fresh mango because it is both oily and fibrous.

Caesarean scars

Your wound will initially be covered by a sterile dressing, which will stay in place for 24 hours or more. Remarkably, even in these first few days, significant healing is taking place and the scar is sufficiently strong to permit the removal of the stitches/wound clips five days after the birth. You will either have the stitches removed the day you are due to leave hospital, or by a community midwife once you are back home. (If your obstetrician used dissolvable sutures, these do not need removal.) Although removal may be a little uncomfortable, it lasts only a few seconds. Before your stitches are removed, depending on what sort of dressing you have been given, you may have to keep the area dry and will not be able to bathe. Thereafter, keep your wound clean and dry it by patting with a clean towel. Make sure your underwear covers it completely, otherwise rubbing from the elastic or from your clothes will be uncomfortable.

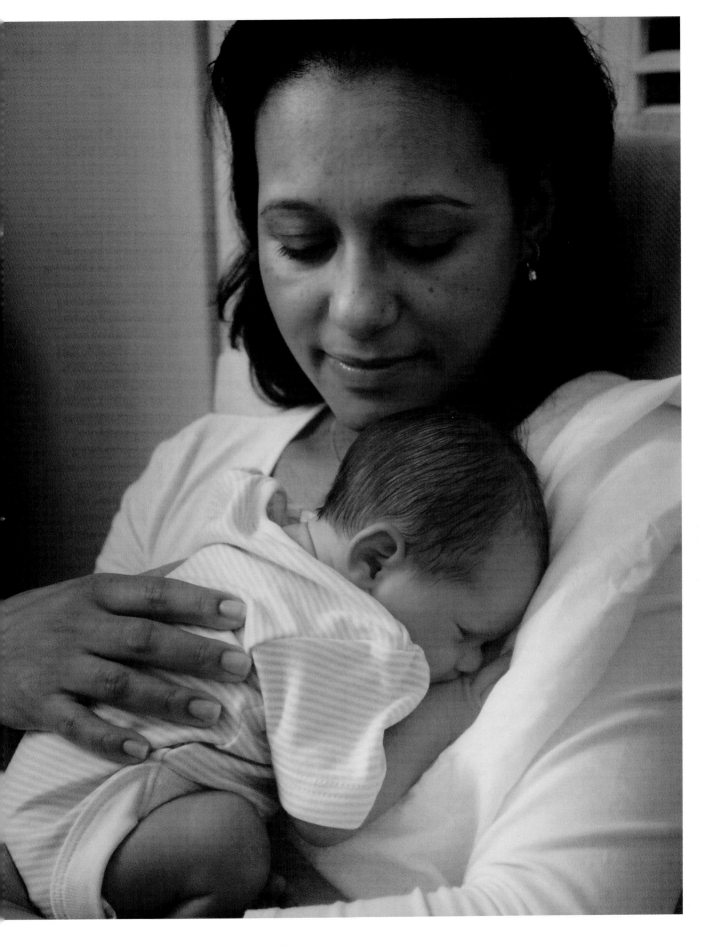

It is important to take care of your back and your posture after you have had a Caesarean section. Avoid lifting anything heavy (including heavy bags, prams and toddlers) for six weeks after the birth and, if you do have to bend down or pick something up, remember to flex your knees and keep your back straight, pushing up through your legs to come to standing again. There is no legal minimum time after which you are allowed to drive after a Caesarean section: you are able to drive safely once you feel well enough and can turn around while reversing and do an emergency stop without discomfort. Also check with your insurance company to see if there are any restrictions.

The scar itself will be red and raised up, and may look and feel quite lumpy for several days after the birth due to slight bleeding and inflammation beneath the skin. Slowly, it should begin to settle down and to flatten out. However, if the scar does not seem to be healing, and continues to be tender or red, or is leaking fluid, speak to your GP or midwife, as you may have developed an infection that requires antibiotics. The skin around the scar will also feel numb, because nerve endings were cut at the time of the operation. This is normal and you will slowly regain the feeling around the incision over the next few months.

How you feel

Tearfulness and irritability are commonly felt around three days after the birth (known as the 'baby blues') and usually last a short while. If you feel low for much longer than this, talk to your partner and family /friends first, then to your midwife or GP, as you could be suffering from postnatal depression and may benefit from further help and support. See Chapter 9, p. 280 for more on your emotional welfare after birth.

Occasionally, women develop an infection (e.g. genital tract, uterine) after they have left hospital and this needs to be treated. If you start to feel unwell in the days following your return home, especially during the first two weeks, call your midwife or your GP (or you can always contact the maternity unit). Symptoms to look out for are:

- feeling hot and shivery
- abdominal pain

- temperature over 37.3°C
- offensive-smelling lochia or heavy bleeding
- breathlessness.

Equally, you should always let your GP or midwife know if anyone in your family is unwell during this time, as this could impact on your own health.

Postnatal exercises

Some gentle exercise after the birth, such as going for a walk, will not only help to reduce the risk of postnatal venous thromboembolism (see Chapter 6, p. 214), but will also make you feel better psychologically, thanks to the mood-enhancing endorphins that are secreted during physical activity. However, you should wait until your bleeding is minimal before doing more specific toning and core strength exercises; if you had a Caesarean section, you should delay until you have been given the all-clear at your six-week check. That said, do start your pelvic floor exercises as soon as possible after delivery (see Chapter 2, p. 37), as these will help your perineum to recover from pregnancy, even if you had a Caesarean section.

Gentle back and abdominal exercises, such as the ones described in Chapter 2, p. 34, are safe to do you after the first week or two if you had a vaginal delivery, depending on how you are recovering. However, if you feel any discomfort or pulling, stop and wait a few days before trying again. Thereafter, you should only resume your normal exercise routine once you feel ready. You should only go swimming once your bleeding has ceased, as you should avoid wearing tampons because they may feel uncomfortable and may increase the risk of infection. As with your regime while you were pregnant, don't force things: listen to your body. It will take some weeks to regain your pre-pregnancy shape and some women do bounce back faster than others.

Your six-week check

You will be seen, usually by your GP, around six weeks after the birth. As well as discussing your contraception plans, they will check the following:

- blood pressure
- your episiotomy or Caesarean scar (if applicable)
- breasts and nipples
- your uterus, to ensure it has returned to its non-pregnant size
- your perineum, to check on the pelvic floor muscles
- weight
- urine, to check for infection or diabetes.

Urinary incontinence can be an issue after birth (see Complications, p. 288), although daily pelvic floor exercises (see opposite) will be essential for improving the strength of your perineum. If you are still having problems by the time of your check-up, ask your GP what can be done and establish a plan of action: no woman should have to put up with incontinence caused by childbirth.

Additionally, if you have any concerns or questions regarding any other aspect of your physical or mental health, this is the ideal opportunity to discuss them.

Pre-pregnancy health check

If you are planning on becoming pregnant again, see your GP for a pre-pregnancy check-up sooner rather than later, especially if you have a pre-existing health condition such as diabetes, obesity or hypertension, or if you developed a pregnancy-related complication such as gestational diabetes. This will enable you to take steps to being as healthy as possible before your next pregnancy.

No one can truly prepare you for the sheer shock of looking after a baby and the sudden change of pace and rhythm that it brings. From now on, it will be your baby's needs that largely dictate what gets done (or not) and it can sometimes be the women that are the most organised or used to being in control who find it hardest to get used to this new way of life.

If this sounds a little familiar, try to embrace the unpredictability of your new existence, to look at it as one big adventure, and to allow yourself to live in a slower, less structured manner for a while. Otherwise, anxiety and tension about what you are unable to achieve can start to sow the seeds of excessive worry and even postnatal depression (*see* Chapter 9, p. 281). Remember also that, despite what parenting books may tell you, it is not really possible to establish routines for your baby in the first few weeks. Tiny babies need feeding little and often, don't know the difference between night and day and won't usually sleep through the night until they are around twelve weeks old. So do what you can to go with the flow – there is nothing you really need to be doing except caring for your baby at this point – and try to accept that this will be a tiring, if not exhausting, time for you and your partner, but that it will not last for ever.

> " **All you can do is take one step at a time until you find your feet with this brand new little person.** " KATE

DID YOU KNOW…?

Survival is key during the first six weeks, so don't fret over the cleaning, cooking balanced home-cooked meals, and any other areas where you normally feel you have to keep up high standards – pragmatism rules! Let yourself off the hook for a while: it is perfectly fine if all you have managed to do that day is post a letter.

Coping without sleep

It is true that trying to cope with everything while suffering from nights of broken sleep is difficult. Some babies are better at settling and sleeping than others (*see* Chapter 8, p. 255) and it can be frustrating if your baby seems more wakeful than those of your friends. However, with a bit of help from others and a resolve to rest when your baby is sleeping during the day, you can help to minimise the effects of sleep deprivation, knowing that one day your baby *will* sleep through the night and you will start to feel like a functioning human being again!

Your partner's role

Your partner will play an important role helping you to cope and their support in the first few weeks and beyond is vital. In fact, establishing a workable division of childcare and household tasks from the start will do much in laying the groundwork for your future life together as a family. In the early days, your partner can field phone calls and limit the number of visits by well-meaning friends and family while you try to rest. And when people do come to visit, your partner can be the one making the tea and washing up afterwards, not you. Similarly, there are many routine domestic tasks that your partner can do until you feel that you can share them more equally (although, remember, your baby is the priority, not whether your home looks immaculate).

Some mothers take over the care of their baby almost entirely, leaving their partners unable to partake in the joy of looking after their newborn or, worse, criticised if they do attempt to help and don't do it 'right'. This can easily alienate them and leave them feeling neglected and resentful. Some partners, however, are scared and daunted at the idea of looking after what appears to be a fragile newborn, and lack the confidence to have a go. Try to remember that you are

a team, and that if your partner doesn't learn how to care for the baby, this can harm their future relationship not only with their child, but also with you. There is rarely a 'right' or 'wrong' way to do things – merely your way and theirs – so, although constructive advice can be of help, try to let them find their own method of bathing, changing and, where possible, feeding the baby. Indeed, leave your partner to look after the baby by themselves while you go out for an hour or so. In this way, they will feel confident that they don't need you to be there. In return, you will be safe in the knowledge that your partner is able to do this and that you don't necessarily need to be around the whole time.

When the midwife visits

Most partners are very keen to be 'hands-on' in the care of their newborn. They are more than happy to do the winding, soothing, nappy-changing and so on and, perhaps, very eager that others recognise their commitment. They can, therefore, be slightly offended when they realise that the visiting midwives are rather more interested in you and the baby than in the role they are performing. A midwife may even ask your partner to hand over the baby to you during this time, which may be particularly upsetting for them. However, your partner should know that seeing how mother and baby relate to each other is an important part of a midwife's postnatal assessment and no judgement at all on their capabilities. And, while their role at this time is a crucial one, they will have a lifetime to show how they can love and care for their child.

Doing it differently the second time around

It seems to be that, generally speaking, women are better able to cope with second and subsequent babies because they are less anxious and more knowledgeable about babycare. If this is not your first baby, you will remember what you felt like during the first few weeks and months after the birth and you will have the advantage of knowing, perhaps, what you could do better or differently this time to make your life easier. You will be more confident as a mother and know that many of the little things that you got upset about first time around don't, in fact, matter. So, if anything, you are likely to find your new baby easier to cope with than you did your first baby, even though you also have other children to look after. You may have to do some logistical organising in order to cater for all your children's needs (*see* below), but as a result you will probably find that your new baby is quite flexible and used to being carted around at the drop of a hat because of older siblings' commitments.

Your other children

The arrival of a baby brother or sister inevitably changes the family dynamics for your other child(ren). However much they might have been prepared, children usually find the arrival of a new baby difficult to adjust to and accept, especially once the novelty has worn off. This is particularly the case when children are very young, as it is harder to explain things to them. It is important to discuss the situation with them: don't dismiss their anxieties as groundless, but take the time to really listen and understand what they are trying to say to you.

The idea of having a sibling might initially have been exciting, but all too often, once the reality dawns of what this means in practice (e.g. you no longer devote all your attention to them, everyone seems to be making an endless fuss of this new baby), toddlers often start saying that they want the baby to be put in the bin, put back in their mother's tummy or returned to hospital. They may also start 'accidentally' hurting the baby by pinching, prodding or even hitting them – so never leave a baby alone with your toddler. They might also try to seek attention by suddenly being naughty, having tantrums, or becoming clingy or whingey. All these are completely normal patterns of behavior, but there are various things you can do which can help children feel more secure about the arrival of a new baby:

▸ Every day, spend some time with your other child(ren), doing something that they enjoy doing and devoting all your attention to them. The new baby must not interrupt these moments.
▸ Provide plenty of cuddles and verbal reassurance to show that you love them as much as ever.
▸ Encourage family members and close friends to bring them a little present (not just one for the baby) when they first visit to make them feel special as well.
▸ Maintain their routine and programme of activities.
▸ Avoid making big changes (e.g. starting nursery, changing from a cot to a 'big' bed, moving bedrooms, potty training) when the baby arrives, but introduce theses either several weeks before or after.

Children need to feel that there is continuity and stability. The arrival of a baby will be a major change and keeping their life as it was for a while longer will help them to feel more secure.

> " If you have other children, prepare for the arrival of the new baby by having a week of fun with them, perhaps at a theme park, before the birth. As having a new little one means you need one-on-one time to get to know them, make plans for someone to look after your other children occasionally, especially to begin with and whenever you need support. If their behaviour starts to get worse, make sure you pick your battles, rather than try to deal with everything at once. And whenever you get the chance, sit and relax with your other children or just have some time alone – the washing-up and the housework will wait! " **KATE**

BREASTFEEDING

Breast milk is the best food for all babies and, even if it is given for a short time, it will be beneficial to their health. However, deciding whether or not to breastfeed is a very personal matter, but if you decide you want to, it is a good idea to ensure you have the appropriate guidance and support.

There are many benefits to breastfeeding. Your breast milk contains antibodies of the infections to which you are immune, which in turn help to protect your baby; it is also thought that the antibodies found in breast milk reduce the risk of Sudden Infant Death Syndrome, or cot death (see p. 255). Colostrum (the very first milk that is produced) is especially high in antibodies, protein and vitamin K – even if you don't continue to breastfeed, it is worth giving your baby colostrum for a few days. Breastfed babies are less likely to be overweight than formula-fed babies, as they are better able to regulate their appetite; breast milk may also reduce the likelihood of children suffering from certain allergies later on. In addition, breastfeeding has some other benefits for you:

- ► If you feed for a minimum of two months, it is thought to reduce your risk of developing breast cancer.
- ► It stimulates the production of oxytocin, a hormone known to play a part in bonding.
- ► It can be done any time, any place and requires no sterilisation of bottles, so is very practical (especially in the dark hours!).
- ► Breast milk is free.

Breastfeeding is the normal way to feed a baby, but it needs to be learned and practised, requiring patience and persistence. If you want to breastfeed, it is good to get as much help as possible at the beginning. Many hospitals offer antenatal breastfeeding classes, either as a group or one-to-one, but you may also need support when your baby is first born. Midwives try to be helpful, but often have several women to look after. Your maternity unit may have a breastfeeding counsellor, whom you should ask to see before you go home, because they offer invaluable advice and encouragement. Because women often leave hospital before their milk has come in, many hospitals also have a breastfeeding team, who can visit you at home, if necessary – ask for their number before you leave. See also the Box below about specific charitable organisations that support women who want to breastfeed.

It is important to recognise that, while some women – and their babies – take to breastfeeding without any problems, many others find it harder than they thought it would be. It may be natural, but it can take a while to establish your milk supply and an efficient technique. However, with perseverance and the right support, you will soon find that you generate a good supply of milk, gain confidence in how to feed your baby and find breastfeeding enjoyable and fulfilling.

Your milk will not 'come in' until the level of progesterone and oestrogen falls after delivery and that of prolactin rises, usually at around three to five days after the birth, although putting your baby to the breast at regular intervals before that will help the process along. Because milk production works on the principle of 'supply and demand' (see Box on p. 245), it is important that milk is extracted from the breast regularly right from the beginning – introducing formula early on (for 'mixed' feeding – see p. 249) can interfere with this process. And although you can express your milk and give it via a bottle (see p. 245), this is best left until your baby has first learnt to suckle effectively from the breast, as the two techniques are quite different.

GETTING THE RIGHT SUPPORT

Unless you receive proper help and support, it can be easy to give up breastfeeding if you encounter any problems. If your hospital offers a home-visiting breastfeeding specialist, do make use of them and you can always speak to your midwife or health visitor. However, problems can occur outside of their visits. There are also several nationwide organisations, such as the National Childbirth Trust (NCT), the La Leche League (LLL) and the Breastfeeding Network (BfN), that can provide vital help, support and information: they have a network of trained volunteers who can be of assistance, either on the phone or in person. The internet can help you to locate a local breastfeeding club and is also a good way to obtain advice on key elements, with videos showing latching on and good positions for breastfeeding. Finally, there are books on breastfeeding that can also be very helpful. See Useful Resources for further information.

Getting started

Firstly, you should find a comfortable position. If you are sitting upright, you may need pillows or cushions behind your back. Your baby should be raised up to breast level on one or more pillows or cushions so that you don't have to stoop or support their weight in your arms, as this puts a strain on your back and shoulders. Alternatively, you can place the baby on a pillow beside you, with their body stretching underneath your arm – this hold is good if you are recovering from a Caesarean section or if you are very overweight. Some women find that lying down on their side with their baby facing them can also be a good breastfeeding position, particularly at night. Before you settle in your chosen position, make sure you have a drink, your telephone and anything else you may need within easy reach.

Latching on

Place your baby so that the whole of their body faces yours, not just the head. The key thing about breastfeeding is learning how to get your baby attached to the breast correctly – this is often called 'latching on' – so that milk can be removed effectively. The baby's mouth must be open wide and sucking on the whole of your nipple, including the areola. To help your baby, hold your breast in your free hand and brush the nipple against the baby's top lip: this stimulates the 'rooting' reflex (*see* Chapter 6, p. 218) and should make your baby open their mouth. Then, gently shape your breast so that the nipple is slightly compressed and – there is nothing delicate about this at the beginning – put as much breast tissue as you can (not just the nipple) in your baby's mouth. You may have to be more proactive in doing this when your baby is newborn.

If your baby is latched on correctly, the top lip is turned upwards and creased over, you will see the jaw moving rhythmically and you should instantly feel that there is

a good suction on the entire areola, rather than simply some sucking on the nipple. If your baby is only attached to the nipple this can quickly lead to soreness (*see* p. 246), so insert your little finger into the corner of their mouth to break the suction, take your baby off the breast and start the process again.

When the time comes for the next feed, latch your baby on to the other breast. This is so that you can be sure that each breast is being properly drained, which will keep up your milk supply, prevent engorgement and ensure that your baby reaches the nutritious hindmilk (*see* Box opposite). You may want to make a note of which breast to begin with next time or fix a safety pin to your bra to remind you.

How often and for how long?

A newborn baby's stomach is tiny and so they need to feed little and often at first: usually at least eight times in 24 hours, for ten to twenty minutes or more each time. Your baby will have different levels of hunger at each feed. In addition, the quality of your breast milk can vary throughout the day: the morning feed is the one with the most supply of milk, because the level of milk-producing hormones is at its highest during the night; conversely, by the early evening, the quality of your milk may have diminished, as your body needs a rest. It is therefore important that you follow the needs of your baby, known as 'feeding on demand', rather than a strict time schedule. Signs that your baby may be hungry include:

▸ moving their head or 'rooting' for the breast when they are held
▸ moving their mouth or licking or smacking their lips
▸ sucking their hand or fingers
▸ crying (although this is usually one of the last signs of hunger).

You may feel that all you are doing in the first few weeks is feeding, but remember that frequent feeding in the early days helps to establish milk supply and that, as your baby grows, they become more efficient at it and you will have greater time between feeds.

How do I know if my baby is getting enough?

It is hard to know how much milk a baby is receiving when they are fed from the breast and this can be a cause of concern for many new mothers. To start with, your baby will only take a little milk from one breast at each feed. Newborns tire easily and may stop sucking after a few minutes, so you can stroke their cheek to stimulate their sucking. If, after a few 'reminders', they seem uninterested in continuing, then they have probably had enough. As your baby grows, they will be able to empty the breast each time, in which case you can offer the second breast as well. A rule of thumb is that if your baby seems satisfied after each feed, is gaining weight after two weeks and has at least six wet nappies and passes two stools per day, then they are getting enough. However, if you have any concerns about this, talk to your midwife or health visitor.

Expressing milk

If you want to feed your babies breast milk from a bottle or you need to relieve engorgement (*see* p. 246) you will need to express your milk. This means removing milk from the breast either by hand or by pump.

Expressing by hand

Hand expression can be useful for removing small amounts of colostrum or milk, or for relieving your engorged breasts between feeds. It is not a technique that allows you to express enough milk for an entire feed, and some women find it harder than others to express even small amounts. It is slow and should not be attempted unless you are already producing copious amounts of milk. First wash your hands and find a comfortable position to sit, with a sterilised container to hand (*see* p. 248 for more on the hygiene of feeding). Make sure your breasts are warm. Massage your breast, working towards the nipple. Cup the container close to the nipple with one hand and hold your breast around the areola in the other, with your thumb on top and fingers underneath to make a 'C'-shape. Squeeze repeated and rhythmically until the milk starts flowing. When the flow ceases or slows, move your fingers to a different part of the breast and resume pumping. If you are having difficulty with this technique, ask for help from your midwife, health visitor or a breastfeeding counsellor.

Expressing with a pump

For more frequent expression or when you require greater quantities of milk, you will need to use a breast pump. Similarly, mechanical extraction is a fast and efficient way to relieve severe engorgement or blocked ducts. The fastest and most effective breast pumps, in my experience, are electric pumps similar to ones used in maternity units (be warned: these are not small, unobtrusive objects!). Some women are able to express successfully using a battery-operated pump, but this is more likely to be the case once milk production is well established. Manual pumps, on the whole, are an inefficient, frustrating, time-and money-wasting method and should be avoided.

The NCT rents out electric pumps at a relatively small cost, and you may also be able to hire them directly from the manufacturers. Speak to your hospital or breastfeeding counsellor, as they may also be able to provide you with useful contact numbers. Be aware, though, that there may be a shortage in your area, so enquire early if you intend to hire.

You can keep expressed breast milk for up to five days in the fridge at 4°C or in the freezer for up to six months at −18°C, using special sterile bags (sold in babycare shops and pharmacies). Defrost it as you would any other liquid and place in sterilised bottles – and remember to label all expressed milk (with date and volume milk), so that the rest of the family do not unwittingly make use of it at some stage.

> ### HOW BREAST MILK PRODUCTION WORKS
>
> Milk production is stimulated by a baby sucking on the breast. It works on a principle of 'supply and demand': the more the breast is emptied, the more milk you will produce. If milk is not removed regularly from the breast, the supply will gradually decrease and then eventually stop altogether. If your breast is stimulated by a sucking baby (or by expressing), milk production will continue and increase as and when necessary to meet your baby's needs.
>
> Each of your breasts contains clusters of alveoli (sacs) that produce and store milk; ducts lead from the alveoli to the nipple. When a baby suckles, the pituitary gland at the base of your brain releases two hormones: prolactin, which produces milk, and oxytocin, which contracts the alveoli inside the breast and forces milk down through ducts and into the nipple. This is known as the 'let-down reflex', also called the 'milk ejection reflex', and some women find that it causes a tingling sensation in their breasts. Triggering the let-down reflex is essential for a baby to get a good amount of milk. Some women have a strong let-down reflex – milk starts flowing before the baby has had time to start sucking – and for many, the let-down reflex begins as soon as they hear their baby start to cry, even if they are nowhere near the breast.
>
> The milk at the beginning of the feed is known as foremilk, and is more watery and thirst-quenching than the creamier hindmilk, which comes after the foremilk has been consumed. This change is gradual, however: the fat content of the milk gradually increases the further the feed progresses. Because hindmilk is more calorie-dense, it is therefore important that your baby feeds until they have had sufficient quantities to satisfy their hunger and that you do not swap breasts while your baby is actively feeding.

Common breastfeeding problems

While many women experience no problems when breastfeeding their baby, others do. Don't worry if you find yourself in this situation: it is much more common than you might have been led to believe. However, with proper help and support, you will invariably find that difficulties can be overcome. Many of these problems arise from poor latching on, so you should always seek help from your midwife, health visitor or a breastfeeding support organisation, as this can be corrected. Remember: breastfeeding should not normally be painful. However, if you are experiencing pain as a result of some of the problems listed below, it is safe to take a simple analgesic, such as paracetamol or ibuprofen.

Breast engorgement

Engorgement can occur when your milk first comes in. Your breasts can swell up and become hard, although this tends to settle down within 24 hours or so. Engorgement can also occur any time the breast is not being drained efficiently. The fuller and harder the breasts get, the more painful they become for you and the more difficult it is for a baby to latch on, so the cycle is perpetuated. In order to relieve engorgement, it is very important that your baby suckles a little and often, so don't keep to a strict time schedule: let your baby take a small amount of milk at regular intervals from the affected breast(s) until it is time for the proper feed. If the baby is not able to latch on, express a little milk first so that your breasts are softer, then try again. When it is time for the feed, start with the breast that is more engorged, as a baby sucks most strongly at the beginning. Don't let your baby drain your milk completely: if your breasts are over-stimulated as a result of a long feed, they will try to refill again as fast as possible, which will not improve the problem of engorgement. If not relieved, engorgement can lead to mastitis (see below), an extremely painful condition that occurs when a breast duct becomes blocked and infected.

Until engorgement improves, you can place a cold green cabbage leaf over the entire breast, as this contains a high concentration of sulphur, known to reduce swelling and inflammation in tissue. Special gel pads sold in chemists can also help calm inflammation. Conversely, a warm flannel helps relieve the pain and can improve milk flow. Finally, always wear a supportive maternity bra.

Sore, cracked nipples

Sore, cracked or bleeding nipples can occur when you are trying to establish breastfeeding and your baby is not latching on properly. This means they are chewing on your nipple rather than suckling. Seek help with latching on as soon as you can, but even though it may be painful, it is important that you continue to feed or express, both to keep up your milk supply and to prevent engorgement.

To help sore nipples to heal, expose them to the air as much as possible when not feeding. Don't use soap or perfumed gels when washing, because these dry out the skin, and allow your nipples to dry naturally without covering them. If necessary, spread a little hypoallergenic, lanolin-based cream on the nipples to help relieve the soreness. Healing can take 24–48 hours.

Nipple shields, moulded silicone that covers the nipple and areola, can help alleviate the pain and allow the healing of sore nipples, because they prevent your nipples rubbing against your bra and because they allow the milk to flow without the entire nipple being inside the baby's mouth. They are very useful and cheap, although their success depends on whether you have a reasonably strong let-down reflex and your milk flow is good. If this is not the case, your baby will find it hard to get as much milk from your breast as when feeding directly from your nipple, so you may need to express as well.

Mastitis

Mastitis is an inflammation of the breast and is usually caused by severe engorgement and/or cracked nipples. If left untreated, the breast may become infected (often the infection enters through the cracked nipple and is not always the result of the initial engorgement). If this happens, an abscess can even develop, which often requires hospitalisation in order to be treated. The first sign of mastitis is often a hard, red and painful lump on your breast, caused by blocked milk ducts. Your breast may also feel hot and tender. If you notice this, you should be vigilant, as you may start to develop flu-like symptoms (e.g. a fever, feeling shivery or achy) soon after. It is very important to empty your breast as you would for symptoms of engorgement, but if your symptoms don't improve within 12–24 hours, consult a doctor, as you may need antibiotics to combat the infection (a small amount will pass through into your breast milk, but will not harm your baby). If at all possible, try to keep breastfeeding or expressing so that your milk supply does not start to dwindle.

Comfort sucking

If your baby is feeding steadily and is correctly latched on, you should not need to feed for longer than twenty minutes or so. If feeds go on for more than 40 minutes, it may be that the breast has already been drained and your baby is now sucking purely for comfort. Comfort sucking can lead to cracked and sore nipples (see above) and should be avoided, however soothing it is for your baby.

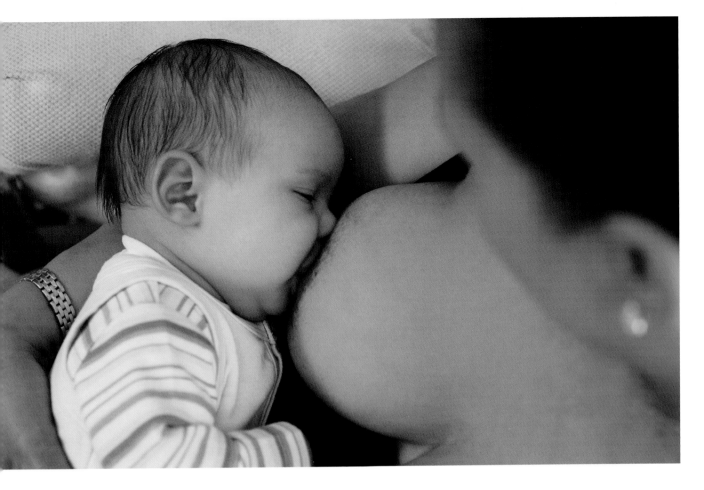

❝ My breastfeeding journey has been one of the most challenging yet enjoyable things I have ever done. I can honestly say that, without the support I had, I wouldn't have been able to carry on. The beginning was very difficult. Billy was three weeks early and he just wouldn't latch on. I had lots of midwives helping me, but he still wouldn't suckle, so I had to hand express my colostrum and syringe-feed him for the first few days. We tried everything, but nothing was working and when he fell to less than 2,500 g, I felt like a failure as a mother. The last option was to try a nipple shield. It worked! We left hospital a week later, still using the nipple shields. They were really fiddly when out and about and Billy was suffering from bad wind, so I was keen to stop using them as soon as I could. My friend's mum is a midwife and she would come round and help me latch him on without the cover. It took a long time and a lot of perseverance, but we got there and now we are successfully breastfeeding without nipple shields! ❞ SARAH

FORMULA FEEDING

Some mothers choose to feed their baby on infant formula immediately from birth or switch to it sometime in the first year. Whatever you decide, don't feel guilty or think that you have somehow short-changed your baby: this is a personal decision and you should be supported in it, because it is the one that feels right for you.

Women use formula for a variety of reasons, including the fact that their baby can be fed by others without the need for expressing. This can allow you to rest more (including having an uninterrupted night's sleep) or to get on with other tasks. In addition, formula-fed babies usually sleep through the night earlier than breastfed ones. This is because formula is less digestible than breast milk, so it stays in the stomach longer and keeps babies feeling fuller. Some women find that it is easier to have a routine with formula feeds, and to know whether their baby has had the correct amount of milk for their weight. Some feed solely on formula from the start; others breastfeed exclusively for a while before gradually switching to formula, or maintain feeding with both breast milk and formula (called 'mixed' or 'combined' feeding – *see* oppostire) until their baby is old enough to be weaned.

Although infant formula is made from cow's milk, it is specially formulated with essential vitamins and minerals to resemble human milk as much as possible. Speak to your health visitor if you are unsure about which particular brand to buy. Formula is available in two forms: ready-made liquid formula (which comes in cartons) and powdered formula (which comes in tins). Ready-made formula is highly practical when you are out and about or travelling, but they work out more expensive than buying the powdered version. In addition, once the carton has been opened, it is not sterile and will need to be thrown away after 24 hours if not used (*see* Box), which is wasteful. Powdered formula is more economical and needs to be made with water that has been boiled and is at least 70°C (but don't use water that has been boiled more than once). Some preparations can be mixed with cooled, boiled water rather than hot, and this can be very useful if you are travelling, although the water must be kept in a sterilised bottle. Babycare shops or departments will advise you on what equipment you need (*see* Chapter 5, p.142 for a suggested list).

Your midwife or health visitor will advise you on how frequently to feed and how much milk your baby needs per feed, as this is calculated according to the baby's weight. Nevertheless, your baby's appetite may vary from one feed to the next, so you should never force them to finish a bottle. Instructions for mixing up the formula will be displayed on the container and it is very important that you follow this: never alter the proportion of formula to water, as this could affect your baby's health and growth. Your baby should also drink cooled, boiled water, as formula is less thirst-quenching than breast milk. Avoid adding juices to the water to make it more palatable, as this gets babies used to sweet drinks.

HYGIENE DOS AND DON'TS

Hygiene is important when dealing with feeding equipment, because both breast milk and formula are breeding grounds for bacteria and your baby could therefore be made unwell by drinking from unclean bottles and/or teats:

▶ Wash and dry your hands before handling feeding/expressing equipment.

▶ Wearing washing-up gloves, wash *and rinse* every bottle, teat and breast pump part thoroughly in hot water, scrubbing the inside of each using a specially designated brush. (Dishwashers can be used to wash, but sterilising is still required afterwards.)

▶ After they have been washed, sterilise all bottles, teats and other equipment used for expressing or to make up feeds (e.g. spoons, knives, containers) for the first six months in a steriliser (or using another suitable method).

▶ Made-up formula can be kept in a fridge for 24 hours, in a coolbag with an ice pack for four hours and at room temperature for two hours; after these times it should be thrown away, even if it is unused.

▶ Throw away any formula or breast milk that is left over after a feed.

▶ Never re-heat formula or breast milk that has already been heated.

How to give a bottle

Your baby needs to be held in a supported, semi-reclined position so that they can breathe and swallow easily. Test the temperature of the formula by pouring a few drops on the inside of your wrist. If it feels hot, either wait for it to cool or run the bottle under the cold tap before testing again. Brush the teat against your baby's mouth, so that they open wide and draw in the teat. Hold the bottle at an angle so that the milk fills the teat (this prevents them taking in too much air). Allow your baby the occasional break from the feed (flow is faster from a bottle than from the breast), so that you can wind them: place them over your shoulder or upright on your lap, and rub your baby's back in a firm, circular motion. If no burp has occurred after a couple of minutes, there is probably no need to continue. Remember to have a muslin cloth or bib to hand to catch any small amounts of milk that are often 'posseted' as a result (see p. 258).

Mixed (combined) feeding

Some mothers choose to feed their babies with both breast milk and formula, a practice known as 'mixed' or 'combined' feeding. This can be done in various ways: for example, you could breastfeed for one feed and feed formula the next, or breastfeed during the day and give formula at night. In this way, your baby continues to benefit from some breast milk, but others can help you with some of the feeds.

You can start mixed feeding by dropping one breastfeed at a time and substituting with formula. Usually the early evening feed works best, because often your milk is the least plentiful as a result of being tired at the end of the day. You can gradually move on to alternating breast and formula feeds, and/or breastfeeding first thing in the morning and last thing at night. Bear in mind that if you are not exclusively breastfeeding, you milk supply will be affected – you still need to breastfeed or express regularly to make sure that your baby's nutritional needs are met. For this reason, it is best not to begin mixed feeding until breastfeeding is well-established.

> **DID YOU KNOW...?**
> If you have warmed up a bottle in a microwave, shake the bottle to ensure that the heat is evenly dispersed before testing the temperature on the inside of your wrist.

CARING FOR YOUR BABY

Looking after your baby on your own for the first time can seem overwhelming, but you will soon get to know your baby's wants and needs. You cannot expect, in the first six weeks, to establish much of a routine, but learning a few techniques in how to bathe and soothe your baby, as well as getting them to sleep, go a long way in helping to make life manageable.

A community midwife will visit you at home after the birth to check on your baby and she can also advise you on any aspect of babycare. Always remember that, if you are concerned about anything outside of her visits, you can ring the maternity unit (the number is on the front of your maternity notes), as they never close and can help and advise you postnatally as well. Thereafter, the health visitor at your local health clinic will take over and she will either visit you at home (e.g. if you have had a Caesarean delivery) or can see you and your baby at the clinic. You can take your baby to be weighed every week and can ask any questions about your baby (or, for that matter, your own recovery). In fact, your health clinic or Children's Centre is an invaluable source of advice and information for all the family.

Nappy-changing

You will probably have thought about whether you want to use cloth nappies or disposables (or both) before your baby was born (*see* Chapter 5, p. 145). Nappy-changing will be a frequent occurrence (a newborn will go through at least ten to twelve nappies every day) and you will soon develop your own technique.

Firstly, wash your hands, rinse and dry them thoroughly and make sure you have all the equipment you will need. Remove the wet or soiled nappy and wash around your baby's bottom with cotton wool dipped in warm water. Baby wipes are convenient when you are out and about, but even hypoallergenic ones can damage a baby's skin when used all the time (and are more expensive than cotton wool and water). Wipe a girl from front to back and, for boys, clean around the scrotum and penis without retracting the foreskin. Pat the area dry with a clean towel or dry cotton wool. Apply barrier cream if necessary (*see* p. 256 for information about nappy rash). Babies still urinate when their nappy is off, so make sure you have another nappy or cloth handy to mop up if necessary. Fit the new nappy according to the manufacturer's instructions and wash your hands afterwards.

Bathing

Bathing can be an enjoyable part of your care routine and is often a calming way to end the day and settle your baby for the night. Check the temperature of the water before you place your baby in it, not with your hand, which can tolerate higher temperatures, but by using either a special bath thermometer or by dipping your elbow into the water. Remember that newborns can lose heat very quickly, so they should not spend a long time in the water and you will need to dry and dress them swiftly afterwards in a warm room.

Whether you have invested in a special baby bath (*see* Chapter 5, p. 142) or are using your normal, full-size bath, you will need to support your baby while they are in the water – you can do this by holding them in the crook of your arm. A special bath support, which cradles the baby in a semi-reclined position in the water, can be used in a full-size bath and this allows you to have two hands free, although you should never leave your baby alone in the water even for a short moment. Avoid using soap, which can dry a baby's skin, but tip a little non-scented, hypoallergenic bath emollient into the water instead to keep their very delicate skin protected, soft and hydrated. Hair can be rinsed once a week with plain warm water, if required (you don't need shampoo).

Some newborns like splashing in a bath, but if yours seems to hate the experience, it is fine to bathe your baby every other day or even less frequently, as long as they are 'topped and tailed' daily (*see* p. 253).

> ### DID YOU KNOW...?
> In general, it is better to change a baby's nappy *after* a feed, as babies often empty their bowels when they have a full stomach. You will soon become expert in recognising your baby's habits in this department!

Topping and tailing

On days when you are not bathing your baby, 'topping and tailing' (cleaning the face and the bottom) is sufficient. Firstly, wash, rinse and dry your hands thoroughly. Dip a piece of cotton wool in some cooled boiled water, squeeze out, then gently wipe from the inner to the outer part of the eye. Use a different piece of cotton wool for the other eye, to avoid spreading bacteria from one eye to the other. Pat dry with a clean towel. For your baby's bottom, wash as you would do when nappy changing, with a fresh piece of cotton wool. Pat dry and leave to air a little if possible.

Interacting with your baby

Very young babies are content to feed, sit and sleep and don't need special entertainment – their new world will be stimulating enough. However, they will benefit from as much physical closeness and eye contact as you can give them, even from the very beginning. To start with, babies can only focus on objects that are very close to them and are unable to detect colours, so they relate more to strong shapes and images rather than toys, which is why black-and-white mobiles or cot bumpers are good stimuli for newborns. Most of all, they focus on faces, so getting close up to look and speak to them will help them to get to know you; holding, rocking and singing to them will also develop their other senses. By about four weeks, babies will start to follow anything that moves within their field of vision, so you could hold and move a rattle or soft toy for them (babies cannot do this for themselves until they are about three months). A baby starts to smile at around six to eight weeks, which is always a special moment for parents, and they will respond to you when you smile at them.

While newborns don't need toys as such, it can be a good idea to introduce a particular soft toy or snuggly blanket that they can learn to associate with comfort and sleep, although it is always useful to have an identical one as a replacement, should a particular favourite get lost or need washing (*see* also the section on crying on p. 254). Try to resist spending too much money on toys yourself: you will be given lots as presents and a baby can be as fascinated by simple, everyday objects as by more sophisticated (and expensive) play equipment.

> " My top tip to mums is to do everything you can to enjoy being pregnant, giving birth and being a mummy. It's a precious gift that some people don't get to experience. I would also say, follow your instincts: don't be afraid to change your mind on things you thought you never wanted to do and don't pressure yourself to do things a certain way if it's not working – try something and if it doesn't work, try something else. You haven't failed – you're just learning about your baby. Babies are little people with personalities, so let them experience your world for themselves, too. Above all, life doesn't end when you become a parent: it opens your eyes to a new kind of love and way of thinking. " HEATHER

Crying

Crying is the normal and natural way for babies to express themselves. A baby's cry is designed to be almost impossible for their parents, and especially their mothers, to resist – this form of communication is essential for their survival, after all. Not all cries indicate that there is something 'wrong' and it can take up to six months for parents to get to know what their baby's different types of cry mean. Some of the reasons babies cry are:

▸ they are hungry (crying tends to start slowly and at low volume, gradually increasing in strength)
▸ their nappy needs changing
▸ they have wind (crying can be sharper, like they may be in pain)

▸ they are too hot or too cold (the back of their neck should feel warm, but not excessively so)
▸ they are tired (the crying is more whiney and they are fractious and easily set off)
▸ they are suffering from colic (a sharper cry – *see* p. 258)
▸ they are unwell (*see* p. 259 for a checklist of symptoms).

It can be frustrating not to know the cause of your baby's crying. Unfortunately, if your baby is still crying after you have tried the relevant measures above, then it is just a matter of trying to soothe them until the crying eventually stops. You will soon learn your own ways to calm your baby, but there are some tried-and-tested methods that can help. A muslin cloth with your smell or milk can help to settle a baby. These are better than a specific soft toy, because if you lose or mislay the latter, it may be difficult to soothe them, whereas a muslin cloth can be washed and exchanged with another one without your baby noticing. Swaddling a newborn in a lightweight cotton sheet or blanket helps to make them feel secure and to calm them, especially when they are trying to get to sleep – ask your health visitor or a friend/family member to show you how to do this. Walking around your home holding your baby, going for a quick walk

DID YOU KNOW…?

If you are worried that your baby's crying may mean that there is something seriously wrong, don't hesitate to seek medical advice as a matter of urgency.

or (last resort) driving with them can help to stop babies crying (although try to avoid getting into the very tempting habit of going for a walk/drive *in order* for your baby to fall asleep). Having other people calming your baby can be more effective than if you try to do so yourself, especially if you are breastfeeding, because even if your baby has been fed, they may nonetheless recognise your smell as the source of comfort. It is best if you leave the room while the other person tries to soothe your baby.

Babies that cry a lot can make life very stressful, so it is important that you have appropriate support. You can talk to your health visitor, a local support group or call a helpline (*see* Useful Resources) if you ever feel overwhelmed. Even giving yourself a break for a few minutes in another room can help you get a sense of perspective – it is very unlikely that any harm will come to your baby in this time. And remember, as babies grow older, they will find new ways of communicating with you.

Sleeping

During the first six weeks, babies can sleep for sixteen to eighteen hours per day, although this varies from one baby to another. However, because they need frequent feeds, they often don't sleep for longer than two to three hours at a time. Until they are about three months old, they are unable to distinguish between day and night; nor are they likely to sleep through the night or develop any kind of night-time sleeping routine, as their ability to do so depends on brain maturity and having the capacity for a large enough feed to keep them sustained for longer periods of time. Reassure yourself, however, that these interruptions will eventually stop, allowing you and your baby to have restful sleep at night.

Although the recommended safest practice is to have your baby in the same room as you for the first six months, whether you do this is a personal decision, which depends on many factors. Many parents prefer to have their baby in their room during the first few weeks while they are getting up so frequently in the night. Some like to have their baby in bed with them (known as 'co-sleeping'), but evidence from a recent study has shown that this may increase the risk of Sudden Infant Death Syndrome, or 'cot death' (*see* below). What is a definite factor in the increase of the risk of SIDS is if one or both of you smokes, has drunk alcohol or taken any drugs that evening or is on medication that makes you drowsy, so never fall asleep with your baby in these circumstances and do try to give up smoking (*see* also Chapter 2, p. 44) or at least make sure that your home is smoke-free. The best way to place your baby in a Moses basket, crib or cot is outlined below.

Sudden Infant Death Syndrome (cot death)

Sudden Infant Death Syndrome (SIDS), also known as 'cot death', is the term used for the sudden and unexpected death of an apparently well baby or infant. SIDS is very rare, occurring in less than one in 2,000 births and mostly in babies of less than three months of age (the peak period is between seven and ten weeks old), but it is still the most common cause of death in babies over one month old. Most at risk are boys, premature babies and those of low birthweight.

Although the specific causes of death are unexplained, it is known that exposure to tobacco smoke (both before and after birth) can significantly increase the risk of SIDS. In addition, a major report analysing thousands of cases of SIDS across five large-scale studies has recently shown that there was a five-fold increase in the risk of SIDS in breastfed babies under the age of three months who slept in their parents' bed, compared with those who slept in a Moses basket/crib/cot in the same room. It was suggested that an increase in body temperature, which may affect a baby's breathing, could be a factor. The report concluded that 81 per cent of SIDS in those under three months old, where there are no other risk factors (e.g. parents who smoke or consume excessive amounts of alcohol), could be prevented if they didn't sleep in the same bed as their parents. Whether or not all experts agree with these findings, it is generally accepted that, while it is fine to feed your baby in an adult bed, it is safer for a baby under three months old to sleep in their own bed rather than in yours. There are some additional measures that parents can take to reduce the risk of SIDS:

▸ Make sure your baby's mattress is new and free from dust and damp.
▸ Always place your baby on their back to sleep.
▸ Position your baby with their feet at the end of the cot, with any sheets or blankets no higher than the shoulders, so that they cannot wriggle under the covers.
▸ If you are using a baby sleeping bag, make sure it is well-fitting so that your baby does not slip down inside.
▸ Don't let your baby get too hot and keep their head uncovered, so that they can lose excess heat.
▸ Breastfeed your babies, if only for a short time, as the antibodies in breast milk may help your babies' immune system, so that they are less likely to be affected by SIDS.
▸ Settle your babies with a dummy, as this is thought to help keep the airways open; however, never force babies to take a dummy if they do not want to.

For further information, contact your health visitor or a relevant support organisation (*see* Useful Resources).

YOUR BABY'S HEALTH

All babies will have minor health issues at some point and you will soon learn to recognise which ones may be more important than others. The key thing to remember is to trust your instinct, because no one knows your baby as well as you. So if you sense something is not right, insist on being taken seriously.

Most newborns encounter some of the problems listed below in their first few weeks of life. Your health visitor will be able to offer advice on how to treat minor complaints, but if you are concerned that an issue may need further investigation, don't hesitate to see your GP – no harm was ever done by discovering that there was no problem after all. For information on more serious health problems, see the A – Z of Complications.

Milia and other skin problems

Babies often develop spots, probably as a result of hormonal changes, and most clear up of their own accord. Superficial white to yellowish spots, typically occurring around the cheeks, nose and eyes, are known as milia. These are benign and disappear naturally within a few weeks of the birth. Babies' skins are very delicate and frequently develop strange, unidentified little rashes, but it is always better to get these checked over by a doctor. Don't use perfumed soaps or gels to wash your baby, however, as these are too astringent and will dry out the delicate skin.

Cradle cap

The condition known as 'cradle cap' is common in newborns. While the greasy, yellowy scales are not particularly attractive, cradle cap is not serious and it is certainly not infectious. Try putting some baby oil on the affected area and leaving it to soak in, as this may help loosen the scales. Try not to pick at the scales, however, as this could cause the skin to become infected. Usually cradle cap disappears on its own within a short space of time.

Nappy rash

A rash around your baby's bottom – 'nappy rash' – is a very common complaint and is caused by the ammonia in urine, which irritates a baby's highly sensitive skin. There may be red patches around the area or the whole bottom may be red, feeling hot to touch and/or with some pimples or spots. Some babies are more prone to nappy rash than others, but try to avoid leaving your baby in a wet nappy. Use cotton wool and water rather than baby wipes, patting the area dry with a soft towel. Airing your baby's bottom as much as possible (e.g. after a bath) is also very beneficial, as it allows the skin to breathe and to heal without being covered up. If necessary, you can apply some proprietary cream or petroleum jelly, as this acts as a barrier between the urine and the skin and can reduce the feeling of soreness. If the rash persists, it may be a sign of thrush, which will need treating with an antifungal cream – ask your health visitor or GP for advice.

Bowel movements

For the first one or two bowel movements after the birth, your baby will pass meconium, the greeny-black sticky liquid that was lining the gut before birth. After that, your baby's stools are quite loose and yellowy-brown (breastfed babies have looser stools than formula-fed ones). However, if the stools become liquid and/or green, your baby has diarrhoea. This needs prompt medical attention, because babies become dehydrated very quickly. In the meantime, try to give cooled, boiled water to keep your baby hydrated.

Constipation can occur in very young babies. You will notice that your baby's stools are firmer and/or less frequent. Give your baby some water to sip, in small and frequent doses, and if this does not improve the situation, consult your GP to rule out other underlying causes.

DID YOU KNOW...?

Get to know your GP, if possible before you give birth, because you will undoubtedly see them afterwards! First-time mothers make regular visits to their doctor's surgery in their child's first year, as babies usually suffer from a range of minor ailments and mothers are understandably anxious about them. However, never worry about 'bothering' the doctor: it is far better to have your baby checked out, rather than risk leaving a worrying health condition to worsen.

Vomiting milk

Babies frequently regurgitate a bit of milk when they are winded, known as 'posseting'. Some do this more than others, and this is entirely normal. If your baby is suddenly unable to keep milk or fluids down, however, seek medical opinion promptly, because babies become very dehydrated very quickly. Occasionally, a baby will vomit up an entire feed in a more violent fashion – this is called 'projectile vomiting'. If this happens as a one-off, it is usually nothing to worry about. But if this starts to happen after every feed over a short period (a rare occurrence), speak to your GP at once. See also entry on pyloric stenosis in Complications, p. 291.

Sticky and watery eyes

A mild eye infection, conjunctivitis is common in newborn babies, as a result of fluid or blood entering their eyes during the birth process. It usually clears up naturally, but if the problem persists, your GP may prescribe a mild antibiotic cream. Sticky eyes can also occur after your baby has been asleep – follow the instructions given in 'topping and tailing' for keeping them clean. If your baby's eyes are watery, this can be a sign of a blocked or underdeveloped tear duct. Again, this will improve in time and is rarely serious.

Colic

Colic is a common but poorly understood condition that tends to begin at some stage between two and twelve weeks and is characterised by prolonged crying. It is thought to involve spasms in the baby's intestines, and often arises in the early evening, at a time when babies may already be fractious because they are tired and are difficult to soothe. However, a colic cry is typically more sharp and piercing than a weary one and a baby will often pull up their knees at the same time. Colic can often be confused with hunger, especially in breastfed babies, because they still seek to suckle as a method of comfort – try to resist allowing your baby to comfort suck at your breast (see p.246), as this can quickly lead to soreness.

There is no fail-safe treatment for colic, although babies can sometimes be calmed by having their abdomen rubbed, or by lying across your arm or lap (but never put them to sleep on their front). Others find it soothing to be rocked or carried around, or to suck on a finger or a dummy. Gripe water, digestive teas (e.g. fennel) and proprietary products given before a feed are among other suggested remedies, but in many cases, it is a question of taking turns with your partner to look after your baby. By the time they are about three months old, the daily episode of colic has invariably passed.

Thrush

Oral thrush, caused by the yeast fungus candida albicans, is a common and usually harmless mouth infection developed by many newborns. One or more curd-like patches of white spots may be seen inside your baby's mouth and babies can also become 'fussy' when it comes to feeding due to the irritation this causes. Thrush often disappears on its own after a few days, but if not, consult your GP or pharmacist, as an oral gel suitable for newborns can be given as treatment. Babies can pass the infection on to you via your nipples if you are breastfeeding, in which case you may find it painful to breastfeed. An antifungal cream can be prescribed to clear up this minor infection.

Common colds

Their immature system makes newborn babies susceptible to the common cold virus. Usually this is nothing to be concerned about, but if your baby's temperature rises above 38°C, consult your GP. If your baby becomes congested and finds it hard to feed, seek advice from your pharmacist. Saline nose drops can help, as can raising your baby's cot/ Moses basket a little at the head end to ease congestion. Avoid decongestant oils before your baby is three months old, and even then do not put any drops directly onto their clothing (and certainly not on their skin).

Your baby's six-week check

When your baby is around six weeks old, your GP or hospital doctor or paediatrician will examine them and assess their general health and development. If the GP carries out this check, your own six-week check will probably be done at the same time (*see* p. 237). The doctor will check the following:

▶ heart, chest and breathing
▶ head circumference, length and weight (these will be plotted on a growth chart)
▶ abdominal organs and genitals
▶ eyes, ears and mouth
▶ hip alignment to check for dislocation (clicky hips)
▶ grasp reflex, head control and muscle tone.

Your baby's feeding and sleeping patterns will be discussed (although few babies are in any sort of routine by this stage), as well as any other issues that you may have.

The first vaccination, due at two months, may be booked in as well, and this is a good opportunity to discuss any concerns or questions you might have regarding the programme of vaccinations for your baby. The Department of Health website has the full schedule (*see* Useful Resources), but your health visitor or GP can also inform you.

Childcare

Depending on your circumstances, what family and other help is available and whether you are planning to go back to work, you may need to consider some form of childcare for your baby. You should start looking into which type might work best for you early in your maternity leave, as there is a shortage of childcare nationally and good-quality options are often in high demand.

You may have a relative or friend who is able to take on some or all of your childcare, either for free or for expenses only. Although this can be a wonderful arrangement, it is worth clarifying exactly what you expect this person to do in order to avoid misunderstandings at a later stage. Some people prefer more formal and regulated childcare and there are a number of different options available. However, paid childcare is not cheap, and some forms are more expensive than others, so it is worth thinking carefully about exactly what you require and when. The following options are suitable from birth onwards:

▸ maternity nurse/night nurse
▸ doula
▸ nanny (live in or live out).

Other types of care are suitable only once your baby is a little older:

▸ registered childminder
▸ au pair
▸ nursery/crèche.

Speak to other mothers for recommendations of good local nanny agencies (which may also have doulas, maternity/night nurses or au pairs on their books). Some magazines and local newspapers can be good sources of childcare advertisements. After you have interviewed potential candidates and have either drawn up a shortlist or reached a decision as to your preferred choice, it is vital that you follow up all the references you have been given and speak to any recent employers or (in the case of childminders and nurseries/crèches) parents who are using them.

Even the very best of childcare will not spare you from the odd emergency, such as your child being ill on the day that you have an important meeting or your normal arrangement suddenly falling through. Make sure that you have agreed with your partner in advance that you will not always be the one taking time off from work to cover this, and remember that other mothers are often fantastic at helping you out in a crisis.

Maternity nurses and night nurses

A maternity nurse helps you to care for your baby in the very early weeks and is the most expensive childcare option, because they usually cover 24 hours a day, six days a week and live in. Maternity nurses are usually employed for between two and eight weeks, although you may want them to do just a few nights or days per week rather than be with you all the time. They don't normally get involved with the household tasks, although some are happy to do this (ask at the interview) and often need to be booked several months in advance (i.e. well before you give birth). In addition to helping you with daytime care, maternity nurses can look after the baby at night, either bringing them to you for breastfeeding and then changing and settling them (which will enable you to sleep for a longer stretch) or giving the baby a feed from a bottle.

Many couples prefer to have the first, intimate days after the birth to themselves before enlisting a maternity nurse. You may also have other have relatives coming to help in the early days and so would prefer them to start at a later date. Always interview potential candidates, as it is important that you have a good working relationship.

As their name implies, night nurses help you with night-time duties, in much the same way as a maternity nurse. However, they then go home during the day, as they do not live in. They, too, can be helpful in the first few weeks when your baby needs feeding more than once a night.

Doulas

The rise of the doula as a caregiver in labour and after the birth is a recent phenomenon (for more on their role in labour, *see* Chapter 5, p. 137). Doulas can be hired for the postnatal period alone and, because they have usually had children themselves, they have good knowledge of childcare. They are also happy to help out around the house and can offer flexible hours, agreed in advance, to suit you. This can range from a few visits to fixed hours for a period of six to eight weeks. They usually charge an hourly fee or, if hired for both pre-and post-birth, often offer a fixed-price package. There are doula qualifications in the UK and a non-profit association, Doula UK, which has a register of qualified caregivers (*see* Useful Resources). Nanny agencies may also have doulas on their books.

Nannies

A nanny looks after your children in your home and can live in or live out. In the past, live-ins were cheaper than live-outs, but this difference has been eroded in more recent years. They may have qualifications such as an NVQ level 2 or 3, a BTEC in childcare or a DCE qualification (formerly NNEB), but none of these is obligatory to work as a nanny. A nanny's salary is paid net of all tax, National Insurance contributions and other benefits, so these must all be met by you, the employer – this can add 30 per cent to the wage bill. However, if you have more than one child, a nanny is often more cost-effective than, say, paying for two nursery places (see below).

You can hire a nanny to look after your children exclusively or you can share them with another family (which is cheaper than having one employed solely by you). The basis on which you nanny-share can vary: you might have a nanny on certain days, while the other family has them for the others; alternatively, the nanny might look after your babies plus a child/children from another family at the same time.

Communication, honesty and respect are key to developing a good relationship with your nanny. It is important to lay out employment terms very clearly and to make your wishes known. Similarly, you may need to be flexible if your nanny needs to take leave for personal circumstances. A happy nanny is more likely to provide a loving, stimulating environment as well as continuity of care for your child. And remember that a strong bond between your nanny and your baby will not make any difference to your baby's love for you. It will simply mean that you have an even happier baby.

There are books and websites with further advice on employing nannies and drafting contracts (see Useful Resources), and if you are hiring one through an agency, check the small print in advance.

Registered childminders

Childminders look after children in their own home rather than yours, and are paid by the hour and per child. They often look after other children as well, and so the home-based care with children of varying ages can feel very much like a family atmosphere. However, the downside of this is that if yours are unwell, your childminder may not be able to look after them until they are better, so that illnesses are not spread to the other children in their care. In addition, their hours are often less flexible, and they may not be able to accommodate your needs if, for example, you work late on certain days. Your local council will have a list of registered childminders, all of whom will have been thoroughly vetted (which includes an inspection of their home).

Au pairs

Au pairs are young people who have come to the UK to improve their language skills and who live with you, have their own room and receive board and lodging, as well as a small amount of money. An au pair is not classed as an employee, but as a member of your family. As such, they have their meals with you and, for example, accompany you on outings and holidays. In return, they undertake some domestic tasks including childcare, but not for more than 30 hours a week. Many do not have particular experience of looking after babies, so it is better to use an au pair when your child is a little older, and to limit their duties to *helping* you with childcare, rather than being left in sole charge.

Au pairs are often hired when they are still abroad – there are specialist au pair agencies and websites that allow you to do this. Always speak to them in advance, as an email exchange will not tell you how good their English is. Clarify as much as possible in advance of their arrival what you require them to do. Au pairs will expect to have several hours off during the day to go to language classes, as well as evenings to themselves, unless pre-arranged by you. Once again, respect and communication are key, and they should not be seen as young people whom you can make use of for very little money.

Nurseries and crèches

Nurseries can be run either privately or by the state and the best ones are usually very oversubscribed. As with childminders, they charge per child, although they may give a small discount for a second child. Many nurseries accept babies from a very young age, either full- or part-time; a crèche tends to take them when they are a few months old and for a few hours at a time on an ad-hoc basis. All crèches and nurseries are tightly regulated regarding safety and the ratio of carers to children, but when you visit, ask about staff turnover, as this gives a good indication of how happy the work environment is.

The advantage of a good nursery is that it provides a stimulating, social environment for your baby and it operates when it says it will, thus avoiding the problem of what to do if your nanny or childminder is unwell. Conversely, if your baby is unwell, the nursery will not accept them, so you may have to take time off work. Many nurseries don't stay open late, so if your job requires you occasionally to work into the evening, or if getting there before closing time is going to be problematic, it may not be the best option for you.

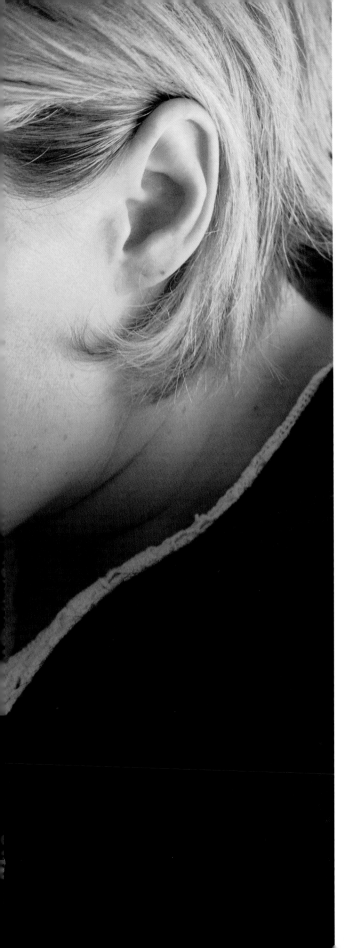

Your emotional welfare

Your emotional well-being is as important in pregnancy and new motherhood as your physical welfare. Mental health is still not much discussed in general and even less so in pregnancy, although there is now more awareness about postnatal depression. Some of the best ways to safeguard your emotional welfare over the months before and after the birth are to nurture your relationship with your partner, start preparing yourself for motherhood and to ensure that you have as much support as you need.

It is very common for women to experience a wide range of emotions at the start of their pregnancy – not all of them positive ones. These are normal feelings that will probably pass as you become more accustomed to this major life event.

Finding out you are pregnant

We all imagine that discovering you are pregnant is a moment of unbridled joy – and for many women this is true. It may be that you conceived easily, at a moment in your life when you feel ready to take on the responsibility of parenthood, are in a stable relationship with a secure income and a comfortable home, and so on. Your great happiness and confidence in the future will be boosted by the excitement of your family and friends at your news.

For others, however, the circumstances of their pregnancy might be less than ideal, and this will naturally create feelings of trepidation for what lies ahead, even more so if the pregnancy was unplanned. Furthermore, those who became pregnant through assisted conception (*see* Box in Chapter 1, p.13) may find their overriding emotion is one of anxiety rather than optimism, especially if they had to undergo several cycles or lost previous pregnancies. It is important to realise that it is entirely normal to be apprehensive about the future, and that pregnant women share many of the same anxieties, regardless of their personal situation.

Your changing moods

Even if yours is a wanted and planned pregnancy, you may find that, past the initial euphoria of discovering you are pregnant, you begin to have unexplained mood swings during the first few weeks. These are believed to be primarily the result of the hormonal surges of early pregnancy (*see* Chapter 4, p.85), possibly combined with some of the anxieties outlined below.

In the initial weeks of the first trimester, irritability, especially with your partner, is a particularly common emotion. Sometimes it seems as if nothing they say or do is right, and you snap at them continually. They can be left bewildered – as can you – at your sudden personality change and frightened at the thought that it might be permanent. You may feel your partner is not sufficiently understanding of what you are going through both physically and emotionally, or is not being helpful or supportive in the way you would

expect. I would urge you to communicate! Your partner cannot be expected to read your mind at all times and, unless you talk, they may never know what is bothering you. If you tell them, they have at least a chance of getting it right. And you can reassure them that your irritability is temporary and you should be back to your old self once the second trimester is under way.

Many women also find themselves unexpectedly bursting into tears in the early part of their pregnancy. For example, you can be watching television as normal, then be in floods at the mention of something that, previously, would never have resulted in such a reaction. Once again, hormones are in all likelihood to blame for your heightened emotional state, and things will return to normal from the second trimester onwards. However, it is also true that many women (and their partners) react more emotionally to sad stories involving children once they become parents themselves – you never see the world in quite the same way again.

Fears about the pregnancy

One of the reasons many women find it difficult to adjust to the idea of having a baby is that they are worried about the pregnancy itself, in particular the risk of miscarriage. This might be especially so if you have had a previous miscarriage or had difficulty getting pregnant. As a result – consciously or not – you might refrain from becoming emotionally attached to your developing baby, or spend the early weeks ticking off each day that passes until you are at the stage where you feel confident the pregnancy is safe. If you had complications in a previous pregnancy, you may be worried that similar problems will occur again, so it is important to discuss this with your midwife or obstetrician, who will be able to inform and reassure you. For more information on the risk of miscarriage, see Feature in Chapter 3, pp.68–9.

Unsurprisingly, these concerns can colour your emotions, although for the majority whose pregnancies do continue, feelings will, by and large, disappear as your pregnancy progresses. Having said that, women going through a second or subsequent pregnancy are often a bit more anxious about it than first-time mothers, because they are more aware of what can potentially go wrong, no matter how unlikely it is to do so. For discussion of the concerns you may have as you approach the end of pregnancy, see pp.276–7.

Worries about your lifestyle

Embarking on parenthood is a major life change and it is natural to be concerned about what it involves. Some of the issues that may preoccupy you are:

▸ whether you can afford to buy everything a child needs or to give up work (even temporarily) to look after your baby
▸ whether you will be able to cope with a young child (including the sleepless nights)
▸ feeling daunted by the responsibility of bringing up a child
▸ the loss of control over your organised life
▸ the effect on your relationship, including your sex life
▸ the effect on your social life
▸ how your body-image may suffer
▸ whether your career will be irrevocably harmed
▸ that you have suffered from postnatal depression in the past and fear you might do so again.

Thinking about the impact of having a child shows that you are taking it seriously. However, becoming unduly stressed is not good for anyone, pregnant or not. And, although the risk is minimal, there is some evidence to suggest that stress can, in some cases, affect a baby's development. So if you are struggling with your anxieties, try to talk things through with your partner, your friends and family or a professional counsellor, who can help you to assess your lifestyle by focusing on one issue at a time and to find a suitable solution. For advice about the baby equipment that you might need, see Chapter 5, p.142. Further information about maternity entitlements is given in the Feature on maternity leave in Chapter 2, pp.50–1.

What have I let myself in for?

When the reality of your pregnancy dawns, you may find yourself asking why on earth you thought it was a good idea. You barely feel responsible enough for yourself, never mind another, vulnerable, human being. Your uneasiness about the prospect of being a parent yourself might be exacerbated if you have a difficult relationship with your own parents. You may also start to examine your partner, their reaction to the pregnancy, their own family relationships and wonder whether they will be a good parent. Again, these are signs that you are feeling a sense of responsibility, which means that you have already taken the first step on the road to parenthood.

For some women, misgivings about their pregnancy also lead to feelings of guilt, as well as fear that this means they will not be good mothers. I should reassure you that, especially if this is your first pregnancy, you may find it very difficult to relate to the fact that you are carrying a baby. It all seems very abstract and unreal, and this feeling is likely to continue until you have seen your growing baby at your first scan (*see* Chapter 3, p.66) or can feel the baby move (at around eighteen to twenty weeks). Indeed, it may not be until the actual birth that the reality of your baby might really sink in. Whatever the case, it absolutely does not mean you will not be a good mother. See also p.277 for more on preparing for motherhood.

Having the right support

Many of the causes of the anxieties listed above are temporary and you will probably be able to rationalise and resolve them yourself. Nevertheless, I do believe that if something is troubling you, then talking it through is often very helpful. Discuss things with your partner, trusted friends and family, or consult parenting websites or internet chat rooms, forums and blogs (*see* below). You may find that joining an antenatal class helps you to get to know other women with whom you can discuss your feelings (*see* Chapter 2, p.56). Some women, however, go on to experience symptoms of antenatal depression, particularly later on in their pregnancy, and these need to be addressed (*see* p.270). If necessary, seek professional help from your midwife, GP or obstetrician. Whatever you do, try not to suppress any feelings that threaten to overwhelm you, as this could spoil what should be one of the most exciting times of your life.

Parenting websites and blogs

There is a plethora of websites and blogs on pregnancy and parenting, and many women find them a valuable source of information for all aspects of parenthood. Pregnancy and new motherhood can be an isolating time, so internet helplines, chat rooms and forums can be a particularly useful form of support when you have little time to get out and about and meet up with people. A few consoling words from a fellow mum-to-be or someone who has been through a similar experience can be enough to put things into perspective when you are feeling overwhelmed. See Useful Resources for recommended sites.

YOUR RELATIONSHIP

Not all pregnant women have a partner, but those who do often start to consider their relationship during pregnancy and how it may alter once they become parents. Discussing these issues now will help you embrace the many changes your life together will undergo.

How your partner may feel

Many partners are thrilled to be joining the world of parenthood. Yet, if it is common for pregnant women to experience a wide range of emotions, it is not surprising that the same is true for their partners at this time. Many of the anxieties that you may encounter (see p.264) can also apply to your partner, but they might additionally experience some of the following thoughts:

▶ Why is she behaving so strangely since discovering she was pregnant and is this change permanent?
▶ What will happen to my relationship with her?
▶ Will this be the end of life as I know it (e.g. no more evenings out with my friends)?
▶ Will I cope with the emotional and financial responsibility of caring for a child?
▶ Can I face going to antenatal classes?
▶ What will happen during labour and do I even want to be there?
▶ Will she and the baby be alright?
▶ Will I be able to cope with seeing her in pain?
▶ Will I be of any help to her?
▶ Will seeing her give birth put me off sex?
▶ Will she ever want sex again?

Some partners also worry that they might not bond with and love their child, but I can reassure you that it is very common to think this and this absolutely does not make them potential bad parents. Hospitals now very much encourage partners to cut the umbilical cord (see Chapter 6, p.176), as well as to have skin-to-skin contact with their baby as soon as possible after the birth and this can help a partner to feel close to their baby. Whether or not this happens, it can take some partners a little longer than others to bond with their baby. However, given time – and especially time on their own with their baby – they

all reach the same stage: they would never want to return to a life without children.

By talking about some of your anxieties concerning your pregnancy and relationship, you will show your partner that it is acceptable to have ambivalent thoughts and emotions and this will hopefully encourage them to voice their own doubts. Indeed, I would say that it is healthy to question these things, because it shows a level of self-awareness as you embark on such a momentous time in your lives, and this will stand you in good stead in times to come. It will also show that you are brave enough as a couple to discuss potentially tricky subjects and this can only bring you closer and improve your communication – something that will be invaluable in the years to come.

Communicating with each other

Having a child can certainly put a strain on a relationship, especially if the two of you don't discuss their respective needs openly and non-confrontationally. For example, many women wonder if their partners are going to be able to help and support them through pregnancy, the birth and the weeks that follow. I would say that, unless you communicate these concerns to your partner and let them know *what* help and support you would value, don't be surprised if they don't do exactly what you want and need. So, if your partner is going to take some time off after the birth, think about what you actually want them to do during this time and make sure they know how to do it (e.g. the internet shopping) – don't let them sit around or potter about in the proverbial garden shed for two weeks.

Baby talk

While many women find the biological details of what happens to their body during pregnancy endlessly fascinating (which is not surprising, since it is nothing short of extraordinary), they can be disappointed to discover that their partners don't share their fascination. Similarly, constant talk about what sort of pram to buy may not be every partner's idea of a scintillating conversation. It is not that they don't care and are not thrilled at the idea of becoming a parent, but you may have to accept that some subjects will simply be more interesting to you than to them.

Sex during pregnancy

Some women find that pregnancy boosts their libido, others that their sex life is adversely affected during this time. Whichever is the case for you, it is important to discuss these issues with your partner to avoid misunderstandings and any feelings of rejection.

Now that you are no longer concerned with 'making a baby' or, conversely, with avoiding getting pregnant, you may experience a greater desire for sex. In addition, the increase in vaginal secretions, the greater blood flow to the genital area and the slight rise in overall body temperature can enhance sexual pleasure and make orgasm more likely for women during pregnancy, particularly in the second trimester before your increasing size is having an impact. Before then, however, you may be suffering from the typical side effects of the first trimester of pregnancy: nausea, vomiting, exhaustion and tender breasts – none of which is conducive to sexual intercourse (see Chapter 4, p.122 onwards for more information). Towards the end of your third trimester, the size of your bump, combined with symptoms such as heartburn, indigestion and backache, can mean that you find it difficult to settle in a comfortable position in bed; as a result, you sleep less well and therefore feel more than normally tired. You may also start to think that your increased size makes you unattractive to your partner. Furthermore, some report feeling as if there is a 'third person' present during intercourse, which can make them very uncomfortable or self-conscious about sex later on in pregnancy.

Even if endless well-known women profess to feeling sexier than ever when they are pregnant, if you have gone off the idea of sex, it is important that you explain to your partner that this is temporary and not personal. Reassure them that you still love them and find them attractive and try to find ways, through massaging, kissing, stroking and cuddling, of keeping a physical connection, so that you don't become distanced from each other – intimacy need not mean having full sexual intercourse. However, if you are still having sex as your pregnancy advances through the third trimester, the size of your bump may mean that you need to find other positions that work for both you and your partner.

When problems arise

Problems within your relationship can come to the surface during pregnancy. Couples who are not supportive of each other or who now appear to have quite different views on child-rearing can start to ask themselves questions about the long-term future of the relationship. It is sadly not uncommon for emotional abuse by a partner to arise or worsen when a woman is pregnant, and this can be manifested in controlling, threatening or jealous/possessive behaviour, in actions that are designed to undermine or humiliate, and in physical violence (see Box). The issues concerned are clearly too wide-ranging to be discussed here, but all women should be aware that they don't have to suffer abuse or violence in their relationship and that your healthcare professionals can help you address this, as they are trained in handling such a situation and are very used to discussing the problem. They will be entirely non-judgemental, and will simply sit and listen to you if that is all you wish, as well as help you in more practical ways if you request it.

ANTENATAL DEPRESSION

For many people, mental illness remains a taboo subject. They might be happy to discuss a physical ailment, but are often reluctant to talk about psychological problems. This is particularly the case during and after pregnancy because, as a society, we assume that this is a time when women should be at their happiest. Yet we now know that antenatal and postnatal depression are much more common than we used to think. Fortunately, as a result of this new awareness, help is now more readily available and women no longer have to suffer in silence.

Women have a one in four chance of developing some sort of mental health problem during their lifetime, and this is most likely to arise during their reproductive years. The fact that you are pregnant or a new mother doesn't shield you from mental health issues; indeed, for some, this is the trigger for excessive anxiety and clinical depression. The reality is that suicide is one of the most common causes of ante- and postpartum death in women. I am therefore very keen to destigmatise depression, as it can cause terrible misery and, at its worst, can have devastating consequences, not just for you, but also for those around you.

Part of the reason for the prevalence of depression may have its roots in the on-going changes to our society. Many women today can feel isolated during pregnancy and especially after the birth. For example, if you work and this is your first baby, and if your family and close friends live far away, you may find that you don't have other women to call on for help, advice and reassurance. As a result, you may go into labour with very little clear idea of what is about to happen. You will rely very much on the medical team you happen to have on the day, as well as on your birth partner, who (unless it is your mother) usually knows even less about what can happen during labour than you do. After the birth, you are expected to leave hospital within a very short space of time and to look after your baby and/or return to work in a way that was completely unthinkable in the past – and still is in many cultures, where women are encouraged to rest for several weeks after the birth (although it should be noted that there

are sound medical reasons for resuming some activity after delivery – *see* Box in Chapter 6, p.214). Feelings of isolation and of being overwhelmed in pregnancy and new motherhood can quickly become acute, which is why it is no surprise that ante- and postnatal depression are on the rise. As a result, the notion of this being a blissful period is often a far cry from reality.

While postnatal depression is now more widely recognised, many people still don't realise that depression during pregnancy – antenatal depression – is just as common, if not more so, and can be as serious. It is true that most women are thrilled to be pregnant and that, although they might occasionally experience periods of tearfulness, irritability or anxiety (*see* pp.264–6), they remain happy at the prospect of having a baby. However, it is now thought that up to one in six women suffers from significant levels of anxiety and depression during some or all of their pregnancy, making it at least as common as postnatal depression. The situation is not helped by the common assumption that women are expected to be ecstatic and to bloom because they are pregnant. And although you undergo regular and varied tests throughout your pregnancy, your mental health is not rigorously assessed. Cursory questions might be asked at an antenatal appointment, but there is insufficient time for an in-depth discussion that might give you the opportunity to talk honestly about how you feel.

What causes antenatal depression?

It is not known exactly what causes antenatal depression, although some experts (but not all) believe that fluctuating hormone levels during pregnancy cause mood swings to be more pronounced, and these can develop into clinical depression. However, what is agreed upon is that there are a number of risk factors, many of which overlap with those thought to cause postnatal depression:

▶ money worries
▶ anxiety about work and how your career may be adversely affected
▶ dread about the (negative) upheaval a child will bring and the consequent loss of control
▶ problems within the relationship with a partner
▶ unresolved issues with your past or with your family, especially with your mother
▶ feeling low at the start of your pregnancy
▶ previous depression or postnatal depression, or a family

TOKOPHOBIA

Most women will, from time to time, feel anxious about giving birth. But if your fears are very severe and debilitating, possibly as a result of a previous birth experience or a long-held fear of childbirth, you may have a condition called tokophobia. With proper support, many of these fears can be overcome, so don't hesitate to seek help via your midwife or obstetrician.

- history of depression
- isolation
- ambivalence about the pregnancy, especially if it was unexpected
- social expectations to be the perfect mother and fears that you will 'fail'
- pressure to produce a baby of a particular sex
- fear of something going wrong during the pregnancy (usually as a result of a past miscarriage, stillbirth or neonatal death)
- difficulty in conceiving (e.g. many rounds of IVF), resulting in severe anxiety that something will go wrong
- extreme fear of childbirth (tokophobia – *see* Box).

Many of these risk factors represent normal and natural concerns that many pregnant women experience from time to time. It is when they take a hold and prevent you from dealing with your situation that problems occur.

Symptoms of antenatal depression

Many of the symptoms listed below are often put down to 'hormones' and are assumed to be part of the emotionally erratic behaviour that women normally experience during pregnancy. Indeed, some of them (e.g. fatigue, loss of appetite due to morning sickness) are actually caused by pregnancy. However, I want to stress that if you have any of these symptoms and feel that they are beginning to prevent you from leading your life or are affecting your mental equilibrium, then don't dismiss them as something you have to put up with – it may be that you are suffering from antenatal depression. Symptoms include:

- unexplained tearfulness
- irritability
- anxiety
- loss of appetite
- loss of libido
- poor sleep over a period of days or weeks, especially early-morning waking and an inability to get back to sleep
- unexplained fatigue or lethargy

" I was diagnosed with antenatal depression during my second pregnancy. I felt absolutely miserable for the entire nine months, which is hard when you're supposed to be happy. My GP and midwifery team were wonderfully supportive and I was referred to a special mental health unit and had extra meetings with a doctor. I was offered antidepressants, but decided not to take them. I had a feeling that I'd feel normal as soon as the baby was born. I was right! The minute I saw her little face, I fell in love and I've been happy ever since. " **DIANE**

- ▸ inability/lack of desire to plan for the future
- ▸ inability to derive excitement or enjoyment from life or from the arrival of the baby (anhedonia)
- ▸ compulsive behaviour (e.g. repeated hand-washing)
- ▸ feelings of isolation
- ▸ excessive possessiveness
- ▸ thoughts about death.

Women who are suffering from antenatal depression often feel enormous shame and guilt at being depressed at a time when you are expected to be at your happiest. You think you have no right to feel as you do. This then causes a vicious circle: because you dare not admit to anyone what you are going through, you find yourself sinking into an ever-greater depression. Maybe you also feel that you cannot tell your partner, because you are afraid they will think less of you as a result and view you as having non-maternal and unnatural feelings. Furthermore, you may worry that if you go to see your GP or midwife, your case might be highlighted to social services. All these fears are understandable but, I can assure you, totally unfounded.

Help for antenatal depression

The earlier you are diagnosed and treated for antenatal depression the better. Getting help can start with your partner – in fact, since you may not realise that your feelings are indicative of depression, it is important that those around you are aware of the signs. Communication is essential: don't shut them out – you may even find that they share some of your anxieties and emotions. In all likelihood, they will be relieved to discover that there is a reason – clinical depression – why you are not your usual self and that they themselves are not to blame. You may find that your symptoms improve simply by talking to and being reassured by your partner, as well as by close family or friends (though be mindful of who you confide in, as some may find antenatal depression difficult to understand). Internet chat rooms and forums can also be invaluable in supporting you (*see* p.266), because you may discover that your feelings are very common.

> **DID YOU KNOW...?**
> Depression can affect your partner, too, both before and after the birth (*see* p.281 for further details), so make sure that you are aware of the signs and that they get appropriate help.

In addition to more formal methods for treating antenatal depression, taking a little exercise on a daily basis can be of benefit, even if this only entails going out for a walk. Exercise stimulates the secretion of endorphins, the body's natural mood-enhancing hormones. See also some of the other self-help measures for postnatal depression outlined on pp.281–3.

If you need more support than your partner can offer you or you are not currently in a relationship, speak to your GP or midwife. There will also be a consultant at your hospital who specialises in mothers-to-be who are at risk of developing depression, who already have symptoms or who are already taking medication for it. In most cases, there is a specialist midwife who works closely with the consultant and who may be able to visit you at home. In addition, hospitals will often have a group meeting for mothers-to-be, which will give you an opportunity to voice your concerns and gain support and reassurance. Equally, you should know that you can go to your maternity unit at any time of the day or night for help and support. Remember, health professionals will have seen mothers in your situation many times before and they will be able to advise you and, if necessary, can arrange for you to be referred so that you can get the right sort of help.

Counselling and support are often all that is required. The fact that you are finally being listened to, helped and not judged is often such a relief that this alone can be enough for your condition to improve. However, a course of psychotherapy may also be appropriate. Cognitive behaviour therapy (CBT) is a form of talking therapy that may be available at your GP surgery or with a therapist approved and paid for by the NHS, although you may wish to pay for such help if the waiting time is too long. Other more long-term counselling or psychotherapy can also be very helpful (this is not available on the NHS), again because it enables you to be listened to at length, to know yourself better and to feel understood.

Although antenatal depression can often be treated by psychotherapeutic means, medication can also be very helpful and should not be ruled out solely because you are pregnant. Your GP or obstetrician can refer you to a specialised perinatal psychiatrist, and this will enable you to discuss your symptoms and feelings at length and, where necessary, to be prescribed antidepressants. Although doctors are invariably reluctant to advise medication unless other options have been tried or the situation is acute, there are antidepressants that are safe to take during pregnancy and that will not harm your baby.

With the proper care and support, there is every chance your symptoms will improve considerably, if not disappear altogether. However, you may need to continue treatment, involving either therapy or medication or both, beyond the end of pregnancy and into the first year of your baby's life, because otherwise you are at considerable risk of developing postnatal depression.

TREATMENT AND MEDICATION FOR DEPRESSION

If you are seeking treatment for mental health problems either during or after your pregnancy, you may wish to ask your healthcare professional the following questions, as appropriate:

▶ Can you explain what the different types of treatment for depression are?
▶ Why is this particular treatment (counselling/ psychotherapy/medication) suitable for me?
▶ What will my treatment involve?
▶ If my treatment involves medication, are there any risks for me or my baby? If so, what are they and can they be reduced?
▶ Might I have withdrawal symptoms or problems when I stop taking the medication?
▶ I am taking other medication: will this new medication affect it?
▶ When should I start to feel better and what happens if I don't by then?

If you were already taking medication for a mental health condition before you got pregnant, speak to your doctor as soon as possible so that you can both decide if it is safe to keep using it, or whether the dose needs to be changed or another drug prescribed. For example, the group of antidepressants known as a selective serotonin reuptake inhibitors (SSRIs), of which paroxetine is an example (Seroxat is a common brand), should be only be used during pregnancy when strictly indicated. However, do *not* stop taking any medication abruptly, as any small risk to your baby by continuing the medication may be outweighed by possible withdrawal symptoms when you cease, some of which can be unpleasant and potentially severe.

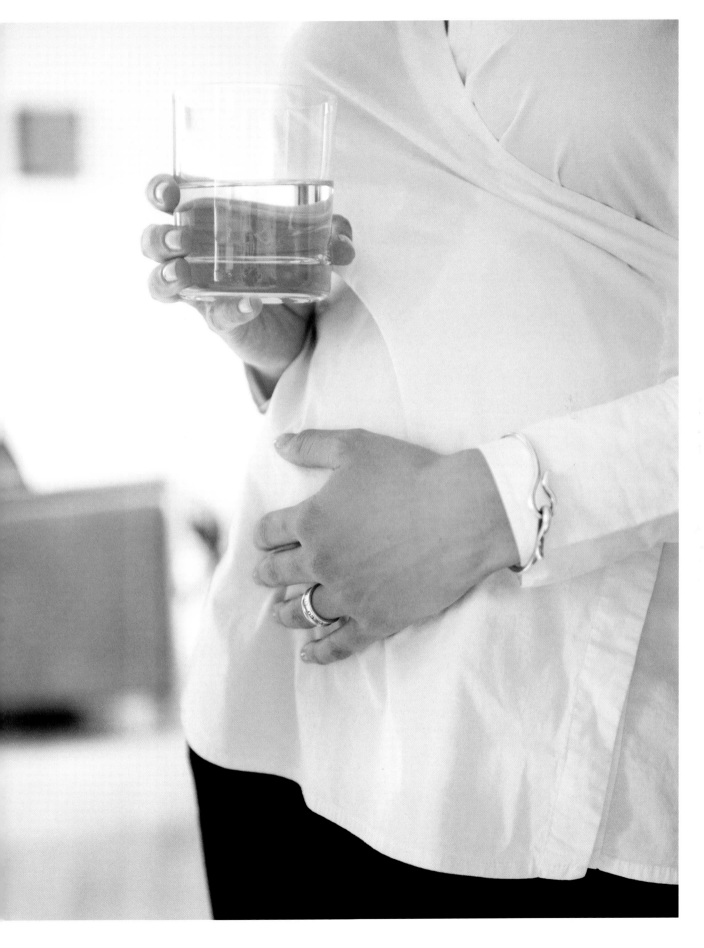

PREPARING FOR MOTHERHOOD

As the end of your pregnancy approaches, your feelings of excitement and impatience are probably growing as you start to prepare for your new life. It is very normal to have some very conflicting and powerful emotions at this time, some of which may be quite out of character, and these may involve concerns regarding your imminent role as a mother.

How you feel in the third trimester

Aside from the physical concerns of late pregnancy, you may find you are beginning to behave in ways that are untypical. For example, the tearfulness you experienced in early pregnancy (see p.264) might resurface. In addition, you might find it increasingly difficult to focus on any task and you are more lethargic and slower to get jobs done – things don't seem quite as pressing as they used to. You may also be more forgetful than usual. Although this is commonly referred to as 'maternal amnesia', research has now dismissed the concept and showed that there is no difference in cognitive function between pregnant and non-pregnant women. Any forgetfulness you may be experiencing is therefore more likely to be the result of simply being distracted by what is happening to your body and by the imminent birth. In order to counter this, try to prioritise your current tasks as much as possible so that you focus only on the essential ones. And make lists of things you have to do so that you reduce the risk of forgetting them.

Your body is changing fast during the final trimester and while, for some women, the sight of their very pregnant shape is something they welcome and revel in, for others it is actually quite distressing: they hate what their bodies have become and are extremely self-conscious, especially in front of their partner. It is not for me to comment on the rights and wrongs of this, but I do think that how you view your body depends on several elements: firstly, how you felt about your body before you got pregnant; secondly, how well you feel at this stage of your pregnancy (if you are suffering from many unpleasant side effects, you are likely to feel worse about your body); and thirdly, how your partner makes you feel about your body.

Towards the end of their pregnancy, some women develop a 'nesting' instinct, cleaning out cupboards that have never previously been emptied, sorting out the baby's room down to the last detail, and generally going into cleaning overdrive (see below). Others prefer to stay calmly at home, put their feet up and avoid venturing too far in case they get caught short. Many first-time mothers work until the last couple of weeks before their delivery date, and this can either make it difficult to focus on work, knowing that they will shortly be going on maternity leave, or, conversely, it can act as a spur to prioritise their work and get to the bottom of their in-tray. Each of us is different, but we all know that, once we are in our final month of pregnancy, there is no more denying the facts: the birth will definitely occur some time soon!

'Nesting instinct'

Many women develop an urge, some time during the final weeks of their pregnancy, to do a lot of clearing out and cleaning in their home. This strange phenomenon is referred to as the 'nesting instinct' and I have no idea why it is that, at a time when you are feeling increasingly weighed down by your bump, you discover a need to spring clean your cupboards for the first time ever. It may be a subconscious way of preparing psychologically for the birth and, unless it leaves you aching or exhausted, there is no reason why you shouldn't give in to your feelings, because it is certainly true that you will not have the time or energy to do any of these tasks once the baby is born! See Chapter 5, p.140 for more on final tasks before the birth.

How will I cope with the birth?

Giving birth for the first time is a great unknown and it is entirely natural to be apprehensive about it. Thoughts can centre on whether you and the baby will have a safe outcome and how you will be able to cope with the pain. Some women may also be embarrassed about the physical side, as well as whether they will behave 'badly' in front of medical staff.

You should try to reassure yourself with the thought that, although emergencies do arise, in almost all cases things do turn out all right and the baby is delivered safely in the end. Have confidence in your midwife or doctor: they too wish for you to have a good birth experience – but one that ends with a healthy mother and a healthy baby. In addition, labour does not need to be excessively painful and Chapter 6, pp.180–191 provides detailed information about the different methods of pain relief available, so that you experience as little pain as possible during your labour.

There is no reason to feel self-conscious about the physical process of birth. Doctors and midwives are so used to being

covered in various bodily fluids that this is one of the reasons they wear scrubs to deliver babies: once you have ruined a suit and/or a pair of shoes helping a mother during labour, you never again forget to change in advance! In fact, all they might remember will be your face and your baby – none of the other body parts. When it comes to the idea that you might disgrace yourself, I can confirm from personal experience that all staff will have seen and heard it all before countless number of times and will have forgotten everything long before you do.

Will I be a good mother?

Aside from the practical aspects of making sure your home is ready for your new arrival, there will undoubtedly be some psychological elements to your preparations and you may be feeling some trepidation about the transition into motherhood. There is simply no way to be fully prepared for the complexities of your forthcoming role, as you will need to continually adapt to the unique and changing behaviours of your new baby, all of which are unknown to you at this point. All I can say is that countless women have gone before you and lived to tell the tale, so try not to be overwhelmed by these feelings and instead look forward to addressing the challenges of each day as you do in every other aspect of your life.

Nowadays, many women (and their partners) have had little experience of looking after babies until they have one of their own. If you are worried that the practicalities of looking after a tiny, fragile-looking infant may be beyond you, I can guarantee you that, once you have been shown how (and don't leave hospital until this is the case, particularly if you wish to breastfeed), you will master the arts of babycare, such as nappy-changing and bathing, very quickly indeed.

You may worry also that you have yet to formulate an idea of how you would like to bring up your child. I can tell you that no parent has it all worked out in advance. In any case, this sort of approach is likely to make it difficult to respond flexibly to all the challenges that parenting presents, which will not make you the best kind of mother. Once you have had your baby, you will be bombarded with advice, some of which will be helpful and some of which will not. By all means ask questions, read books and listen to other people's experiences and opinions. But, in the end, you should trust your own instincts and do what feels right for you and your child: then you will know you have made the right decision. In reality, there is no such thing as a 'perfect mother'. All you should be aiming for is being a 'good enough' mother, and it is almost certain that you will fall into that category.

As the whirlwind that accompanies the birth of a new baby subsides, you may find that your daily life now barely resembles the one you were living before. It will take some time for you to adjust to your new role and to work out how you can find the space to be 'you' as well as a mother and a partner.

If you were used to being stimulated by an interesting job, the contrast between your old life and your new one will be enormous. The day-to-day demands of looking after a newborn can be relentless and not very rewarding and this can seem like quite some way from the rosy existence you imagined before you had a child. For some women, this can even lead to difficulties with bonding with their baby (*see* Box). Remember, however, that any feelings you have at this time are likely to be exacerbated by some of the physical and hormonal changes taking place in your body after the birth. See also Chapter 8, p.238 for more on managing life at home.

The 'baby blues'

The physical demands of giving birth, combined with the enormous hormonal changes that are happening in your body, not to mention significant sleep deprivation, can make you feel drained and emotionally fragile. This is referred to as the 'baby blues': you feel vulnerable, easily tearful, irritable and generally rather low. These feelings often occur at the time your milk comes in, around three to five days after the birth.

The baby blues are entirely normal and usually improve within a couple of weeks. Not all women experience these feelings, but if you do, make sure you tell your partner and close family, because they need to know how you are feeling in order for them to be able to support you, not only emotionally but in practical ways. It is important to let people help you, even if this doesn't come naturally to you.

You may be surprised to be feeling low after the birth, either because this may be a new experience or because, in general, women are led to believe that nothing can dim their elation at having a baby. Reassure yourself that what you are going through is extremely common and is no reflection on you whatsoever. However, if your feelings persist or worsen, it is worth seeking the advice of your midwife or GP, as you may be suffering from postnatal depression (*see* p.281).

BONDING WITH YOUR BABY

There is a misconception among many people that good mothers 'bond' with their babies as soon as they are born, feeling an instant, boundless love for them. Moreover, that for this bond to be strong and for the long-term benefit of the mother-child relationship, it is essential that mothers are constantly with their babies in the weeks following the birth, preferably in close physical contact with them, and breastfeeding them as well. This is a total misapprehension that only serves to make countless new mothers feel guilty, either because they do not yet feel this all-consuming love, or because they feel happier if they can sometimes have time for themselves away from their baby.

I feel very strongly that it is important to dispel the notion of how important immediate bonding is. Some mothers do feel an overwhelming passion for their baby from the moment they are born, but for many others, these feelings take longer to emerge. Bonding instantly with your baby is no indication whatsoever of your ability to be a good mother. Equally, research has shown that there is no difference in the bonding process between women who have had a vaginal birth or a Caesarean section. And there is no evidence to suggest that mothers who are separated from their babies at birth – for example, if their baby is premature or sick and has to spend time in the neonatal unit – develop any less of a bond than those who are permanently with their babies from the start. This shows that there is no link at all between the closeness of contact to your baby in the early weeks and having a good, healthy and loving relationship with your child in years to come.

The pressure to be 'perfect'

The high expectations that women sometimes have of themselves post-birth are not helped by the abundant and widespread messages in the media to be the perfect mother, to gain a bikini body within weeks of giving birth and to get back to work in even less time than that. Not surprisingly, most women don't manage to do this, leaving them to feel they are 'failing' and not coping. In reality, you cannot achieve these goals (even if you wanted to) without enormous amounts

of money, paid help and contracting out vast areas of your life, from childcare to cooking, shopping and general household duties. Remember that instead of focusing on being the 'perfect' mother (not that she even exists) or trying to aspire to 'celebrity' standards, you should be aiming to be a 'good enough' mother, to obtain help where you can (and pay for it if necessary) and to decide what is best for you, your partner and your baby when it comes to going back to work.

Your relationship

You might have gained a new role as a mother and this will, quite naturally, take up the majority of your time and emotional input, but you still have a partner and it is essential that you nurture this relationship, too. It is very easy to become swallowed up by parenthood and to lose sight of who you and your partner are as people, not just as parents, so it is important that you give yourselves time away from the baby. While your social life will undoubtedly be affected, that doesn't mean that it has to end altogether. It may take greater forethought and planning, but if you enlist the help of friends, family or (if you can) good-quality childcare, there is no reason why you cannot have a few hours away from your baby during the day or evening, even as early as a few weeks after the birth.

It is easy to underestimate how much the arrival of a new baby changes your partner's life as well. It can also take partners some time to adjust to their new role and it can be a harder process than they had anticipated. They, too, are likely to be tired for much of the time – especially if they are juggling work with broken nights – and possibly mourning the carefree life they used to have. Indeed, some partners develop symptoms of postnatal depression themselves (*see* opposite).

There is no doubt that the birth of a child does, at least initially, change the dynamic of any relationship: you no longer have only each other to consider, but another person, too. Aim at all times to keep the lines of physical and verbal communication open between the two of you, because your relationship will benefit in the long run.

Your sex life

There is no doubt that birth does affect a couple's sex life, at least initially. There are significant changes after the birth of a baby, some physical, some emotional, and these may affect your experience of and desire to have sex. This is especially the case in the first six months after the birth and, for women, this is usually caused by one or more of the following factors:

▸ Breastfeeding is causing vaginal dryness (because of the low levels of oestrogen and high levels of prolactin) and making intercourse uncomfortable.

▸ Perineal scars from tearing or an episiotomy is making penetrative sex painful (although sexual intercourse is very effective at improving the flexibility of the scar).
▸ Tiredness reduces libido and means that you often crave a good night's sleep rather than sex.
▸ Changes in your body shape have left you feeling less confident about your attractiveness.
▸ While you are not at work, you have assumed a more traditional domestic role, and this has made you feel under-appreciated and resentful towards your partner.
▸ Postnatal depression has lowered your libido.

Partners can also feel exhausted, under-appreciated and depressed. The arrival of a baby can mean that they now view you as more of a mother and less of a lover. Alternatively, their memory of the birth can remain with them and it may take a while for the previous passion to be rekindled; they may also be concerned about causing you pain during intercourse.

These factors are very common, yet so rarely talked about. Some of the painful symptoms of penetrative sex (e.g. vaginal dryness, scars) can be allieviated by lubricant (there are plenty to choose from), which may in turn increase your desire to have sex. Ultimately, though, if you can be open and honest with your partner, you can each understand how the other is feeling and can support each other. Verbal and physical reassurance that you love each other is important. Physical closeness (e.g. kissing, cuddling) is important to maintain even if you are not having sex. Usually, if verbal and physical communication are maintained, sex follows naturally within two or three months of the birth, but if this is not the case, you may need to discuss your feelings further with your partner. With communication, understanding and sensitivity, your sex life can survive and even improve after the birth of a child. Sex may never be as frequent as before, but many couples find that its intensity and level of fulfilment is increased.

Rediscovering you

It may be unrealistic to carve out some time for yourself in the early weeks of new motherhood, but try not to leave it too long before you do so. At the very least, make sure that you talk to an adult every day, even if you have only got a couple of minutes to spare. Remember those friends that you promised to continue to see after you became a mother (*see* Chapter 2, p.47)? Set yourself a target date – not too far in the future – when you think you might manage a night out together. It may have to be a modest affair to begin with, but if you get into the habit of planning time away from your baby (and your partner), it will help you to retain the sense of your own identity that can so easily be lost when caring for others.

POSTNATAL DEPRESSION

The arrival of a new baby is a time of enormous change and can be a psychological upheaval, as you adjust to your new role as a mother. In some women, this can lead to postnatal depression, particularly if they have previously suffered from depression in the past.

Around ten per cent of women develop postnatal depression, which is defined as depression beginning from a few weeks to up to a year after the birth. The symptoms are the same as for antenatal depression (see pp. 271–3). Women may not be aware that they have a problem, or may be reluctant to admit to one, perhaps because they are afraid of what might happen if they do. Yet postnatal depression is an illness that needs to be taken seriously and treated by experienced professionals, and the earlier it is diagnosed, the better it is for you, your baby and those around you. Left untreated, it can affect your interactions with your baby and curtail your ability to function normally.

It is important that you realise that postnatal depression is a common illness and that you are not to blame for it occurring. Furthermore, don't feel embarrassed to talk about it: women often feel ashamed or guilty about their depression, but hiding it from others makes you feel worse. Voice your feelings, complain if necessary, and avoid concealing your emotions in a bid to soldier on gamely – women are very good at not making a fuss, but you are allowed to do so in these circumstances! Yes, you may have wanted your baby, but no, you don't have to suffer in silence if all is not well. So, make an appointment to see your GP or health visitor sooner rather than later: speaking up about how you feel is often the first step towards getting better.

What causes postnatal depression?

As with antenatal depression, the causes of postnatal depression are not fully understood, although hormonal changes after the birth probably play a part. What is known is that if women have suffered from previous episodes of depression, there is a greater likelihood that they will develop postnatal depression, and those who have suffered in the past from postnatal depression have a one in four chance of the condition recurring. In addition, the following may also be contributory factors:

- ▸ tiredness
- ▸ grieving for the life you once had
- ▸ strains in your relationship
- ▸ social isolation
- ▸ lack of emotional and practical support
- ▸ a difficult birth.

Postnatal depression can be treated in several ways, using similar methods to those employed for antenatal depression (see p.273). Support from your partner and close family, and/or with counselling or psychotherapy, can prove sufficient for milder cases. In more severe ones, antidepressant medication may be prescribed (see Box on p.274).

Depression in your partner

Although ante- and postnatal depression are usually considered to affect only women, around four to seven per cent of partners (figures quoted are for men) are now thought to suffer from it too. Symptoms are similar to those described for antenatal depression and there is no single reason why some are affected but not others. However, the increased pressure of parenthood, responsibility (financial or otherwise) for another person, as well as a strained relationship with their partner all contribute. Their own personality, medical and family history are also factors. Coping strategies, such as staying late at work or drinking to excess, can be a sign that your partner is finding parenthood, or its prospects, difficult to cope with. If you think that your partner is developing depression during or after your pregnancy, encourage them to speak openly to you about how they are feeling, try to support them and not to judge them. Suggest that they seek help by speaking to their GP – treatment options will be similar to those for pregnant women and new mothers. They could also consider some of the self-help strategies set out below, such as doing some exercise or having some time to themselves either to socialise or to do something they enjoy.

Self-help for postnatal depression

In addition to seeking professional help, there are several measures you can take yourself to help reduce the severity of your postnatal depression and aid your recovery.

Finding other mothers

Try to build a network of mothers in your area whom you can see on a regular basis (it is not very practical to have to travel

POSTPARTUM PSYCHOSIS

It is thought that around one in 500 women develops a form of severe postnatal depression – called postpartum psychosis (PPP) – that, if left untreated, can leave them at risk of harming themselves and/or their baby. If you have had previous mental health problems, the likelihood of developing PPP increases significantly, and you should be monitored antenatally and postnatally by specialists. However, not all women who develop PPP have had previous mental health issues.

Symptoms vary (and can change rapidly); they include mania, confusion, hallucinations and delusions. This should be treated as an emergency and help should be sought as soon as possible. Treatment involves admittance to a specialist mother-and-baby unit (with the baby) until the condition improves. If it is diagnosed early and women are given appropriate specialist perinatal psychiatric care, involving medication and psychological support, they almost always recover fully and their long-term ability to be good mothers is not affected. For more information, see Useful Resources.

long distances to see other friends). There are usually many places to meet other women in your situation, such as NCT groups, baby swimming classes, playgroups and so on. Ask around or speak to your health visitor; there may also be support groups at your local Children's Centre that can provide helpful advice. In addition, internet chat rooms/forums for new mothers also provide much-needed support and practical advice and can make you feel less isolated (*see* p.266).

Getting some help at home

The amount of domestic tasks you have to do when you are at home with a baby can easily undermine your morale. The physical and emotional changes you experience after giving birth make help a necessity, not a luxury. If you don't want to ask friends or family, consider paying for help, even temporarily. Having someone else do the ironing, shopping online and having it delivered, and doing whatever else is necessary to lighten your burden of dull chores, can stop you feeling daunted and overwhelmed. Don't feel guilty about this or that you are somehow failing.

Exercising to lift your spirits

Do a little light exercise every day and go out at least once. This may simply mean going for a short walk, but it is essential for your mental health to get those mood-enhancing endorphins going with a bit of fresh air and exercise. Mother-and-baby yoga and Pilates classes not only provide a good way of toning your post-pregnancy body, but they enable you to meet other women near to your home who, like you, have young babies.

Treating yourself

Give yourself regular little treats – not just once a week, but every day if possible. Do whatever makes you feel good: this can mean anything from going for an indulgent cup of hot chocolate in your local café to getting your partner to look after the baby while you soak in a relaxing bath at the end of the day. Factor in longer breaks by leaving your baby with family or friends, even for an hour, while you have time for yourself – you will find that people are often queuing up to do this for you. This is essential for you to rediscover the person you were before all the interrupted sleep and round-the-clock nappy-changing came along, although make sure that 'time for yourself' does *not* mean going to the supermarket to do the weekly food shopping!

Eating sensibly

Being deprived of calories and nutrients can depress your mood and leave you feeling exhausted. Try to stick to a healthy diet, but make sure it is an enjoyable one, and allow yourself some occasional treats as well (*see* Chapter 2, p.22 for more information on eating healthily). Having regular meals and small, nutritious snacks will help avoid the highs and lows caused by poor, irregular eating habits. If your body image is contributing to your depression, bear in mind that you are unlikely to shift your baby weight by going on a drastic diet, especially if you are breastfeeding, because you will probably end up bingeing on all sorts of unhealthy foods after a few days and putting all the weight back on. It is better to lose weight gradually by adjusting your diet sensibly, seeking the advice of a nutritionist, if necessary. See also the Feature on obesity in Chapter 2, pp.30 –1 for some helpful suggestions on managing your weight.

Contacting a support organisation

Staying connected with the adult world reduces the isolation that can cause depression. If you don't have a friend you can ring on a regular basis, consider ringing a helpline of one of the organisations that help and support women suffering from postnatal depression (*see* Useful Resources).

Listed below is a range of some of the more serious complications of pregnancy and birth, as well as conditions that can affect either you or your baby in the postnatal period and beyond.

CEREBRAL PALSY

Cerebral palsy (CP) is caused by an injury to a baby's brain or a problem with brain development before, during or after birth. It affects one in 400 children, but is more common in babies born prematurely (the earlier they are born, the higher the risk of having CP). Other risk factors include:

▸ a difficult labour
▸ a breech birth
▸ a baby of low birthweight (under 2,500 g)
▸ twin or multiple pregnancies (because of the high percentage of premature births)
▸ maternal age over 40.

CP is an umbrella term that covers a range of conditions, from mild to severe, affecting muscle control, movement, speech, posture, walking, sight and hearing. Children born with CP have the same range of intelligence as those born without, but they often have learning difficulties as a result of the particular way in which CP affects them. Around one-third suffer from epilepsy. Cerebral palsy cannot be detected antenatally and may only be diagnosed in infancy, rather than at birth. There may be no known reason for a child being born with cerebral palsy, but causes include lack of oxygen to the brain, abnormal brain development or infection (such as rubella) in the early part of pregnancy.

There are three main types of cerebral palsy, and many of those affected have a mixture of these types, with no two people being affected in the same way. Cerebral palsy does not get worse as a child gets older, although the condition can lead to health problems that can cause increasing difficulties in the future. Some children diagnosed with CP have very minor symptoms that are barely noticeable, while others have a severe form of the condition, including intellectual and physical disabilities that require life-long care and support with every aspect of daily life.

CHROMOSOMAL ABNORMALITIES

An explanation of what a chromosomal abnormality is and how they can be passed on from parents to baby, as well as details about how they are screened for and diagnosed, is given in the Feature in Chapter 3, p.75.

Down's syndrome (Trisomy 21) is the most common chromosomal abnormality, and occurs when there are three copies of chromosome 21. It can be diagnosed antenatally, but will also become apparent soon after birth. Newborn babies suspected of having Down's syndrome are floppy at birth (as a result of reduced muscle tone) and will have certain physical characteristics, including a flatter facial profile and nasal bridge and a single crease across their palm. Definitive diagnosis will be by blood test, which produces a visual display of the chromosomes (known as a karyotype). Children with Down's syndrome usually (but not always) have specific health issues. Around half have heart disorders, ranging from mild to severe (babies are usually screened for this soon after diagnosis); other problems can include bowel abnormalities, respiratory, thyroid, eye and hearing problems, and a higher incidence of infection. Your baby will be followed from birth by a paediatrician and other relevant specialists and, with appropriate care, most children lead healthy lives. Parents are given help and support by medical staff and there are local and nationwide support groups to provide other sources of information and advice.

Edward's syndrome (Trisomy 18) occurs when there are three copies of chromosome 18 and it is usually incompatible with life. Three-quarters of affected babies are miscarried or stillborn, and when diagnosed antenatally (in 90 per cent of cases, the anomaly is picked up at the fetal anomaly scan and confirmed with amniocentesis) parents are offered a termination of pregnancy. Approximately 94 per cent of babies with Edward's syndrome have the full form of the disease and, of those born alive, a third die within the first month, and only five to ten per cent survive beyond one year and will have severe physical and learning disabilities. Those with partial forms of the syndrome can and do survive for longer, and the extent of their disabilities depend on their particular form of Trisomy 18.

Patau's syndrome (Trisomy 13) is the third most common chromosomal abnormality, although it only affects around 1 in 10,000 births. It is caused by having three copies of chromosome 13 and is the most severe of the three viable trisomies. In around 80 per cent of cases, the pregnancy ends in miscarriage. Of those who are born alive, most die within the first few days and have severe disabilities. A small percentage do survive longer than a year, but usually these babies do not have the full syndrome. Patau's syndrome is usually visible on the fetal anomaly scan, as the fetus will be seen to have structural anomalies together with a failure to grow. Diagnostics tests will be offered to confirm the condition and a termination will be offered.

Turner syndrome (45 X) is a monosomy, where the absence of one of the sex chromosomes leaves a single copy of the X (female) chromosome. It is only detected antenatally if you have an amniocentesis for another reason. Unlike most chromosomal abnormalities, it is not associated with increased maternal age, and occurs in around one in 2,500 births. A high percentage of fetuses miscarry during the first trimester, but of those that survive, many are not diagnosed until childhood. Physical features can include a broad chest with widely spaced nipples, webbing or loose skin at the neck and a low hairline. Girls are short in stature and, in later childhood, lack any signs of puberty, including menstruation. They are infertile, although oestrogen treatment can enable secondary sexual development and menstruation to take place. In some cases, the girl has a version of the syndrome that can mean she is not necessarily infertile.

CYSTIC FIBROSIS

One in 25 people carries the recessive gene for cystic fibrosis (CF), and one baby in 2,500 live births has the disease. CF causes the body to produce thick mucus, which affects many organs, especially the lungs, pancreas and digestive system. As a result, sufferers are prone to regular chest infections; they can also develop malnutrition as a result of the mucus in their pancreas and digestive system, which disrupts the production of digestive enzymes. A rigorous daily regime of treatments, including physiotherapy and medication to reduce the risk of lung infections, limits the build-up of mucus and provides the enzymes required to digest food.

ECTOPIC PREGNANCY

Just over one per cent of pregnancies are ectopic. This means that the fertilised egg starts to grow inside the Fallopian tube, where fertilisation takes place, rather than moving into the uterus in order to grow (although occasionally the embryo can develop in the cervix, ovary or abdomen). An ectopic pregnancy invariably manifests itself between the sixth and tenth weeks of pregnancy (most commonly during the sixth week) and always results in the end of the pregnancy. It is potentially extremely serious and, if not diagnosed in time, can be life-threatening. You are at increased risk of an ectopic pregnancy if you have had one previously ectopic pregnancy, have a damaged Fallopian tube (e.g. as a result of pelvic inflammatory disease), are over 40 years old or are a smoker. However, in the majority of cases, women who have ectopic pregnancies don't fall into the higher risk category. Some women get no early symptoms, while others get some or all of the following:

▸ bleeding (from light spotting to heavy bleeding, with or without clots)
▸ abdominal pain; this can develop over a few days or arise suddenly, may be on one side only, and feels like a sharp, cramping pain
▸ pain in the tip of your shoulder, due to blood leaking into your abdomen; doesn't go away if you change position
▸ diarrhoea/pain on having a bowel movement
▸ dizziness
▸ extreme pain, fainting or collapse; this symptom, in particular, should be treated as an emergency, as it can be a sign of internal bleeding caused by a ruptured Fallopian tube – go to your nearest hospital.

If you suspect you may have an ectopic pregnancy, contact your GP immediately or, if symptoms occur out of hours, go to your nearest Accident and Emergency department. You should be referred at once to an Early

Pregnancy Unit (EPU) or an out-of-hours gynaecology service. If you have had a previous ectopic pregnancy or have had previous surgery on a Fallopian tube, you can go straight to an EPU. In order to diagnose an ectopic pregnancy, you will need to give urine and blood samples (to confirm that you are pregnant) and an abdominal and a vaginal examination will be carried out. Finally, a transvaginal ultrasound scan will be done to establish whether an intrauterine pregnancy is present and, if so, whether a fetal pole and fetal heartbeat can be detected (*see* Chapter 4, p.87).

The presence of an ectopic pregnancy does inevitably mean that the embryo will not develop into a viable fetus and, in order not to put your health at risk, options for treatment will be discussed with you. You could wait to see if the pregnancy ends on its own, but this is only suitable in a minority of cases. In some cases, a drug can be administered by injection that prevents the pregnancy from continuing and the embryo is gradually reabsorbed. As with the previous option, the pregnancy needs to be detected very early and show no signs of a fetal heartbeat or tissue rupture. Surgery is the most likely treatment for removing the embryo because, in many cases, symptoms of an ectopic pregnancy only appear once the Fallopian tube has been damaged – at this point it is your only option and is often life-saving.

FEMALE GENITAL MUTILATION

It is estimated that 130 million women worldwide have undergone genital mutilation, and around two million currently do so annually. Because female genital mutilation (FGM) is so common in certain parts of the world, if you originate from a country that practises FGM, you are likely to be asked antenatally (e.g. at the booking appointment) if you have had some form of FGM. The midwife will be respectful of your cultural traditions, but it is important that your healthcare professionals know whether you have had FGM, as it can affect how the birth of your baby is managed. Referral to a psychologist should be made available to you and, depending on what sort of FGM you have had, reversal surgery may be offered in order to enable a vaginal delivery to take place (every effort will be made to have an all-female medical team attending you during the operation). It is better for this to take place by the eighteenth week of pregnancy in order to allow plenty of time before the birth for the affected tissue to heal.

FGM increases the risk of a range of obstetric complications, including those arising from a Caesarean section (which may be advised, depending on your circumstances), problems with vaginal/perineal scarring both before and after delivery, and an increased likelihood of an episiotomy, vaginal tearing and PPH. It can also be harder to perform a vaginal examination during labour, making fetal scalp monitoring and blood sampling more difficult. There are several hospital-run clinics around the country dedicated to FGM (*see* Useful Resources). These are staffed only by women, who can help and inform you during and after your pregnancy.

FIBROIDS

Benign uterine growths, known as fibroids, are very common and are often symptomless: 40 per cent of women aged over 40 have them and they are present in all women who live to 90 years old (if they have not had a hysterectomy). There are different types of fibroid, depending on exactly where in the uterus they are situated. A fibroid needs to measure at least 4 cm in order to significantly interfere with the implantation of an embryo, although if a fibroid protrudes into the uterine cavity (a submucosal fibroid), it may increase the risk of miscarriage and reduce the success rate of IVF. Fibroids do not usually cause problems during pregnancy, but sometimes they decrease in size (known as 'red degeneration') because their blood supply is diverted to the placenta and this can cause episodes of abdominal pain. Conversely, some fibroids grow during pregnancy, but these will be seen and monitored during routine ultrasound scans and it is rare for fibroids to become so large that they invade the uterine cavity or obstruct the passage of the baby down the birth canal. If a Caesarean section takes place and the fibroid is sited low in the uterus, a higher incision or even a vertical one (*see* Box in Chapter 6, p.210) may be required. Whether a delivery is vaginal or by Caesarean, fibroids increase the risk of PPH. Indeed, because of this, fibroids are never removed electively during a Caesarean section. Women with diagnosed fibroids should be offered an ultrasound scan twelve to sixteen weeks after delivery to see if any treatment should be considered.

GROUP B STREPTOCOCCUS

About one in five pregnant women carries the bacterium Group B streptococcus (GBS) in their digestive system and vagina. It is usually harmless and many babies come into contact with it during labour and birth and are unaffected by it. However, a very small percentage do develop an infection that can be serious: it is fatal in about ten per cent of affected babies and twenty per cent will suffer long-term harm. Most babies who become infected do so within twelve hours of the birth, and those born prematurely or following a delivery more than eighteen hours after the mother's membranes ruptured are at particular risk. Symptoms tend to arise within two days of infection and include:

▸ being floppy and unresponsive
▸ not feeding well
▸ high or low temperature
▸ irritability
▸ unusually fast/slow breathing
▸ grunting when breathing.

Women in the UK are not routinely screened for GBS (although you can have a test done privately if you are delivering in a private hospital), but if you are known to be carrying GBS, you will be given antibiotics intravenously during delivery, especially if your membranes rupture before you start your labour, in order to protect your baby.

HIP DYSPLASIA
Dislocation of the hips, called 'hip dysplasia', affects around one in 200 babies and is a condition checked for at birth by the paediatrician. It is more common in girls and in breech deliveries and is a result of the hip socket being too shallow, enabling the head of the femur to slip out (this does not cause babies any pain). The condition is rarely serious and can be corrected with exercises and by the use of splints, braces or a harness until the baby is a few months old. See also Useful Resources for more information.

HYPERTENSION
High blood pressure, clinically termed 'hypertension', is becoming more prevalent in women of reproductive age and makes pregnancy more complicated to manage. It reduces blood flow to the placenta and therefore restricts the amount of oxygen and nutrients your baby can receive. Left untreated, hypertension can result in serious risks to your health and/or that of your baby, such as late miscarriage, premature birth, babies that are small for gestational age, placental abruption and maternal stroke or death. Women with

pre-existing hypertension, or those who develop hypertension before twenty weeks of pregnancy (chronic hypertension), account for one to five per cent of all pregnancies. Pregnancy-induced hypertension (gestational hypertension) is defined as arising after the twentieth week of pregnancy and it occurs in a further five to ten per cent of all pregnancies, but in up to 25 per cent of first pregnancies. Risk factors for gestational hypertension include:

▸ having a BMI of more than 35
▸ being aged 40 or over
▸ having diabetes
▸ being a smoker
▸ a gap of more than ten years between your current and previous pregnancy
▸ hypertension in a previous pregnancy.

Of the women who develop gestational hypertension before 34 weeks, 40 per cent will go on to develop pre-eclampsia, a potentially serious problem that, if undetected, can lead to eclampsia, which (rarely) can be fatal. See individual entries on these conditions.

If you are at risk of developing hypertension during pregnancy, you will be advised to take a low dose of aspirin (75 mg) every day. If hypertension of whichever type is diagnosed, you will be monitored in a hospital-based obstetric clinic at least once a month during your pregnancy. Depending on the severity, this could range from having your blood pressure and urine checked twice a week, having blood tests, or being admitted to hospital in order to have a range of tests performed at least once a day. In addition, your baby's size will be monitored using an ultrasound scan, as fetal growth can be impaired. You will be offered medication that will help to lower your blood pressure and keep it within an appropriate range for you (any drugs you take during pregnancy will be safe for your baby). In addition, try to reduce the amount of salt in your diet, be active throughout your pregnancy and control your weight gain.

The following figures enable you to know whether your blood pressure reading falls into the mild, moderate or severe category of hypertension:

▸ **mild:** blood pressure between 140/90 and 149/99; does not usually require treatment
▸ **moderate:** blood pressure between 150/100 and 159/109
▸ **severe:** blood pressure of 160/110 and higher.

Some women have a higher reading when a midwife or doctor takes their blood pressure, so an average of three readings is taken, usually over at least two visits, in order to try and reduce the effect of 'white coat' hypertension. If you go into labour naturally and your blood pressure is very high, this will be monitored at points throughout labour, or even continually, and you may be advised to have an assisted delivery (see Chapter 6, p.198); alternatively, a Caesarean section may be offered. If at any stage during pregnancy you develop severe hypertension or symptoms of pre-eclampsia, you will be admitted to hospital and, depending on how far advanced your pregnancy is, delivered by induction or Caesarean section.

INTRAUTERINE GROWTH RESTRICTION
A baby whose growth slows or ceases in the womb (i.e. doesn't follow the expected pattern) is defined as having intrauterine grown restriction (IUGR). This is part of a wider group of babies that are 'small for gestational age' (SGA), where their size, or estimated fetal weight (EFW), in the womb is in the bottom tenth percentile for that gestation. The lower the percentile for SGA, the greater the likelihood of IUGR. A low level of amniotic fluid (or oligohydramnios – see entry opposite) may also indicate IUGR.

IUGR can be caused by a variety of factors, including:

▸ maternal age of 35 and over
▸ smoking (which is responsible for 30–40 per cent of cases)
▸ excessive alcohol intake
▸ hypertension, diabetes (including gestational) or pre-eclampsia
▸ placental insufficiency (see entry on p.288)
▸ chromosomal abnormality, such as Down's syndrome (see entry on p.284)
▸ congenital abnormality (see Feature in Chapter 3, p.75)
▸ infections such as rubella and toxoplasmosis (see Chapter 2, pp.42 and 43), as well as syphilis (see entry on sexually transmitted diseases, p.291).

IUGR can increase the risk of stillbirth or neonatal death (see Feature on pp.294–6), premature birth, fetal compromise during labour and impaired fetal neurological or cognitive development, usually related to prematurity. If your baby's growth appears to be slowing down, your healthcare professionals may offer one or more ultrasound scans to assess the EFW more accurately. Your developing baby's growth should always be plotted on a *customised*, rather than a general chart, as the former takes account of your ethnicity, your height and weight, and the number of babies you have had. This could affect whether your baby is diagnosed as being SGA (either because they have failed to achieve their full growth potential or because they are *constitutionally* small) or having IUGR.

If IUGR has been diagnosed, you will be monitored and scanned on a regular basis so that your carers can assess how your baby is developing and can discuss with you when the optimum time for delivery might be. It may be better to deliver your baby prematurely, in which case, if this is earlier than 34 weeks, you will be given a dose of steroids prior to delivery to help your baby's lungs to mature as much as possible before birth. Depending on your baby's circumstances, a Caesarean section may be offered. If vaginal delivery is decided upon, your doctors may offer induction rather than wait for you to go into spontaneous labour. In either case, continuous fetal heart rate monitoring of your baby will be advised throughout labour. Delivery will be in a hospital with appropriate neonatal facilities, and an experienced paediatrician will attend the birth so that your baby's needs can be met from birth.

JAUNDICE

Jaundice is a blood condition that occurs in around half of all newborn babies, and premature babies are especially prone because their livers are immature at birth. The excess red blood cells that the baby had while in the womb need to be broken down at birth. A yellow pigment, bilirubin, is produced during this process, and when it is not cleared fast enough by the liver and kidneys, it turns the baby's skin a yellowish colour. This 'physiological jaundice' becomes apparent between one and four days after the birth and clears up on its own within ten days. Doctors will monitor the bilirubin levels in your baby's blood (using a drop of blood from a heel prick) and, if it gets too high, your baby will be placed under ultraviolet light (phototherapy) for a few hours every day, as this breaks down the bilirubin in the skin. Treatment will stop as soon as the bilirubin levels fall below a certain level.

Occasionally, breastfed babies develop mild jaundice, but this is harmless and disappears once breastfeeding ceases. Very occasionally,

jaundice is a sign of another underlying problem. It can be caused, for example, by an infection, a liver or thyroid problem, or a blood group incompatibility causing anaemia. Phototherapy is usually used to treat the jaundice, but in some cases a blood transfusion may also be necessary.

OBSTETRIC CHOLESTASIS

Obstetric cholestasis is a rare liver condition that affects less than one per cent of pregnancies, invariably occurring after 24 weeks. Symptoms include itchy skin all over the body, but mainly on the hands and feet, with no accompanying rash. It is caused by bile salts leaking out into the bloodstream, and women who have been previously affected have a high chance of developing it in subsequent pregnancies. IVF also increases the risk.

It used to be thought that obstetric cholestasis increased the risk of stillbirth and premature birth, but research is now inconclusive. The risk of stillbirth may be very slightly raised, but the increased number of premature births is more likely a reflection of scheduled early delivery in order to protect babies from any possible effects. If you develop the condition, your obstetrician will discuss with you the advantages or not of delivering your baby early – unless your symptoms are intolerable, your baby is probably best left in the womb for as long as possible.

Itchiness can be alleviated by keeping cool both during the day and at night and by applying non-scented hypoallergenic moisturising cream; some women find that aqueous menthol cream can also calm symptoms. Symptoms will disappear very soon after delivery when the levels of bile salts in your blood stream return to normal.

OLIGOHYDRAMNIOS

Oligohydramnios is defined as an insufficient amount of amniotic fluid. It may be diagnosed at the fetal anomaly scan, in which case you will be offered further scans to monitor fluid levels, or later in your pregnancy. When diagnosed at the scan, it may also indicate a renal malformation in your baby. Oligohydramnios can also occur in pregnancies that continue after 41 weeks because, after peaking at about 34–6 weeks, the volume of amniotic fluid gradually decreases thereafter. Oligohydramnios is also an indicator for IUGR (*see* entry opposite) and for premature rupture of membranes.

PLACENTA ACCRETA

Placenta accreta is a condition where the placenta grows into the wall of the uterus and cannot separate normally. It is rare, and usually occurs if you have placenta praevia at 32 weeks and have had a previous Caesarean section or other uterine surgery:

▸ For women who have had one previous Caesarean section, the risk of placenta accreta occurring as a result of placenta praevia is eleven per cent.
▸ For those who have had two previous Caesarean sections, the risk is 40 per cent.
▸ For those who have had three, the risk is 61 per cent.

If placenta accreta is suspected, the remainder of your pregnancy will be managed as high-risk, due to the potential for haemorrhage before, during or after delivery. (Placenta percreta, where the placenta grows through the uterine wall and extends outside the uterus is even rarer, occurring in around one in 2,500 births, but will also be managed as a high-risk delivery.) You will be delivered by Caesarean section by a consultant obstetrician and consultant anaesthetist in a hospital with appropriate intensive care facilities (in case of haemorrhage during the operation). Your consultant will discuss with you the options for treatment in the event of either severe bleeding or the placenta not separating from the uterine wall. These include embolisation of the uterine arteries (a procedure that blocks the blood supply to the uterus), use of a cell salvage machine (which recycles your blood and reduces the need for blood transfusions) or a hysterectomy. There are also situations where it may be the best option to leave the placenta inside the uterus and wait for the tissue to be re-absorbed by your body over several months. Ideally, your doctors will aim to deliver your baby at 36–7 weeks.

PLACENTA PRAEVIA

When the placenta is lying low in the uterus, over or near the internal cervical opening (or 'os'), it is referred to as 'placenta praevia'. This is associated with a higher rate of pregnancy complications, notably preterm delivery and antepartum haemorrhage (bleeding). In addition, if you have placenta praevia at term, you will need to be delivered by Caesarean section, as your baby will not be able to descend through the birth canal.

A low-lying placenta is usually first seen at the fetal anomaly scan and, at this point, affects up to one in three pregnancies. As the pregnancy progresses, however, the lower segment of the uterus expands and, as it does so, the placenta 'migrates' away from the cervix. By full term, placenta praevia occurs in less than one in 200 pregnancies. Risk factors for placenta praevia at term include:

▸ previous Caesarean sections (it is thought the scar on the uterine wall somehow interferes with baseline muscular activity and, as a result, the placenta settles in this area during implantation)
▸ increasing maternal age (probably also related to repeated pregnancies)
▸ previous history of placenta praevia.

If your placenta is found to be near the 'os' (the internal part of the cervical opening) but is not covering it at your fetal anomaly scan, you will be offered further ultrasound scanning, usually at around 36 weeks. If your placenta reaches/overlaps the os completely, there is a higher chance that this will still be the case as you approach full term and, as this carries a higher risk of antenatal haemorrhage, you should be monitored during the third trimester, firstly with a transvaginal scan at 32 weeks, and then, if diagnosis is confirmed, with a follow-up abdominal ultrasound scan. You should contact your maternity unit at once if you develop any vaginal bleeding at any stage after twenty weeks. Bleeding is usually (though not always) painless and often initially profuse, though it may not last long. It may also begin as spotting.

If placenta praevia is confirmed in later pregnancy, you may need to be admitted to hospital, depending on your situation. As the baby cannot be delivered vaginally, a Caesarean section will be performed by 38 weeks, possibly even earlier if you experience bleeding. The procedure is usually carried out by a consultant obstetrician and consultant anaesthetist. A decision to deliver these pregnancies earlier than 38 weeks is often made in order to avoid an emergency Caesarean section in the middle of the night (because you have gone into labour spontaneously) when the full operating team may not be present.

PLACENTAL ABRUPTION

In up to two per cent of pregnancies, part of the placenta starts to separate from the uterine wall before the third stage of labour (see Chapter 6, p.176), a condition termed 'placental abruption'. It is not really known why it occurs, but risk factors include previous smoking, increased maternal age, hypertension and pre-eclampsia. Placental abruption is a serious condition and you should always call your maternity unit if you have any of the following symptoms:

▸ vaginal bleeding (either bright red blood or darker in colour, indicating older blood); the bleeding comes from the space between the placenta and the uterine wall and can range from a bit of spotting to a sudden gush
▸ back pain
▸ abdominal pain/tenderness
▸ contractions.

If, after calling the maternity unit to describe your symptoms, placental abruption is suspected, you will need to come into hospital to be examined as a matter of urgency. If diagnosis is confirmed, you will be admitted and your doctors will discuss with you what the options are, as these will depend on how close to term you are, how much you are bleeding, your overall health and whether your baby's well-being will be better safeguarded by delivery or by continuing with the pregnancy. Delivery will be by induction or by Caesarean section, depending on the severity of the abruption. Sometimes, if placental abruption is minor (often called a 'marginal bleed') the bleeding will stop on its own and, after a period of monitoring, you may be allowed home.

PLACENTAL INSUFFICIENCY

The placenta is your baby's support system during pregnancy, providing oxygen and nutrients, and when it does not work well, your baby's development and well-being can be harmed. There are many reasons why a placenta may not develop or function properly, some of which concern maternal lifestyle:

▸ diabetes
▸ hypertension and pre-eclampsia
▸ smoking
▸ excessive alcohol intake
▸ being past your estimated delivery date
▸ taking certain types of medication
▸ taking cocaine or other recreational drugs.

Sometimes, however, none of these factors apply: the placenta may simply have an abnormal shape or may not grow large enough for no apparent reason; it can also fail to attach properly to the uterine wall or, conversely, may come away from it (placental abruption – see entry above), causing bleeding.

Placental insufficiency does not cause any symptoms in the mother, but it can cause IUGR in the baby (see entry on p.286) and increase the chances of complications occurring later in pregnancy and during the birth. If a baby's growth appears to be slow or to have decreased, an ultrasound scan can assess the placenta's size. In some cases, placental insufficiency can be improved: for example, treating or managing diabetes and hypertension can enable a baby's growth to normalise. If the problem with the placenta is serious, however, delivery of the baby may be required before term, and this may be by induction or by Caesarean section, depending on the circumstances. These options will also be offered if the placental insufficiency occurs after your estimated delivery date.

POLYHYDRAMNIOS

The condition of polyhydramnios is defined as an abnormally large volume of amniotic fluid surrounding the baby and is usually detected either by ultrasound scan (usually at the fetal anomaly scan) or because your uterus is larger than expected for your stage of gestation, in which case the condition will be confirmed by ultrasound scan. Polyhydramnios can arise for a variety of reasons, including:

▸ poorly-controlled maternal diabetes
▸ a defect in the baby's gastrointestinal tract or central nervous system that prevents the fetus from swallowing or absorbing the amniotic fluid
▸ a lack of red blood cells in the baby (fetal anaemia).

Often, however, the cause is not clear. Polyhydramnios increases the risk of preterm birth (pressure on the uterus by the large amounts of fluid can cause membranes to rupture), umbilical cord prolapse (see entry on p.293) and abnormal fetal presentation (see Chapter 5, p.148), so in some instances, draining of the excessive amniotic fluid may be advised to reduce these risks. You will be scanned regularly to assess the volume of fluid and early delivery may be advised.

POSTNATAL INCONTINENCE

While it is a common side effect of pregnancy (see Chapter 4, p.128), urinary incontinence also affects around one in three women postnatally. Although the problem returns to normal within a year of childbirth for 84 per cent of them, a year can seem a long time to wait and most women can be shown ways to overcome this distressing condition. Incontinence can be divided into three categories:

▸ stress incontinence, where a leak of urine occurs, typically after laughing, coughing, sneezing, running, jumping or lifting
▸ urge incontinence (or overactive bladder), where you need to urinate frequently and sometimes have to rush to get to the toilet in time
▸ a combination of both the above.

If you are still experiencing leakage or an urgent need to pass urine despite regularly practising pelvic floor exercises for a few weeks, you should make an appointment with your GP. You will be referred to your nearest continence service, run by specialist nurses and urologists/ gynaecologists. Depending on what type of incontinence you are suffering from, different options can be offered. If your BMI is over 30, you will benefit from losing weight. Stress incontinence responds well to regular pelvic floor exercises done over a period of three months (and thereafter for the rest of your life – see Feature in Chapter 2, p.37). Urge incontinence can be caused by the compression of the bladder during pregnancy, so you may need to 'train' yourself to extend the intervals between going to the toilet, so that the bladder wall is stretched and capacity is increased. If these measures do not help, medication can be given in certain situations. If surgery is advised – and surgical techniques are now more effective and less invasive than in the past – ensure that the surgeon and uro-gynaecology centre you choose have regular, specialist experience of the specific procedure you are going to have (you can ask the surgeon directly or get your GP to find out). Don't consider having surgery if there is a chance that you plan to have more children, as both the pregnancy and the delivery will impact on its effectiveness.

Faecal incontinence, where you struggle to have control over your bowels, is less common than urinary incontinence and mainly affects women who have suffered third- or fourth-degree perineal tearing during childbirth (see Chapter 6, p.174). It is not uncommon, however, for women to experience minor faecal incontinence in the week or so following

delivery, but this usually disappears within a few days, especially if you do pelvic floor exercises and reduce your intake of high-fibre foods until the situation improves. In the case of severe problems, surgery may be required, and you will be referred to a specialist as soon as possible. Again surgery is best considered when you are sure you have completed your family.

POSTPARTUM HAEMORRHAGE (PPH)

Excessive loss of blood from the uterus or vagina after birth is known as postpartum haemorrhage (PPH). This is defined as the loss of 500 ml of blood following a vaginal delivery or 1,000 ml after a Caesarean section. If this happens within 24 hours, it is called primary PPH; if sudden loss of blood (irrespective of how much) occurs after 24 hours and up to twelve weeks following delivery, it is termed secondary PPH.

Primary PPH affects around six per cent of births in the UK. It is more common following a prolonged labour, an assisted delivery (ventouse or forceps) or a Caesarean section. PPH can arise because:

▸ the uterus has failed to contract sufficiently fast following the baby's birth
▸ part of the placenta has been retained in the uterus
▸ the placenta has not detached from the uterine wall
▸ there is continued bleeding from perineal tears
▸ there is a blood-clotting problem.

PPH can therefore occur more frequently with 'traditional' management of the third stage of labour (when the placenta is delivered) than with an 'active' one, which uses drugs to ensure that contractions remain strong and the uterus shrinks quickly. See Chapter 6, p.176 for more information on the third stage of labour. With a 'traditional' third stage, the placenta may stay in place for longer, so the womb can sometimes not contract quickly enough and this leaves blood vessels unable to 'close off' and still able to bleed.

Rarely, PPH is so serious that your blood pressure starts to drop and your pulse rate increases. Assuming you are in hospital when this occurs, a doctor or midwife will measure your blood loss and administer intravenous fluids and possibly a blood transfusion if required. Once the reason(s) for the

haemorrhage is recognised, removed or dealt with, the blood loss should stop (unless there is a blood-clotting problem). If bleeding continues, surgical assessment is required and this may mean that you need to go to the operating theatre. Drugs to make the uterus contract may also be administered, in a higher dose than would be given during labour. In some cases, antibiotics are also given to reduce the chance of a future infection.

Secondary PPH affects 0.5 per cent of births. It is often caused by pieces of retained placenta or membranes that have become infected, or a more generalised infection in the womb (e.g. endometritis). In addition to bleeding, symptoms may include abdominal pain or extreme tenderness, fever and an offensive-smelling vaginal discharge. Infection, if present, increases the risk of haemorrhaging, so significant amounts of retained tissue will probably be removed under general anaesthetic and antibiotics will be given.

PRE-ECLAMPSIA AND ECLAMPSIA

Pre-eclampsia is a serious complication of pregnancy and the related condition of eclampsia is potentially life-threatening.

Pre-eclampsia is a combination of hypertension (high blood pressure) and proteinuria (protein in the urine) that usually occurs after the twentieth week of pregnancy. Although its cause is not yet understood, pre-eclampsia affects two to eight per cent of women, with around one in 200 developing severe pre-eclampsia. Although pre-eclampsia does affect many women who have no known risk factors, it is more common if you have hypertension, diabetes, are aged 40 or above, or have a BMI of more than 35. It is also more likely to occur if this is your first pregnancy or if you developed pre-eclampsia in your last pregnancy (one in six women with previous pre-eclampsia develop it in their next pregnancy). If you have more than one known risk factor, you will be advised to take a low dose (75 mg) of aspirin once a day from the twelfth week of your pregnancy onwards.

Although mild pre-eclampsia may not cause any symptoms, at every antenatal check-up your urine will be checked for protein and your ankles, feet and hands will be examined for signs of swelling, another common symptom. Symptoms of more severe pre-eclampsia include:

- severe headache (not alleviated by painkillers)
- blurred vision or flashing lights before the eyes, often in peripheral vision
- severe pain below the ribs
- rapid swelling of feet, ankles, hands or face
- feeling very unwell
- nausea, vomiting or severe heartburn.

If you experience any of these symptoms during the second half of your pregnancy, call your midwife or maternity unit or go to your nearest hospital; also call if you have been given urine-testing kits to use at home and the stick indicates protein in the urine sample.

Pre-eclampsia affects the development of the placenta and can therefore affect your baby's development and well-being; it also increases the risk of placental abruption (see entry on p.288). In severe cases, your baby can die in in the womb, which is why you will be closely monitored, even if your pre-eclampsia is mild. This will include more regular hospital appointments, where your blood pressure will be measured (you may be given medication to lower it), your urine will be tested for protein and you will have blood tests to assess your renal function and any changes to your blood-clotting system. In addition, you may be offered additional ultrasound scans to monitor your baby's growth and the development of the placenta. If you develop severe pre-eclampsia, the senior midwife and obstetrician looking after you will advise bed rest and will prescribe medication to lower your blood pressure. If your baby continues to grow well, your pregnancy can continue as normal, but you may be advised to have your baby at 37 weeks, or earlier if necessary. If this is the case, your obstetrician may prescribe magnesium sulphate, which is administered intravenously usually for at least 24 hours, as evidence shows that it significantly reduces the risk of eclampsia (see below) either before or in the 24 hours after delivery. The method of delivering your baby will depend on the health of you both, but will involve either induction or a planned Caesarean section. In the severest circumstances, delivery by emergency Caesarean section will be the only option.

In most cases, pre-eclampsia disappears after the birth, although this can take up to six weeks. If yours was severe, you are likely to require monitoring for a few days after the birth. In rare cases, pre-eclampsia can develop postnatally, usually within 48 hours of delivery; symptoms are similar to antenatal pre-eclampsia and should be treated without delay.

Left undetected, pre-eclampsia can lead to **eclampsia**, a rare but potentially fatal condition for both mother and baby, which causes epileptic-type seizures or fits. It affects one in 2,000–4,000 pregnancies and can occur antenatally or, in 45 per cent of cases, postnatally, when symptoms usually manifest themselves within four days of delivery. The maternal mortality rate is 1.8 per 100 cases.

Other complications include kidney, liver and/or lung failure, or a combination of these, known as **HELLP syndrome**. HELLP stands for haemolysis (the destruction of red blood cells), elevated liver enzymes and low platelet count. This combination of conditions may arise before or after delivery, on its own or in conjunction with pre-eclampsia, and it can be life-threatening. HELLP syndrome reflects a failing liver and women can quickly become severely ill and may need intensive medical support.

PREMATURITY

Premature babies, especially those born before 32 weeks, are more likely to suffer from a range of complications and the earlier they are born, the greater the likelihood they will be affected (especially if they are small for gestational age). The section in Chapter 7. p.230 deals with minor complications of prematurity, and some of the more serious ones are covered below.

Babies born before 34 weeks lack surfactant and, as a result, the lungs collapse at the end of each breath and fail to provide enough oxygen for the baby; this can lead to **neonatal respiratory distress syndrome** (NRDS) and serious health complications. A baby that may be developing NRDS displays signs such as shallow breathing, a grunting sound when breathing, flared nostrils and blue lips, fingers and toes. Around half of babies born before 32 weeks are affected with NRDS, but the nearer they are born to full term, the less likely this becomes. Premature babies are helped to breathe using a variety of methods and machines, but artificial surfactant may be applied in tiny quantities directly into the baby's airways via a small tube. Depending on the baby's response, the medical team will then adjust the treatment until they are able Δ292to breathe unaided. NRDS is usually successfully treated in the neonatal unit.

Necrotising enterocolitis (NEC) describes an inflammation of the intestines that can

damage it and cause some parts to become ischaemic (i.e. lack oxygen and die). About three in 1,000 babies in neonatal units are thought to develop NEC and they usually have an additional underlying condition that makes them more vulnerable to it. The cause is unclear, but may be due to bacteria or insufficient blood flow to the bowel at some stage of the baby's development before or after birth. Symptoms include pain or a tender abdomen, blood in the stools, vomiting of greenish bile and generally appearing unwell. Treatment usually involves stopping milk feeds and feeding the baby intravenously, thus giving the bowel time to repair itself. Antibiotics may also be given. Babies usually recover, but NEC is a potentially serious complication, and surgery may be required to remove the affected part of the bowel. Sadly, not all babies recover following surgical intervention.

Bleeding on the brain is not uncommon in premature babies, but if born after 30 weeks and of a good weight for gestational age, most can cope with these incidents. For babies that are small for gestational age (see entry on IUGR on p.286), especially those born before 30 weeks, the extent of the bleeding determines if and how they are affected, although in the majority of cases, babies recover with minor or no long-term neurological consequences. For some, however, the problem can lead to a range of developmental issues, including cerebral palsy (see entry on p.284). Although doctors will monitor and treat any bleeds accordingly, the medical team are often not able to say at this early stage to what extent a baby has been affected by serious bleeding.

Premature babies before 32 weeks and weighing less than 1,500 g are more likely than babies born at term to have **sight and hearing problems**, although in the case of hearing, the risk is nonetheless low (their hearing is always tested before they leave hospital). Sight is assessed weekly or fortnightly when they are in the neonatal unit to ensure they do not develop a complication known as retinopathy of prematurity, which is caused by oxygen damage to the retina. In most cases, this leads to minor, temporary consequences, or to a mild visual impairment such as long-sightedness. More severe cases requiring surgery are rare. In the most serious cases, the retina detaches from the eyeball and (very rarely) this can cause blindness.

PYLORIC STENOSIS

Between the bottom of the stomach and the small intestine is an opening, or muscular valve (the pylorus), which keeps food in the stomach until it is ready to pass into the small intestine. In approximately three in 1,000 babies, this outlet becomes thicker and narrower, preventing milk from passing into the intestine, a condition called 'pyloric stenosis'. It is not clear why this happens, nor why boys are more affected than girls. Symptoms will involve the baby starting to bring up small amounts of milk after a feed. These amounts increase over the next few days and may be yellow and curdled in appearance. Projectile vomiting may occur as the milk is brought up more forcefully. Bowel movements will also become infrequent and the baby becomes lethargic due to dehydration.

The condition usually manifests itself at around three to six weeks and, once diagnosed, will require a short operation under general anaesthetic to widen the passage once again. This is often done as keyhole surgery (laparoscopically), so is minimally invasive. Pyloric stenosis is not possible to detect antenatally from an ultrasound scan. It is a fairly common reason for surgery after birth (see entry on p.292) and is invariably very successful, enabling babies to feed and grow problem-free thereafter.

SEPSIS

Women are said to be immunocompromised in pregnancy – their immunity to infection is lowered, so that their body doesn't reject the baby. This makes you more susceptible to infections, such as vaginal, urinary or streptococcal infections (see below), and also to associated complications. Symptoms of sepsis are outlined in the Box in Chapter 2, p.42, but since they are similar to flu, you should be examined by your midwife or GP for a diagnosis. Always let your doctor or midwife know if you have a temperature above 37.5°C while pregnant or in the first six weeks after delivery. Equally, if anyone in your house or immediate family has an infection, you should take steps to minimise its spread to you or your baby. Because of possible contact with toxoplasmosis, you should also follow sensible hygiene precautions when emptying cat litter, gardening or handling fruit or vegetables (see Chapter 2, p.42).

SEXUALLY TRANSMITTED DISEASES

Sexually transmitted diseases (STDs) in pregnancy can be harmful to you and your baby, and certain precautions may need to be taken to minimise their effects, particularly during labour and birth.

There are two types of **herpes** virus and both are highly infectious. Type 1 (herpes simplex) manifests itself in cold sores on the mouth and lips; type 2 (genital herpes) causes ulcers or sores on the vulva, vagina or even cervix. Herpes sores that appear on the genital area are often spread during oral sex and are caused by the type 1 virus. Tell your midwife or obstetrician if you already have the herpes virus or if you think you may have become infected with it at any stage during pregnancy. Whatever the type of herpes, if the first infection occurs before you become pregnant, there is no risk to the baby and any outbreaks can be treated with antiviral medication. If it occurs during the first trimester, there is a slightly increased chance of miscarriage. If you contract it in the last six weeks of pregnancy, there is a two in five chance of passing the virus on to your baby in a vaginal birth, because they will not have had time to develop immunity to the virus while in the womb. Neonatal herpes can, in rare cases, cause serious complications, so a Caesarean section will be offered and your baby will be given antiviral drugs after birth. If this is not your first outbreak, it is safe to have a vaginal delivery. Once your baby is born, avoid skin-to-skin contact between your baby and anyone with an active herpes simplex infection, such as a cold sore on the mouth or nose, and make sure that the infected person washes their hands before coming into contact with your baby.

The common bacterial infection of **chlamydia** is a largely symptomless STD for women, but if undetected and untreated, it can lead to Fallopian tube damage and a greater chance of having an ectopic pregnancy. If detected during pregnancy, you should be referred to a genito-urinary clinic so that the most appropriate treatment can be given. If chlamydia is present during delivery, about 40 per cent of babies will develop an eye infection (conjunctivitis) within three to fourteen days of birth. This can easily be treated with antibiotics, but if left untreated, it can cause blindness, so seek medical help if your baby's eyes begin to show signs of watery or yellowy discharge, or become swollen or tender to the touch.

Gonorrhoea may be symptomless or can include vaginal discharge and pain when urinating, and is another cause of Fallopian tube damage and ectopic pregnancy. It does not affect the developing fetus, but if present during delivery, it can cause conjunctivitis in the newborn (see the entry on chlamydia above for symptoms and treatment).

Although it is uncommon in the pregnant population in the UK, all women are screened for **syphilis** at the first antenatal blood test (see Chapter 3, p.62). If undetected, it can cause congenital and developmental problems in the baby (e.g. IUGR – see entry on p.286), stillbirth or miscarriage. Once detected, however, it can successfully be treated by a single penicillin injection to the mother.

All women are offered screening for **HIV** at their booking appointment and are offered counselling if the test is positive. Currently, appropriate antiretroviral therapy is highly effective in preventing the HIV virus from developing into AIDS, and certain additional measures can be taken that are very successful in preventing the virus from passing to the baby. Mothers who continue to take their antiretroviral therapy, deliver in the manner most suitable to their medical situation and avoid breastfeeding their baby now have a transmission rate of less than one per cent. A decision on whether to have a vaginal delivery or an elective Caesarean section should be made in discussion with your specialist team of doctors by 36 weeks of pregnancy.

SHOULDER DYSTOCIA

Around 0.6 per cent of vaginal cephalic deliveries result in shoulder dystocia, where the head has been delivered but one of the baby's shoulders becomes stuck in the pelvis, preventing the body from emerging. Gentle traction on the part of the midwife or obstetrician has not succeeded and additional medical staff (including a consultant obstetrician) and obstetric manoeuvres are urgently needed to deliver the baby. The risk factors for shoulder dystocia include maternal diabetes or obesity, a baby who is estimated to weigh over 4,500 g, delivering after your estimated delivery date and a prolonged second stage of labour.

Shoulder dystocia is potentially extremely serious, because umbilical cord compression between the baby's body and the maternal pelvis can lead to oxygen deprivation, which can cause permanent neurological damage or, in the worst case, death; the baby can also suffer a nerve injury due to the pressure exerted on the stuck shoulder, although in most cases this is temporary. Shoulder dystocia can also cause severe complications for the mother, including PPH (see entry on p.289) in over ten per cent of cases and third- or fourth-degree perineal tears (see Chapter 6, p.174).

If shoulder dystocia occurs, you will be asked to stop pushing and move into a position that increases the diameter of the pelvis (lying flat on the bed with both knees bent up towards your chest). An episiotomy may be performed to enlarge the vaginal opening and enable the obstetrician to free the shoulder manually from the inside. This also reduces the risk of severe perineal tearing and heavy bleeding. One of the medical staff will put pressure on one of the baby's shoulders by pressing down externally just above your pubic bone. If this is not effective, the obstetrician will attempt to rotate the baby's shoulders internally or try and deliver the posterior arm first.

Occasionally, nerve damage occurs to the shoulder and arm, or a fractured clavicle (collar bone) or (very rarely) an arm fracture may occur. However, the neonatologist present at the birth will check for any signs of damage and, in almost all cases, any injury to your baby is temporary and heals well.

As obstetric manoeuvres need to be done quickly if longer term damage is to be avoided, it can sometimes feel as if you are not fully informed or involved. You and your partner will be given a full explanation of events after the delivery and the opportunity to ask questions of the obstetrician, midwife and paediatrician.

SICKLE-CELL DISEASE
Sickle-cell disease (SCD) is a group of conditions that affect the oxygen-carrying red blood cells. The most common of these are sickle-cell anaemia and thalassaemia. SCD is associated with maternal and fetal complications, including an increased incidence of miscarriage and premature labour, IUGR (see entry on p.286) and perinatal mortality.

SCD is a genetic (inherited) condition, largely affecting those of African, South Asian, Mediterranean and Middle-eastern origin, and those pregnant women deemed to be at higher risk are offered a blood test to screen for the condition. About one in 2,400 babies are born with SCD and both parents need to be carriers of the gene (they have what is referred to as the 'sickle-cell trait') for it to be passed on to their

child (see Feature in Chapter 3, p.75 for how genetic abnormalities are inherited). If you and your partner are both found to be carriers of the SCD gene, you will be offered genetic counselling to help you decide if you wish to have an antenatal diagnostic test to determine if your baby has the condition. In addition, all mothers are offered testing for their newborn babies by means of a heel prick test five to eight days after birth, the results of which are available about six weeks later.

If you already have SCD before getting pregnant, you should be seen before conceiving by a sickle specialist and your partner should be encouraged to have a blood test to establish if they have the sickle-cell trait, so that any future pregnancy can be managed as well as possible. In all cases, antenatal care should include additional antenatal monitoring and testing, including ultrasound scans. In addition, your doctor or midwife will prescribe a higher dose folic acid supplement for you to take: 5 mg, rather than 0.4 mg (see Chapter 2, p.24 for more information).

If SCD is diagnosed in your baby while they are still in the womb, you can be reassured that they will not be affected by the condition during pregnancy; symptoms usually appear once they are around three months old, with treatment beginning at that stage. Your child will be referred to a medical team in a specialist sickle-cell centre, which will provide a treatment plan adapted to your child's specific requirements.

SPINA BIFIDA
Spina bifida is a neural tube defect that occurs during the first few weeks of an embryo's development. The spinal column fails to fully close around the developing spinal cord, leaving a gap in the spine. There are different forms of spina bifida, some more severe than others. The causes are not fully known, but a lack of folic acid in the maternal diet before and during the first three months of pregnancy is known to be a significant risk factor. If you are at risk of having a baby with spina bifida (e.g. if you have a close family member affected, have had a previous baby diagnosed, are taking anti-epileptic medication), you will be prescribed a higher dose (5 mg) folic acid supplement.

The condition is usually first seen at the fetal anomaly scan. After birth, surgery can usually be carried out to close up the gap in the spine, but nerve damage has usually occurred by this stage, leading to a variety of complications,

including paralysis of the lower limbs, infections and incontinence.

SURGERY AT BIRTH
The knowledge that your newborn will need surgery soon after birth is very upsetting for parents: your baby will be separated from you and, in some cases, may not survive, even with surgery. Your healthcare professionals are trained to deliver the news and explain the situation in a sensitive but clear way, and to allow you all the time you need to ask questions. If your baby needs to be transferred to another hospital, they will also explain how this will take place.

Plan for the day of the surgery as best you can, including arranging to breastfeed your baby before the operation, and decide whether or not you want to have someone to accompany you. There are usually rooms for parents to use during this time, so that they can stay close to their baby, but if the operation is lengthy, you may be better off leaving the hospital premises and attempting, however difficult, to do something else.

Try to prepare for the fact that, initially, your baby may look very different afterwards and may be covered with tubes, dressings and bandages. The medical staff will be available at all times to reassure you and explain the situation. However, there will be many procedures (both before and after surgery), such as the siting of IV lines or intubation (e.g. the insertion of a tube for ventilation), that may be too upsetting for you to see. Indeed, for your own benefit, you may be gently asked by the medical team to leave the room while these are carried out. You are within your rights to stay, but be aware that this may hinder the staff, will be of no help to your baby and may lead you to look back on the process negatively.

Having a newborn baby in hospital leaves many couples in limbo: on the one hand, they are parents to this baby, on the other, they are not able to do any of the 'normal' things they had planned to do. It is important that you don't feel responsible for what is happening – it is not your fault. In addition, if your baby is in hospital for a while, don't feel guilty about taking time away – you are allowed to take care of yourself, to go for a walk or to see friends and family.

Many parents feel that no one understands what they are going through – which may actually be true. Getting the right support is crucial in helping you to cope with this difficult time, so do accept offers of help from friends and family (but make sure they know to stay away from you, your partner and any other children if they are unwell). There are also online support groups and helplines that can be invaluable for answering questions – often on the specific condition that your baby suffers from – and the medical staff are usually very knowledgeable about how to access these (see Useful Resources).

TERMINATION

The decision to have a termination, usually as a result of a fetal abnormality, is invariably a distressing one, even if you are clear that you do not wish to proceed with the pregnancy. There are several ways in which termination can be carried out, depending on how far advanced your pregnancy is.

Medical abortion can be carried out up to 24 weeks of pregnancy and involves taking a combination of two drugs. The first drug you will be given, in tablet form, blocks the hormones that enable your pregnancy to continue. The following day, you will be given a prostaglandin vaginal pessary, after which your uterus will expel the fetus. If yours is a second trimester termination, you may require additional doses of prostaglandin before this happens. For this reason, and also because you are likely to require pain relief, you will usually stay in hospital. After the nineteenth week of pregnancy, a drug will need to be administered to the fetus before the above process starts in order to stop the fetal heart. This is usually performed at a specialist fetal medicine centre. The remainder of the termination process can then take place at your preferred hospital.

Suction/surgical termination can be carried out until nineteen weeks. If yours is a first trimester termination, you should be offered either a general anaesthetic or a local anaesthetic/sedation. Your cervix will be gently opened until the contents of your uterus can be removed using a suction device. If carried out between thirteen and nineteen weeks, you may also be given a vaginal pessary to help your cervix to soften and minimise any damage to it and you will be given a general anaesthetic. In both cases, the procedure itself takes about ten to fifteen minutes.

Surgical dilation and evacuation ('D and E') is used from nineteen to 23+6 weeks of pregnancy (the legal limit for termination) and is performed in two stages. The first involves administering a vaginal pessary, which enables your cervix to gently dilate over the course of a few hours. Once that has happened, you will undergo a general anaesthetic so that the obstetrician can remove the contents of the uterus with a suction tube and forceps. Ultrasound scanning is done at the same time as a guide and to ensure everything is removed.

You should expect to bleed heavily for the first week following a termination and to experience some cramping. Bleeding should stop within two weeks, but make sure you rest as much as possible during this time. Complications caused by terminations are rare and most commonly include infection (symptoms to look out for are fever, excessive bleeding, abdominal pain and smelly vaginal discharge). Most women recover very well physically from a termination, even a late second trimester termination, but they may take a lot longer to recover emotionally. Feelings of guilt and bereavement are common, with the added burden of having consciously ended your pregnancy. Counselling can be very helpful, as can charities and support groups aimed specifically at helping women who terminate their pregnancies (see Useful Resources).

UMBILICAL CORD PROLAPSE

Umbilical cord prolapse is when the cord precedes the baby down the birth canal during a vaginal birth. It is a relatively common complication, occurring in about one in 300 births, but it can potentially be extremely serious: if the cord is in front of the descending baby, pressure from the baby (especially from the head) can compress the cord and cut off vital blood supply and oxygen. Equally, if the cord slips through the cervix and is exposed to air before the baby has been delivered, the cord constricts and this can lead to oxygen deprivation before the birth. Umbilical cord prolapse is a known risk factor of breech deliveries (see Chapter 6, p.202), but it can also occur if you have had several previous vaginal deliveries (because it is easier for the baby to lie in an oblique or transverse position – see Chapter 5, p.148), if the birth is premature, with cases of polyhydramnios (see entry on p.288) or premature rupture of the membranes. Options for the management of prolapsed cord vary, depending on circumstances, but include removing or reducing pressure from the baby on the cord, fast vaginal delivery using forceps or ventouse, or emergency Caesarean section.

UNDESCENDED TESTES

Testes (testicles) develop inside a male fetus' abdominal cavity and, by the end of the pregnancy, have usually descended into the scrotum. However, in about one per cent of babies, one or both testes have not done so (this is more common in premature babies). In most cases, the testes have both descended by the time the baby is twelve months old, but if this does not happen, it is important to have the problem corrected when a baby is still young, as undescended testicles increase a man's chances of being infertile (sperm are not produced or are damaged) or of developing testicular cancer in later life. The surgery to rectify the problem involves a minor operation under local anaesthetic, with the testicle(s) gently repositioned inside the scrotal sac.

WEAK OR INCOMPETENT CERVIX

A weak or incompetent cervix is rare and difficult to define, but occurs when the cervix begins to efface and dilate at some stage during the second or third trimester, causing either painless contractions or the premature rupture of the membranes, followed by a late miscarriage, very premature delivery or stillbirth. It is usually diagnosed retrospectively after one or more of these occurrences, where other possible causes have been ruled out. See Box in Chapter 4, p.106 for more information on very premature birth. If you have a history of late second trimester or early third trimester delivery, you may be monitored in a subsequent pregnancy via transvaginal ultrasound, and if your cervix is seen to be less than 25 mm long before 24 weeks, insertion of a suture (stitch) may be recommended (known as cervical cerclage – see Chapter 7, p.223). However, the efficacy of this procedure in preventing premature effacement or rupture of membranes is not guaranteed, and the procedure does itself carry a risk of stimulating contractions and/or rupturing the membranes. There are different types of suture and your obstetrician will discuss with you the advantages of possible intervention and which sort of suture may be best suited to your particular circumstances. Occasionally, a 'rescue suture' may be offered, although this has a higher rate of failure, as the cervix has usually started to dilate significantly by this stage.

Stillbirth and neonatal death

Nothing can prepare parents for the distress that losing a baby causes. No grief is greater than that of losing a child, at whatever age or at whatever stage of pregnancy. If you are suffering this sort of bereavement, you will need a lot of support and information to help you through what will inevitably be a devastating time.

A stillbirth is defined as a baby born dead after the 24th week of pregnancy (i.e. the baby is delivered with no sign of life at birth). A neonatal death is the death of a baby within the first four weeks of life. Perinatal death is sometimes used as a term to refer to babies who are stillborn or who die within seven days of birth. In the UK and Northern Ireland:

▶ one in 200 babies is stillborn – eleven each day, or 4,000 per year
▶ one in 300 babies dies within the first four weeks of life – six per day, or 2,200 per year.

Towards the end of the third trimester, the risk of stillbirth increases with each ensuing week of pregnancy (*see* Useful Resources for further information):

▶ at 38 weeks, the risk is one in 1922
▶ at 40 weeks, it is one in 1148
▶ at 41 weeks, it is one in 786
▶ at 42 weeks, it is one in 644
▶ at 43 weeks, it is one in 486.

This is one of the reasons that doctors recommend induction before 42 weeks if you are overdue. Although these figures are distressing, it is worth noting that they still represent only around 0.8 per cent of total births.

What are the causes of death?

Every parent who suffers the death of their baby wants to know why it occurred. Although it is not always possible to fully determine what happened, a cause can be found in roughly two-thirds of cases.

Stillbirth
▶ Around 30 per cent are caused by the baby not growing properly inside the womb (intrauterine growth restriction, or IUGR – *see* Complications, p.286).
▶ About six per cent are caused by a chromosomal abnormality of the baby.
▶ Maternal infection, diabetes, placental abruption and pre-eclampsia are the most common other causes.
▶ About 500 babies a year die during labour.

Neonatal death
▶ Congenital anomalies account for 23 per cent.
▶ Twenty per cent are the result of premature rupture of membranes (*see* Chapter 6, p.157), IUGR or lack of oxygen/ birth trauma during labour.
▶ Thirteen per cent are due to neonatal infection.
▶ The remaining known causes are prematurity, poor placental function and haemorrhage.

You may know in advance of delivery that your baby is already dead or will only survive a short time after the birth; in other instances, your baby will be born apparently healthy, only to become ill soon after and to die despite the best efforts of the medical professionals. Whatever the circumstances, all staff will be acutely aware of how devastating your loss is.

Giving birth

If it is suspected that your baby has died in the womb, an ultrasound scan will be used to confirm this. After expressing their sadness for you and allowing you and your partner time alone, as well as plenty of opportunity to ask questions, an obstetrician and midwife will talk you and your partner through the birth process, as there are various options of when and how to have your baby. A vaginal birth rather than a Caesarean section is recommended, as you are less likely to compromise future deliveries and you will be able to go home sooner. However, you may prefer, after discussion with an obstetrician concerning the risks and benefits, to have a Caesarean section.

If you choose a vaginal birth, you will be offered induction in order to avoid further complications with infection or bleeding. (You may choose to let nature take its course by going into labour naturally, but you will need regular checks to ensure there are no signs of infection.) The first part of the induction process – usually taking an oral tablet – can start soon after the death has been confirmed, or you may prefer to go home for a night first. Once again, all options will be explained to you so that you can choose the one that best suits your preferences and your medical situation.

Each labour ward has a delivery room adapted for deliveries of stillbirths and where your partner can stay overnight to be with you. Furthermore, there will be a specialist midwife who will look after you during your stay in hospital. You do not need to be in pain throughout this procedure. There are several options, ranging from intramuscular or intravenous morphine to a person-controlled analgesia (PCA) pump similar to that used with an epidural, and the anaesthetist will spend time ensuring that your chosen method is effective.

After the birth, the staff will ensure that you are given all the time you want in a private environment with your baby. You will be able to dress and hold your baby, take photographs and, if you wish, gather mementoes, such as hand and feet prints (a midwife will help you to do this), a lock of hair, your baby's hospital wristband, their baby blanket/soft toys and whatever else you would like. These, along with any cards and letters you receive, can be put in a memory box to commemorate your baby's journey, which many parents come to treasure. Of course, if you prefer not to, then do not feel obliged to do this.

Your physical recovery

Your body will go through the same processes after the birth as outlined in Chapters 6 and 8. This will include your milk will coming through a few days after the birth, and this is often very distressing, so do ask for medication if it has not already been offered (in tablet form), which you can take to stop the production of milk. Be aware, though, that occasionally you may still get some milk coming through once you stop the medication. You will have heavy bleeding as you would after a normal delivery, but if in the week or so following the birth you develop a fever, flu-like symptoms, smelly vaginal discharge, abdominal pain, or bleeding that becomes heavier, or if you develop pain/swelling in your legs or shortness of breath/ chest pain, contact your hospital at once, as you may need treatment or to be readmitted for treatment of an endometrial infection. Bleeding should stop in about two weeks.

You will be offered a postnatal appointment with your consultant obstetrician, usually about six weeks after the birth. Do feel free to ask for it sooner, although the reason for this scheduling is to ensure that all test results are back. Try to write down any questions you might have in advance of the appointment.

Finding out why your baby died

As well as the appointment with your obstetrician, you will be given one with the paediatrician who looked after your baby, so that you can receive support and information. This will include discussing what can be done to try to find out the precise cause of death. Various tests and investigations involving you and/or your baby will be offered, and these will be explained to you in detail. Some of these will require samples of your blood, others from the fetus or placenta. As infection is a common cause, a range of blood tests that screen for several different infections can be conducted. This is known as a TORCH screen (it stands for toxoplasmosis, rubella, cytomegalovirus, herpes simplex and HIV). A post-mortem of your baby may be suggested (see below), which will require your written consent. You will given plenty of time to decide what course of action to take and to ask further questions if necessary, and will be supported fully in your choices by trained medical staff. If you are able to discover the cause of death (remember, this may not be possible in all cases), this can be helpful if you plan to get pregnant again in the future.

What does a post-mortem involve?
A post-mortem gives you your best chance of an answer as to why your baby has died. There are different options for post-mortems. These include an external examination only, an MRI scan or a full post-mortem, where tissue samples will be taken for examination microscopically. The funeral may need to be delayed until the post-mortem has been carried out. Your midwife or doctor will explain these different procedures to you and give you time to discuss with your partner what is best for you as a couple.

Registering the death and planning the funeral

Your GP will be informed when you leave hospital, and your midwife will explain the formalities of registering your baby's death and will provide the paperwork. A stillbirth needs to be registered within 42 days in England and Wales, 21 days in Scotland, but it is not compulsory to do so in Northern Ireland. The member of staff will also discuss the funeral with you: most hospitals offer funeral services, but you may prefer to make your own arrangements. Each hospital has personnel of differing faiths to help support you during this time, should you wish, and your midwife will ensure you know how to contact them.

Coping with your loss

Before you leave hospital, bereavement counselling will be offered to you and you may want to take this up straight away or at some stage in the future. All relevant contact numbers of hospital staff will also be provided. You may also wish to contact specialist charities that deal specifically with parents who have lost babies in similar circumstances to you (see Useful Resources).

There is no set pattern or time for grieving and every person goes through the process differently. Grieving parents are often told by well-meaning people that time will heal their wounds and that they can always have another baby. Yet parents do not 'get over' the death of a baby, whatever happens in the future. It becomes a part of who they are and they eventually learn to live with it. However, anniversaries or key dates relevant to that baby, as well as other, sometimes unconnected events, can lift the lid on your grief and make the immense sadness of bereavement resurface. Because others can find your grief difficult and embarrassing, you can feel isolated. It is therefore important that you surround yourself with people who understand what you are going through, who are truly able to listen non-judgmentally to what you are feeling, and who can offer help and practical support to you and your partner at this time. Don't be afraid to ask for psychological help, as professional, 'neutral-party' counselling and therapy can make you feel listened to and more positive.

Your partner will be grieving as much as you, but they may do so in a way that is very different from yours. They may want to talk constantly about what has happened, throw themselves into work (many people's response to trauma) or say very little at all. It doesn't mean they are not hurting just as much as you. As ever in times of difficulty, communication is key. If you can keep each other aware, in an honest, non-accusatory way, of how you are feeling, then you may at least understand that your partner's way of grieving is simply different from yours. And hopefully, with time, patience, and maybe professional help for one or both of you, your relationship need not be permanently affected.

Your other children

Children will need appropriate information on what happened in words that they can understand, as well as support wherever necessary. Do explain to them that they are not in any way to blame (younger children, especially, often think they are in part responsible for bad events in their life). Children react to loss differently from adults: they verbalise their emotions far less and are more likely to show their feelings through changes in behaviour (this applies as much to young children as to teenagers, who often begin to act like 'adults' in an effort to spare their parents further grief). Consequently, don't suggest counselling unless they specifically request it. You should not feel that you must hide your own emotions from them or avoid talking about the baby, as this will make them subconsciously feel that the baby's death is something to be ashamed of and to hide. With open, honest communication, you will be doing everything you can to help your children grieve for their sibling.

Moving forward

You will eventually resume your previous life, perhaps by starting to go back to work after your period of maternity leave (you are still entitled to this after experiencing a stillbirth – *see* Feature in Chapter 2, pp.50–1). This is bound to be difficult at first, but everyone will be extremely concerned for your welfare and this may help to give you strength. Remember that it is up to you what and how much you wish to say: your colleagues will take their lead from you.

In time, your thoughts may turn to whether or not you should try for another baby. Physically, there is no time barrier for conceiving again, apart from the resumption of menstruation. It is more a question of when you are emotionally ready. Given that you know that pregnancies do not always go to plan, you will need to feel strong enough to cope with any eventuality that the pregnancy may bring.

Index

Useful Resources

The following are good sources of information about pregnancy and birth:
National Institute for Care and Health Excellence: www.nice.org.uk
Royal College of Obstetricians and Gynaecologists: www.rcog.org.uk
National Institutes of Health (US): www.nih.gov
You can also access research undertaken by the Centre for Maternal and Child Enquiries (CMACE) from a number of online sources.

Chapter 1

Independent midwives
www.independentmidwives.org.uk

Assisted conception
IVF: perinatal risks and early childhood outcomes scientific impact paper no.8, May 2012: www.rcog.org.uk/womens-health/clinical-guidance/perinatal-risks-associated-ivf

Home births
Perinatal and maternal outcomes by planned place of birth for healthy women with low risk pregnancies: the Birthplace in England national prospective cohort study: www.bmj.com/content/343/bmj.d7400

Chapter 2

Healthy family eating and snack delivery
www.fit4life.com
www.marksandspencer.com
www.waitrose.com
www.graze.com
www.change4life.icnetwork.co.uk
www.which.co.uk/campaigns/food-and-health/healthy-eating-for-all/healthy-breakfasts

Weight loss
www.slimmingworld.com

Back pain
www.osteopathy.org.uk

Exercise
www.pregnancyyogaapp.com

Immunisations
www.nathnac.org/travel

Smoking
Allen Carr's Easy Way to Stop Smoking by Allen Carr

Alcohol
RCOG paper, from BJOG vol. 118/issue 12 Nov 2011: www.onlinelibrary.wiley.com/doi/10.1111/j.1471-0528.2011.03050.x/abstract

Maternity/paternity leave
www.gov.uk/browse/working/time-off

www.maternityaction.org.uk
www.citizensadvice.org.uk

Elastic waistband kit
Belly Belt by Gro-Group (can be bought online from several different suppliers)

Antenatal classes and information
www.antenatalonline.co.uk
www.babycentre.co.uk
www.bounty.com
Pregnancy for men: the whole nine months by Mark Woods

Chapter 3

Diabetes
www.guidance.nice.org.uk/CG63

Miscarriage
www.miscarriageassociation.org.uk

Antenatal tests and results
www.fetalanomaly.screening.nhs.uk
www.arc-uk.org

35+ mothers
www.ons.gov.uk/ons/rel/vsob1/characteristics-of-Mother-1--england-and-wales/2011/sb-characteristics-of-mother-1.html
www.rcog.org.uk/what-we-do/campaigning-and-opinions/statement/rcog-statement-later-maternal-age
www.rcog.org.uk/womens-health/clinical-guidance/induction-labour-term-older-mothers-scientific-impact-paper-34

Chapter 4

Cord blood banking
www.rcog.org.uk/news/rcogrcm-statement-cord-blood-collection-and-banking

Fetal immune system
Fetal and adult hematopoietic stem cells give rise to distinct T cell lineages in humans: www.ncbi.nlm.nih.gov/pmc/articles/PMC3276679/

Fetal and maternal circulations
Thomas et al., 1994; Bianchi et al., 1996; Ariga et al., 2001; O'Donoghue et al., 2004

Chapter 5

Doulas
www.doula.org.uk

Ready-meal delivery
www.abelandcole.co.uk
www.oakhousefoods.co.uk
www.cookfood.net

Nappies
www.which.co.uk/baby-and-child/nursery-and-feeding/guides/disposable-vs-reusable-nappies

Chapter 6

Hiring TENS machines
www.pregnancytens.co.uk
www.tens.co.uk

Epidurals
(risk of spinal damage)
British Journal of Anaesthesia, Jan 2010
(increasing the risk of instrumental delivery)
British 2005 review of 21 studies into epidurals involving 6,600 women

Vaginal delivery of breech babies
www.sogc.org/wp-content/uploads/2013/01/gui226CPG0906.pdf

Risks of stillbirth in postmaturity
Prolonged pregnancy: evaluating gestation-specific risks of fetal and infant mortality: www.bmj.com/content/320/7232/444.2

Induction
www.publications.nice.org.uk/induction-of-labour-ifp70/more-information

Use of pain relief in labour
Towards Better Births: a review of maternity services in England (Care Quality Commission): www.archive.cqc.org.uk/_db/_documents/Maternity_services_survey_report.pdf

Chapter 7

Support groups for families of premature babies
www.bliss.org.uk
www.tommys.org

Survival and later health of extremely premature babies
www.epicure.ac.uk

Location map of neonatal units
England and Wales: www1.imperial.ac.uk/departmentofmedicine/divisions/infectiousdiseases/paediatrics/neonatalmedicine/ndau/nnu_networks/map/
Scotland: www.scotland.gov.uk/Publications/2009/04/30153006/3

Vaginal versus Caesarean deliveries of babies born before 32 weeks
Research carried out by U Reddy, J Zhaang, L Sun, Z Chen, T Raju, SK Laughon, at National Institute of Child Health and Human Development: www.nih.gov/news/health/sep2012/nichd-21a.htm

Chapter 8

Postnatal control underwear
www.bopeep.com

Breastfeeding
www.nct.org.uk
www.laleche.org.uk
www.thetruthaboutbreastfeeding.com
www.letsbreastfeed.com
www.breastfeedingnetwork.org.uk
www.abm.me.uk
www.breastfeeding.co.uk
*What to expect when you're breastfeeding…
and what if you can't* by Clare Byam-Cook

Expressing
www.expressyourselfmums.co.uk

Breast pumps
www.medela.co.uk

Crying
www.cry-sis.org.uk

Sleep
www.mill-pond.co.uk

Schedule of vaccinations
www.gov.uk/government/organisations/
department-of-health

Childcare
www.doula.org.uk
www.childcare.co.uk
www.home-start.org.uk
www.oneparentfamilies.org.uk

Each local authority has a Family Information
Service that can provide a list of all Ofsted-
registered providers in the area.

Chapter 9

Parenting websites
www.netmums.com
www.mumsnet.com
www.mumsmeetup.com
www.mama.bm
Single parents: www.gingerbread.co.uk

Domestic abuse
National Domestic Violence Helpline:
0808 2000 247
www.womensaid.org.uk

Mental health
apni.org
www.app-network.org
www.mind.org.uk
www.pndsupport.co.uk

www.pni.org.uk
www.pandasfoundation.org.uk

Psychotherapy
www.bacp.co.uk
www.psychotherapy.org

A–Z of Complications

Female genital mutilation
www.forwarduk.org.uk/resources/support/
well-woman-clinics

Hip dysplasia
www.hipdysplasia.org

Surgery at birth
www.bestbeginnings.org.uk

Termination
www.bpas.org
www.mariestopes.org.uk

Stillbirth
RCOG Scientific Paper no.34 2013: www.rcog.org.
uk/womens-health/clinical-guidance/
when-your-baby-dies-birth-information-you
www.uk-sands.org
www.winstonswish.org.uk
www.childbereavement.org.uk

Acknowledgements

Photographs

Many thanks to the parents and babies who kindly
allowed themselves to be photographed for this book:

Penelope Wincer, Deji Akerele, Ben Richardson, Natasha,
Matt, Louis and Soraya Hatton, Jacqui Noels, Anne and
Nick Caine, Anandarajah Maelle and Camille Gutapfel

Many thanks Queen Charlotte's & Chelsea Hospital
Neonatal Unit staff and patients.

Pages 84, 85, 86, 89, 90, 93, 94, 97, 98, 105, 109
© Nucleus Medical Media/Visuals Unlimited/Corbis

Pages 100, 102, 112, 116, 118, 119 SCIEPRO/SCIENCE PHOTO LIBRARY

Personal stories

Many thanks to the mums featured on *One Born Every Minute*
for sharing their personal stories:

Kirri Bradley, Kerry Brodie, Diane Carlita, Katie Coultas,
Kate Craven, Tracy David, Carolyne Desvignes, Heather Grieg,
Sam Hall, Bethany Harrion, Shannon Jackson, Donna Kirkbridge,
Leah Longley, Rowena Michelle, Julie Murrish, Vicky Pape,
Jenna Sharp, Dawn Stanislawski-Doyle, Sarah Towler,
Becky Veal, Anna Williams and Sarah Wise.

Thanks also to Maggie Poe, Jessica Brookes, Anna Thompson
and Becca Baker.

Dragonfly

Lucy Bowden, Lucinda Hicks, Hannah Shrives and
Iain Walmsley

Shine 360

Frances Adams, David Christopher, Lori Heiss, Kathryn Holland
and Ben Liebmann

My thanks to Dr Penny Law for being such fun to work with (her patients are lucky to have her), to my agent David Luxton for always staying so calm, to Quadrille for their ongoing enthusiasm and support, and above all to Victoria Marshallsay and Pauline Savage, without whom this book would never have reached full gestation, and whose patience, skill and wisdom were quite extraordinary.

DEBBIE BECKERMAN

In writing this book, many friends, colleagues and patients have encouraged me with their enthusiasm, and provided invaluable insights and support. In particular, I would like to thank various colleagues including: Wendy Savage who inspired me whilst a medical student and was my obstetrician; my fellow consultants at Hillingdon Hospital Foundation Trust; the so-friendly Irish Consultant Obstetricians at the Coombe, and The National Maternity Hospital, who showed me how to manage a really busy labour ward; the midwifery team at Hillingdon; special thanks goes to Laura for all of her commitment to the Wednesday Project.

Thanks to all those interesting women who have allowed me to share their pregnancies. I do hope I have answered most of your questions.

Thanks to Debbie Beckerman, for showing me how to describe medical procedures and concepts in a clear and concise manner; to Victoria Marshallsay for masterminding all the information in so little time; to Pauline Savage for her patience with the many, many changes. To Jim Smith and Tiffany Mumford for design and photography and for producing such a beautiful book. Thanks to Anne Furniss at Quadrille for her confidence in me and Rebecca Winfield for introducing me to the new and exciting world of books.

Thanks to my obstetrician sister, Hannah, for helping me with the newborn section (I did know but has been a while). Thanks to Tamsyn Hamilton for her help with the section on exercise (and for motivating me in that department).

For Maddie – my best birthday present ever!

Thanks to Richard for sharing his holidays with my laptop.

DR PENELOPE LAW

Disclaimer

Editorial Director Anne Furniss
Creative Director Helen Lewis
Project Editors Victoria Marshallsay and Pauline Savage
Design Jim Smith
Illustrations Annamaria Dutto
Photography Tiffany Mumford
Production Director Vincent Smith
Production Controller Sasha Taylor

First published in 2013 by
Quadrille Publishing Ltd
Alhambra House
27–31 Charing Cross Road
London WC2H 0LS
www.quadrille.co.uk

British Library Cataloguing-in-Publication Data. A catalogue record of this book is available from the British Library.

ISBN: 978 184949 315 4

Printed in China